S0-BRY-705

FILMMAKERS SERIES

edited by
ANTHONY SLIDE

In Preparation

D. W. Griffith and the Biograph Company

by
Cooper C. Graham
Steven Higgins
Elaine Mancini
João Luiz Vieira

Filmmakers, No. 10

The Scarecrow Press, Inc.

Metuchen, N.J., and London

1985

11841709

8-92

Library of Congress Cataloging in Publication Data
Main entry under title:

D.W. Griffith and the Biograph Company.

(Filmmakers ; no. 10)
Filmography: p.
Bibliography: p.
Includes index.
1. Griffith, D. W. (David Wark), 1875-1948.
2. Biograph Company.   I. Graham, Cooper C., 1938-
II. Series: Filmmakers (Scarecrow Press) ; no. 10.
PN1998.A3G7335 1985   791.43'0233'0924   85-2170
ISBN 0-8108-1806-X

for

JAY LEYDA

and

PATRICK LOUGHNEY

CONTENTS

EDITOR'S FOREWORD

Aside from including critical biographies on filmmakers not already the subjects of book-length studies, the Scarecrow Filmmakers Series should serve as a publication outlet for major research volumes which might not otherwise see the light of day. These books do not necessarily focus on the life and work of an individual filmmaker, but rather document one or more aspects of that person's career.

Such a volume is the present work, D. W. Griffith and the Biograph Company. There are countless books and articles on D. W. Griffith, but none that adopts the focus of this work, a unique cooperative project by a group of (now former) students in the Department of Cinema Studies of New York University. Taking into account the continuing--indeed permanent--importance of D. W. Griffith in the history of world cinema, these four students set out to document all the films created by Griffith as both a director and production supervisor at the American Biograph Studios from 1908 through 1913. What they have accomplished is a major, awe-inspiring task, involving primary research at both the Museum of Modern Art and the Library of Congress, along with willing and helpful cooperation--as the acknowledgments indicate--from librarians and scholars across the United States.

There are quite a number of us who are critical of what appears to be, and usually is, the low standard, or non-existence, of film scholarship at many American universities. Some of that criticism can be laid to rest thanks to the efforts of Cooper C. Graham, Steven Higgins, Elaine Mancini, and João Luiz Vieira, along with their mentor, Jay Leyda. As more volumes such as this are published, it may very well be that film study in American universities can be said to have come of age.

Anthony Slide

vii

INTRODUCTION

This volume fills a gap in film scholarship. Since
the Biograph Company is the only early American film studio
for which substantial visual and written records survive, we
found it unfortunate that no attempt to bring them all to light
has ever been concluded. We have happily succeeded in doing
so. The reader will find in this volume a chronicle of the
Biograph studio during its proudest years.

The initial idea behind this project was simply to
compile as much production information as seemed useful for
the study of D. W. Griffith's Biograph films. These data
were then to be transferred to the films themselves, copies
of which are in the collection of N. Y. U. 's Department of
Cinema Studies. It soon became clear that this aspect of the
project was too limited in scope. We felt our research to
be of such a nature that students and scholars would find it
valuable in their study of Griffith's career, as well as in
their attempts to reconstruct the workings of the early American film industry. We therefore decided to expand the scope
of the project, embracing Griffith's several functions at Biograph and, in so doing, recreating the day-to-day workings
of the entire company. This process highlighted some aspects of Griffith's and his colleagues' activities that would
otherwise have remained hidden.

During the period from 1908 to 1913, Biograph regularly released up to three reels a week, a staggering output
by any standard. This could not have been done by one person alone. The joint efforts of the technicians and performers, under the guidance of various directors, made this possible. However, most of the scholarly literature dealing with
D. W. Griffith at Biograph has focussed on his role as director. We wish to shift the emphasis from Griffith as director to Griffith as production supervisor--a job he per-
formed whether he was the company's sole director, or one
of several.

From THE ADVENTURES OF DOLLIE, filmed on 18
and 19 June, 1908, through THE CALL, filmed on 7, 8 and

10 December, 1909, Griffith was the studio's only director.
With ALL ON ACCOUNT OF THE MILK, filmed 9, 10 and
11 December, 1909, the first non-Griffith unit began operating
at Biograph. The activity of non-Griffith production units
continued until Griffith left Biograph, to the point where, in
the autumn of 1913, six directors other than Griffith were
working at the new Bronx studio. In fact, from early July
1913 until his official departure on 1 October, Griffith per-
sonally directed no films but rather supervised the output
of these other units.

Historians have always acknowledged D. W. Griffith's
preeminence as a director, but we must also account for the
several stages of his development. It is no longer enough to
recognize the fact that Griffith directed fewer and fewer films
while at Biograph, without also citing the increased number
of films that he oversaw as production supervisor. Unlike the
later Reliance-Majestic and Triangle periods, Griffith seems
to have been an active participant in the decision-making process at Biograph, and the administrative leverage he acquired
through the commercial and critical success of his own pro-
ductions was used to gain more freedom for himself. With
the appearance of the various comedy and "melodrama" units
at the studio, Griffith allowed himself the luxury of concen-
trating on the kinds of stories with which he felt most com-
fortable.

New directors were carefully groomed, usually starting
as actors and then becoming assistants to Griffith before
directing their own films. In the cases of Frank Powell and
Wilfred Lucas, they also retained the unofficial job of company manager after starting their own units. Anthony
O'Sullivan returned to the company in late 1912 as an established director and quickly filled the gaps created when
Griffith began to spend more time in preparing his own films.
W. Christy Cabanne, another actor and the first true protégé,
became Griffith's alter-ego in the summer of 1913 when it
was apparent that Biograph valued Griffith more as a producer than as a director. It is also clear that Griffith came
to depend on the talent and business acumen of Mack Sennett
and his successors in the comedy unit, for even though he
never truly appreciated the genre that Sennett almost single-
handedly created at Biograph, Griffith was perceptive enough
to recognize Sennett's abilities and use them to his, and the
company's, advantage.

The gradual emergence of different production units at
Biograph brought with it a transformation of the acting com-

pany. In the 1908-1909 period, actors and actresses can be
seen functioning as a true stock company, one day playing
the lead in a prestigious film, and the next day filling out a
crowd scene in a split-reel comedy. Griffith, as Biograph's
only director at this time, depended upon such versatility in
his performers to meet the company's crowded release sched-
ule. This "democratic" system had changed by 1912, however, and the fact that we were unable to identify so many
of the secondary players in the later films is a good indica-
tion of how firmly the star system had taken hold at Biograph.
Character actors continued to move back and forth between
lead and supporting roles, of course (e.g., Charles Hill
Mailes), and Griffith remained true to his penchant for casting
certain roles by type, and not by star status. Still, by 1912-
1913 one is struck by the consistency with which most performers are used at Biograph; they rarely move back down
the ladder once their positions are established.

All of this is discernible by examining the "Films"
section of this book. The "Filmographies" section helps the
reader to isolate individual careers and judge more clearly
the importance of the contributions made by the creative and
technical personnel at Biograph. Unlike the "Films" section,
which is arranged according to release sequence, the "Filmographies" section is arranged in order of production; thus,
one is better able to trace the growth of an actor or director,
or may concentrate on the development of certain themes
found in a particular author's work. Biograph, like other
early American film companies, was a virtual assembly line
of film product ("sausages," as Griffith himself once described them), and the career of a Kate Toncray or a William
J. Butler vividly demonstrates this fact. We hope that by
extracting these filmographies we will stimulate further research into obscure or unjustly neglected careers.

A close reading of the text will give the reader a new
sense of the many collaborations that developed at Biograph.
Scholars have always been aware of the Griffith-Bitzer team,
and of the staggering achievements it produced, even well
beyond the Biograph years. Other relationships existed at
the studio, however, and they encourage new study and fresh
evaluations.

What role did Arthur Marvin play in Griffith's first
months as a director, when Bitzer was not Griffith's cameraman and Marvin was? What contributions did Harry McClelland, the company's set designer, make toward achieving the
famous "Biograph look"? What was it about the dozens of

stories submitted to Biograph by George Hennessy that at-
tracted Griffith? Is one able to make a case for a Sennett-
Higginson team, such as is generally accepted with Griffith
and Bitzer? Why did Harry Carey, Claire McDowell, and
Charles H. West form an acting trio under the direction of
Anthony O'Sullivan, a collaboration that continued well into
1915, long after Griffith's departure? These questions are
only a few of the many that are raised by the information
presented in this book. Other areas of inquiry will occur to
the reader, depending upon his or her particular interests.
It is our hope that new ways of understanding the Biograph
Company will result from the fresh data we have uncovered.

Biograph is unique among early film studios, not only
because of D. W. Griffith's fruitful association with it, but
also because it regularly deposited paper print rolls with the
U.S. Copyright Office, thus allowing future generations a
second look at this influential body of work. When we began
this project, we were struck by a curious phenomenon: even
though virtually all the Biograph Company's output was available for examination in some form or other, and even though
the company's records had survived, no one had ever edited
these sources into the type of basic production history that
this book constitutes. It seemed a glaring omission in film
scholarship, one that we felt should be rectified. More work
needs to be done in reconstructing similar histories for other
early studios, for with each passing day more of that history
is lost due to time and simple neglect. If this book encour-
ages others to undertake such efforts, we believe we will have
accomplished a great deal toward improving our understanding
of the cinema and its origins.

* * * * *

Since we wished to account for Griffith's and his colleagues' presence at the studio in their various capacities,
we decided to begin the text with YALE LAUNDRY, filmed
at Biograph 7, 8 and 9 October, 1907, because this film
marks an early screen appearance by Anthony O'Sullivan, the
first actor to become an important part of Griffith's repertory
company, and later to become a significant director of melo-
dramas for the studio. Griffith's two acting credits for the
Edison Company have also been included in the text, as have
all the films released before THE ADVENTURES OF DOLLIE
that survive and that show some evidence of Griffith's or his

subsequent stock company's involvement. The last entry is
a Klaw and Erlanger film, THE WIFE, copyrighted on 28 May,
1914, though produced during Griffith's last days at the Bronx
studio before his departure for Harry Aitken's Reliance-
Majestic company.

We supply production information for each film. Except in rare instances, these data are derived solely from
primary sources. The most important primary source for
our purposes was the D. W. Griffith Papers at the Museum
of Modern Art in New York, which include such Biograph
Company records as the Cameraman's Register (1899-1911),
the Story Register (1910-1916), and the Long Book. The
Cameraman's Register, which ends with WHO GOT THE
REWARD?, filmed 10 and 16 November, 1911, lists the films
in production order, with the cameraman, shooting dates and
locations noted for each entry. The Story Register lists the
original stories in the order in which they were purchased
by the company, along with their authors' names, the title
under which each was bought, the date the shooting of the
film was "finished," release lengths, as well as occasional
notations identifying the directors. The Long Book comple-
ments the Cameraman's Register through A REAL ESTATE
DEAL, finished August 1912, listing the film titles in alpha-
betical order along with their cameramen.

Other sources augmented the Griffith Papers. Eileen
Bowser's Biograph Bulletins: 1908-1912, Kemp Niver and
Bebe Bergsten's Biograph Bulletins: 1896-1908, and the
weekly advertisements in the New York Dramatic Mirror
provided us with the accurate release titles, release dates
and lengths. Copyright information came from Catalogue of
Copyright Entries (1894-1912 and 1912-1939), giving copyright
date and number. Beginning with A CHANGE OF SPIRIT,
copyrighted 11 October, 1912, the applications for copyright,
deposited with the Copyright Office of the Library of Congress,
provided us with the names of previously uncredited authors.

Cast identifications required unusual solutions. Except
for certain reissues by the studio in the 1915-1917 period,
no Biograph of the Griffith years was released with credits
of any kind. Our first step was to compile the names of
performers who claimed to have worked for the studio. We
consulted the trade papers of the era, including their various
"Studio Directory" sections, personal memoirs, published and
unpublished, relevant encyclopedias of the performing arts,
as well as G. W. Bitzer's own notations on the Bulletins

themselves. When this list of approximately five hundred names was assembled, we used it as a guide for the acquisition of portraits and biographical information of the performers. We obtained photographs from:

> Billy Rose Theatre Collection. Library for the Performing Arts at Lincoln Center, New York Public Library.
> Harvard Theatre Collection. Harvard University, Cambridge, Massachusetts.
> Daniel Blum Collection. State Historical Society of Wisconsin, Madison.
> Martin Quigley Collection. Georgetown University, Washington, D. C.
> Prints and Photograph Division. Library of Congress, Washington, D. C.

In addition, we turned to the trade papers of the time, especially the New York Dramatic Mirror of 19 March, 1913, in which the identities of the leading Biograph players were revealed to the public for the first time. Once we ascertained that the photographs were roughly contemporary to 1908-1913, we then proceeded to examine the films themselves.

Surviving prints were studied at New York University's Department of Cinema Studies, the Motion Picture, Broadcasting and Recorded Sound Division of the Library of Congress, and the Museum of Modern Art, New York. The films were obtained from the various collections of these institutions, as well as from private collectors. Each film was analyzed, frame by frame whenever necessary, on an editing table by the authors as a group. We discovered that working as a committee better enabled us to recognize and confirm the identities of performers. No performer was finally identified without the approval of the entire group. Reliable cast identifications required multiple viewings. We had the gallery of photographs with us at all times, referring to it whenever questions arose. We are certain of our identifications, and if a question mark is placed next to the name of a performer, it denotes a reasonable assumption.

Although all the Biograph films exist in some form, they are not all accessible as positive reference prints. When the copyright laws applicable to film were amended in 1912, Biograph no longer deposited complete paper print rolls, as had been their practice since 1896. They elected instead to submit positive photographic fragments consisting of the first few frames of every shot, including all title cards, for each film. These fragments survive and formed the basis for cast identifications for films not otherwise extant. We employed the same process in examining these as we had for prints: decision by committee.

Finally, for those titles that do not survive in any viewable form, especially 1911 releases, we relied upon the photographs accompanying the Bulletins and trade paper advertisements.

* * * * *

Key to entries:

We have supplied only available production information. If a production function is not included in an entry, it is because no verifiable information could be listed. For example, very few of the 1907-1909 films have an author credit attached to them because only scant information was to be found for those films pre-dating the period covered by the Story Register (1910-1916).

The format of the entries is as follows:

1. Title: The form of the titles is taken from the main title of the original film itself. When the film does not survive we use the Bulletin, or the weekly advertisements of the New York Dramatic Mirror.

2. Director [d]: D. W. Griffith is the director for all releases from 14 July 1908 through 10 January 1910. At this point, the reader will encounter overlapping filming dates which confirm the existence of more than one production unit. For the identification of directors other than Griffith, we used the primary sources at our disposal, especially the Story Register, which frequently makes note of a release's director, either by full name or by initial.

3. Author [au]: Derived from the Story Register, the copyright records and, especially for the 1907-1909 films, from published and unpublished memoirs. Because it is impossible to determine with any degree of certainty whether an individual submitted an outline, a synopsis, or an actual script, we have elected to use the designation "au" for author.

The reader should always remember that Biograph employed
a scenario staff, and that this department within the studio
was an integral part of the production process--Stanner E.
V. Taylor himself claimed to be responsible for eighty-five
percent of the stories produced by Biograph in the 1908-
1909 period. For the releases of the 1910-1914 period for
which no author is cited, it is quite possible that the author
was a member of the scenario staff, or the director himself.
We have also noted those story titles that differ significantly
from the film's final release title.

4. Source [s]: Literary and dramatic works upon
which the films were based, or that served as inspiration
for the films' narratives. The Biograph Company may have
used many sources for their films; we have listed only those
sources that are clearly verifiable. Since this category is
subject to interpretation, we submit it to the reader as a
guide for further research.

5. Cameraman [c]: G. W. Bitzer, by his own testimony, said he worked exclusively for D. W. Griffith while
at Biograph, and this has been totally accepted. We have
found no evidence to refute this claim (in fact, we have found
Bitzer, upon careful examination, to be reliable in most
cases), and so we have used Bitzer's statement as a guide
for determining his credits after the Long Book ends. Be-
sides Bitzer, none of the cameramen of the other units at
Biograph is known for this later period; the reader should
refer to the "Filmographies" section for possible production
personnel. All other information is derived from the Cameraman's Register (1899-1911) and the Long Book.

6. Filming date [f]: Taken from the Cameraman's
Register and the Story Register; the former supplies exact
filming dates, while the latter supplies only "finished" filming
dates. All other shooting dates are approximations by the
authors derived from additional primary sources and internal
evidence; these are identified by "c." for circa. Dates separated by slashes are distinct dates (e. g., 7/8/9 December),
and those separated by a hyphen denote a period of time during which a film was in production (e. g., 7-10 December).

7. Location [l]: Taken from the Cameraman's Register, notations in the trade press, memoirs and examination
of the films themselves. For those films begun on the East
Coast and finished in California, or vice versa, the distant
locations are clearly noted; otherwise, all films were shot

entirely either in California or on the East Coast. For example, when the word "studio" is attached to an exterior location on the East Coast, the film was also shot in the New York studio. After the Cameraman's Register ends in November of 1911, the simple identifications "New York" and "California" are employed, unless more specific information is available. The addresses of the various Biograph studios, and the period each was in use, are as follows:

New York:
    a) 11 East 14th Street, New York, New York
        (1906-1912)
    b) 807 East 175th Street, Bronx, New York
        (1913-1917)

California:
    c) Grand Avenue & Washington Street, Los
        Angeles (January-April, 1910)
    d) Georgia Street & Girard Street, Los Angeles
        (1911-1915)

8. Release date [r] and Release length [rl]: Derived from Biograph Bulletins: 1908-1912, the advertisements in the New York Dramatic Mirror, and the weekly release schedules published in the Moving Picture World. Release lengths not noted in these sources come from the Story Register.

9. Copyright: Taken from the 1894-1912 and 1912-1939 volumes of the Catalogue of Copyright Entries, copyright application forms and the paper print rolls themselves.

10. Cast information: Unless otherwise noted, all identifications are from the films themselves, following the method described above. Character names come from the synopses published in the Bowser volume or the trade press, as well as from the films' original intertitles. Whenever we deemed it necessary to designate a character not found in the above sources, we have done so. This is especially true of secondary characters and members of groups, such as "wedding guests" and those "in bar." We have identified the actors according to their most commonly used professional names. Whenever appropriate, however, we have used full given names rather than professional nicknames (e.g., Jack Dillon is identified as John T. Dillon so as not to confuse him with Jack Dillon, a director of the period). Nicknames and variant spellings are noted in the "Filmographies" section.

The reader will frequently find question marks within the cast. They appear alone, or attached to names. In the latter case, this indicates that we felt confident, but could not be absolutely certain of a particular performer's identity. In the former case, the question marks are of two kinds: individual and group. For individuals, it means that the performer could not be identified. For groups, we have simply identified whom we could, and have used words such as "among," "in," or "on" to imply the presence of others.

11. NOTE: This category accounts for explanations of cast and/or production anomalies, reissue dates, or other miscellaneous information which may be of use or of interest to the reader.

* * * * *

Acknowledgments:

This book was written over a six-year period, traveling with us through several other projects and over three continents to reach its final form. We have many people to thank for their professionalism and scholarship, as well as for their interest and enthusiasm.

New York University's Department of Cinema Studies was our starting point. We took on this project at the urging of Jay Leyda, in whose Griffith Biograph class we first met, and Jay's constant encouragement and meticulous standards have guided us ever since. Others in the department who took the time to help us included William K. Everson, Robert Sklar, Elena Pinto Simon, Leger Grindon, and Ann Harris and Ed Simmons of the Study Center.

The National Endowment for the Arts and the American Film Institute provided financial assistance during these early months. The two grants received by N.Y.U. were critical, allowing us the time and resources to establish our methodology and the scope of the project.

The staff of the Motion Picture, Broadcasting and Recorded Sound Division of the Library of Congress saw us come and go more times than we can count, as we followed their move from the Annex to the new Madison Building. Patrick Loughney was instrumental in pointing us in the right direction

time after time, finding important records that would otherwise have remained inaccessible, and alerting us to the existence of the paper print fragments, without which this book
would have been woefully incomplete.   Barbara Humphrys and
Emily Sieger fielded questions and located films for us, in
addition to explaining the intricacies of the Library and its
workings.   Paul Spehr encouraged us in pursuing the publication of an earlier version of the book, and Pat Sheehan and
Scott Simmon made themselves available for help and advice.
Joseph Balian showed us the panic button, and made sure we
never ran out of films.

Eileen Bowser of the Museum of Modern Art's Department of Film granted us access to the previously unknown
THE HEART OF AN OUTLAW, as well as sharing with us her
own research and years of experience with MOMA's Griffith
material.   Charles Silver, coordinator of the Study Center
(and good friend), knew when to help us and when to ignore
us, and it is largely through his efforts that we accomplished
so much at MOMA.   Jon Gartenberg, Catherine Ann Surowiec,
Lee Amazonas, Robert Summers (currently with John E. Allen) and Ron Magliozzi of the Film Department were always
there when we needed them.   Pearl Moeller and the staff of
the MOMA Library helped us in our many searches through
the D. W. Griffith Papers.

The staffs of various archives gave of their time and
energies, including the Performing Arts Library at Lincoln
Center, the Harvard Theatre Collection, the Georgetown
University Library, Culver Services, and the State Historical
Society Of Wisconsin, Madison (especially Maxine Fleckner).

Many individuals helped us.   The following people
stand out: William K. Everson (for films), Tom Gunning (for
the print of FIGHTING BLOOD and careful proofreading),
Blanche Sweet (for her memories and her friendship), George
C. Pratt (for his scholarship), Gunnar Lundquist and Einar
Lauritzen (for correspondence).   Susan Fawcett Sosin was our
colleague in the project's early stages; we thank her for her
enthusiastic and diligent work.

At Scarecrow Press, we have had invaluable assistance
from Anthony Slide, our editor, and William Eshelman, the
president.   Their commitment to publish this book gave us
the impetus to complete it to our mutual satisfaction.

Luis Antonio Coelho, Patricia Graham, Mary Clerkin
Higgins and Alan Morrice were always with us, helping us in

a thousand different ways. Their support for the project was unwavering throughout the six years during which we struggled to complete it. They made suggestions, criticized the text, and offered their hospitality, often sacrificing their privacy and comfort.

Finally each of us would like to thank the others. Rarely do group members interact so warmly, respect each other so fully, and share responsibility so equally. When we started the project, we never imagined the years and complications that would ensue but, from the beginning, we all understood the necessity of commitment. At the end, the four of us consider ourselves lucky to have worked with such congenial collaborators.

Cooper C. Graham, Baltimore
Steven Higgins, New York City
Elaine Mancini, New York City
João Luiz Vieira, Rio de Janeiro

September 1984

FILMS

(In order of release)

YALE LAUNDRY

? (d); G. W. Bitzer (c); 7/8/9 October 1907 (f); Studio (l); 28 October 1907 (r); 805 feet (rl); H101825 / 30 October 1907 (copyright)

Anthony O'Sullivan (Ole)

DR. SKINUM

? (d); G. W. Bitzer (c); 26/27 November 1907 (f); Studio (l); 14 December 1907 (r); 592 feet (rl); no copyright registration

Robert Harron (Boy at door); Anthony O'Sullivan (Female assistant)

MR. GAY AND MRS.

? (d); Arthur Marvin, G. W. Bitzer (c); 3/4 December 1907 (f); Studio (l); 21 December 1907 (r); 762 feet (rl); H104043 / 24 December 1907 (copyright)

Anthony O'Sullivan (Waiter); Linda Arvidson? (Manicurist); Robert Harron (Messenger)

PROFESSIONAL JEALOUSY

? (d); Arthur Marvin, G. W. Bitzer (c); 22 December 1907 (f); Studio (l); 4 January 1908 (r); 609 feet (rl); no copyright registration

D. W. Griffith (Extra on stage); Robert Harron (Backstage messenger)

RESCUED FROM AN EAGLE'S NEST

Edison Company (co); J. Searle Dawley (d); Edwin S. Porter (c); 2/3/6/7/8/9/11 January 1908 (f); Studio/Palisades, New Jersey (l);

13

one reel (rl); H105145-49 / 16 January 1908 (copyright)

D. W. Griffith (Father); Miss Earl (Mother); Jeannie (Baby)

FALSELY ACCUSED!

? (d); G. W. Bitzer (c); 26/27/28 December 1907 (f); Studio (l);
18 January 1908 (r); 990 feet (rl); no copyright registration

Edward Dillon (Inventor); D. W. Griffith (Cop in court)

LONESOME JUNCTION

? (d); G. W. Bitzer (c); 8 January 1908 (f); Studio (l); 22 January
1908 (r); 574 feet (rl); H105288 / 20 January 1908 (copyright)

John T. Dillon (Englishman); Anthony O'Sullivan (Heinrich Spitzel-
perger); Edward Dillon (Bandit)

CLASSMATES

Wallace McCutcheon, Sr. (d); G. W. Bitzer, Arthur Marvin (c);
15-20 January 1908 (f); Studio (l); 1 February 1908 (r); 800 feet
(rl); H105590 / 27 January 1908 (copyright)

D. W. Griffith, Linda Arvidson (Extras); Edward Dillon (A Class-
mate)

NOTE: Incorporates THE INSTALLATION OF PRESIDENT BUTLER,
a newsreel photographed by Arthur Marvin in April 1902 and THE
HARVARD-PENNSYLVANIA FOOTBALL GAME, a newsreel photographed by G. W. Bitzer, Wallace McCutcheon, Sr. and A. E.
Weed in November 1903. The 1902 newsreel includes shots of Theodore Roosevelt and Andrew Carnegie. McCutcheon's return to
Biograph, after several years with Edison, is reported in "McCutcheon Rejoins Old Firm," Variety, 25 October 1908, p. 11.

BOBBY'S KODAK

Wallace McCutcheon, Sr. (d); G. W. Bitzer (c); 22/24 January
1908 (f); Studio (l); 10 February 1908 (r); 518 feet (rl); H105983 /
7 February 1908 (copyright)

Edward Dillon (Father); Robert Harron (Son)

THE SNOWMAN

Wallace McCutcheon, Sr. (d); G. W. Bitzer (c); 30/31 January 1908 (f); Studio (l); 19 February 1908 (r); 717 feet (rl); H106282 / 17 February 1908 (copyright)

Robert Harron (A child)

CUPID'S PRANKS

Edison Company (co); J. Searle Dawley (d); Edwin S. Porter (c); 5/7/9/10 February 1908 (f); Studio (l); one reel (rl); H106508-14 / 19 February 1908 (copyright)

Violette Hill (Cupid); Miss Murray (Woman); Mr. Barry (Lover); D. W. Griffith (Extra at ball)

THE PRINCESS IN THE VASE

Wallace McCutcheon, Sr. (d); G. W. Bitzer (c); 10/14 February 1908 (f); Studio (l); 27 February 1908 (r); 938 feet (rl); H106575 / 25 February 1908 (copyright)

D. W. Griffith (Lover); Linda Arvidson? (Lady-in-waiting); Edward Dillon (Waiter)

THE YELLOW PERIL

Wallace McCutcheon, Sr. (d); G. W. Bitzer (c); 19/20 February 1908 (f); Studio (l); 7 March 1908 (r); 542 feet (rl); H106924 / 3 March 1908 (copyright)

D. W. Griffith (Mr. Phlipp); Anthony O'Sullivan (Bridget, the cook)

THE BOY DETECTIVE--OR--THE ABDUCTORS FOILED

Wallace McCutcheon, Sr. (d); G. W. Bitzer (c); 26/28 February 1908 (f); Studio/Hoboken, New Jersey (l); 11 March 1908 (r); 497 feet (rl); H107074 / 7 March 1908 (copyright)

Robert Harron (Swifty); Edward Dillon (A Villain)

HER FIRST ADVENTURE

Wallace McCutcheon, Sr. (d); G. W. Bitzer (c); 9 March 1908 (f); Studio/Leonia Junction, New Jersey (l); 18 March 1908 (r); 509 feet (rl); H107372 / 13 March 1908 (copyright)

D. W. Griffith? (Father); Robert Harron (In crowd)

NOTE: The first appearance of the Biograph Company logo (AB) within a shot.

CAUGHT BY WIRELESS

Wallace McCutcheon, Sr. (d); G. W. Bitzer (c); 11/13 March 1908 (f); Studio (l); 21 March 1908 (r); 969 feet (rl); H107672 / 18 March 1908 (copyright)

Edward Dillon (Land agent); D. W. Griffith (Policeman)

OLD ISAACS, THE PAWNBROKER

Wallace McCutcheon, Sr. (d); D. W. Griffith (au); G. W. Bitzer (c); 17/19 March 1908 (f); Studio (l); 28 March 1908 (r); 969 feet (rl); H107936 / 26 March 1908 (copyright)

? (Isaacs); Edward Dillon (Debt collector); D. W. Griffith (Doctor); D. W. Griffith, Edward Dillon, Mack Sennett? (Charity workers)

NOTE: Bitzer identifies Griffith as the author of this film (D. W. Griffith Papers, The Museum of Modern Art, New York).

A FAMOUS ESCAPE

Wallace McCutcheon, Sr. (d); G. W. Bitzer (c); 27/30 March 1908 (f); Studio (l); 7 April 1908 (r); 730 feet (rl); H108356 / 3 April 1908 (copyright)

Harry Solter (Prison guard); D. W. Griffith, Anthony O'Sullivan (Prisoners)

KING OF THE CANNIBAL ISLANDS

Wallace McCutcheon, Sr. (d); G. W. Bitzer (c); 3/4/6 April 1908 (f); Studio/Fort Lee, New Jersey/Hudson River (l); 15 April 1908 (r); 692 feet (rl); H109315 / 11 April 1908 (copyright)

Harry Solter (Heinie Holtzmeyer); ? (Lena); Anthony O'Sullivan (In bar); Linda Arvidson (In chase); D. W. Griffith (Cannibal in top hat)

HULDA'S LOVERS

Wallace McCutcheon, Sr. (d); Gene Gauntier? (au); G. W. Bitzer (c); 10 April 1908 (f); Studio (l); 22 April 1908 (r); 398 feet (rl); H109471 / 16 April 1908 (copyright)

D. W. Griffith? (Handy Hank); ? (Hulda); Anthony O'Sullivan, Harry Solter (Extras)

THE KING'S MESSENGER

Wallace McCutcheon, Sr. (d); G. W. Bitzer (c); 15/17 April 1908
(f); Studio/Asbury Park, New Jersey (l); 29 April 1908 (r); 876 feet
(rl); H109927 / 28 April 1908 (copyright)

D. W. Griffith (Messenger); Mack Sennett (Soldier); Linda Arvidson
(In Court)

THE MUSIC MASTER

Wallace McCutcheon, Sr. (d); D. W. Griffith (au); G. W. Bitzer (c);
7/9 April 1908 (f); Studio (l); 6 May 1908 (r); 500 feet (rl); no copyright registration

NOTE: No material survives from which the cast may be determined.
Bitzer identifies Griffith as the author and "star" of this film (D. W.
Griffith Papers, The Museum of Modern Art, New York).

THE SCULPTOR'S NIGHTMARE

Wallace McCutcheon, Sr. (d); G. W. Bitzer (c); 18/20 April 1908 (f);
Studio (l); 6 May 1908 (r); 679 feet (rl); H110169 / 4 May 1908
(copyright)

? (Sculptor); Florence Auer? (Model); Mack Sennett, Harry Solter,
Anthony O'Sullivan, Edward Dillon [three roles], D. W. Griffith [two
roles] (Extras)

WHEN KNIGHTS WERE BOLD

Wallace McCutcheon, Sr. (d); D. W. Griffith (au); G. W. Bitzer (c);
22 April 1908 (f); Studio (l); 20 May 1908 (r); 905 feet (rl); H110506
/ 13 May 1908 (copyright)

Harry Solter (Nobleman)

NOTE: Bitzer identifies Griffith as the author of this film (D. W.
Griffith Papers, The Museum of Modern Art, New York).

HIS DAY OF REST

Wallace McCutcheon, Sr. (d); Frank E. Woods (au); G. W. Bitzer
(c); 20/21 April 1908 (f); Studio (l); 29 May 1908 (r); 391 feet (rl);
H110428 / 9 May 1908 (copyright)

Edward Dillon (Mr. Jones)

18 / D. W. Griffith

NOTE: This is the first film in the Biograph "Jones" series and
the only one not directed by Griffith. Woods is identified as the
author of the "Jones" series by Epes Winthrop Sargent in "The
Literary Side of Pictures," Moving Picture World, 11 July 1914, p.
201.

THOMPSON'S NIGHT OUT

Wallace McCutcheon, Sr. (d); G. W. Bitzer (c); 1/5 May 1908 (f);
Studio (l); 2 June 1908 (r); 713 feet (rl); H111067 / 26 May 1908
(copyright)

Anthony O'Sullivan (William Thompson); Edward Dillon (John Smith);
Gene Gauntier? (Mrs. Smith); Robert Harron (Sign changer); Mack
Sennett (Theatre bouncer); Harry Solter (Theatre patron)

THE ROMANCE OF AN EGG

Wallace McCutcheon, Sr. (d); G. W. Bitzer (c); April 1908 (f); Little
Falls, New Jersey/Studio (l); 5 June 1908 (r); 617 feet (rl); H111068
/ 26 May 1908 (copyright)

Edward Dillon (Si Green); Gene Gauntier (College student)

'OSTLER JOE

Wallace McCutcheon, Sr. (d); D. W. Griffith (au); G. W. Bitzer (c);
7/8/9 May 1908 (f); Studio (l); 9 June 1908 (r); 877 feet (rl); H111373
/ 4 June 1908 (copyright)

? (Wife); Edward Dillon (Husband); D. W. Griffith (Lover); Harry
Solter, Anthony O'Sullivan (Wedding guests)

NOTE: Bitzer identifies Griffith as the author of this film (D. W.
Griffith Papers, The Museum of Modern Art, New York).

MIXED BABIES

Wallace McCutcheon, Sr. (d); D. W. Griffith (au); G. W. Bitzer (c);
27 April 1908 (f); Studio (l); 12 June 1908 (r); 550 feet (rl); H111646
/ 10 June 1908 (copyright)

Edward Dillon (Father); Robert Harron (Boy in front of store)

NOTE: Bitzer identifies Griffith as the author of this film (D. W.
Griffith Papers, The Museum of Modern Art, New York).

THE INVISIBLE FLUID

Wallace McCutcheon, Sr. (d); G. W. Bitzer (c); 16 May 1908 (f); Studio/Grantwood, New Jersey (l); 16 June 1908 (r); 662 feet (rl); H111674 / 11 June 1908 (copyright)

Edward Dillon (Messenger); D. W. Griffith (Mailman); Mack Sennett (Mover); Anthony O'Sullivan (Fruit vendor)

THE MAN IN THE BOX

Wallace McCutcheon, Sr. (d); Arthur Marvin, G. W. Bitzer (c); 22/24 May 1908 (f); Studio (l); 19 June 1908 (r); 544 feet (rl); H111673 / 11 June 1908 (copyright)

Edward Dillon (Bank clerk); D. W. Griffith (Station agent); George Gebhardt (Wells Fargo clerk); D. W. Griffith (Messenger); George Gebhardt, Anthony O'Sullivan, Mack Sennett, Gene Gauntier (Gang members)

THE OUTLAW

Wallace McCutcheon, Sr. (d); D. W. Griffith (au); G. W. Bitzer (c); 19/25 May 1908 (f); Coytesville, New Jersey (l); 23 June 1908 (r); 677 feet (rl); H111672 / 11 June 1908 (copyright)

? (Outlaw); Edward Dillon (Stage driver)

NOTE: Bitzer identifies Griffith as the author of this film (D. W. Griffith Papers, The Museum of Modern Art, New York).

OVER THE HILLS TO THE POORHOUSE

Stanner E. V. Taylor (d); "Over the Hills to the Poorhouse," the poem by Will Carleton (s); Arthur Marvin, G. W. Bitzer (c); 15-21 May 1908 (f); Studio/Location not noted (l); 26 June 1908 (r); 790 feet (rl); H112129 / 20 June 1908 (copyright)

Florence Auer? (Old woman); Edward Dillon (Son); Mack Sennett (Mover); Mack Sennett (Bartender); Anthony O'Sullivan (Bailiff); Anthony O'Sullivan (In bar)

NOTE: Taylor is identified as the director of this film in Billy Bitzer, His Story, p. 51.

AT THE FRENCH BALL

Wallace McCutcheon, Sr. (d); G. W. Bitzer (c); 28/29 May 1908 (f); Studio (l); 30 June 1908 (r); 670 feet (rl); H112127 / 20 June 1908 (copyright)

? (Wife); D. W. Griffith (Husband); Edward Dillon, Robert Harron (Extras)

AT THE CROSSROADS OF LIFE

Wallace McCutcheon, Jr. (d); D. W. Griffith (au); G. W. Bitzer, Arthur Marvin (c); 2/4 June 1908 (f); Studio/Location not noted (l); 3 July 1908 (r); 778 feet (rl); H112128 / 20 June 1908 (copyright)

? (Father); Marion Leonard, Florence Auer (Daughters); Edward Dillon (Manager); Charles Inslee (Singer); D. W. Griffith (Suitor); Edward Dillon, Anthony O'Sullivan (Theatre patrons); Robert Harron (Messenger)

NOTE: Copyrighted as CROSSROADS OF LIFE. Marion Leonard identifies McCutcheon, Jr. as the director, and Bitzer identifies Griffith as the author of this film (D. W. Griffith Papers, The Museum of Modern Art, New York).

THE KENTUCKIAN

Wallace McCutcheon [Sr?/Jr?] (d); Arthur Marvin, G. W. Bitzer (c); 9/11 June 1908 (f); Coytesville, New Jersey/Studio (l); 7 July 1908 (r); 757 feet (rl); H112470 / 27 June 1908 (copyright)

Edward Dillon, Florence Auer, D. W. Griffith, George Gebhardt, Harry Solter, Mack Sennett, Anthony O'Sullivan

THE STAGE RUSTLER

Wallace McCutcheon [Sr?/Jr?] (d); G. W. Bitzer, Arthur Marvin (c); 10/13 June 1908 (f); Studio/Shadyside, New Jersey (l); 10 July 1908 (r); 670 feet (rl); H112792 / 3 July 1908 (copyright)

D. W. Griffith (Phil Bowen); Edward Dillon (His accomplice); ? (Roulette Sue); George Gebhardt, Mack Sennett, Harry Solter, Anthony O'Sullivan (In bar); Linda Arvidson (Mother on street); George Gebhardt (In posse)

THE ADVENTURES OF DOLLIE

D. W. Griffith (d); Arthur Marvin (c); 18/19 June 1908 (f); Sound Beach, Connecticut (l); 14 July 1908 (r); 713 feet (rl); H113248 / 10 July 1908 (copyright)

Arthur Johnson (Father); Linda Arvidson (Mother); ? (Dollie); Charles Inslee (Gypsy); Madeline West (Gypsy's wife)

THE FIGHT FOR FREEDOM

D. W. Griffith? (d); Arthur Marvin, G. W. Bitzer (c); 23/24 June 1908 (f); Studio/Shadyside, New Jersey (l); 17 July 1908 (r); 729 feet (rl); H113480 / 16 July 1908 (copyright)

? (Pedro); Florence Auer (Juanita); ? (Mother); Anthony O'Sullivan (Bartender); Edward Dillon, George Gebhardt (In bar); George Gebhardt (Guard); Edward Dillon (In posse)

NOTE: Since this film was photographed after THE ADVENTURES OF DOLLIE, and since Griffith is the only known director for Biograph after DOLLIE (until December 1909), he is the only logical choice for director. However, there is no primary evidence to confirm the fact.

THE BLACK VIPER

Wallace McCutcheon [Sr?/Jr?], D. W. Griffith (co-d); Arthur Marvin, G. W. Bitzer (c); 6/22 June 1908 (f); Studio/Shadyside, New Jersey (l); 21 July 1908 (r); 724 feet (rl); H113479 / 16 July 1908 (copyright)

Edward Dillon (Mike); ? (Jennie); George Gebhardt (Viper); Mack Sennett, D. W. Griffith (Rescuers); Anthony O'Sullivan (Gang member)

NOTE: The delay between the two shooting dates strongly suggests the involvement of two different directors. Since the latter date (June 22) follows the completion of THE ADVENTURES OF DOLLIE, and since Griffith is the only known director for Biograph after DOLLIE (until December 1909), he and the McCutcheons are the only logical choices for co-directors.

THE TAVERN-KEEPER'S DAUGHTER

D. W. Griffith (d); Arthur Marvin (c); 2/13 July 1908 (f); Studio (l); 24 July 1908 (r); 410 feet (rl); H113770 / 22 July 1908 (copyright)

George Gebhardt (Mexican); Edward Dillon (Father); Florence Auer (Mother); Marion Leonard (Daughter); Harry Solter (Old man)

THE REDMAN AND THE CHILD

D. W. Griffith (d); Arthur Marvin (c); 30 June/3 July 1908 (f); Passaic River, Little Falls, New Jersey (l); 28 July 1908 (r); 857 feet (rl); H113769 / 22 July 1908 (copyright)

Charles Inslee (The Sioux); John Tansey (Child); George Gebhardt, Harry Solter (Villains); Linda Arvidson (Woman); ? (Surveyors); ? (Fisherman)

DECEIVED SLUMMING PARTY

Wallace McCutcheon [Sr?/Jr?], D. W. Griffith (co-d); G. W. Bitzer,
Arthur Marvin (c); 27 May, 14 July 1908 (f); Studio/Times Square,
New York City (l); 31 July 1908 (r); 483 feet (rl); H113968 / 28 July
1908 (copyright)

Edward Dillon (Guide); D. W. Griffith (Reginald O. C. Wittington);
? (Ezra and Matilda Perkins); Mack Sennett (Policeman); Harry Sol-
ter, George Gebhardt, Charles Inslee, Anthony O'Sullivan (Chinese);
Mack Sennett (In restaurant); Mack Sennett (Waiter)

NOTE: The first shooting date precedes THE ADVENTURES OF
DOLLIE by nearly one month and thus it is unlikely that Griffith was
the only director of this film.

THE BANDIT'S WATERLOO

D. W. Griffith (d); Arthur Marvin (c); 6/8 July 1908 (f); Shadyside,
New Jersey/Studio (l); 4 August 1908 (r); 738 feet (rl); H113969 / 28
July 1908 (copyright)

Charles Inslee (Bandit leader); Linda Arvidson (Accomplice); Marion
Leonard (Kidnapped woman); Linda Arvidson (Woman at inn); Harry
Solter (Police sergeant); ? (Bandits); ? (Mexicans); ? (Priests)

A CALAMITOUS ELOPEMENT

D. W. Griffith (d); G. W. Bitzer, Arthur Marvin (c); 9/11 July 1908
(f); Studio/11 East 14th Street, New York (l); 7 August 1908 (r); 738
feet (rl); H113967 / 28 July 1908 (copyright)

Harry Solter (Frank); Linda Arvidson (Jennie); Charles Inslee (Her
father); George Gebhardt (Bill, a thief); D. W. Griffith, ? (Policemen); Robert Harron (Bellboy); ? (Mover); ? (In police station)

NOTE: Street location (the Biograph studio) taken from internal
evidence.

THE GREASER'S GAUNTLET

D. W. Griffith (d); Arthur Marvin (c); 14/15 July 1908 (f); Studio/
Shadyside, New Jersey (l); 11 August 1908 (r); 1027 feet (rl); H114338
/ 6 August 1908 (copyright)

Wilfred Lucas (Jose); Arthur Johnson (Tom Berkeley); ? (His friend);
Marion Leonard (Mildred West); Charles Inslee (Bill Gates); ? (Jose's
mother); George Gebhardt (Chinese waiter); Anthony O'Sullivan (Bartender); Linda Arvidson (Woman on street); Harry Solter (Kidnapper);

George Gebhardt, Linda Arvidson, Harry Solter (Party guests); Linda Arvidson, George Gebhardt, Harry Solter? (In lynch mob)

THE MAN AND THE WOMAN

D. W. Griffith (d); Arthur Marvin, G. W. Bitzer (c); 17/18 July 1908 (f); Studio/Fort Lee, New Jersey (l); 14 August 1908 (r); 776 feet (rl); H114339 / 6 August 1908 (copyright)

Linda Arvidson (Gladys); George Gebhardt (Tom Wilkins); Harry Solter (Priest); Charles Inslee (False clergyman); ? (Extras)

THE FATAL HOUR

D. W. Griffith (d); Arthur Marvin (c); 21/27 July 1908 (f); Studio/Fort Lee, New Jersey (l); 18 August 1908 (r); 832 feet (rl); H114372 / 8 August 1908 (copyright)

George Gebhardt (Hendricks); Harry Solter (Pong Lee); Linda Arvidson (Kidnapped woman); Florence Auer? (Detective); Mack Sennett, D. W. Griffith (Policemen); John Tansey? (Boy); Anthony O'Sullivan (Chinese driver); ? (Rescuer)

FOR LOVE OF GOLD

D. W. Griffith (d); "Just Meat," the story by Jack London (s); Arthur Marvin (c); 21 July 1908 (f); Studio (l); 21 August 1908 (r); 548 feet (rl); H114479 / 11 August 1908 (copyright)

Harry Solter, George Gebhardt (Thieves); ? (Rich man); Harry Solter (Butler)

BALKED AT THE ALTAR

D. W. Griffith (d); Arthur Marvin (c); 29/30 July 1908 (f); Studio/Fort Lee, New Jersey (l); 25 August 1908 (r); 703 feet (rl); H114598 / 15 August 1908 (copyright)

Mabel Stoughton (Female lead); Arthur Johnson, George Gebhardt, Robert Harron, Linda Arvidson (Among supporting players)

FOR A WIFE'S HONOR

D. W. Griffith (d); Arthur Marvin (c); 28/30 July 1908 (f); Studio (l); 28 August 1908 (r); 474 feet (rl); H114858 / 19 August 1908 (copyright)

Charles Inslee (Irving Robertson); Harry Solter (Frank Wilson);

George Gebhardt (Henderson, the manager); ? (Mrs. Robertson); Linda Arvidson (Maid); Arthur Johnson, ? (Friends)

BETRAYED BY A HANDPRINT

D. W. Griffith (d); Arthur Marvin, G. W. Bitzer (c); 6/19 August 1908 (f); Studio (l); 1 September 1908 (r); 833 feet (rl); H115136 / 27 August 1908 (copyright)

Florence Lawrence (Myrtle Vane); ? (Mrs. Wharton); Harry Solter (Mr. Wharton); George Gebhardt (The palmister); Linda Arvidson (Maid); Mack Sennett (Butler); Gene Gauntier, Linda Arvidson (Party guests)

NOTE: Copyrighted as BETRAYED BY HAND PRINTS.

MONDAY MORNING IN A CONEY ISLAND POLICE COURT

D. W. Griffith (d); G. W. Bitzer (c); 7 August 1908 (f); Studio (l); 4 September 1908 (r); 414 feet (rl); H115087 / 25 August 1908 (copyright)

John R. Cumpson (Hon. Patrick McPheeney); Harry Solter (His aide); Anthony O'Sullivan, ? (Ignatius O'Brien and Diogenes Cassidy, Attorneys); Mack Sennett, ? (Policemen); ? (Regina, the maid); Robert Harron (Young man); ? (Streetwalker Flossy); ? (Serpentine Sue); George Gebhardt ("Happy Hooligan" character); ? (Scrappy Rosenberg and Izzy McManus, Fighters); ? (Boys)

NOTE: Copyrighted as CONEY ISLAND POLICE COURT.

THE GIRL AND THE OUTLAW

D. W. Griffith (d); Arthur Marvin (c); 31 July, 2/4 August 1908 (f); Fort Lee, New Jersey (l); 8 September 1908 (r); 835 feet (rl); H115212 / 29 August 1908 (copyright)

Charles Inslee (Bill Preston); Gene Gauntier? (Nellie Carson); Harry Solter (Her father); Florence Lawrence (Woman); George Gebhardt, Arthur Johnson, Mack Sennett? (Indians)

BEHIND THE SCENES

D. W. Griffith (d); Arthur Marvin (c); 10/13 August 1908 (f); Studio (l); 11 September 1908 (r); 530 feet (rl); H115211 / 29 August 1908 (copyright)

Florence Lawrence (Mrs. Bailey); Gladys Egan (Her daughter); Robert Harron (Messenger); Charles Inslee (Manager); George O. Nicholls

(Doctor); George Gebhardt? (In audience); George Gebhardt, Mack
Sennett (Backstage)

THE RED GIRL

D. W. Griffith (d); Arthur Marvin (c); 1-12 August 1908 (f); Studio/
Little Falls, New Jersey (l); 15 September 1908 (r); 1014 feet (rl);
H115322 / 3 September 1908 (copyright)

? (Villainess); Florence Lawrence (The Red Girl); Charles Inslee
(Her husband); ? (Kate Nelson); Harry Solter (Bartender); George
Gebhardt (Indian); D. W. Griffith (On footpath); Mack Sennett, George
Gebhardt (In first bar); Linda Arvidson, Mack Sennett, George Geb-
hardt (In second bar)

THE HEART OF O YAMA

D. W. Griffith (d); Tosca, the play by Victorien Sardou (s); Arthur
Marvin (c); 14 August 1908 (f); Studio (l); 18 September 1908 (r); 881
feet (rl); H115483 / 9 September 1908 (copyright)

Florence Lawrence (O Yama); George O. Nicholls? (Grand Daimio);
George Gebhardt (O Yama's lover); Mack Sennett, D. W. Griffith?
(Footmen); ? (O Yama's mother); Harry Solter? (Spy)

NOTE: Contains plot elements from The Girl of the Golden West,
the play by David Belasco, and The Darling of the Gods, the play by
David Belasco and John Luther Long.

WHERE THE BREAKERS ROAR

D. W. Griffith (d); G. W. Bitzer, Arthur Marvin (c); 21/25 August
1908 (f); Studio/New York City (l); 22 September 1908 (r); 566 feet
(rl); H115623 / 15 September 1908 (copyright)

Arthur Johnson (Tom Hudson); Linda Arvidson (Alice Fairchild);
Charles Inslee (Villain); Florence Lawrence, George Gebhardt, Harry
Solter (At beach); George Gebhardt (Assaulted man); Mack Sennett,
Edward Dillon (Policemen); Robert Harron, Mack Sennett (On board-
walk)

A SMOKED HUSBAND

D. W. Griffith (d); Frank E. Woods (au); G. W. Bitzer (c); 26/27
August 1908 (f); Studio/West 12th Street, New York City (l); 25 September 1908 (r); 470 feet (rl); H115986 / 21 September 1908 (copyright)

John R. Cumpson (Mr. Bibbs); Florence Lawrence (Mrs. Bibbs); ?

(Mother); Linda Arvidson (Maid); Robert Harron (Messenger); Harry Solter (Maid's accomplice); Arthur Johnson (Policeman); Mack Sennett, George Gebhardt (Men in top hats)

NOTE: The first "Jones series" comedy directed by D. W. Griffith. Although the married couple is here called Bibbs, the situations and characterizations are identical to those found in the "Jones series."

THE STOLEN JEWELS

D. W. Griffith (d); G. W. Bitzer (c); 24 August/15 September 1908 (f); Studio/New York Curb Exchange (l); 29 September 1908 (r); 630 feet (rl); H116138 / 24 September 1908 (copyright)

Harry Solter (Mr. Jenkins); Florence Lawrence (Mrs. Jenkins); Linda Arvidson (Nurse); ? (Children); George Gebhardt (Detective); ? (Bailiff); John R. Cumpson (Smithson); John R. Cumpson, Charles Inslee (At broker's); George Gebhardt (Mover); D. W. Griffith (In crowd)

NOTE: Griffith can be seen directing the crowd at the Exchange.

THE DEVIL

D. W. Griffith (d); The Devil, the play by Ferenc Molnar (s); G. W. Bitzer (c); 12 September 1908 (f); Studio/Street location not noted (l); 2 October 1908 (r); 570 feet (rl); H116154 / 25 September 1908 (copyright)

Harry Solter (Harold Thornton); Claire McDowell (His wife); Florence Lawrence (Model); Arthur Johnson (Wife's companion); Mack Sennett (Waiter); George Gebhardt (Devil)

NOTE: The only time Griffith and Bitzer used stop-motion photography in a Biograph film.

THE ZULU'S HEART

D. W. Griffith (d); G. W. Bitzer (c); 28/29 August 1908 (f); Cliffside, New Jersey (l); 6 October 1908 (r); 776 feet (rl); H116155 / 25 September 1908 (copyright)

Charles Inslee (Zulu chief); George Gebhardt (Zulu warrior); Harry Solter (Boer); Florence Lawrence (His wife); Gladys Egan (Their daughter); John R. Cumpson, Arthur Johnson (Zulu warriors)

FATHER GETS IN THE GAME

D. W. Griffith (d); G. W. Bitzer (c); 3 September 1908 (f); Studio/Central Park, New York City (l); 10 October 1908 (r); 604 feet (rl); H116386 / 1 October 1908 (copyright)

Mack Sennett (Bill Wilkins); ? (Mrs. Wilkins); Harry Solter (Son); ? (Daughter); George Gebhardt (Professor Dyem); Charles Avery (Butler); George Gebhardt, Florence Lawrence (First couple); ? (Son's sweetheart); Charles Inslee? (Clumsy waiter)

THE BARBARIAN, INGOMAR

D. W. Griffith (d); Der Sohn der Wildniss, the play by Friederich Halm; English version, Ingomar, the Barbarian, by Maria Lovell (s); G. W. Bitzer (c); 4/5 September 1908 (f); Cos Cob, Connecticut (l); 13 October 1908 (r); 806 feet (rl); H116387 / 1 October 1908 (copyright)

Charles Inslee (Ingomar); Harry Solter (Myron); ? (Actea); Florence Lawrence (Parthenia); ? (Myron's companion); George Gebhardt (Polydor, the merchant); Arthur Johnson, Mack Sennett, ? (Barbarians)

THE VAQUERO'S VOW

D. W. Griffith (d); G. W. Bitzer (c); 31 August/1 September 1908 (f); Studio (l); 16 October 1908 (r); 805 feet (rl); H116506 / 3 October 1908 (copyright)

? (Manuella); Charles Inslee (Renaldo); Harry Solter (Gonzales); Mack Sennett, Florence Lawrence, Arthur Johnson, George Gebhardt (In wedding party); George Gebhardt (Bartender); Arthur Johnson, Mack Sennett, Florence Lawrence (In bar); ? (Manuella's mother); ? (Little girls)

THE PLANTER'S WIFE

D. W. Griffith (d); G. W. Bitzer (c); 8/10 September 1908 (f); Little Falls, New Jersey/Studio (l); 20 October 1908 (r); 865 feet (rl); H117027 / 14 October 1908 (copyright)

Arthur Johnson (John Holland); Claire McDowell (His wife); Harry Solter (Tom Roland); Florence Lawrence (Tomboy Nellie); George Gebhardt (Boatman)

ROMANCE OF A JEWESS

D. W. Griffith (d); G. W. Bitzer (c); 15/25 September 1908 (f); Studio/Location not noted (l); 23 October 1908 (r); 964 feet (rl); H117093 / 16 October 1908 (copyright)

Florence Lawrence (Ruth Simonson); ? (Her father); George Gebhardt (Solomon Bimberg); Gladys Egan (The daughter); John R. Cumpson, Mack Sennett, Harry Solter, Mabel Stoughton? (Customers); Arthur Johnson, Mack Sennett (In bookstore); Harry Solter (Rubinstein); Arthur Johnson (Matchmaker); Mack Sennett (Doctor)

THE CALL OF THE WILD

D. W. Griffith (d); G. W. Bitzer, Arthur Marvin (c); 17-25 September 1908 (f); Studio/Coytesville, New Jersey (l); 27 October 1908 (r); 988 feet (rl); H117205 / 19 October 1908 (copyright)

Charles Inslee (George Redfeather); Harry Solter (Lieutenant Penrose); Florence Lawrence (Gladys, his daughter); George Gebhardt (Indian agent); John R. Cumpson (Chinese servant); Mack Sennett, Arthur Johnson, Claire McDowell (Party guests); Arthur Johnson, Mack Sennett, George Gebhardt (Indians)

CONCEALING A BURGLAR

D. W. Griffith (d); G. W. Bitzer (c); 26/28 September 1908 (f); Studio (l); 30 October 1908 (f); 663 feet (rl); H117340 / 22 October 1908 (copyright)

Arthur Johnson (Mr. Brown); Florence Lawrence (Mrs. Brown); Harry Solter (Mr. Wells); Mack Sennett (Waiter); George Gebhardt, Jeannie MacPherson, ? (Dinner guests); Robert Harron (Valet); Mack Sennett (Policeman)

AFTER MANY YEARS

D. W. Griffith (d); Frank E. Woods (au); "Enoch Arden," the poem by Alfred Lord Tennyson (s); Arthur Marvin, G. W. Bitzer (c); 22 September, 8/10 October 1908 (f); Sea Bright, New Jersey/Atlantic Highlands, New Jersey/Studio (l); 3 November 1908 (r); 1033 feet (rl); H117541 / 28 October 1908 (copyright)

Charles Inslee (John Davis); Florence Lawrence (Mrs. Davis); Harry Solter (Tom Foster); Mack Sennett, George Gebhardt (Sailors); Gladys Egan (Daughter); Arthur Johnson, Mack Sennett (Rescue party)

THE PIRATE'S GOLD

D. W. Griffith (d); Arthur Marvin, G. W. Bitzer (c); 8/10 October 1908 (f); Sea Bright, New Jersey/Studio (l); 6 November 1908 (r); 966 feet (rl); H117952 / 6 November 1908 (copyright)

George Gebhardt (Young Wilkinson); ? (His mother); Mack Sennett, ? (Pirates); Linda Arvidson (Mrs. Wilkinson); ? (Daughter); Charles Inslee? (Creditor)

TAMING OF THE SHREW

D. W. Griffith (d); The Taming of the Shrew, the play by William Shakespeare (s); Arthur Marvin, G. W. Bitzer (c); 1/7 October

1908 (f); Studio/Coytesville, New Jersey (l); 10 November 1908 (r); 1048 feet (rl); H118185 / 11 November 1908 (copyright)

Florence Lawrence (Kate); ? (Petruchio); Linda Arvidson (Bianca); Harry Solter (Father); George Gebhardt, Charles Inslee (Bianca's suitors); Mack Sennett (Petruchio's servant); Charles Avery (Music teacher); Arthur Johnson, Jeannie MacPherson, Gene Gauntier (In wedding party); ? (Petruchio's houseservants)

THE GUERRILLA

D. W. Griffith (d); Arthur Marvin, G. W. Bitzer (c); 12/14 October 1908 (f); Studio/Coytesville, New Jersey (l); 13 November 1908 (r); 898 feet (rl); H118186 / 11 November 1908 (copyright)

Arthur Johnson (Jack Stanford); ? (Confederate renegade); ? (Dorothy); Mack Sennett, Harry Solter, George Gebhardt (Confederate soldiers); Charles Inslee (Servant); Mack Sennett, Harry Solter (Union soldiers)

THE SONG OF THE SHIRT

D. W. Griffith (d); "The Song of the Shirt," the poem by Thomas Hood (s); G. W. Bitzer (c); 19/20 October 1908 (f); Studio (l); 17 November 1908 (r); 638 feet (rl); H118293 / 14 November 1908 (copyright)

Florence Lawrence (Woman); Linda Arvidson (Dying woman); Robert Harron (Stock boy); Mack Sennett (Foreman); George Gebhardt, Mack Sennett (In office); Harry Solter (Employer); Arthur Johnson (Waiter); ? (Daisy Tuttle); Mack Sennett, Harry Solter (In second restaurant); George Gebhardt (Waiter); ? (Second employer)

THE INGRATE

D. W. Griffith (d); Stanner E. V. Taylor? (au); G. W. Bitzer, Arthur Marvin (c); 2/28 October, 2 November 1908 (f); Studio/Cos Cob, Connecticut (l); 20 November 1908 (r); 893 feet (rl); H118294 / 14 November 1908 (copyright)

Arthur Johnson (The trapper); Florence Lawrence (The wife); George Gebhardt (The Canuck)

NOTE: This film was remade by Biograph as IN THE NORTH WOODS. The later film, released 2 September 1912, was authored by Taylor.

A WOMAN'S WAY

D. W. Griffith (d); Arthur Marvin (c); 3/6 October 1908 (f); Coytesville, New Jersey/Little Falls, New Jersey (l); 24 November 1908 (r); 676 feet (rl); H118461 / 18 November 1908 (copyright)

George Gebhardt (Woodsman); Mabel Trunelle? (His daughter); ?
(Trapper); Harry Solter (Camper); Linda Arvidson (His wife); Arthur
Johnson (Man with rifle)

THE CLUBMAN AND THE TRAMP

D. W. Griffith (d); G. W. Bitzer (c); 21/29 October, 16 November
1908 (f); Studio/West 12th Street, New York City (l); 27 November 1908 (r); 994 feet (rl); H118716 / 21 November 1908 (copyright)

? (Sniffins); Florence Lawrence (Bridget); ? (Tramp); Mack Sennett,
Florence Lawrence, Arthur Johnson (Dinner guests); Mack Sennett
(Policeman); Arthur Johnson, ? (Moneylenders); Florence Lawrence,
Linda Arvidson, Jeannie MacPherson (Guests at second dinner);
George Gebhardt (Waiter); Arthur Johnson, ? (Guests at third din-
ner); ? (Wife); ? (Mother); Robert Harron, Harry Solter (On street)

THE VALET'S WIFE

D. W. Griffith (d); Arthur Marvin, G. W. Bitzer (c); 10/13 November 1908 (f); Studio/Location not noted (l); 1 December 1908 (r); 508
feet (rl); H118992 / 28 November 1908 (copyright)

Mack Sennett (Reggie Van Twiller); Harry Solter (Postman); Robert
Harron (Valet); George Gebhardt, ? (Dinner guests); Charles Avery
(Mr. Tubbs); ? (Mrs. Tubbs); Arthur Johnson (Reverend Haddock);
Harry Solter (Adoption agent); Florence Lawrence (Nurse); ? (Boy)

MONEY MAD

D. W. Griffith (d); "Just Meat," the story by Jack London (s); G.
W. Bitzer (c); 28 October, 2/16 November 1908 (f); Studio/Location
not noted (l); 4 December 1908 (r); 684 feet (rl); H118991 / 28 November 1908 (copyright)

Charles Inslee (Miser); Harry Solter, George Gebhardt (Villains);
Mack Sennett (Man on street); ? (Accosted girl); Arthur Johnson, ?
(Bank clerks); Mack Sennett, Florence Lawrence, Jeannie MacPherson
(Bank customers); Florence Lawrence (Landlady)

THE FEUD AND THE TURKEY

D. W. Griffith (d); Arthur Marvin, G. W. Bitzer (c); 4?/6/7 November 1908 (f); Studio/Shadyside, New Jersey (l); 8 December 1908 (r);
904 feet (rl); H119109 / 3 December 1908 (copyright)

Harry Solter (Mr. Caufield); Linda Arvidson (Mrs. Caufield); Arthur
Johnson (Colonel Wilkinson); Robert Harron (George Wilkinson);
George Gebhardt (Bobby Wilkinson, as an adult); ? (Bobby Wilkinson,

as a child); Marion Leonard (Nellie Caufield, as an adult); Gertrude
Robinson (Nellie Caufield, as a child); Florence Lawrence (Her sis-
ter); Mack Sennett, Harry Solter (In the Wilkinson clan); ? (Aunt
Dinah); Charles Inslee (Uncle Daniel); ? (Tillie, the cook)

THE RECKONING

D. W. Griffith (d); G. W. Bitzer (c); 9/10 November 1908 (f); Studio/
Hoboken, New Jersey (l); 11 December 1908 (r); 462 feet (rl);
H119108 / 3 December 1908 (copyright)

Harry Solter (Husband); Florence Lawrence (Wife); Mack Sennett
(Lover); George Gebhardt (Bartender); Arthur Johnson, ? (Policemen);
Robert Harron (In crowd)

THE TEST OF FRIENDSHIP

D. W. Griffith (d); G. W. Bitzer (c); 6-25 November 1908 (f); Hoboken, New Jersey/Studio (l); 15 December 1908 (r); 775 feet (rl);
H119491 / 10 December 1908 (copyright)

Arthur Johnson (Edward Ross); Harry Solter (Butler); George Gebhardt (Valet); Mack Sennett, Linda Arvidson, Marion Leonard, Gertrude Robinson, Charles Inslee, Tom Moore? (Guests); Charles Inslee (Employer); Florence Lawrence (Jennie Colman); Harry Solter
(Foreman); Robert Harron (Leaving factory); Mack Sennett (Man in
fight); Marion Leonard, Linda Arvidson (At wigmaker's); ? (Wedding
guests)

AN AWFUL MOMENT

D. W. Griffith (d); Arthur Marvin (c); 19/21 November 1908 (f);
Studio/Location not noted (l); 18 December 1908 (r); 737 feet (rl);
H119490 / 10 December 1908 (copyright)

George Gebhardt (Matteo Rettazzi); Marion Leonard (Fiammetta, his
wife); Harry Solter (Judge Mowbray); Florence Lawrence (His wife);
? (Their daughter); Linda Arvidson (Maid); Gertrude Robinson, Mack
Sennett, Tom Moore? (In court); Mack Sennett, George Gebhardt
(Policemen)

THE CHRISTMAS BURGLARS

D. W. Griffith (d); G. W. Bitzer (c); 28/30 November 1908 (f);
Studio/8th Avenue and 14th Street, New York City (l); 22 December
1908 (r); 679 feet (rl); H120042 / 17 December 1908 (copyright)

Florence Lawrence (Mrs. Martin); Adele De Garde (Margie, her
daughter); Tom Moore, Jeannie MacPherson, Marion Leonard (Cus-

tomers); Charles Inslee (Mike McLaren); George Gebhardt, Arthur Johnson, Harry Solter, Mack Sennett (His assistants); ? (Policeman); ? (Neighbor)

MR. JONES AT THE BALL

D. W. Griffith (d); Frank E. Woods (au); G. W. Bitzer (c); 23/24 September 1908 (f); Studio (l); 25 December 1908 (r); 503 feet (rl); H120041 / 17 December 1908 (copyright)

John R. Cumpson (Mr. Jones); Florence Lawrence (Mrs. Jones); Mack Sennett (Butler); George Gebhardt (Man in blackface); ? (Hostess); Mack Sennett (Policeman); Arthur Johnson, Marion Sunshine?, Harry Solter, George Gebhardt, Charles Inslee, Jeannie MacPherson (At the ball)

NOTE: Copyrighted as JONES AT THE BALL.

THE HELPING HAND

D. W. Griffith (d); Arthur Marvin (c); 23/27 November 1908 (f); Studio/Central Park, New York City (l); 29 December 1908 (r); 841 feet (rl); H120043 / 17 December 1908 (copyright)

Flora Finch (Mrs. Harcourt); Linda Arvidson (Daisy Harcourt); George Gebhardt (Man with letter); Anita Hendrie (Jessie Marshall); Tom Moore?, David Miles, Charles Inslee, Florence Lawrence, George Gebhardt, Mack Sennett, Charles Avery (At brothel); Harry Solter (Bill Wolfe); Arthur Johnson (Mr. Miller); Robert Harron (Messenger); Tom Moore (In office); George Gebhardt, Mack Sennett, Marion Leonard, Florence Lawrence, Tom Moore (Wedding guests); ? (Priest)

ONE TOUCH OF NATURE

D. W. Griffith (d); G. W. Bitzer, Arthur Marvin (c); 13-18 November 1908 (f); Studio (l); 1 January 1909 (r); 724 feet (rl); H120834 / 30 December 1909 (copyright)

Arthur Johnson (John Murray); Florence Lawrence (His wife); ? (Their daughter); Marion Leonard (Sicilian woman); Charles Inslee (Her accomplice); ? (Stolen child); Harry Solter (Doctor); Linda Arvidson (Nurse); Gertrude Robinson, ? (Girls on street); Harry Solter, ? (Their parents); George Gebhardt, ? (Passersby); ? (Drunk); Jeannie MacPherson, ? (First couple); Dorothy West, Mack Sennett (Second couple); Mack Sennett, ? (Policemen); George Gebhardt (Man at stage door)

THE MANIAC COOK

D. W. Griffith (d); G. W. Bitzer (c); 25/27 November 1908 (f);
Studio (l); 4 January 1909 (r); 533 feet (rl); H120836 / 30 December
1908 (copyright)

Anita Hendrie (Margie, the cook); Marion Leonard (Mrs. Holland);
Harry Solter (Mr. Holland); Mack Sennett, George Gebhardt (Policemen)

MRS. JONES ENTERTAINS

D. W. Griffith (d); Frank E. Woods (au); G. W. Bitzer (c); 21
October, 2 November 1908 (f); Studio (l); 7 January 1909 (r); 635
feet (rl); H120835 / 30 December 1908 (copyright)

John R. Cumpson (Mr. Jones); Florence Lawrence (Mrs. Jones);
Jeannie MacPherson (Maid); Flora Finch, ? (Guests); Harry Solter
(Delivery man)

NOTE: Copyrighted as JONES ENTERTAINS

THE HONOR OF THIEVES

D. W. Griffith (d); G. W. Bitzer (c); 4/10 December 1908 (f); Hudson Street, New York City/Studio (l); 11 January 1909 (r); 681 feet
(rl); H120976 / 2 January 1909 (copyright)

Florence Lawrence (Rachel Einstein); Harry Solter (Mr. Einstein);
Arthur Johnson, ? (Customers); Owen Moore (Ned Grattan); ? (Mike
Murphy); David Miles, Mack Sennett, Anita Hendrie (At dance);
George Gebhardt, Arthur Johnson? (Musicians); Mack Sennett, George
Gebhardt (Policemen)

LOVE FINDS A WAY

D. W. Griffith (d); Arthur Marvin, G. W. Bitzer (c); 31 December
1908/4 January 1909 (f); Studio (l); 11 January 1909 (r); 319 feet (rl);
H121529 / 12 January 1909 (copyright)

Anita Hendrie (Duchess); ? (Duke); Marion Leonard (Their daughter);
Harry Solter, Charles Inslee (Her suitors); Mack Sennett, John R.
Cumpson (Footmen); David Miles (Minister); Florence Lawrence
(Among wedding guests); Dorothy West, Linda Arvidson (Ladies-in-
waiting); George Gebhardt, Charles Avery (Plotters)

A RURAL ELOPEMENT

D. W. Griffith (d); G. W. Bitzer (c); 16 December 1908 (f); Coytes-

ville, New Jersey (l); 14 January 1909 (r); 546 feet (rl); H121530 /
12 January 1909 (copyright)

Linda Arvidson (Cynthia Stebbins); George Gebhardt (Hank Hopkins);
Harry Solter (Hungry Henry); David Miles (Dad Stebbins); Mack Sennett, Marion Leonard, Owen Moore, John R. Cumpson (In crowd)

THE SACRIFICE

D. W. Griffith (d); "The Gift of the Magi," the story by O. Henry
(s); G. W. Bitzer (c); 11-21 December 1908 (f); Studio (l); 14 January 1909 (r); 438 feet (rl); H121590 / 14 January 1909 (copyright)

Harry Solter (Mr. Hardluck); Florence Lawrence (Mrs. Hardluck);
Arthur Johnson, Linda Arvidson, Marion Leonard, Mack Sennett (At
wigmaker's); Mack Sennett, John R. Cumpson, George Gebhardt (At
jeweler's); Mack Sennett, George Gebhardt (At pawnshop)

THE CRIMINAL HYPNOTIST

D. W. Griffith (d); G. W. Bitzer (c); 8/21 December 1908 (f); Studio
/Street location not noted (l); 18 January 1909 (r); 626 feet (rl);
H121531 / 12 January 1909 (copyright)

Owen Moore (Man); Marion Leonard (His fiancee); Arthur Johnson
(The hypnotist); David Miles (Robbery victim); Charles Inslee (Professor); George Gebhardt (His assistant); Harry Solter (Doctor); Florence Lawrence (Maid); George Gebhardt (Policeman); Mack Sennett,
Tom Moore?, Herbert Yost, Linda Arvidson, David Miles, George
Gebhardt, Jeannie MacPherson, Anita Hendrie, Charles Inslee (Party
guests)

THOSE BOYS

D. W. Griffith (d); G. W. Bitzer, Arthur Marvin (c); 5 January 1909
(f); Studio (l); 18 January 1909 (r); 342 feet (rl); H121795 / 19 January 1909 (copyright)

Anita Hendrie (Mother); ? (Father); Linda Arvidson, Dorothy West,
? (Daughters); ? (Sons); Florence Lawrence (Maid)

MR. JONES HAS A CARD PARTY

D. W. Griffith (d); Frank E. Woods (au); G. W. Bitzer (c); 17-23
December 1908 (f); Studio/Grand Central Station, New York City (l);
21 January 1909 (r); 583 feet (rl); H121796 / 19 January 1909 (copyright)

John R. Cumpson (Mr. Jones); Florence Lawrence (Mrs. Jones);

Linda Arvidson (Maid); Robert Harron (Messenger); Arthur Johnson,
Mack Sennett, Charles Inslee, Harry Solter (Men); Flora Finch,
Anita Hendrie, ? (Women)

THE FASCINATING MRS. FRANCIS

D. W. Griffith (d); G. W. Bitzer (c); 9 January 1909 (f); Studio (l);
21 January 1909 (r); 417 feet (rl); H121876 / 22 January 1909 (copyright)

Marion Leonard (Mrs. Francis); Herbert Yost (Young man); Anita
Hendrie, Harry Solter (His parents); Gertrude Robinson (Maid);
Florence Lawrence (Visitor); John R. Cumpson, Mack Sennett, Guy
Hedlund, Gertrude Robinson, George Gebhardt, Charles Inslee,
Arthur Johnson (Party guests)

THE WELCOME BURGLAR

D. W. Griffith (d); G. W. Bitzer (c); 11/12/29 December 1908 (f);
Fort Lee, New Jersey/Studio (l); 25 January 1909 (r); 790 feet (rl);
H121797 / 19 January 1909 (copyright)

Marion Leonard (Alice Pierce); Harry Solter (Ben Harris); Charles
Inslee (Employer); Charles Inslee (Husband); Owen Moore, George
Gebhardt, Anita Hendrie, Mack Sennett, Arthur Johnson, David Miles
(In office); Linda Arvidson (Maid); Mack Sennett (Butler); Mack Sen-
nett, Owen Moore, Arthur Johnson (In bar); David Miles (Bartender);
Robert Harron (Messenger); George Gebhardt (Burglar)

THOSE AWFUL HATS

D. W. Griffith (d); G. W. Bitzer (c); 11/12 January 1909 (f); Studio
(l); 25 January 1909 (r); 185 feet (rl); H122037 / 27 January 1909
(copyright)

Flora Finch, Linda Arvidson, Mack Sennett, Arthur Johnson, Florence
Lawrence, John R. Cumpson, Anita Hendrie, George Gebhardt, Dorothy West, Charles Inslee, Robert Harron, Gertrude Robinson (In
theater)

NOTE: This is the only use of a traveling matte in a Griffith Biograph film. The film being projected is an excerpt from AT THE
CROSSROADS OF LIFE.

THE CORD OF LIFE

D. W. Griffith (d); G. W. Bitzer, Arthur Marvin (c); 6/8/13 January
1909 (f); Studio/Location not noted (l); 28 January 1909 (r); 857 feet
(rl); H121877 / 22 January 1909 (copyright)

Charles Inslee (Galora); Marion Leonard (His wife); George Gebhardt
(Antonine); Anita Hendrie, David Miles, Florence Lawrence, Dorothy
West, John R. Cumpson, Linda Arvidson (In tenement); Mack Sen-
nett, Arthur Johnson, ? (Policemen); Gertrude Robinson, Harry
Solter (On street)

NOTE: Location is probably Fort Lee, New Jersey.

THE GIRLS AND DADDY

D. W. Griffith (d); Arthur Marvin, G. W. Bitzer (c); 31 December
1908, 1-14 January 1909 (f); Fort Lee, New Jersey/Studio (l); 1
February 1909 (r); 901 feet (rl); H122510 / 3 February 1909 (copyright)

David Miles (Doctor Payson); Florence Lawrence, Dorothy West (His
daughters); Gertrude Robinson (On street); Anita Hendrie (In post of-
fice); Robert Harron (Messenger); Mack Sennett, Arthur Johnson,
D. W. Griffith, John R. Cumpson, Marion Leonard (At "Black &
Tan" ball); ? (Black burglar); Charles Inslee (White burglar); Arthur
Johnson, Mack Sennett (Policemen)

THE BRAHMA DIAMOND

D. W. Griffith (d); G. W. Bitzer (c); 14-19 January 1909 (f); Studio
(l); 4 February 1909 (r); 1036 feet (rl); H122508 / 3 February 1909
(copyright)

Harry Solter (A tourist); George Gebhardt (A guard); Florence Lawrence (His sweetheart); David Miles (Her father); Charles Inslee
(Unscrupulous Hindu); Arthur Johnson (Executioner); Arthur Johnson
(Guide?); Mack Sennett (Guard); Mack Sennett (Servant); Mack Sennett (Hotel Manager); Robert Harron (Native servant); Marion Leonard? (Dancer); Arthur Johnson (In hotel); John R. Cumpson, Anita
Hendrie, Dorothy West, Herbert Yost (Tourists)

NOTE: Reference print in the AFI Collection at the Library of Congress is incomplete (476 feet--35 mm). Missing material includes
first prison scene and Yogi seer scene, as well as all but one original intertitle.

A WREATH IN TIME

D. W. Griffith (d); G. W. Bitzer (c); 1-8 December 1908 (f); Studio/
8th Avenue and 14th Street, New York City (l); 8 February 1909 (r);
558 feet (rl); H122629 / 8 February 1909 (copyright)

Mack Sennett (John Goodhusband); Florence Lawrence (Mrs. Goodhusband); Harry Solter (Drinking partner); ? (Maid); Arthur Johnson,
George Gebhardt, Charles Inslee, David Miles (In bar); Robert Harron

(Messenger); Anita Hendrie, Arthur Johnson, Flora Finch, George Gebhardt (On stage); Arthur Johnson (Waiter); Linda Arvidson, Jeannie MacPherson, Anita Hendrie, Charles Avery (At stage door)

EDGAR ALLEN POE

D. W. Griffith (d); G. W. Bitzer (c); 21/23 December 1908 (f); Studio (l); 8 February 1909 (r); 450 feet (rl); H122509 / 3 February 1909 (copyright)

Herbert Yost (Edgar Allan Poe); Linda Arvidson (His wife); Arthur Johnson (First publisher); Charles Perley (Resident poet); David Miles, Anita Hendrie (Second publishers)

NOTE: "Allan" is misspelled in the Biograph title.

TRAGIC LOVE

D. W. Griffith (d); Arthur Marvin, G. W. Bitzer (c); 28/30 December 1908, 12 January 1909 (f); Studio/Fort Lee, New Jersey (l); 11 February 1909 (r); 893 feet (rl); H122691 / 8 February 1909 (copyright)

Arthur Johnson (Bob Spaulding); David Miles (Mr. Rankin); Linda Arvidson (Mrs. Rankin); Florence Lawrence (Maid); John R. Cumpson, Mack Sennett (Bartenders); George Gebhardt, Charles Inslee (Thieves); Anita Hendrie (Landlady/Thieves' accomplice); Mack Sennett, ? (Policemen); Raymond Hatton? (Detective); Robert Harron (Paperboy); Marion Leonard, Harry Solter, Florence Lawrence, Mack Sennett, George Gebhardt, Raymond Hatton?, Anita Hendrie, Charles Avery (In factory)

THE CURTAIN POLE

D. W. Griffith (d); G. W. Bitzer (au); G. W. Bitzer (c); 16/22 October 1908 (f); Fort Lee, New Jersey/Studio (l); 15 February 1909 (r); 765 feet (rl); H120977 / 2 January 1909 (copyright)

Mack Sennett (M. Dupont); Harry Solter (Mr. Edwards); Florence Lawrence (Mrs. Edwards); Linda Arvidson, Jeannie MacPherson (Party planners); ? (Drinking partner); ? (Store owner); Linda Arvidson (Woman on street); ? ("Hick" couple); Arthur Johnson (In bar); George Gebhardt (Man in top hat); Jeannie MacPherson (Nurse with buggy); Arthur Johnson (Vegetable vendor); Arthur Johnson (Party guest); ? (Maid)

HIS WARD'S LOVE

D. W. Griffith (d); G. W. Bitzer (c); 29 January 1909 (f); Studio (l);

15 February 1909 (r); 235 feet (rl); H122930 / 13 February 1909
(copyright)

Arthur Johnson (Reverend Howson); Florence Lawrence (His ward);
Owen Moore (Gerald Winthrop); Linda Arvidson (Maid)

THE HINDOO DAGGER

D. W. Griffith (d); G. W. Bitzer (c); 23/29 December 1908 (f);
Studio/Fort Lee, New Jersey (l); 18 February 1909 (r); 583 feet (rl);
H123060 / 17 February 1909 (copyright)

Harry Solter (Jack Windom); Marion Leonard (Woman); Arthur Johnson (Tom); Robert Harron (Messenger); John R. Cumpson (Doctor);
George Gebhardt (Second lover)

THE JONESES HAVE AMATEUR THEATRICALS

D. W. Griffith (d); Frank E. Woods (au); G. W. Bitzer (c); 19/20
December 1908 (f); Studio (l); 18 February 1909 (r); 400 feet (rl);
H122929 / 13 February 1909 (copyright)

John R. Cumpson (Mr. Jones); Florence Lawrence (Mrs. Jones);
Anita Hendrie, George Gebhardt, Owen Moore, Herbert Prior, Dorothy West, David Miles, Mack Sennett (Theater people); Marion Leonard (Mrs. Trouble); Linda Arvidson (Maid)

POLITICIAN'S LOVE STORY

D. W. Griffith (d); Arthur Marvin, G. W. Bitzer (c); 18/19 January
1909 (f); Central Park, New York City/Studio (l); 22 February 1909
(r); 526 feet (rl); H123061 / 18 February 1909 (copyright)

Mack Sennett (Boss Tim Crogan); Marion Leonard (Peter, the car-
toonist); Herbert Prior (Crogan's friend); George Gebhardt, Arthur
Johnson, David Miles, Herbert Yost (Newspaper employees); ?
(First couple); Dorothy West, ? (Second couple); Arthur Johnson,
Linda Arvidson (Third couple); Anita Hendrie, David Miles (Fourth
couple); ? (Masher)

THE GOLDEN LOUIS

D. W. Griffith (d); G. W. Bitzer? (c); 28/29 January 1909 (f); Studio
(l); 22 February 1909 (r); 474 feet (rl); H123059 / 17 February 1909
(copyright)

Anita Hendrie (Mother); Adele De Garde (Child); Owen Moore (Good
Samaritan); Charles Inslee (Gambler); Herbert Yost, Mack Sennett,
Arthur Johnson (Gamblers); Mack Sennett, Herbert Yost, Dorothy
West, George Gebhardt, Marion Leonard, Linda Arvidson (Revellers)

NOTE: The production records at the Museum of Modern Art are unclear in attributing the cameraman's credit.

AT THE ALTAR

D. W. Griffith (d); G. W. Bitzer, Arthur Marvin (c); 30 January, 8 February 1909 (f); Studio/Edgewater, New Jersey (l); 25 February 1909 (r); 972 feet (rl); H123389 / 26 February 1909 (copyright)

Marion Leonard (Minnie, the daughter); Charles Inslee (Grigo, the suitor); Herbert Yost (Giuseppe Cassella); David Miles, Anita Hendrie (Parents); Dorothy West (Minnie's friend); Arthur Johnson, Mack Sennett (Policemen); Robert Harron, Harry Solter (On street); Florence Lawrence (At wedding); Herbert Prior (Priest); Mack Sennett, John R. Cumpson, Dorothy West, George Gebhardt (Dinner guests)

HIS WIFE'S MOTHER

D. W. Griffith (d); Frank E. Woods (au); G. W. Bitzer, Arthur Marvin (c); 25/26 January 1909 (f); Bleecker Street, New York City /Studio (l); 1 March 1909 (r); 523 feet (rl); H123539 / 1 March 1909 (copyright)

John R. Cumpson (Mr. Jones); Florence Lawrence (Mrs. Jones); Dorothy West (Maid); Anita Hendrie (Mrs. Jones' mother); Mack Sennett, Charles Inslee (Waiters); Robert Harron (Busboy); Arthur Johnson, Owen Moore, Linda Arvidson (Restaurant patrons); David Miles (At confectioner's)

THE PRUSSIAN SPY

D. W. Griffith (d); G. W. Bitzer (c); 1 February 1909 (f); Studio (l); 1 March 1909 (r); 465 feet (rl); H123540 / 1 March 1909 (copyright)

Marion Leonard (Lady Florence); Harry Solter (Count Lopes); Owen Moore (The spy); Arthur Johnson, Mack Sennett, David Miles (Soldiers); Florence Lawrence (Maid)

A FOOL'S REVENGE

D. W. Griffith (d); Rigoletto, the opera by Giuseppe Verdi; Le Roi S'Amuse, the novel by Victor Hugo (s); Arthur Marvin, G. W. Bitzer (c); 11/12 February 1909 (f); Studio (l); 4 March 1909 (r); 1000 feet (rl); H123743 / 8 March 1909 (copyright)

Owen Moore (The Duke); Charles Inslee (The Fool); Marion Leonard (The daughter); Anita Hendrie, Herbert Prior? (Fool's accomplices); Mack Sennett (Minstrel); Mack Sennett (Servant); Dorothy West, John

R. Cumpson, David Miles, Arthur Johnson, Linda Arvidson, Harry Solter, Raymond Hatton? (At court)

THE ROUE'S HEART

D. W. Griffith (d); G. W. Bitzer (c); 23/24 December 1908 (f); Studio (l); 8 March 1909 (r); 755 feet (rl); H123744 / 8 March 1909 (copyright)

Harry Solter (Monsieur Flamant); John R. Cumpson, Owen Moore, David Miles?, Herbert Yost, Charles Inslee, Arthur Johnson (Noblemen); Linda Arvidson, Anita Hendrie, Florence Lawrence (Ladies); Marion Leonard (Sculptress); Adele De Garde (Her model); Dorothy West, Linda Arvidson (Her friends); Arthur Johnson, Mack Sennett (Servants)

THE WOODEN LEG

D. W. Griffith (d); Arthur Marvin, G. W. Bitzer (c); 13/19 February 1909 (f); Studio (l); 8 March 1909 (r); 240 feet (rl); H123745 / 8 March 1909 (copyright)

David Miles (Harry); Florence Lawrence (Claire); John R. Cumpson (Father); Mack Sennett (Tramp); ? (Boyfriend); ? (Maid)

THE SALVATION ARMY LASS

D. W. Griffith (d); Salvation Nell, the play by Edward Sheldon (s); G. W. Bitzer, Arthur Marvin (c); 26/28 December 1908, 27 January, 18 February 1909 (f); Studio/Fort Lee, New Jersey (l); 11 March 1909 (r); 926 feet (rl); H123873 / 11 March 1909 (copyright)

Florence Lawrence (Mary Wilson); Harry Solter (Bob Walton); Charles Inslee (Harry Brown); Anita Hendrie, Dorothy West, Herbert Prior, Mack Sennett, John R. Cumpson, Owen Moore (Salvation Army members); Arthur Johnson, John R. Cumpson, Linda Arvidson, Charles Avery (In first bar); David Miles, ? (Medical orderlies); Marion Leonard (Landlady); Marion Leonard (Shoplifter); Arthur Johnson, David Miles (Shoplifter's companions); John R. Cumpson, Linda Arvidson, Anita Hendrie, Charles Inslee, Charles Avery (In factory); Mack Sennett, Owen Moore, Herbert Prior (Outside factory); Arthur Johnson, George Gebhardt, David Miles, Guy Hedlund (In second bar); George Gebhardt, Linda Arvidson, Robert Harron, Arthur Johnson, Charles Inslee, Adele De Garde (In street crowds)

THE LURE OF THE GOWN

D. W. Griffith (d); Arthur Marvin, G. W. Bitzer (c); 9/10/18

February 1909 (f); Fort Lee, New Jersey/Studio (l); 15 March 1909 (r); 547 feet (rl); H123872 / 11 March 1909 (copyright)

Marion Leonard (Isabelle); Harry Solter (Enrico); Florence Lawrence (Veronica); Anita Hendrie (Her partner); Charles Inslee (Second suitor); Owen Moore (Rich man); Linda Arvidson (Rich woman); David Miles (Butler); Adele De Garde, David Miles, John R. Cumpson (On street); Mack Sennett, John R. Cumpson, Herbert Prior, Arthur Johnson, Dorothy West (At dance)

I DID IT, MAMMA

D. W. Griffith (d); G. W. Bitzer (c); 15 February 1909 (f); Studio (l); 15 March 1909 (r); 372 feet (rl); H123871 / 11 March 1909 (copyright)

Anita Hendrie (Mother); Adele De Garde (Gladys); ? (Claude); Dorothy West (Maid); Linda Arvidson (Visitor)

THE VOICE OF THE VIOLIN

D. W. Griffith (d); G. W. Bitzer, Arthur Marvin (c); 19/23 February 1909 (f); West 12th Street, New York City/Studio (l); 18 March 1909 (r); 978 feet (rl); H124289 / 17 March 1909 (copyright)

Arthur Johnson (Herr Von Schmitt); Marion Leonard (Helen Walker); ? (Mr. Walker); David Miles (Communist leader); ? (Friend); Mack Sennett, John R. Cumpson, Dorothy West, Linda Arvidson, Herbert Prior, Adele De Garde (At party meeting); Anita Hendrie (Maid); Dorothy West, Owen Moore, Herbert Prior, Tom Moore (Servants)

THE DECEPTION

D. W. Griffith (d); "A Service of Love," the story by O. Henry (s); G. W. Bitzer (c); 5/6 February 1909 (f); Studio (l); 22 March 1909 (r); 653 feet (rl); H123959 / 13 March 1909 (copyright)

Herbert Yost (Harvey Colton); Florence Lawrence (Mabel Colton); Adele De Garde, Anita Hendrie, Dorothy West, David Miles, Min Johnson (At laundry); Arthur Johnson (Man in top hat); Harry Solter (Harvey's friend); Owen Moore (Rich patron); Arthur Johnson (His secretary); Mack Sennett (Doctor); Charles Inslee (Landlord); David Miles, ? (At Conservatory); ? (Grocer)

NOTE: Bitzer identifies Min Johnson in this film.

"AND A LITTLE CHILD SHALL LEAD THEM"

D. W. Griffith (d); G. W. Bitzer (c); 22/24 February 1909 (f);

Studio (l); 22 March 1909 (r); 340 feet (rl); H123958 / 13 March 1909 (copyright)

Marion Leonard (Mother); Arthur Johnson (Father); Adele De Garde (Daughter); David Miles (Lawyer); Anita Hendrie (Maid); Mack Sennett (Servant)

A BURGLAR'S MISTAKE

D. W. Griffith (d); G. W. Bitzer, Arthur Marvin (c); 16/18 February, 3/5 March 1909 (f); Studio (l); 25 March 1909 (r); 959 feet (rl); H124687 / 25 March 1909 (copyright)

Harry Solter (Henry Newman); Charles Inslee (Dick Folson); Marion Leonard (Mrs. Newman); Gertrude Robinson, Dorothy West, Adele De Garde (Children); Robert Harron (Messenger); Mack Sennett, Owen Moore, David Miles, Raymond Hatton? (At Folson's); Arthur Johnson, Herbert Prior, Mack Sennett (Policemen); Raymond Hatton? (Secretary)

THE MEDICINE BOTTLE

D. W. Griffith (d); G. W. Bitzer (c); 3/4/10/16 February 1909 (f); Studio (l); 29 March 1909 (r); 472 feet (rl); H124890 / 26 March 1909 (copyright)

Florence Lawrence (Mrs. Ross); Adele De Garde (Her daughter); Marion Leonard (Mrs. Parker); Linda Arvidson (Telephone operator); ? (Maid); ? (Old woman); Owen Moore, Anita Hendrie, Herbert Yost, Dorothy West, Mack Sennett, David Miles, Linda Arvidson, Min Johnson (At party)

NOTE: Bitzer identifies Min Johnson in this film.

JONES AND HIS NEW NEIGHBORS

D. W. Griffith (d); Frank E. Woods (au); G. W. Bitzer (c); 24/25 February 1909 (f); Studio/Perry Street, New York City (l); 29 March 1909 (r); 452 feet (rl); H124891 / 26 March 1909 (copyright)

John R. Cumpson (Mr. Jones); Florence Lawrence (Mrs. Jones); Anita Hendrie, ? (Neighbors); Mack Sennett (Policeman); Gertrude Robinson (Maid); Owen Moore, David Miles, Linda Arvidson, Herbert Prior?, Gertrude Robinson, Charles Inslee, Charles Avery (In crowd)

A DRUNKARD'S REFORMATION

D. W. Griffith (d); G. W. Bitzer (c); 25/27 February, 1 March 1909 (f); Studio (l); 1 April 1909 (r); 983 feet (rl); H125114 / 31 March 1909 (copyright)

Arthur Johnson (John Wharton); Linda Arvidson (His wife); Adele De
Garde (Daughter); Robert Harron (Theater usher); Florence Lawrence,
David Miles, Mack Sennett, Marion Leonard, Anita Hendrie, Owen
Moore, Harry Solter, Charles Avery (In play); Anita Hendrie, Tom
Moore (In audience); John R. Cumpson, Mack Sennett (In orchestra);
Mack Sennett, Herbert Prior, John R. Cumpson, David Miles (In
bar)

THE ROAD TO THE HEART

D. W. Griffith (d); Arthur Marvin (c); 4/5 March 1909 (f); Studio (l);
5 April 1909 (r); 618 feet (rl); H125115 / 31 March 1909 (copyright)

Anita Hendrie (Vinuella); Herbert Yost (Jose); David Miles (Miguel);
Florence Lawrence (Mexican woman); John R. Cumpson (Chinese
man); Arthur Johnson, Mack Sennett (Cowboys)

TRYING TO GET ARRESTED

D. W. Griffith (d); "The Cop and the Anthem, " the short story by
O. Henry (s); G. W. Bitzer, Arthur Marvin (c); 13 January, 26
February 1909 (f); Palisades Park, New Jersey (l); 5 April 1909 (r);
344 feet (rl); H125118 / 31 March 1909 (copyright)

John R. Cumpson (Tramp); Anita Hendrie (Assaulted woman); Florence
Lawrence (Nanny); Owen Moore (Passerby); Herbert Prior, Mack
Sennett ("Tough" couple); Arthur Johnson (Fugitive); Robert Harron,
David Miles, Owen Moore (In fight); Marion Leonard (Extra); Charles
Inslee (Policeman)

A RUDE HOSTESS

D. W. Griffith (d); G. W. Bitzer (c); 3 March 1909 (f); Studio (l);
8 April 1909 (r); 439 feet (rl); H125116 / 31 March 1909 (copyright)

Marion Leonard (Mrs. Leffingwell); Anita Hendrie, ? (Visitors); Arthur Johnson (Thief); ? (Maid); Owen Moore (Footman); Mack Sennett,
? (Policemen)

SCHNEIDER'S ANTI-NOISE CRUSADE

D. W. Griffith (d); Arthur Marvin, G. W. Bitzer (c); 8/9 March
1909 (f); Studio (l); 8 April 1909 (r); 556 feet (rl); H125117 / 31
March 1909 (copyright)

John R. Cumpson (Schneider); Florence Lawrence (His wife); Anita
Hendrie (Lena); ? (Maid); Arthur Johnson (Violinist); Owen Moore,
Herbert Prior (Thieves); ? (Fritz, the son)

THE WINNING COAT

D. W. Griffith (d); G. W. Bitzer (c); 2 March 1909 (f); Studio (l);
12 April 1909 (r); 767 feet (rl); H125503 / 8 April 1909 (copyright)

Owen Moore (Courtier); Marion Leonard (Noblewoman); Harry Solter
(Duke?); Florence Lawrence (Lady-in-waiting); Anita Hendrie, Mack
Sennett, Linda Arvidson? (Servants); Jeannie MacPherson? (Page);
John R. Cumpson (Innkeeper); David Miles, Arthur Johnson, John R.
Cumpson (Extras)

NOTE: No print of this film exists. Identifications have been taken
from the original paper print roll, which is badly deteriorated.

A SOUND SLEEPER

D. W. Griffith (d); G. W. Bitzer, Arthur Marvin (c); 18 March 1909
(f); Fort Lee, New Jersey (l); 12 April 1909 (r); 214 feet (rl);
H125502 / 8 April 1909 (copyright)

Anthony O'Sullivan (Tramp); Mack Sennett (Gentleman); Anita Hendrie,
Florence Lawrence (Women); Arthur Johnson, Herbert Prior, Robert
Harron (In fight); Owen Moore (Policeman)

CONFIDENCE

D. W. Griffith (d); G. W. Bitzer, Arthur Marvin (c); 12/13/20 March
1909 (f); Studio/Location not noted (l); 15 April 1909 (r); 990 feet
(rl); H125501 / 8 April 1909 (copyright)

Florence Lawrence (Nellie Burton); David Miles, Herbert Yost (Mexi-
cans); Charles Inslee (Jim Colt); Arthur Johnson (Doctor); Owen
Moore, Herbert Prior, Anthony O'Sullivan, Linda Arvidson, Charles
Avery (Dinner guests); Herbert Prior, John R. Cumpson, Owen
Moore, Anthony O'Sullivan, Raymond Hatton? (In bar); Owen Moore,
Anita Hendrie (In hospital); Mack Sennett, George Siegmann (Foot-
men)

LADY HELEN'S ESCAPADE

D. W. Griffith (d); G. W. Bitzer (c); 10/11 February 1909 (f); Studio
/Location not noted (l); 19 April 1909 (r); 765 feet (rl); H125727 /
14 April 1909 (copyright)

Florence Lawrence (Lady Helen); David Miles (Musician); Anita Hend-
rie (Friend); Owen Moore (Boyfriend); Dorothy West, ? (Maids);
Herbert Prior (Footman); Charles Inslee (Father); ? (First suitor);
Herbert Prior (Policeman); Mack Sennett, Arthur Johnson, John R.
Cumpson (Dinner guests)

A TROUBLESOME SATCHEL

D. W. Griffith (d); G. W. Bitzer, Arthur Marvin (c); 18 March 1909 (f); Fort Lee, New Jersey (l); 19 April 1909 (r); 212 feet (rl); H125729 / 14 April 1909 (copyright)

John R. Cumpson (Man with satchel); ? (Auctioneer); Mack Sennett, Florence Lawrence, Robert Harron, Anita Hendrie (In crowd); Owen Moore (Policeman); Herbert Yost (Pharmacist); Arthur Johnson, Herbert Prior (Thieves)

THE DRIVE FOR A LIFE

D. W. Griffith (d); Arthur Marvin, G. W. Bitzer (c); 15 January, 23/30 March 1909 (f); Studio/Fort Lee, New Jersey (l); 22 April 1909 (r); 940 feet (rl); H125726 / 14 April 1909 (copyright)

Arthur Johnson (Harry Walker); Marion Leonard (Mme. Lebrun); Florence Lawrence (Mignon); Dorothy West, Gertrude Robinson, Linda Arvidson (Mignon's sisters); Anita Hendrie (Mignon's mother); ? (Chauffeur); ? (Butler); Gertrude Robinson (Maid); Robert Harron (Messenger)

LUCKY JIM

D. W. Griffith (d); G. W. Bitzer, Arthur Marvin (c); 17 March 1909 (f); Studio (l); 26 April 1909 (r); 502 feet (rl); H125728 / 14 April 1909 (copyright)

Marion Leonard (Gertrude); Mack Sennett (Jack); Herbert Yost (Jim, the first husband); Anita Hendrie (Mother); David Miles (Father); Harry Solter (Jim's friend); ? (Maid); Herbert Prior (Minister); Arthur Johnson, Owen Moore, John R. Cumpson, Charles Inslee, Florence Lawrence, Anthony O'Sullivan, Linda Arvidson (Wedding guests)

TWIN BROTHERS

D. W. Griffith (d); Arthur Marvin (c); 10/12 March 1909 (f); Studio (l); 26 April 1909 (r); 437 feet (rl); H125730 / 14 April 1909 (copyright)

David Miles (Father); Arthur Johnson, Herbert Prior (Brothers); Owen Moore, Anita Hendrie, John R. Cumpson, Adele De Garde, Linda Arvidson, Anthony O'Sullivan, Charles Inslee (Museum visitors); Charles Avery (In bar)

'TIS AN ILL WIND THAT BLOWS NO GOOD

D. W. Griffith (d); G. W. Bitzer, Arthur Marvin (c); 20/24 March,
6 April 1909 (f); Fort Lee, New Jersey/Studio (l); 29 April 1909 (r);
876 feet (rl); H126009 / 20 April 1909 (copyright)

Herbert Prior (Tim Noonan); Florence Lawrence (Mary Flinn); Mack
Sennett, Anthony O'Sullivan, John R. Cumpson, David Miles, Charles
Avery (At factory); Marion Leonard (Landlady); Mack Sennett, David
Miles, Herbert Yost (In restaurant); Arthur Johnson (Policeman);
Owen Moore, Robert Harron, John R. Cumpson, Harry Solter, Linda
Arvidson (In crowd); Anita Hendrie (Wife); Charles Inslee (Husband);
Adele De Garde, ? (Children); Owen Moore, Anthony O'Sullivan (In
police station); Anthony O'Sullivan (Superintendent)

THE EAVESDROPPER

D. W. Griffith (d); G. W. Bitzer, Arthur Marvin (c); 5/8 March
1909 (f); Studio (l); 3 May 1909 (r); 644 feet (rl); H126278 / 28 April
1909 (copyright)

Charles Inslee (Hidalgo); David Miles (Manuelle); Marion Leonard
(Mercedes); Linda Arvidson (Mercedes' friend); Herbert Yost (Carlos);
? (Servant); Owen Moore (Man)

THE SUICIDE CLUB

D. W. Griffith (d); Arthur Marvin, G. W. Bitzer (c); 25/26 March
1909 (f); Studio (l); 3 May 1909 (r); 318 feet (rl); H126280 / 28
April 1909 (copyright)

Herbert Yost (The Chosen One); Violet Mersereau (Woman); Anthony
O'Sullivan, Herbert Prior, Owen Moore, Mack Sennett, John R.
Cumpson, David Miles, Charles Avery (Members of the Suicide Club)

THE NOTE IN THE SHOE

D. W. Griffith (d); G. W. Bitzer (c); 13/16 March 1909 (f); Studio
(l); 6 May 1909 (r); 711 feet (rl); H126279 / 28 April 1909 (copyright)

Florence Lawrence (Ella Berling); Anita Hendrie (Mother); Anthony
O'Sullivan (Messenger); George Siegmann (Butler); ? (Ella's employ-
er); Charles Inslee (Customer who finds note); Mack Sennett, Marion
Leonard, Anthony O'Sullivan (Factory employees); Owen Moore, Mack
Sennett, David Miles, Robert Harron (In store); Arthur Johnson, John
R. Cumpson (In office)

ONE BUSY HOUR

D. W. Griffith (d); G. W. Bitzer, Arthur Marvin (c); 2 April 1909
(f); Studio/Fort Lee, New Jersey (l); 6 May 1909 (r); 279 feet (rl);
H126642 / 6 May 1909 (copyright)

John R. Cumpson (Jim Smith); Herbert Prior (Hiram Greengage);
Mack Sennett, Harry Solter, Charles Avery (In store); ? (Passerby);
Charles Inslee, George O. Nicholls, Anita Hendrie, Anthony O'Sulli-
van, David Miles, Florence Lawrence, Owen Moore, Harry Solter,
Robert Harron, Violet Mersereau (Customers)

JONES AND THE LADY BOOK AGENT

D. W. Griffith (d); Frank E. Woods (au); G. W. Bitzer (c); 12/14/20
January 1909 (f); Studio (l); 10 May 1909 (r); 585 feet (rl); H126829
/ 10 May 1909 (copyright)

John R. Cumpson (Edward Jones); Florence Lawrence (Mrs. Jones);
Mack Sennett (Dick Smith); Flora Finch (Book agent); Owen Moore,
George Gebhardt, Harry Solter (In office); Robert Harron (Messen-
ger); Gertrude Robinson (Maid)

THE FRENCH DUEL

D. W. Griffith (d); G. W. Bitzer, Arthur Marvin (c); 23 February,
11 March 1909 (f); Studio/Coytesville, New Jersey (l); 10 May 1909
(r); 407 feet (rl); H127177 / 18 May 1909 (copyright)

John R. Cumpson (Leon Martinel); Arthur Johnson (Gaston Tortoni);
Charles Avery (Alphonse de Signoles); Florence Lawrence, Anita
Hendrie (Nurses); David Miles, Mack Sennett (In club); Charles Inslee,
Owen Moore, Harry Solter (At duel)

A BABY'S SHOE

D. W. Griffith (d); Arthur Marvin, G. W. Bitzer (c); 5/6/12 April
1909 (f); Studio/Central Park, New York City (l); 13 May 1909 (r);
999 feet (rl); H126827 / 10 May 1909 (copyright)

Florence Lawrence (Poor mother); Owen Moore (Son); Linda Arvidson
(Daughter); George O. Nicholls (Priest); Anita Hendrie (Adoptive
mother); Harry Solter (Adoptive father); Arthur Johnson (Doctor);
Mack Sennett, Herbert Prior (Butlers); David Miles (Second priest);
Anthony O'Sullivan (Rectory doorman)

THE JILT

D. W. Griffith (d); G. W. Bitzer, Arthur Marvin (c); 13/16 April

1909 (f); Studio/Riverside Drive, New York City (l); 17 May 1909 (r); 997 feet (rl); H126828 / 10 May 1909 (copyright)

Arthur Johnson (John Hale); Owen Moore (Frank Allison); Florence Lawrence (Mary, his sister); Marion Leonard (Dorothy Kirk); Mack Sennett (Her first suitor); ? (Maid); George O. Nicholls, Herbert Prior (Movers); ? (Landlord); Anthony O'Sullivan, Mack Sennett (Bartenders); David Miles (Man in park); Anthony O'Sullivan, George O. Nicholls (Thieves); Anthony O'Sullivan (Butler); Herbert Prior, Harry Solter, Mack Sennett, Anthony O'Sullivan, David Miles (At stock exchange); Herbert Prior, George O. Nicholls, Anita Hendrie, Linda Arvidson, David Miles, Violet Mersereau (Wedding guests); Herbert Prior, Herbert Yost, Charles Avery (At college); Mack Sennett, Charles Avery (Extras)

NOTE: This film marks the changeover from "American Mutoscope and Biograph Company" to "Biograph Company," noted in Moving Picture World, 15 May 1909, p. 629.

RESURRECTION

D. W. Griffith (d); Resurrection, the novel by Lev Tolstoy (s); G. W. Bitzer, Arthur Marvin (c); 26-30 March, 23 April 1909 (f); Studio (l); 20 May 1909 (r); 999 feet (rl); H127268 / 19 May 1909 (copyright)

Arthur Johnson (Prince Dmitri); Florence Lawrence (Katusha); Marion Leonard (A prisoner); David Miles, Mack Sennett, Owen Moore, Charles Avery (At court); Owen Moore, David Miles, Linda Arvidson (At prison); Mack Sennett (Guard); John R. Cumpson, Herbert Prior, Mack Sennett, Anthony O'Sullivan (At inn); Herbert Prior, John R. Cumpson, Anita Hendrie, George Siegmann? (Servants); Anita Hendrie (Lady); Charles Avery (A prisoner)

ELOPING WITH AUNTY

D. W. Griffith (d); G. W. Bitzer, Arthur Marvin (c); 6/7/21 April 1909 (f); Studio (l); 24 May 1909 (r); 614 feet (rl); H127383 / 22 May 1909 (copyright)

Florence Lawrence (Margie); ? (Her fiance); David Miles (Father); Anita Hendrie (Aunty); Arthur Johnson (Minister); Anthony O'Sullivan (Butler); ? (Maid); Mack Sennett, Arthur Johnson, Violet Mersereau (In store)

TWO MEMORIES

D. W. Griffith (d); G. W. Bitzer (c); 23/27 April, 1 May 1909 (f); Studio (l); 24 May 1909 (r); 318 feet (rl); H127384 / 22 May 1909 (copyright)

Marion Leonard (Marion Francis); David Miles (Henry Lawrence); Mary Pickford (Marion's sister); ? (Maid); Anthony O'Sullivan (Servant); Herbert Prior, Anita Hendrie, Owen Moore, Mack Sennett, Florence Lawrence, John R. Cumpson, Arthur Johnson, Gertrude Robinson?, Charles Avery (Party guests)

THE CRICKET ON THE HEARTH

D. W. Griffith (d); The Cricket on the Hearth, the novel by Charles Dickens (s); Arthur Marvin, G. W. Bitzer (c); 8/9/10/24 April 1909 (f); Studio/Fort Lee, New Jersey (l); 27 May 1909 (r); 965 feet (rl); H127599 / 26 May 1909 (copyright)

Owen Moore (Edward Plummer); Violet Mersereau (May Fielding); Linda Arvidson (Sister Dorothy); Dorothy West? (Sister Bertha); David Miles (Caleb Plummer); George O. Nicholls (Mr. Fielding); Anita Hendrie (Mrs. Fielding); Herbert Prior (John Peerybingle); Mack Sennett (Merry Andrew); Harry Solter (Tackleton); John R. Cumpson (Innkeeper); Arthur Johnson (Minister)

ERADICATING AUNTY

D. W. Griffith (d); Arthur Marvin, G. W. Bitzer (c); 15/16/26 April 1909 (f); Studio/Fort Lee, New Jersey (l); 31 May 1909 (r); 545 feet (rl); H127700 / 28 May 1909 (copyright)

? (Matilda Scroggins); Florence Lawrence (Flora, her ward); Owen Moore (Tom Norton); Arthur Johnson (Reverend Joshua Wittington); Herbert Prior (Bill Corker); ? (Maid); David Miles, Charles Avery (Servants)

HIS DUTY

D. W. Griffith (d); Arthur Marvin, G. W. Bitzer (c); 10/12 May 1909 (f); 31 May 1909 (r); 429 feet (rl); H127701 / 28 May 1909 (copyright)

Kate Bruce (Mrs. Allen); Frank Powell (Jack Allen); Owen Moore (Bob, their son); Arthur Johnson, Marion Leonard (In store); David Miles (Proprietor); Mary Pickford, Violet Mersereau, Robert Harron (Children on street)

NOTE: The production records at the Museum of Modern Art do not list a location for this film.

WHAT DRINK DID

D. W. Griffith (d); Edward Acker (au); Suggested by Ten Nights in a

Barroom (s); G. W. Bitzer (c); 19/28 April 1909 (f); Studio/Fort
Lee, New Jersey (l); 3 June 1909 (r); 913 feet (rl); H127702 / 28
May 1909 (copyright)

David Miles (Alfred Lucas); Florence Lawrence (His wife); Gladys
Egan, Adele De Garde (Their children); Mack Sennett, George O.
Nicholls, Herbert Prior, Anthony O'Sullivan, Owen Moore, Charles
Avery (Workmen); Harry Solter (Boss); Anthony O'Sullivan, ? (Com-
panions); Arthur Johnson, John R. Cumpson (Bartenders); Anita Hend-
rie (Extra)

NOTE: Edward Acker claimed credit as the author of this film in
the "Studio Directory" section of Motion Picture News, October 1916.

THE VIOLIN MAKER OF CREMONA

D. W. Griffith (d); Le Luthier de Crémone, the one-act play in verse
by François Coppée (s); G. W. Bitzer (c); 21-23 April 1909 (f); Studio (l); 7 June 1909 (r); 963 feet (rl); H128159 / 9 June 1909 (copyright)

Herbert Prior (Taddeo Ferrari); Mary Pickford (Giannina, his daugh-
ter); Owen Moore (Sandro); David Miles (Filippo, the cripple); Harry
Solter (Judge); Marion Leonard (His companion); Anthony O'Sullivan,
Charles Avery (Workers); Mack Sennett, John R. Cumpson, Arthur
Johnson, Violet Mersereau, Charles Avery (In crowd)

THE LONELY VILLA

D. W. Griffith (d); Mack Sennett?, Stanner E. V. Taylor? (au); G.
W. Bitzer, Arthur Marvin (c); 29/30 April, 4/6/14 May 1909 (f);
Studio/Fort Lee, New Jersey (l); 10 June 1909 (r); 750 feet (rl);
H128182 / 10 June 1909 (copyright)

David Miles (Robert Cullison); Marion Leonard (Mrs. Cullison);
Gladys Egan, Mary Pickford, Adele De Garde (Their children); Owen
Moore, Anthony O'Sullivan, Herbert Prior (Burglars); Anita Hendrie
(Maid); Mack Sennett (Butler); Mack Sennett (Policeman); John R.
Cumpson, Arthur Johnson, Violet Mersereau, Charles Avery (At inn);
James Kirkwood (Among rescuers)

NOTE: This film was based upon Au téléphone, the play by André
de Lorde. However, it is more likely that the immediate source of
THE LONELY VILLA was the Pathé Frères film released in the U.S.
as A NARROW ESCAPE (March 1908). Surviving prints of the Pathé
film bear the British release title, PHYSICIAN OF THE CASTLE.
The author's credit is derived from various secondary sources.

A NEW TRICK

D. W. Griffith (d); G. W. Bitzer (c); 11 May 1909 (r); Edgewater, New Jersey (l); 10 June 1909 (r); 223 feet (rl); H128181 / 10 June 1909 (copyright)

Marion Leonard (Woman); Mack Sennett (Thief); Herbert Prior, Arthur Johnson (Helpers)

THE SON'S RETURN

D. W. Griffith (d); G. W. Bitzer, Arthur Marvin (c); 5/7/8 May 1909 (f); Studio/Leonia, New Jersey/Coytesville, New Jersey (l); 14 June 1909 (r); 993 feet (rl); H128255 / 12 June 1909 (copyright)

? (Will Sanderson); Herbert Prior (His father); Anita Hendrie (His mother); Mary Pickford (Mary Clark); Harry Solter (Employer); Mack Sennett, Anthony O'Sullivan (Creditors); Owen Moore, Arthur Johnson (On stairs); Frank Powell, Arthur Johnson, Owen Moore (In bank); David Miles, Mack Sennett (Neighbors); Charles Avery (Extra)

HER FIRST BISCUITS

D. W. Griffith (d); Frank E. Woods (au); G. W. Bitzer (c); 20 April 1909 (f); Studio (l); 17 June 1909 (r); 514 feet (rl); H128254 / 12 June 1909 (copyright)

John R. Cumpson (Mr. Jones); Florence Lawrence (Mrs. Jones); Anita Hendrie, Arthur Johnson, Mack Sennett, Marion Leonard, Owen Moore, David Miles, Herbert Prior, Mary Pickford, Violet Mersereau, Charles Avery (Biscuit victims); George O. Nicholls (Policeman); Anthony O'Sullivan (Workman); ? (Thief); Jeannie MacPherson (Secretary); Anita Hendrie (In crowd)

THE FADED LILLIES

D. W. Griffith (d); Arthur Marvin, G. W. Bitzer (c); 15/17 May 1909 (f); Studio (l); 17 June 1909 (r); 481 feet (rl); H128253 / 12 June 1909 (copyright)

David Miles (Francois); ? (His loved one); James Kirkwood (Doctor); Anthony O'Sullivan (Butler at second party); ? (Nurse); Charles Hill Mailes? (Francois' butler); Owen Moore, Frank Powell, William A. Quirk, Mack Sennett, Mary Pickford, Gladys Egan, Herbert Prior (At party)

NOTE: "Lillies" misspelled in title. Copyrighted as FADED LILIES.

WAS JUSTICE SERVED?

D. W. Griffith (d); Arthur Marvin, G. W. Bitzer (c); 20/21/24 May 1909 (f); Studio/Englewood, New Jersey (l); 21 June 1909 (r); 962 feet (rl); H128592 / 19 June 1909 (copyright)

James Kirkwood (George Wallace); ? (His wife); ? (His mother); Gladys Egan (His daughter); Herbert Prior (Policeman); Herbert Prior (Bailiff); Frank Powell (Finder of wallet); Harry Solter (Judge); David Miles (Prosecutor); Mack Sennett, ? (Guards); Owen Moore, Mack Sennett (On street); Mack Sennett, ? (In court); Arthur Johnson, Anthony O'Sullivan, William A. Quirk, John R. Cumpson, Raymond Hatton?, Charles Avery (Jurors)

THE PEACHBASKET HAT

D. W. Griffith (d); Frank E. Woods (au); Arthur Marvin, G. W. Bitzer (c); 1/6 May 1909 (f); Fort Lee, New Jersey/Studio (l); 24 June 1909 (r); 666 feet (rl); H128739 / 24 June 1909 (copyright)

John R. Cumpson (Mr. Jones); Florence Lawrence (Mrs. Jones); Anita Hendrie (Maid); Marion Leonard, Herbert Prior (Gypsies); Linda Arvidson, Violet Mersereau, ? (Visitors); Arthur Johnson, Mack Sennett (Policemen); Owen Moore, Robert Harron, Mary Pickford, Anthony O'Sullivan, Charles Avery (On street); Owen Moore, Mary Pickford, Mack Sennett, Herbert Prior, Arthur Johnson, Jeannie MacPherson, Anthony O'Sullivan (In store)

THE MEXICAN SWEETHEARTS

D. W. Griffith (d); G. W. Bitzer (c); 28 May 1909 (f); Studio (l); 24 June 1909 (r); 309 feet (rl); H128738 / 24 June 1909 (copyright)

? (The señorita); Charles Perley? (Her sweetheart); William A. Quirk (American soldier); James Kirkwood, Mack Sennett (Mexicans in bar)

THE WAY OF MAN

D. W. Griffith (d); G. W. Bitzer, Arthur Marvin (c); 13/24 May 1909 (f); Edgewater, New Jersey/Studio (l); 28 June 1909 (r); 986 feet (rl); H129205 / 28 June 1909 (copyright)

Arthur Johnson (Tom Herne); Florence Lawrence (Mabel Jarrett); Mary Pickford (Winnie, her cousin); Flora Finch (Mother); Gladys Egan (Child); James Kirkwood (Father); Mack Sennett, Anthony O'Sullivan (Butlers); Marion Leonard, Owen Moore, Gladys Egan, Herbert Prior, Gertrude Robinson, David Miles, Violet Mersereau, Frank Powell (Wedding guests); Gladys Egan (At Bide-A-Wee)

THE NECKLACE

D. W. Griffith (d); "La Parure," the story by Guy de Maupassant
(s); G. W. Bitzer, Arthur Marvin (c); 12-27 May 1909 (f); Studio (l);
1 July 1909 (r); 969 feet (rl); J129504 / 3 July 1909 (copyright)

Rose King (Harriet Leroque Kendrick); Herbert Prior (John Kendrick);
Caroline Harris? (Owner of necklace); Mary Pickford (Maid); Anthony
O'Sullivan (Servant); ? (Thieves); Anthony O'Sullivan (Loan clerk);
Frank Powell (Employer); Mary Pickford, Mack Sennett, William A.
Quirk, Arthur Johnson, Charles Avery (In pawn shop); Owen Moore,
Mack Sennett (In jewelry store); Arthur Johnson (Doctor?); Arthur
Johnson, William A. Quirk, Owen Moore, James Kirkwood, David
Miles, Mack Sennett, Frank Powell (Party guests)

THE MESSAGE

D. W. Griffith (d); G. W. Bitzer, Arthur Marvin (c); 15/26 May, 1
June 1909 (f); Studio/Greenwich, Connecticut (l); 5 July 1909 (r); 944
feet (rl); J129505 / 6 July 1909 (copyright)

? (Effie Harris); Frank Powell (Harold Woodson); James Kirkwood
(David Williams); Robert Harron (Farm boy); Mack Sennett, Owen
Moore, Gladys Egan, Anthony O'Sullivan, Jack Pickford (In crowd)

THE COUNTRY DOCTOR

D. W. Griffith (d); G. W. Bitzer (c); 29/31 May, 7 June 1909 (f);
Studio/Greenwich, Connecticut (l); 8 July 1909 (r); 942 feet (rl);
J129513 / 9 July 1909 (copyright)

Frank Powell (Doctor Harcourt); Florence Lawrence (His wife);
Gladys Egan (Edith, their daughter); Kate Bruce (Poor mother); Mary
Pickford (Elder daughter); Adele De Garde (Sick daughter); Rose King
(Maid)

THE CARDINAL'S CONSPIRACY

D. W. Griffith (d); G. W. Bitzer (c); 3/4/12 June 1909 (f); Studio/
Greenwich, Connecticut (l); 12 July 1909 (r); 999 feet (rl); J129525
/ 12 July 1909 (copyright)

Herbert Yost? (The King); Frank Powell (Visiting nobleman); Florence
Lawrence (Princess); Lottie Pickford, ? (Her servants); James Kirk-
wood (The cardinal); ? (Two ladies); William A. Quirk (Barber); Ar-
thur Johnson, Anthony O'Sullivan, Mack Sennett, John R. Cumpson,
(Musketeers); Mary Pickford (Disguised servant); ? (Two spies); John
R. Cumpson, Rose King, William A. Quirk, Owen Moore, Charles
Avery (Members of court)

THE FRIEND OF THE FAMILY

D. W. Griffith (d); Arthur Marvin, G. W. Bitzer (c); 17/18/19 May 1909 (f); Studio (l); 15 July 1909 (r); 749 feet (rl); J129548 / 16 July 1909 (copyright)

Frank Powell (Jack Hudson); Owen Moore (Robert Edmonds); ? (Estelle Morse); ? (Mrs. Edmonds)

NOTE: The original paper print roll is too deteriorated for examination. No reference copy of this film is known to exist. Identifications have been taken from the Bulletin photograph.

TENDER HEARTS

D. W. Griffith (d); G. W. Bitzer (c); 7/15 June 1909 (f); Greenwich, Connecticut/Fort Lee, New Jersey (l); 19 July 1909 (r); 233 feet (rl); J129547 / 16 July 1909 (copyright)

Mary Pickford (Nellie); James Kirkwood (Simple farmer lad); Frank Powell (Handsome dressy chap); Arthur Johnson (Hunter); Lottie Pickford (Nellie's friend); Florence Lawrence, Rose King (Extras)

THE RENUNCIATION

D. W. Griffith (d); G. W. Bitzer, Arthur Marvin (c); 2/14/18 June 1909 (f); Studio/Shadyside, New Jersey (l); 19 July 1909 (r); 982 feet (rl); J129610 / 21 July 1909 (copyright)

Mary Pickford (Kittie Ryan); Anthony O'Sullivan (Steve Ryan, her uncle); James Kirkwood (Joe Fielding); Harry Solter (Sam Walters); William A. Quirk (Kittie's fiancé)

SWEET AND TWENTY

D. W. Griffith (d); G. W. Bitzer (c); 19/21 June 1909 (f); Studio/ Greenwich, Connecticut (l); 22 July 1909 (r); 572 feet (rl); no copyright registration

Mary Pickford (Alice); James Kirkwood (Her father); William A. Quirk (Frank); Florence Lawrence (Alice's sister); ? (Maid)

JEALOUSY AND THE MAN

D. W. Griffith (d); G. W. Bitzer (c); 31 May, 15 June 1909 (f); Studio/Fort Lee, New Jersey (l); 22 July 1909 (r); 418 feet (rl); J129609 / 21 July 1909 (copyright)

James Kirkwood (Jim Brooks); Florence Lawrence (Mrs. Brooks);

Gladys Egan (Their daughter); Anthony O'Sullivan (John West); Mack Sennett (Workman); Arthur Johnson, Owen Moore (At dinner)

A CONVICT'S SACRIFICE

D. W. Griffith (d); G. W. Bitzer (c); 10/16 June 1909 (f); Studio/ Fort Lee, New Jersey (l); 26 July 1909 (r); 977 feet (rl); J129772 / 26 July 1909 (copyright)

James Kirkwood (Convict); Henry B. Walthall (His friend); Stephanie Longfellow (His friend's wife); Gladys Egan, ? (Their children); Anthony O'Sullivan, Owen Moore, Mack Sennett (Workmen); Harry Solter (Foreman); Arthur Johnson, Owen Moore, Mack Sennett, George Siegmann (Guards); Owen Moore (Loiterer); Arthur Johnson (A convict); William A. Quirk (In prison office)

THE SLAVE

D. W. Griffith (d); G. W. Bitzer (c); 22/23 June 1909 (f); Studio (l); 29 July 1909 (r); 998 feet (rl); J129866 / 30 July 1909 (copyright)

Florence Lawrence (Nerada); Harry Solter (Deletrius); James Kirkwood (Alachus); Frank Powell (Old man); Arthur Johnson, Owen Moore (Greeks); Mack Sennett, Alfred Paget (Barbarians); Henry B. Walthall (Messenger); Kate Bruce (Woman in black); Lottie Pickford, ? (Dancers); George Siegmann (Soldier); William J. Butler (Patrician); Mary Pickford (Young girl at court)

A STRANGE MEETING

D. W. Griffith (d); G. W. Bitzer (c); 11/17 June 1909 (f); Studio (l); 2 August 1909 (r); 967 feet (rl); J130279 / 5 August 1909 (copyright)

Stephanie Longfellow (Mary Rollins); Arthur Johnson (Reverend John Stanton); William A. Quirk (Drunk); Frank Powell, Henry B. Walthall (Thieves); Mack Sennett, George Siegmann, Anthony O'Sullivan (In congregation); Owen Moore, John R. Cumpson, Kate Bruce, James Kirkwood, Lottie Pickford, Charles Avery (At party)

THE MENDED LUTE

D. W. Griffith (d); G. W. Bitzer (c); 28/29/30 June, 2 July 1909 (f); Cuddebackville, New York (l); 5 August 1909 (r); 996 feet (rl); J130411 / 7 August 1909 (copyright)

Florence Lawrence (Rising Moon); Frank Powell (Chief Great Elk Horn); Owen Moore (Little Bear); James Kirkwood (Standing Rock); Arthur Johnson, Mack Sennett, Alfred Paget, Henry B. Walthall, Red Wing, James Young Deer (Indians)

THEY WOULD ELOPE

D. W. Griffith (d); G. W. Bitzer, Percy Higginson (c); 24/25 June,
15 July 1909 (f); Studio/Little Falls, New Jersey (l); 9 August 1909
(r); 572 feet (rl); J130485 / 10 August 1909 (copyright)

William A. Quirk (Harry); Mary Pickford (Bessie); James Kirkwood
(Father); Kate Bruce (Mother); Robert Harron, Harry Solter (At
stable); Anthony O'Sullivan (Butler); ? (Sister); ? (Maid); Owen Moore
(In car); William J. Butler, Gladys Egan, John R. Cumpson, Henry
B. Walthall, Gertrude Robinson (In group); Arthur Johnson (Preacher);
Mack Sennett (Man with wheelbarrow); ? (At dock)

JONES' BURGLAR

D. W. Griffith (d); Frank E. Woods (au); Arthur Marvin, G. W.
Bitzer (c); 26 June, ? July 1909 (f); Studio/Coytesville, New Jersey
(l); 9 August 1909 (r); 388 feet (rl); J130484 / 10 August 1909 (copyright)

John R. Cumpson (Mr. Jones); Florence Lawrence (Mrs. Jones); ?
(Maid); Mack Sennett (Burglar); Owen Moore, Arthur Johnson, William
J. Butler, Anthony O'Sullivan, Frank Powell (At club)

NOTE: Copyrighted as MR. JONES' BURGLAR.

THE BETTER WAY

D. W. Griffith (d); G. W. Bitzer (c); 9/10/12 July 1909 (f); Studio/
Coytesville, New Jersey (l); 12 August 1909 (r); 990 feet (rl); J130564
/ 13 August 1909 (copyright)

Stephanie Longfellow (Elizabeth Parker); Kate Bruce (Her mother);
Henry B. Walthall (Oliver Sylvester); James Kirkwood (Squire Calvin
Cartwright); William J. Butler, ? (His parents); Verner Clarges
(Minister); Arthur Johnson, Mack Sennett, Owen Moore, Anthony
O'Sullivan, Lottie Pickford (Puritans)

WITH HER CARD

D. W. Griffith (d); G. W. Bitzer (c); 7 July 1909 (f); Studio (l); 16
August 1909 (r); 1000 feet (rl); J130708 / 17 August 1909 (copyright)

Owen Moore (Henry Larkin); Frank Powell (Randolph Churchill);
Marion Leonard (Adele); ? (Maid); Mack Sennett, Arthur Johnson,
Charles Avery, Henry B. Walthall (At Larkin's); John R. Cumpson,
Verner Clarges?, William A. Quirk, William J. Butler, Anthony
O'Sullivan (At Churchill's); Anthony O'Sullivan (Footman); Frank
Evans (Extra)

HIS WIFE'S VISITOR

D. W. Griffith (d); G. W. Bitzer (c); 13 July 1909 (f); Studio (l); 19 August 1909 (r); 526 feet (rl); J130779 / 19 August 1909 (copyright)

William A. Quirk (Harry Wright); Mary Pickford (Bessie Wright); Frank Powell (Friend); James Kirkwood, Owen Moore, Mack Sennett, William J. Butler (At club)

NOTE: Sequel to THEY WOULD ELOPE.

MRS. JONES' LOVER; or, "I WANT MY HAT"

D. W. Griffith (d); Frank E. Woods (au); G. W. Bitzer (c); 27 May, 18 June 1909 (f); Studio (l); 19 August 1909 (r); 467 feet (rl); J130780 / 19 August 1909 (copyright)

John R. Cumpson (Mr. Jones); Florence Lawrence (Mrs. Jones); ? (Maid); Anthony O'Sullivan (Repairman); ? (Friends)

NOTE: Copyrighted as MRS. JONES' LOVER. This is the last film in the Biograph "Jones" series.

THE INDIAN RUNNER'S ROMANCE

D. W. Griffith (d); G. W. Bitzer (c); 29/30 June, 2/3 July 1909 (f); Cuddebackville, New York (l); 23 August 1909 (r); 994 feet (rl); J130843 / 24 August 1909 (copyright)

Owen Moore (Blue Cloud); Frank Powell (Prospector); Mary Pickford (Squaw); Mack Sennett, Lottie Pickford? (Indians); Frank Powell, Arthur Johnson, James Kirkwood (Cowboys); James Kirkwood (Dying man); Anthony O'Sullivan (At stable)

NOTE: The reference copy in the Paper Print Collection is of such poor quality that it was difficult to identify minor players.

THE SEVENTH DAY

D. W. Griffith (d); G. W. Bitzer (c); 5/8 June 1909 (f); Studio (l); 26 August 1909 (r); 693 feet (rl); J130912 / 27 August 1909 (copyright)

James Kirkwood (Mr. Herne); Rose King (Mrs. Herne); Gladys Egan, John Tansey (Their children); Mary Pickford (Maid); Frank Powell (Lawyer); Mack Sennett, Charles Avery (Clerks); Anthony O'Sullivan (Butler); ? (Nurses); Owen Moore, ? (Visitors); Owen Moore, Arthur Johnson (At parties)

"OH, UNCLE"

D. W. Griffith (d); G. W. Bitzer (c); 21/22 July 1909 (f); Studio (l);
26 August 1909 (r); 292 feet (rl); J130911 / 27 August 1909 (copyright)

James Kirkwood (Zeke Wright); William A. Quirk (Tom, his nephew);
Mary Pickford (Bessie); ? (Maids)

NOTE: Copyrighted as OH, UNCLE!

THE MILLS OF THE GODS

D. W. Griffith (d); G. W. Bitzer (c); 17 July 1909 (f); Studio (l); 30
August 1909 (r); 672 feet (rl); J131133 / 31 August 1909 (copyright)

Arthur Johnson (Henry Woodson); Linda Arvidson (Hulda, the maid);
Marion Leonard (Nellie); John R. Cumpson (Delivery man); ? (Landlady); Frank Powell, William J. Butler, Verner Clarges (In editor's
office); Henry B. Walthall, Mack Sennett, Owen Moore, Anthony O'-
Sullivan (At party)

PRANKS

D. W. Griffith (d); Arthur Marvin (c); 19/20/28 July 1909 (f); Little
Falls, New Jersey (l); 30 August 1909 (r); 328 feet (rl); J131132 /
31 August 1909 (copyright)

Arthur Johnson (Tom); Marion Leonard (Ethel); Robert Harron, Jack
Pickford (Boys); Linda Arvidson, ? (On porch); Henry B. Walthall,
William A. Quirk (Sunbathers); Anthony O'Sullivan (Mr. Tramp); ?
(Ladies)

THE SEALED ROOM

D. W. Griffith (d); "La Grande Bretêche," the story by Honoré de
Balzac (s); G. W. Bitzer (c); 22/23 July 1909 (f); Studio (l); 2 September 1909 (r); 779 feet (rl); J131224 / 3 September 1909 (copyright)

Arthur Johnson (Count); Marion Leonard (Countess); Henry B. Wal-
thall (Minstrel); Mary Pickford, Gertrude Robinson, Linda Arvidson
(Ladies at court); George Siegmann, Owen Moore, William J. Butler,
Verner Clarges (Noblemen at court); George O. Nicholls, Anthony
O'Sullivan (Workmen); Mack Sennett (A soldier)

THE LITTLE DARLING

D. W. Griffith (d); G. W. Bitzer (c); 27 July, 3 August 1909 (f);

Studio/Cuddebackville, New York (l); 2 September 1909 (r); 211 feet (rl); J131223 / 3 September 1909 (copyright)

? (Lillie Green); Mary Pickford (Little Darling); Mack Sennett, John R. Cumpson, Owen Moore, Arthur Johnson, William A. Quirk, Henry B. Walthall, Anthony O'Sullivan, Verner Clarges, Charles Avery (In boarding house); Gertrude Robinson, George O. Nicholls, James Kirkwood (In store); ? (Maid)

"1776" or, THE HESSIAN RENEGADES

D. W. Griffith (d); Arthur Marvin, G. W. Bitzer (c); 26 July, 2/3 August 1909 (f); Studio/Cuddebackville, New York (l); 6 September 1909 (r); 965 feet (rl); J131458 / 9 September 1909 (copyright)

Owen Moore (American soldier); James Kirkwood, Kate Bruce, Mary Pickford, Gertrude Robinson (His family); Frank Powell, William A. Quirk, George O. Nicholls, Anthony O'Sullivan, Arthur Johnson, Mack Sennett, George Siegmann, Henry B. Walthall? (Hessians); Verner Clarges, Robert Harron, Linda Arvidson, William J. Butler (Farmers)

COMATA, THE SIOUX

D. W. Griffith (d); Edmund S. Hirsch (au); G. W. Bitzer (c); 6/7 August 1909 (f); Cuddebackville, New York (l); 9 September 1909 (r); 963 feet (rl); J131568 / 13 September 1909 (copyright)

James Kirkwood (Comata); Marion Leonard (Clear Eyes); Arthur Johnson (Bud Watkins); Linda Arvidson (Nellie Howe); Verner Clarges (Father); Verner Clarges? (Indian chief)

NOTE: Hirsch claimed credit as the author of this film in the "Studio Directory" section of Motion Picture News (1917), p. 158.

GETTING EVEN

D. W. Griffith (d); Mary Pickford (au); G. W. Bitzer (c); 9/10/12 August 1909 (r); Studio/Edgewater, New Jersey (l); 13 September 1909 (r); 587 feet (rl); J131612 / 14 September 1909 (copyright)

William A. Quirk (Bud); Mary Pickford (Miss Lucy); James Kirkwood (Jim Blake); Mack Sennett, Anthony O'Sullivan, Henry B. Walthall, John R. Cumpson, George O. Nicholls (Miners); Verner Clarges, Gertrude Robinson, Kate Bruce, Lottie Pickford, Arthur Johnson (Party guests)

NOTE: Pickford is identified as the author of this film in Billy Bitzer, His Story, p. 74.

THE CHILDREN'S FRIEND

D. W. Griffith (d); G. W. Bitzer (c); 30 July, 12 August 1909 (f);
Sea Breeze, New Jersey/Edgewater, New Jersey (l); 13 September
1909 (r); 386 feet (rl); J131611 / 14 September 1909 (copyright)

Frank Powell, Verner Clarges, Marion Leonard, Linda Arvidson,
Owen Moore (Adults); Gladys Egan (Among children)

THE BROKEN LOCKET

D. W. Griffith (d); G. W. Bitzer (c); 10/11/19 August 1909 (f); Edgewater, New Jersey/Studio (l); 16 September 1909 (r); 999 feet (rl);
J131862 / 17 September 1909 (copyright)

Frank Powell (George Peabody); Mary Pickford (Ruth King); Kate
Bruce (Her mother); Gertrude Robinson (Her friend); Arthur Johnson
(Mr. Joplin); Mack Sennett (Peabody's companion); Marion Leonard
(Mexican woman); Henry B. Walthall (Mexican man); George O.
Nicholls (Doctor); ? (Bartender); James Kirkwood, Owen Moore (At
bar table); William A. Quirk, Owen Moore, Robert Harron, Anthony
O'Sullivan, George O. Nicholls (Outside company office)

IN OLD KENTUCKY

D. W. Griffith (d); G. W. Bitzer (c); 29 July, 3/5/6 August 1909 (f);
Cuddebackville, New York/Studio not noted (l); 20 September 1909 (r);
983 feet (rl); J131613 / 14 September 1909 (copyright)

Verner Clarges (Mr. Wilkinson); Kate Bruce (Mrs. Wilkinson); Henry
B. Walthall (Robert, the Confederate son); Owen Moore (Union son);
Mack Sennett (Union sentry); Frank Powell, George Siegmann, William
J. Butler (Union soldiers); Frank Powell (Confederate officer); William
J. Butler (His aide); William J. Butler, ? (Servants [in blackface]);
Mary Pickford, Gertrude Robinson, James Kirkwood, Linda Arvidson,
George O. Nicholls, Anthony O'Sullivan, John R. Cumpson [in black-
face] (At homecoming party); Robert Harron (Extra)

A FAIR EXCHANGE

D. W. Griffith (d); "Freely adapted" from Silas Marner, the novel
by George Eliot (s); G. W. Bitzer (c); 14/23 August 1909 (f); Studio/
Cuddebackville, New York (l); 23 September 1909 (r); 995 feet (rl);
J132094 / 22 September 1909 (copyright)

James Kirkwood (Silas Marner); Mack Sennett (William Dane); Henry
B. Walthall (Peasant); Anthony O'Sullivan (Nobleman); Verner Clarges
(Minister); John R. Cumpson, Frank Evans, Kate Bruce, William A.
Quirk (At church); George O. Nicholls, Arthur Johnson (Thieves);
Gertrude Robinson (Mother); Edith Haldeman (Her child); Gladys

Egan (Visiting child); Kate Bruce (Old woman); Owen Moore
(Father of child); William A. Quirk (Marner's landlord); Frank Evans
(Helpful peasant); ? (Old dying man)

LEATHER STOCKING

D. W. Griffith (d); Adapted from the novels by James Fenimore
Cooper (s); G. W. Bitzer, Arthur Marvin (c); 7/24/25/26 August
1909 (f); Cuddebackville, New York (l); 27 September 1909 (r); 996
feet (rl); J132315 / 29 September 1909 (copyright)

George O. Nicholls (Colonel); Marion Leonard, Linda Arvidson (His
nieces); Mack Sennett (Big Serpent); Owen Moore (Leather Stocking);
James Kirkwood (Trapper); William A. Quirk, Frank Powell, Anthony
O'Sullivan (Soldiers); Guy Hedlund, Arthur Johnson, Frank Evans
(Indians); Edith Haldeman (Child); ? (Escort)

THE AWAKENING

D. W. Griffith (d); Mary Pickford (au); G. W. Bitzer (c); 16/17/20
August 1909 (f); Studio/Edgewater, New Jersey (l); 30 September
1909 (r); 691 feet (rl); J132453 / 2 October 1909 (copyright)

Arthur Johnson (Major); ? (Widow); Mary Pickford (Her daughter);
Anthony O'Sullivan (Lawyer); Kate Bruce (Nun); Owen Moore (Major's
friend); George O. Nicholls (Priest); Mack Sennett (Butler)

NOTE: Pickford is identified as the author of this film in Billy
Bitzer, His Story, p. 74.

WANTED, A CHILD

D. W. Griffith (d); G. W. Bitzer (c); 31 August 1909 (f); Studio (l);
30 September 1909 (r); 296 feet (rl); J132957 / 2 October 1909 (copyright)

George O. Nicholls (Father); Kate Bruce (Mother); Anthony O'Sullivan? (Postman); Gladys Egan, Jack Pickford, Edith Haldeman
(Children)

PIPPA PASSES OR, THE SONG OF CONSCIENCE

D. W. Griffith (d); "Pippa Passes," the poem by Robert Browning
(s); G. W. Bitzer, Arthur Marvin, Percy Higginson (c); 17-21 August
1909 (f); Edgewater, New Jersey/Studio (l); 4 October 1909 (r); 983
feet (rl); J132585 / 2 October 1909 (copyright)

Gertrude Robinson (Pippa); George O. Nicholls (Husband); ? (His
family); ? (In bar); James Kirkwood (Jules); Linda Arvidson (Greek

model); William A. Quirk, Mack Sennett, Anthony O'Sullivan, ? (In studio); Arthur Johnson (Luca); Marion Leonard (Ottima); Owen Moore (Sibald)

NOTE: Reissued by Biograph, 15 October 1915.

FOOLS OF FATE

D. W. Griffith (d); G. W. Bitzer (c); 27/30 August 1909 (f); Studio/ Cuddebackville, New York (l); 7 October 1909 (r); 972 feet (rl); J132811 / 7 October 1909 (copyright)

James Kirkwood (Ben Webster); Marion Leonard (Fanny Webster); Frank Powell (Ed Hilton); ? (Outside store); ? (Couple in forest)

THE LITTLE TEACHER

D. W. Griffith (d); G. W. Bitzer, Arthur Marvin (c); 1/3/8 September 1909 (f); Greenwich, Connecticut/Leonia [Station], New Jersey/ Studio (l); 11 October 1909 (r); 982 feet (rl); J132812 / 7 October 1909 (copyright)

Mary Pickford (The little teacher); Arthur Johnson (Jack Browning); Edward Dillon (Dave, the bully); Kate Bruce (The mother); George O. Nicholls, ? (Men in schoolroom); William A. Quirk, Gladys Egan, Gertrude Robinson, Edith Haldeman (Students); ? (Browning's fiancée)

A CHANGE OF HEART

D. W. Griffith (d); G. W. Bitzer (c); 2/4 September 1909 (f); Studio/ Greenwich, Connecticut (l); 14 October 1909 (r); 977 feet (rl); J133141 / 14 October 1909 (copyright)

Owen Moore (Howard Norris); William A. Quirk, Edward Dillon, ? (His companions); ? (Country girl); George O. Nicholls (Her father); James Kirkwood (The farmer); Kate Bruce (Howard's mother); Arthur Johnson (Real minister); Anthony O'Sullivan (Cafe owner); Mack Sennett (Outside cafe); Anthony O'Sullivan, ? (Servants)

HIS LOST LOVE

D. W. Griffith (d); G. W. Bitzer (c); 7/8/10 September 1909 (f); Studio (l); 18 October 1909 (r); 968 feet (rl); J133276 / 19 October 1909 (copyright)

James Kirkwood (Luke); Owen Moore (James); Mary Pickford (Mary); George O. Nicholls (Her father); Kate Bruce, ? (Maids); Marion Leonard (Sister); Gertrude Robinson (Grown child); Anthony O'Sullivan (In cabin); Dorothy West, Mack Sennett, Lottie Pickford?, Gladys

Egan, Anthony O'Sullivan, Violet Mersereau, Frank Evans, Marion
Leonard (At wedding); ? (Church caretaker); ? (Doctor); ? (Minister)

THE EXPIATION

D. W. Griffith (d); G. W. Bitzer (c); 15/16 September 1909 (f);
Studio (l); 21 October 1909 (r); 992 feet (rl); J133582 / 23 October
1909 (copyright)

Owen Moore (John Waterbury); Marion Leonard (Helen, his wife);
Arthur Johnson (William Trevor); Anthony O'Sullivan, Frank Evans
(Servants); Mack Sennett (Trevor's friend); ? (Maids); Guy Hedlund?
(Trevor's servant); George O. Nicholls, Frank Evans (Men in cabin)

IN THE WATCHES OF THE NIGHT

D. W. Griffith (d); G. W. Bitzer (c); 13/14/20 September 1909 (f);
Edgewater, New Jersey/Studio (l); 25 October 1909 (r); 996 feet (rl);
J133855 / 27 October 1909 (copyright)

Frank Powell (Henry Brainard); George O. Nicholls (John Whitney);
Marion Leonard (His wife); Gladys Egan (Child); Kate Bruce, ?
(Maids); Anthony O'Sullivan, Mack Sennett (Policemen); Dorothy West,
Mary Pickford (At Brainard's)

LINES OF WHITE ON A SULLEN SEA

D. W. Griffith (d); "Lines of White on a Sullen Sea," (s); G. W.
Bitzer (c); 11/18 September 1909 (f); Studio/Highlands, New Jersey
(l); 28 October 1909 (r); 975 feet (rl); J133854 / 27 October 1909
(copyright)

Linda Arvidson (Emily); George O. Nicholls (Joe); James Kirkwood
(Bill); Kate Bruce (Mother); Marion Leonard (Second wife); Dorothy
West (Her friend); William A. Quirk, Gertrude Robinson (First
couple); Mary Pickford, ? (Second couple); Frank Powell (Doctor);
Mack Sennett, Frank Evans, William A. Quirk, Anthony O'Sullivan
(Fishermen in first port); Owen Moore (In second port)

THE GIBSON GODDESS

D. W. Griffith (d); G. W. Bitzer (c); 11/17 September 1909 (f);
Highlands, New Jersey/Studio (l); 1 November 1909 (r); 576 feet (rl);
J134044 / 1 November 1909 (copyright)

Marion Leonard (Nanette Ranfrea); ? (Her valet); James Kirkwood,
Mack Sennett, William A. Quirk, J. Waltham, Arthur Johnson (Her
admirers); Anthony O'Sullivan (Commodore Fitzmorrice); Kate Bruce,
Mary Pickford, Gertrude Robinson (On sidewalks); Dorothy West

(Maid); Frank Evans (On pier); George O. Nicholls (Manager of beach house)

WHAT'S YOUR HURRY?

D. W. Griffith (d); G. W. Bitzer (c); 21/27 September 1909 (f); Fort Lee, New Jersey/Studio (l); 1 November 1909 (r); 403 feet (rl); J134043 / 1 November 1909 (copyright)

Mary Pickford (Mary); George O. Nicholls (Her father); Kate Bruce (Her mother); Gladys Egan, ? (Her sisters); William A. Quirk (Harry); Bessie McCoy?, ? (Maids); Frank Evans (Butler); Dorothy West, Gertrude Robinson, Anthony O'Sullivan, Violet Mersereau, Mack Sennett, J. Waltham (On street)

NURSING A VIPER

D. W. Griffith (d); G. W. Bitzer (c); 24/29 September 1909 (f); Studio/Englewood, New Jersey (l); 4 November 1909 (r); 920 feet (rl); J134294 / 5 November 1909 (copyright)

Arthur Johnson (Husband); Marion Leonard (Wife); Frank Powell (The Viper); William A. Quirk, Gertrude Robinson, Owen Moore (Fleeing aristocrats); Ruth Hart, Mabel Trunelle (Victimized women); George O. Nicholls, James Kirkwood, Mack Sennett, Frank Evans, Anthony O'Sullivan, Owen Moore, Henry Lehrman, J. Waltham (In mob)

THE RESTORATION

D. W. Griffith (d); G. W. Bitzer (c); 22 September, 1/7 October 1909 (f); Studio/Little Falls, New Jersey (l); 8 November 1909 (r); 964 feet (rl); J134602 / 10 November 1909 (copyright)

James Kirkwood (Mr. Morley); Marion Leonard (Mrs. Morley); Owen Moore (Jack); Mary Pickford (Alice Ashford); George O. Nicholls (Doctor); Kate Bruce, Gertrude Robinson, Guy Hedlund, Frank Evans, Ruth Hart (Servants)

THE LIGHT THAT CAME

D. W. Griffith (d); G. W. Bitzer (c); 30 September, 2/4 October 1909 (f); Studio (l); 11 November 1909 (r); 998 feet (rl); J134658 / 13 November 1909 (copyright)

Marion Leonard, Mary Pickford (Vivian and Daisy); Ruth Hart (Grace); Kate Bruce (Their mother); Owen Moore (Carl Wagner); George O. Nicholls (Doctor); Arthur Johnson (Young doctor); Anthony O'Sullivan, William A. Quirk, Mack Sennett, Francis J. Grandon

(Suitors); James Kirkwood, Arthur Johnson, Guy Hedlund, Dorothy West, Gertrude Robinson, Frank Powell, Anthony O'Sullivan, Mabel Trunelle, Frank Evans, J. Waltham (At the ball)

TWO WOMEN AND A MAN

D. W. Griffith (d); G. W. Bitzer (c); 25 September, 6/12 October 1909 (f); Studio/Fort Lee, New Jersey (l); 15 November 1909 (r); 988 feet (rl); J134952 / 17 November 1909 (copyright)

Frank Powell (John Randolph); Kate Bruce (Molly Randolph); Ruth Hart, Anthony O'Sullivan (Servants); Owen Moore (Friend); Mabel Trunelle (The show girl); ? (Her maid); Mack Sennett, Gertrude Robinson, Ruth Hart, Francis J. Grandon, Dorothy West (At party); George O. Nicholls, James Kirkwood, William A. Quirk, Francis J. Grandon (At lawyer's); Arthur Johnson, Mack Sennett, Charles H. West, Francis J. Grandon, Ruth Hart, Owen Moore, Verner Clarges? (At reception)

A MIDNIGHT ADVENTURE

D. W. Griffith (d); G. W. Bitzer, Arthur Marvin (c); 5/6/8 October 1909 (f); Studio/Location not noted (l); 18 November 1909 (r); 519 feet (rl); J135022 / 20 November 1909 (copyright)

Dorothy West (Mercedes); William A. Quirk (Frank, her suitor); Mary Pickford (Eleanor); Kate Bruce (Mother); ? (Mercedes' maid); Ruth Hart (Eleanor's maid); George O. Nicholls (Frank's friend); Mack Sennett (Sergeant Reginald Vandyke Worthington); Anthony O'Sullivan, Arthur Johnson, Frank Evans (Policemen)

SWEET REVENGE

D. W. Griffith (d); G. W. Bitzer (c); 11/13 October 1909 (f); Studio/Central Park, New York City (l); 18 November 1909 (r); 471 feet (rl); J135021 / 20 November 1909 (copyright)

Arthur Johnson (Paul Hiller); Marion Leonard (His fiancée); Jeannie MacPherson (Alice Baross, the second fiancée); Frank Powell (Alice's father); ? (Alice's mother); ? (Telegraph boy); Robert Harron (On bridge)

THE OPEN GATE

D. W. Griffith (d); G. W. Bitzer (c); 9/12 October 1909 (f); Studio/Coytesville, New Jersey (l); 22 November 1909 (r); 988 feet (rl); J135125 / 24 November 1909 (copyright)

George O. Nicholls (George); Kate Bruce (Hetty); Edith Haldeman

(Mary, as a child); Gertrude Robinson (Mary, as an adult); Owen Moore (Jack); Ruth Hart, Jeannie MacPherson, Dorothy West, ? (Hetty's relatives); Mack Sennett (Hetty's brother-in-law); Anthony O'Sullivan (Messenger); Anthony O'Sullivan (Gardener)

THE MOUNTAINEER'S HONOR

D. W. Griffith (d); G. W. Bitzer (c); 14/19/20 October 1909 (f); Studio/Cuddebackville, New York (l); 25 November 1909 (r); 977 feet (rl); J135135 / 26 November 1909 (copyright)

Mary Pickford (Harum-Scarum); Owen Moore (Her suitor); James Kirkwood (Her brother); Kate Bruce (Her mother); George O. Nicholls (Her father); Arthur Johnson (The man from the valley); Anthony O'Sullivan (Sheriff); Mack Sennett, Frank Evans (In posse); Ruth Hart, William A. Quirk, Gertrude Robinson (Townsfolk); Dorothy West (Also at dance)

THE TRICK THAT FAILED

D. W. Griffith (d); G. W. Bitzer (c); 23 October 1909 (f); Studio (l); 29 November 1909 (r); 645 feet (rl); J135517 / 3 December 1909 (copyright)

Mary Pickford (Nellie Burt); Arthur Johnson (Billy Hart); Anthony O'Sullivan (Hans Kessler); George O. Nicholls (Gallery owner); Dorothy West, Gertrude Robinson, Guy Hedlund, Jeannie MacPherson, Owen Moore, Frank Evans, Ruth Hart? (At gallery); Mack Sennett, William A. Quirk, Kate Bruce (Buyers)

IN THE WINDOW RECESS

D. W. Griffith (d); G. W. Bitzer (c); 15/16/28 October 1909 (f); Studio/Fort Lee, New Jersey (l); 29 November 1909 (r); 337 feet (rl); J135516 / 3 December 1909 (copyright)

George O. Nicholls (Officer Wallace); Marion Leonard (Mrs. Wallace); Adele De Garde (Their child); James Kirkwood (Convict); Jeannie MacPherson, ? (Callers); Arthur Johnson, Anthony O'Sullivan, Frank Evans (Guards)

THE DEATH DISC

D. W. Griffith (d); "The Death Disk," the story by Mark Twain (s); G. W. Bitzer (c); 26/28 October 1909 (f); Coytesville, New Jersey/ Studio (l); 2 December 1909 (r); 995 feet (rl); J135518 / 3 December 1909 (copyright)

George O. Nicholls (The Catholic); Marion Leonard (His wife); Edith

Haldeman (Their child); Frank Powell (Oliver Cromwell); James Kirkwood (His advisor); ? (His valet); Gertrude Robinson, Adele De Garde,
Dorothy West, Jeannie MacPherson (The wife's companions); Ruth
Hart, Dorothy West (Ladies at court); Owen Moore, Anthony O'Sullivan, Frank Evans, Arthur Johnson, Charles Craig (Soldiers)

NOTE: According to Mark Twain, based on a "touching incident
mentioned in Carlyle's Letters and Speeches of Oliver Cromwell. "

THROUGH THE BREAKERS

D. W. Griffith (d); G. W. Bitzer (c); 29/30 October, 1/10 November
1909 (f); Edgewater, New Jersey/Studio (l); 6 December 1909 (r);
974 feet (rl); J135642 / 8 December 1909 (copyright)

James Kirkwood (Mr. Nostrand); Marion Leonard (Mrs. Nostrand);
Adele De Garde (Their child); Kate Bruce (Nurse); George O. Nicholls
(Doctor); Charles Craig, Arthur Johnson, William A. Quirk, Henry
Lehrman, Mack Sennett, Lottie Pickford? (At the ball); Ruth Hart,
Jeannie MacPherson, Grace Henderson (Callers); Grace Henderson,
Ruth Hart (At the whist party); Donald Crisp, Owen Moore, Robert
Harron, Mack Sennett, Henry Lehrman (At the club); Gertrude Rob-
inson, Henry Lehrman, Ruth Hart, Charles Craig, Arthur Johnson,
Frank Evans, Grace Henderson, Jeannie MacPherson, J. Waltham
(At the soirée); Frank Evans (Among servants); ? (Butler)

THE REDMAN'S VIEW

D. W. Griffith (d); G. W. Bitzer (c); 4/5/6 November 1909 (f); Mount
Beacon, New York (l); 9 December 1909 (r); 971 feet (rl); J135835 /
11 December 1909 (copyright)

? (Minnewanna); Owen Moore (Silver Eagle); James Kirkwood (His
father); W. Chrystie Miller, Dorothy West, Kate Bruce, Ruth Hart,
Edith Haldeman (Indians); Charles H. West, Henry Lehrman, Mack
Sennett, George O. Nicholls, William A. Quirk, Arthur Johnson,
Anthony O'Sullivan, Frank Evans, Charles Craig (Conquerors)

A CORNER IN WHEAT

D. W. Griffith (d); The Octopus, the novel by Frank Norris/"A Deal
in Wheat, " the story by Frank Norris (s); G. W. Bitzer (c); 3-13
November 1909 (r); Studio/Jamaica, New York (l); 13 December 1909
(r); 953 feet (rl); J135969 / 15 December 1909 (copyright)

Frank Powell (The Wheat King); Grace Henderson (His wife); James
Kirkwood, Linda Arvidson, W. Chrystie Miller, Gladys Egan (Farm
family); Henry B. Walthall (Wheat King's assistant); Mack Sennett,
George O. Nicholls, Frank Evans, Arthur Johnson, Charles Craig,
William A. Quirk, Robert Harron, Owen Moore, Anthony O'Sullivan,

Henry Lehrman?, William J. Butler (On the floor of the Exchange);
Owen Moore, Arthur Johnson, William A. Quirk, Charles Craig,
Frank Evans, Jeannie MacPherson (Banquet guests); Gertrude Robin-
son, Kate Bruce, Ruth Hart, Edith Haldeman (In store); Jeannie
MacPherson, Dorothy West, Blanche Sweet (Visitors to the grain
elevator); Frank Evans (Grain elevator attendant); ? (Petitioner to
Wheat King); ? (Breadline rioters); ? (Baker); ? (Policemen); ?
(Wheat King's employees)

IN A HEMPEN BAG

D. W. Griffith (d); G. W. Bitzer (c); 2/9 November 1909 (f); Studio
/Edgewater, New Jersey (l); 16 December 1909 (r); 455 feet (rl);
J136054 / 20 December 1909 (copyright)

Grace Henderson (Mother); Ruth Hart (Maid); Dorothy West (Daughter);
Kate Bruce (Nursemaid); Adele De Garde, Gladys Egan (Children);
Jack Pickford (On road); Mack Sennett (Gardener); Robert Harron
(Young man); Henry B. Walthall, Jeannie MacPherson (Couple on
road)

THE TEST

D. W. Griffith (d); Arthur Marvin, G. W. Bitzer (c); 11/13 November
1909 (f); Studio/Coytesville, New Jersey (l); 16 December 1909 (r);
545 feet (rl); J136053 / 20 December 1909 (copyright)

William A. Quirk (Harry); Mary Pickford (Bessie); ? (Maid); Marion
Leonard, Arthur Johnson, Charles Craig, Anthony O'Sullivan, William
J. Butler, Henry B. Walthall (At hotel); ? (Hotel maid); Ruth Hart
(Salvation Army member); ? (Porter)

A TRAP FOR SANTA CLAUS

D. W. Griffith (d); G. W. Bitzer (c); 13/15/16/20 November 1909
(f); Studio/Fort Lee, New Jersey (l); 20 December 1909 (r); 989 feet
(rl); J136186 / 23 December 1909 (copyright)

Henry B. Walthall (Arthur Rogers); Marion Leonard (Helen Rogers);
Gladys Egan (Their daughter); ? (Their son); Mack Sennett, Anthony
O'Sullivan, Charles Craig, William J. Butler (In bar); W. Chrystie
Miller (Old man); Kate Bruce (Maid); William J. Butler (Attorney)

IN LITTLE ITALY

D. W. Griffith (d); G. W. Bitzer (c); 17-20 November 1909 (f); Fort
Lee, New Jersey/Studio (l); 23 December 1909 (r); 956 feet (rl);
J136491 / 29 December 1909 (copyright)

Marion Leonard (Marie Cadrone); ? (Her companions); George O.
Nicholls (Tony Guiletto); Henry B. Walthall (Victor); Gladys Egan, ?
(Children); W. Chrystie Miller, Mack Sennett, William J. Butler,
J. Waltham? (In bar); Anthony O'Sullivan (Peddlar); Charles Craig,
Owen Moore, William A. Quirk, Gertrude Robinson, Dorothy West,
Kate Bruce, Jeannie MacPherson, Mack Sennett, Ruth Hart, Henry
Lehrman, Blanche Sweet, Stephanie Longfellow?, Guy Hedlund? (At
the ball); James Kirkwood (Sheriff); Frank Evans, ? (His deputies)

TO SAVE HER SOUL

D. W. Griffith (d); G. W. Bitzer, Arthur Marvin (c); 22-27 November 1909 (f); Studio/Fort Lee, New Jersey (l); 27 December 1909 (r);
986 feet (rl); J136450 / 28 December 1909 (copyright)

Arthur Johnson (Paul Redmond); Mary Pickford (Agnes Halley); ?
(Her mother); W. Chrystie Miller (Church organist); George O. Nich-
olls (Manager); Kate Bruce (Housekeeper); Jack Pickford, Robert
Harron (Stagehands); James Kirkwood, Mack Sennett, Blanche Sweet,
? (Backstage at debut); Frank Evans (Stage manager); Jeannie Mac-
Pherson, Gertrude Robinson, Henry Lehrman, Paul Scardon, Linda
Arvidson (In audience); Ruth Hart, James Kirkwood, Dorothy West,
Owen Moore, Blanche Sweet (At party); Robert Harron (Usher);
Charles Craig, ? (Bumpkins)

THE DAY AFTER

D. W. Griffith (d); Mary Pickford? (au); G. W. Bitzer (c); 24/26
November 1909 (f); Studio (l); 30 December 1909 (r); 460 feet (rl);
J136612 / 3 January 1910 (copyright)

Arthur Johnson (Mr. Hilton); Marion Leonard (Mrs. Hilton); George
O. Nicholls (Friend); James Kirkwood, Mack Sennett, Henry B.
Walthall, Jeannie MacPherson, Gertrude Robinson, Anthony O'Sullivan,
Frank Evans, Henry Lehrman, Dorothy West, Paul Scardon? (Party
guests); W. Chrystie Miller (The Old Year); Blanche Sweet (The New
Year); Linda Arvidson, ? (Servants)

NOTE: Pickford is identified as the author of this film in Sweetheart,
the biography by Robert Windeler.

CHOOSING A HUSBAND

D. W. Griffith (d); G. W. Bitzer (c); 27 November 1909 (f); Studio
(l); 30 December 1909 (r); 531 feet (rl); J136613 / 3 January 1910
(copyright)

Florence Barker (Gladys); Mack Sennett, William A. Quirk, Charles
Craig, Anthony O'Sullivan (Bachelors); Dorothy West, Blanche Sweet,
? (Gladys' friends); Kate Bruce (Maid); Henry B. Walthall (Harry)

THE ROCKY ROAD

D. W. Griffith (d); Arthur Marvin, G. W. Bitzer (c); 29/30 November, 1/4 December 1909 (f); Studio/Hackensack, New Jersey/ Edgewater, New Jersey (l); 3 January 1910 (r); 990 feet (rl); J136775 / 6 January 1910 (copyright)

Frank Powell (Ben); Stephanie Longfellow (His wife); George O. Nicholls (Farmer); ? (His wife); Edith Haldeman (The daughter, as a child); Blanche Sweet (The daughter, at eighteen); Charles Craig (Farmhand); Kate Bruce (Maid); W. Chrystie Miller (Minister); Gladys Egan, Charles Craig, Dorothy West? (At church); James Kirkwood (Best man); Anthony O'Sullivan, Frank Evans, J. Waltham (In bar); Henry Lehrman (Outside bar); ? (Lumberyard foreman)

THE DANCING GIRL OF BUTTE

D. W. Griffith (d); G. W. Bitzer (c); 2/3/4 December 1909 (f); Studio/Edgewater, New Jersey (l); 6 January 1910 (r); 984 feet (rl); J136851 / 8 January 1910 (copyright)

Florence Barker (Bella); Owen Moore (Howard Raymond); Mack Sennett (In newsroom); W. Chrystie Miller, Charles Craig, William A. Quirk, Frank Evans, Francis J. Grandon (In music hall)

HER TERRIBLE ORDEAL

D. W. Griffith (d); G. W. Bitzer (c); 6/9 December 1909 (f); Studio/Fort Lee, New Jersey (l); 10 January 1910 (r); 952 feet (rl); J137169 / 13 January 1910 (copyright)

George O. Nicholls (Mr. Curtis); Owen Moore (Jack); Florence Barker (Alice); Charles Craig (Jack's rival); Anthony O'Sullivan (Peddlar); ? (Office boy); Robert Harron (At station); W. Chrystie Miller (Extra)

ALL ON ACCOUNT OF THE MILK

Frank Powell (d); Mrs. Laurie Mackin (au); Arthur Marvin (c); 9/10/ 11 December 1909 (f); Studio/Fort Lee, New Jersey (l); 13 January 1910 (r); 989 feet (rl); J137280 / 15 January 1910 (copyright)

Mary Pickford (Young woman); Kate Bruce (Her mother); Blanche Sweet (Maid); Mack Sennett (Farmhand); Arthur Johnson (Young contractor); ? (His mother); Jack Pickford, ? (At construction site); ? (Minister and friends)

NOTE: A possible working title for this film may have been "Loretta and Leander," as found next to the title in the production records at the Museum of Modern Art. In an interview with Iris Barry

(Columbia University, November 1939), Frank Powell claimed this as the first film he directed at Biograph. Mackin is identified as the author of this film by Epes Winthrop Sargent in "The Literary Side of Motion Pictures," Moving Picture World, 11 July 1914, p. 201.

ON THE REEF

D. W. Griffith (d); G. W. Bitzer (c); 13/14 December 1909 (f); Studio (l); 17 January 1910 (r); 988 feet (rl); J137450 / 19 January 1910 (copyright)

Verner Clarges (Rupert Howland); Gladys Egan (Elsie, his daughter); Marion Leonard (Grace Wallace); ? (Her mother); Henry B. Walthall (Mr. Wilson); W. Chrystie Miller, ? (Grandparents); ? (Howland's servants); Frank Evans, ? (Wilson's servants); Adolph Lestina (Priest); Charles Craig, Ruth Hart (At deathbed)

THE CALL

D. W. Griffith (d); G. W. Bitzer (c); 7/8/10 December 1909 (f); Fort Lee, New Jersey/Studio (l); 20 January 1910 (r); 989 feet (rl); J137557 / 22 January 1910 (copyright)

Florence Barker (Edith Lawson); Henry B. Walthall (Billy Harvey); James Kirkwood (Amos Holden); ? (Old woman); Mack Sennett, Gladys Egan, Kate Bruce, W. Chrystie Miller, William A. Quirk, Charles Craig, Anthony O'Sullivan, Ruth Hart, Frank Evans, Jack Pickford (At show); Frank Evans? (Among performers); ? (Stage manager); Charles Craig, Francis J. Grandon?, W. Chrystie Miller (Backstage); Robert Harron (Boy passing handbills)

THE HONOR OF HIS FAMILY

D. W. Griffith (d); Arthur Marvin, G. W. Bitzer (c); 10/17/18 December 1909 (f); Coytesville, New Jersey/Studio (l); 24 January 1910 (r); 988 feet (rl); J137729 / 26 January 1910 (copyright)

Henry B. Walthall (George Pickett, Jr.); Verner Clarges (Colonel Pickett); Ruth Hart, Kate Bruce, Charles Craig, Linda Arvidson, Dorothy West (At farewell); George O. Nicholls, Anthony O'Sullivan, James Kirkwood, Francis J. Grandon? (Officers); Alfred Paget, James Kirkwood (Among soldiers); W. Chrystie Miller (Among friends); Adolph Lestina [blackface]? (Servant); ? (Servants)

THE LAST DEAL

D. W. Griffith (d); G. W. Bitzer (c); 15/16 December 1909 (f); Studio (l); 27 January 1910 (r); 991 feet (rl); J137856 / 29 January 1910 (copyright)

Owen Moore (Husband); Ruth Hart (Wife); Edith Haldeman (Their
child); George O. Nicholls (Employer); James Kirkwood (Westerner);
William A. Quirk, Charles H. West? (Bank tellers); Mack Sennett
(In bank); ? (Maid); Frank Powell, Dell Henderson, Guy Hedlund,
Anthony O'Sullivan, Charles Perley, Charles Craig, Frank Evans,
Gus Pixley?, Adolph Lestina, W. Chrystie Miller, Henry Lehrman?
(At card game)

THE CLOISTER'S TOUCH

D. W. Griffith (d); G. W. Bitzer, Arthur Marvin (c); 20/21 December
1909 (f); Studio (l); 31 January 1910 (r); 993 feet (rl); J137957 / 2
February 1910 (copyright)

Henry B. Walthall (Father); Marion Leonard (Elsa, the mother); Edith
Haldeman (Their child); Arthur Johnson (The duke); Owen Moore, Dell
Henderson, ? (The duke's men); Mack Sennett, Ruth Hart, Charles
Craig, Francis J. Grandon, Alfred Paget, Frank Evans, Henry
Lehrman, Dorothy West, Kate Toncray? (At the palace); George O.
Nicholls, W. Chrystie Miller (Monks); Kate Bruce (Old woman)

THE WOMAN FROM MELLON'S

D. W. Griffith (d); G. W. Bitzer (c); 22/24 December 1909 (f); Studio (l); 3 February 1910 (r); approx 988 feet (rl); J138028 / 5 February 1910 (copyright)

William A. Quirk (Harry Towsend); George O. Nicholls (James
Petersby); Mary Pickford (Mary, his daughter); Gertrude Robinson,
Lottie Pickford, ? (Young women); Anthony O'Sullivan, Francis J.
Grandon (In first office); Mack Sennett, Dell Henderson, Alfred Paget,
Francis J. Grandon, Henry Lehrman (Stockbrokers in second office);
James Kirkwood (Minister); Frank Evans, Alfred Paget, Guy Hedlund
(Butlers); Kate Bruce, Ruth Hart, Dorothy West (Maids); Linda Ar-
vidson (Detective); Charles Craig, ? (Detectives); Charles Craig, ?
(Policemen)

THE COURSE OF TRUE LOVE

Frank Powell (d); Arthur Marvin (c); 23/31 December 1909 (f); Fort
Lee, New Jersey/Studio (l); 7 February 1910 (r); approx 987 feet
(rl); J138088 / 8 February 1910 (copyright)

Florence Barker (Florabel Thurston); Owen Moore (Ben Lawrence);
Elinor Kershaw (Flower girl); ? (Florabel's parents); Francis
J. Grandon, Dell Henderson, ? (Ben's friends); ? (Visitors); Henry
Lehrman, ? (Servants)

THE DUKE'S PLAN

D. W. Griffith (d); G. W. Bitzer (c); 27/28 December 1909 (f); Studio
(l); 10 February 1910 (r); approx 985 feet (rl); J138229 / 12 February
1910 (copyright)

Francis J. Grandon (The Duke); Marion Leonard (Fiametta, his
daughter); Owen Moore (Raoul); James Kirkwood, W. Chrystie Miller,
Alfred Paget, Dell Henderson? (Duke's men); Ruth Hart, Kate Bruce,
Gertrude Robinson [as a boy] (Fiametta's attendants); ? (Second suitor); Dorothy West (At the inn)

ONE NIGHT, AND THEN---

D. W. Griffith (d); G. W. Bitzer (c); 30 December 1909 (f); Studio
(l); 14 February 1910 (r); approx 992 feet (rl); J138316 / 16 February 1910 (copyright)

Henry B. Walthall (Henry Ravol); Kate Bruce (Mother); Gladys Egan,
? (Her children); George O. Nicholls (Doctor); William A. Quirk
(Workman); James Kirkwood, Gertrude Robinson, Mack Sennett,
Charles Craig, Florence Barker, Francis J. Grandon, Ruth Hart,
Dell Henderson, W. Chrystie Miller, Dorothy West, Elinor Kershaw
(At party)

NOTE: Paper print contains only one-half of the original footage.
The final card in the paper print indicates the "Bal. of Prod." was
to be deposited at a later date. This apparently was never done.

THE ENGLISHMAN AND THE GIRL

D. W. Griffith (d); G. W. Bitzer (c); 31 December 1909, 4 January
1910 (f); Studio (l); 17 February 1910 (r); approx 975 feet (rl);
J138587 / 21 February 1910 (copyright)

George O. Nicholls (Mr. Thayer); Kate Bruce (Mrs. Thayer); Charles
Craig (Arthur Wilberforce); Mary Pickford (The girl); Gladys Egan
(Child); Dorothy West, Ruth Hart, ? (Friends); Francis J. Grandon,
Mack Sennett, Anthony O'Sullivan (In store); ? (Delivery man); Mack
Sennett, Anthony O'Sullivan, W. Chrystie Miller, Francis J. Grandon,
Dell Henderson, Dorothy West, Gertrude Robinson, Linda Arvidson
(Members of drama club)

HIS LAST BURGLARY

D. W. Griffith (d); Stanner E. V. Taylor (au); G. W. Bitzer (c); 7
January 1910 (f); Studio/Coytesville, New Jersey (l); 21 February
1910 (r); approx 995 feet (rl); J138678 / 26 February 1910 (copyright)

Henry B. Walthall (William Standish); Dorothy Bernard (His wife); Dorothy West (Maid); James Kirkwood (The Burglar); Kate Bruce (His wife); George O. Nicholls (Minister); Stephanie Longfellow (His housekeeper); Francis J. Grandon (Doctor)

TAMING A HUSBAND

D. W. Griffith (d); G. W. Bitzer (c); 10/12 January 1910 (f); Studio (l); 24 February 1910 (r); approx 986 feet (rl); J138677 / 26 February 1910 (copyright)

Elinor Kershaw (Lady Margaret); Arthur Johnson (Her husband); Dorothy Bernard (Lady Clarissa); ? (Her fencing partner); Mack Sennett, Francis J. Grandon (Soldiers); Anthony O'Sullivan, Guy Hedlund (Servants); Ruth Hart, Dell Henderson (Nobles)

THE FINAL SETTLEMENT

D. W. Griffith (d); G. W. Bitzer, Arthur Marvin (c); 5/8 January 1910 (f); Coytesville, New Jersey/Fort Lee, New Jersey/Studio (l); 28 February 1910 (r); approx 981 feet (rl); J138843 / 3 March 1910 (copyright)

James Kirkwood (Jim); Dorothy Bernard (Ruth); Arthur Johnson (John); Edith Haldeman (Child); Anthony O'Sullivan (Woodsman)

THE NEWLYWEDS

D. W. Griffith (d); Arthur Marvin, G. W. Bitzer (c); 14/26 January 1910 (f); Studio [New York]/Los Angeles, California (l); 3 March 1910 (r); approx 981 feet (rl); J138954 / 7 March 1910 (copyright)

Arthur Johnson (Dick Harcourt); Mary Pickford (Alice Vance); Florence Barker (Dora Dean); Charles H. West (Harry); Frank Powell, Henry B. Walthall, Dell Henderson (Friends); Kate Bruce (Maid); George O. Nicholls, ? (Parents); Alfred Paget, W. Chrystie Miller, Mack Sennett, Dorothy West, Anthony O'Sullivan, Guy Hedlund, Dell Henderson, Frank Evans, Gertrude Robinson, Charles Craig, Ruth Hart (On train); William A. Quirk, Francis J. Grandon, ? (Conductors); Alfred Paget, Jack Pickford, Frank Opperman, Henry B. Walthall, Frank Powell, Robert Harron (At station reception); Gladys Egan (Child on street)

NOTE: 26 January 1910 is the first filming date of the Biograph company's initial California trip.

THE THREAD OF DESTINY

D. W. Griffith (d); G. W. Bitzer (c); 28 January 1910 (f); San Gabriel

Mission, California (l); 7 March 1910 (r); approx 977 feet (rl); J138986 / 9 March 1910 (copyright)

Mary Pickford (Myrtle); Francis J. Grandon (Gus); Henry B. Walthall (Estrada); Linda Arvidson (Hotelkeeper's wife); W. Chrystie Miller (Priest); Mack Sennett, Charles H. West, Anthony O'Sullivan, Charles Craig, Alfred Paget, Frank Opperman, George O. Nicholls (In bar); Dorothy West (On street)

IN OLD CALIFORNIA

D. W. Griffith (d); G. W. Bitzer (c); 2/3 February 1910 (f); Holly-wood, California (l); 10 March 1910 (r); approx 991 feet (rl); J139101 / 12 March 1910 (copyright)

Frank Powell (Governor Manuella); Arthur Johnson (Cortes); Marion Leonard (Perdita); Henry B. Walthall (Her son); Mack Sennett, Francis J. Grandon, Charles H. West, Alfred Paget, Anthony O'Sullivan, Charles Craig (Soldiers); Charles H. West, Frank Opperman (Governor's servants); W. Chrystie Miller (Indian messenger)

THE MAN

D. W. Griffith (d); Stanner E. V. Taylor (au); G. W. Bitzer (c); 4/5 February 1910 (f); Studio/Sierra Madre, California (l); 12 March 1910 (r); approx 983 feet (rl); J139354 / 22 March 1910 (copyright)

Frank Powell (Steve Clark); Florence Barker (Mildred, his wife); Francis J. Grandon (The Wanderer)

THE CONVERTS

D. W. Griffith (d); G. W. Bitzer (c); 8/9 February 1910 (f); Studio/ San Gabriel Mission, California (l); 14 March 1910 (r); approx 986 feet (rl); J139195 / 16 March 1910 (copyright)

Linda Arvidson (The woman); Henry B. Walthall (The man); Charles H. West, Mack Sennett, ? (His friends); Arthur Johnson, Dell Henderson, George O. Nicholls (In bar); Robert Harron, Charles Craig, Frank Opperman (Bystanders); Dorothy West (Leaving bar); Kate Bruce (In doorway); Anthony O'Sullivan (Minister); W. Chrystie Miller (Old man); Alfred Paget (Chauffeur); George O. Nicholls? (On street); ? (Servant)

THE LOVE OF LADY IRMA

Frank Powell (d); Arthur Marvin (c); 5/6/7 January 1910 (f); Studio [New York] (l); 17 March 1910 (r); approx 988 feet (rl); J139353 / 22 March 1910 (copyright)

Florence Barker (Lady Irma); Dell Henderson (Her husband); Mack
Sennett, Henry Lehrman (Rogues); Dorothy West, Gertrude Robinson,
Ruth Hart, Stephanie Longfellow, Francis J. Grandon, Elinor Ker-
shaw (Party guests); Guy Hedlund?, Alfred Paget (Servants); ?
(Doctor); ? (Maid)

FAITHFUL

D. W. Griffith (d); Arthur Marvin, G. W. Bitzer (c); 10/11/12/16
February 1910 (f); Studio/Hollywood, California (l); 21 March 1910
(r); approx 994 feet (rl); J139617 / 28 March 1910 (copyright)

Arthur Johnson (John Dobbs [Adonese]); Mack Sennett (Zeke [Faithful]);
Florence Barker (John's sweetheart); Kate Bruce (Her mother); ?
(Butler); Dell Henderson, Anthony O'Sullivan (Bystanders); Anthony
O'Sullivan, W. Chrystie Miller, William A. Quirk, Dorothy West,
Francis J. Grandon (Neighbors)

THE TWISTED TRAIL

D. W. Griffith (d); G. W. Bitzer (c); 15-18 February 1910 (f); Sierra
Madre, California (l); 24 March 1910 (r); approx 988 feet (rl); J139618
/ 28 March 1910 (copyright)

Mary Pickford (Molly Hendricks); Arthur Johnson (Bob Gorman);
George O. Nicholls (Mr. Hendricks); Kate Bruce (Mrs. Hendricks);
W. Chrystie Miller (Grandfather); Mack Sennett, Dell Henderson
(Ranch hands); ? (Doctor); Charles H. West, Alfred Paget (Among
pursuers); Anthony O'Sullivan (Escort); ? (Coroner); Dorothy West
(Girl on farm); Alfred Paget, Frank Opperman (Indians)

GOLD IS NOT ALL

D. W. Griffith (d); G. W. Bitzer (c); 18/19/21/24 February 1910 (f);
Studio/Pasadena, California (l); 28 March 1910 (r); approx 988 feet
(rl); J139986 / 1 April 1910 (copyright)

Marion Leonard (Mabel, the heiress); Dell Henderson (Tomm Darrell,
her husband); Gladys Egan (Their child); Linda Arvidson (Ruth); Kate
Bruce (Her mother); Mack Sennett (Steve); Kathlyn Williams (Tomm's
mistress); W. Chrystie Miller (Grandfather); George O. Nicholls
(Doctor); Anthony O'Sullivan, Alfred Paget, Frank Opperman (Servants); ? (Maid); Francis J. Grandon, Henry B. Walthall, Charles
Craig, Charles H. West (At party)

THE SMOKER

Frank Powell (d); Arthur Marvin (c); 4/10/11/21 February 1910 (f);
Studio/Glendale, California (l); 31 March 1910 (r); approx 595 feet
(rl); J140142 / 4 April 1910 (copyright)

William A. Quirk (George); Mary Pickford (His wife); Frank Opperman (Farmer); ? (Father); Jack Pickford (Boy); ? (Farmer's daughter)

HIS LAST DOLLAR

Frank Powell (d); Arthur Marvin (c); 9 February 1910 (f); Glendale, California (l); 31 March 1910 (r); approx 397 feet (rl); J140314 / 4 April 1910 (copyright)

Charles Craig (Man); Marion Leonard (Woman); Anthony O'Sullivan (Waiter); Francis J. Grandon, ? (Friends); William A. Quirk (Boyfriend)

AS IT IS IN LIFE

D. W. Griffith (d); G. W. Bitzer (c); 22/23 February 1910 (f); California Pigeon Farm (l); 4 April 1910 (r); approx 981 feet (rl); J140186 / 6 April 1910 (copyright)

George O. Nicholls (George Forrester); Gladys Egan (His daughter, as a child); Mary Pickford (His daughter, as an adult); Mack Sennett (Owner of pigeon farm?); Marion Leonard (Forrester's lover); Charles H. West (Daughter's husband); Frank Opperman (His companion); Anthony O'Sullivan (Worker on farm); Kate Bruce (Maid); W. Chrystie Miller (Old man)

A RICH REVENGE

D. W. Griffith (d); Stanner E. V. Taylor (au); G. W. Bitzer (c); 25/26 February 1910 (f); Edendale, California (l); 7 April 1910 (r); approx 980 feet (rl); J140366 / 11 April 1910 (copyright)

William A. Quirk (Harry); Francis J. Grandon (Bill); Mary Pickford (Jennie); Anthony O'Sullivan (Merchant); Mack Sennett, Frank Opperman (In store); George O. Nicholls (Oil speculator); Charles H. West (Henchman)

A ROMANCE OF THE WESTERN HILLS

D. W. Griffith (d); G. W. Bitzer (c); 1/2 March 1910 (f); Sierra Madre, California/Pasadena, California (l); 11 April 1910 (r); approx 980 feet (rl); J140416 / 13 April 1910 (copyright)

Mary Pickford, Alfred Paget, Arthur Johnson (Indians); Dorothy West, Dell Henderson, Kate Bruce (Tourists); Charles H. West (The nephew); Kathlyn Williams (Second woman)

THE KID

Frank Powell (d); Arthur Marvin (c); 16/17/18 February, 2/8 March 1910 (f); Studio/Fullerton, California (l); 14 April 1910 (r); approx 981 feet (rl); J140598 / 18 April 1910 (copyright)

Henry B. Walthall (Walter Holden); Jack Pickford (His son); Florence Barker (Doris Marshall)

THOU SHALT NOT

D. W. Griffith (d); G. W. Bitzer (c); 3/4/5/11 March 1910 (f); Studio/Pasadena, California (l); 18 April 1910 (r); approx 987 feet (rl); J140639 / 20 April 1910 (copyright)

Henry B. Walthall (Edgar Thurston); Marion Leonard (Laura Edmonds); Kathlyn Williams (Actress); Charles H. West (Friend); George O. Nicholls (Doctor); W. Chrystie Miller, Gladys Egan (On street); Dell Henderson, Linda Arvidson (At party); ? (Butler); Dorothy West (Laura's friend)

THE TENDERFOOT'S TRIUMPH

Frank Powell (d); Stanner E. V. Taylor ["It's in the Surprise"] (au); Arthur Marvin (c); 23/24 February 1910 (f); Verdugo, California (l); 21 April 1910 (r); approx 989 feet (rl); J140758 / 23 April 1910 (copyright)

Florence Barker (The Girl); Arthur Johnson (Tenderfoot); Henry B. Walthall, ? (Horse thieves); Dell Henderson, Charles Craig (Cowboys); Frank Opperman? (Sheriff); Jack Pickford (Boy)

THE WAY OF THE WORLD

D. W. Griffith (d); G. W. Bitzer (c); 12/14 March 1910 (f); San Gabriel Mission, California/Glendale, California (l); 25 April 1910 (r); approx 950 feet (rl); J140899 / 27 April 1910 (copyright)

Henry B. Walthall (Young priest); George O. Nicholls (Old priest); Florence Barker (The Modern Magdalene); Gertrude Claire (Landlady); Dorothy West (Young girl); ? (Her mother); Francis J. Grandon?, ? (Farmers); Francis J. Grandon, Robert Harron, Frank Opperman (Hayers); Gladys Egan (Child); Dell Henderson (Foreman); Alfred Paget, ? (Policemen); W. Chrystie Miller (Bell ringer); Mack Sennett, Charles Craig, Linda Arvidson, Anthony O'Sullivan (At dance)

UP A TREE

Frank Powell (d); Arthur Marvin (c); 3/4 March 1910 (f); Glendale,

California? (l); 28 April 1910 (r); approx 981 feet (rl); J141018 / 30 April 1910 (copyright)

William A. Quirk (Country lout); Florence Barker, Francis J. Grandon, Mack Sennett, Anthony O'Sullivan, Charles Craig (Victims); Frank Opperman (Farmer)

NOTE: Location unclear in the production records at the Museum of Modern Art.

THE GOLD-SEEKERS

D. W. Griffith (d); G. W. Bitzer, Arthur Marvin (c); 18/19/21 March 1910 (f); Sierra Madre, California/Studio (l); 2 May 1910 (r); approx 976 feet (rl); J141120 / 5 May 1910 (copyright)

Henry B. Walthall (Prospector); Florence Barker (His wife); ? (His son); Anthony O'Sullivan, Francis J. Grandon (Prospectors); Dell Henderson (Claim agent); Kate Bruce (Old woman); Mack Sennett (Drunkard); Charles Craig, Frank Opperman (Farmers); Charles H. West, Alfred Paget, W. Chrystie Miller (In claim agent's office)

THE UNCHANGING SEA

D. W. Griffith (d); "The Three Fishers," the poem by Charles Kingsley (s); G. W. Bitzer (c); 16/17 March 1910 (f); Port Los Angeles, California/Santa Monica, California (l); 5 May 1910 (r); approx 952 feet (rl); J141155 / 7 May 1910 (copyright)

Linda Arvidson (Woman); Arthur Johnson (Fisherman); Gladys Egan (Daughter, as a child); Mary Pickford (Daughter, as an adult); Charles H. West (Her suitor); Dell Henderson (Rescuer); Alfred Paget, Dorothy West, Kate Bruce (Villagers); Frank Opperman? (In second village)

LOVE AMONG THE ROSES

D. W. Griffith (d); Arthur Marvin, G. W. Bitzer (c); 22/23/24 March 1910 (f); Hollywood, California (l); 9 May 1910 (r); approx 983 feet (rl); J141266 / 12 May 1910 (copyright)

Henry B. Walthall (The lord); Marion Leonard (The lady); Dorothy West (Handmaiden); Arthur Johnson (Gardener); Mary Pickford (Lacemaker); Kate Bruce (Her mother); Charles H. West, Alfred Paget, Francis J. Grandon (Footmen)

THE TWO BROTHERS

D. W. Griffith (d); Eleanor Hicks (au); G. W. Bitzer, Arthur Marvin (c); 25/26/29 March, 4 April 1910 (f); San Juan Capistrano, California (l); 12 May 1910 (r); approx 993 feet (rl); J141292 / 14 May 1910 (copyright)

Arthur Johnson (Jose); Dell Henderson (Manuel); Kate Bruce (Their mother); Marion Leonard (Red Rose); Charles H. West (A suitor); Henry B. Walthall (Pedro); Mack Sennett, ? (Pedro's men); W. Chrystie Miller (Priest); Florence Barker, Linda Arvidson, Mary Pickford, Charles H. West, Alfred Paget, William A. Quirk, Dorothy West, Anthony O'Sullivan, Gertrude Claire (Mexicans)

OVER SILENT PATHS

D. W. Griffith (d); G. W. Bitzer (c); 5/6 April 1910 (f); San Fernando, California (l); 16 May 1910 (r); approx 980 feet (rl); J141397 / 18 May 1910 (copyright)

Marion Leonard (Daughter); Dell Henderson (Wanderer); W. Chrystie Miller (Father); Arthur Johnson (Marshall); Alfred Paget (Deputy?)

AN AFFAIR OF HEARTS

Frank Powell (d); Arthur Marvin (c); 16/17 March, 2 April 1910 (f); Verdugo, California (l); 19 May 1910 (r); approx 967 feet (rl); J141593 / 23 May 1910 (copyright)

William A. Quirk (Monsieur Borni); Mack Sennett (Monsieur Renay); Florence Barker (The woman); Francis J. Grandon (Her husband); Anthony O'Sullivan (Policeman); ? (Man on bicycle); ? (Hunter); ? (Maid); Jack Pickford (Boy)

RAMONA

D. W. Griffith (d); Ramona, the novel by Helen Hunt Jackson (s); G. W. Bitzer (c); 30/31 March, 1/2 April 1910 (f); Peru, California /Studio (l); 23 May 1910 (r); approx 995 feet (rl); J141683 / 26 May 1910 (copyright)

Mary Pickford (Ramona); Henry B. Walthall (Alessandro); Francis J. Grandon (Felipe); Kate Bruce (Mother); W. Chrystie Miller (Priest); Charles H. West, Dorothy West, Gertrude Claire (In chapel); Anthony O'Sullivan, Frank Opperman (Ranch hands); Mack Sennett (White exploiter); Dell Henderson (At burial); Jack Pickford (Boy)

NOTE: Location noted on first intertitle: Camulos, Ventura County, California.

A KNOT IN THE PLOT

Frank Powell (d); Arthur Marvin (c); 5/6 April 1910 (f); Verdugo,

California (l); 26 May 1910 (r); approx 980 feet (rl); J141733 / 28 May 1910 (copyright)

Florence Barker (Milly Howard); Mack Sennett (Jim Doyle); Francis J. Grandon (Mexican); Kate Bruce (Mother); Anthony O'Sullivan, William A. Quirk (Cowboys); Frank Opperman (At store)

THE IMPALEMENT

D. W. Griffith (d); Stanner E. V. Taylor (au); Arthur Marvin, G. W. Bitzer (c); 21/23/28 April 1910 (f); Studio/Stamford, Connecticut (l); 30 May 1910 (r); approx 987 feet (rl); J141757 / 31 May 1910 (copyright)

Frank Powell (Mr. Avery); ? (Mrs. Avery); Florence Barker (Virgie); Charles Craig, Charles H. West, Dell Henderson, Henry B. Walthall (At first party); Alfred Paget (Butler); Kate Bruce (Maid); Francis J. Grandon (Doctor); Dell Henderson, Henry B. Walthall, Guy Hedlund, Verner Clarges, Charles H. West, Dorothy West (At second party); Frank Evans (Servant)

IN THE SEASON OF BUDS

D. W. Griffith (d); Stanner E. V. Taylor (au); G. W. Bitzer, Arthur Marvin (c); 27/28 April 1910 (f); Stamford, Connecticut (l); 2 June 1910 (r); approx 990 feet (rl); J142083 / 6 June 1910 (copyright)

Mack Sennett (Henry); Mary Pickford (Mabel); Charles H. West (Steve); W. Chrystie Miller (Uncle Zeke); Kate Bruce (Aunt)

A CHILD OF THE GHETTO

D. W. Griffith (d); Stanner E. V. Taylor ["Officer Riley - Man"] (au); Arthur Marvin, G. W. Bitzer (c); 29/30 April, 2/4 May 1910 (f); Studio/Westerfield, Connecticut (l); 6 June 1910 (r); approx 989 feet (rl); J142132 / 8 June 1910 (copyright)

Dorothy West (Ruth); Kate Bruce (Her mother); Dell Henderson (Proprietor); Charles H. West (His son); W. Chrystie Miller (Old man); George O. Nicholls (Officer Quinn); Henry B. Walthall (Farmer); Clara T. Bracey (Farm woman); Gladys Egan, ? (Girls with flowers); Anthony O'Sullivan, Charles Craig, Guy Hedlund, Henry Lehrman, J. Waltham (In sweatshop); Ruth Hart, William J. Butler, Alfred Paget (In second shop); ? (Landlady); Francis J. Grandon (Doctor); Frank Evans (Policeman)

NOTE: Location noted on intertitle: Rivington Street, New York City.

A VICTIM OF JEALOUSY

D. W. Griffith (d); Stanner E. V. Taylor ["Victims of Jealousy"] (au); G. W. Bitzer (c); 6/7 May 1910 (f); Studio (l); 9 June 1910 (r); approx 987 feet (rl); J142237 / 11 June 1910 (copyright)

James Kirkwood (The husband); Florence Barker (The wife); Mary Pickford (Her friend); ? (Artist); Mack Sennett, Anthony O'Sullivan (Milliners); Verner Clarges (Minister); Ruth Hart (Maid); Charles H. West, Charles Craig, Alfred Paget, Joseph Graybill, Henry Lehrman, Edward Dillon, Grace Henderson (At reception); ? (Dancer); Charles Craig, Joseph Graybill, Guy Hedlund (In office); Dorothy West (Visitor); Alfred Paget (Artist's servant); William J. Butler (Valet)

IN THE BORDER STATES

D. W. Griffith (d); Stanner E. V. Taylor (au); G. W. Bitzer (c); 3-14 May 1910 (f); Studio/Delaware Water Gap, New Jersey (l); 13 June 1910 (r); approx 990 feet (rl); J142348 / 15 June 1910 (copyright)

Charles H. West (Young father); ? (Young mother); Gladys Egan, ? (Children); W. Chrystie Miller, Dorothy West (At farewell); Henry B. Walthall, Frank Evans, William J. Butler, Guy Hedlund, Edward Dillon (Confederate soldiers); John T. Dillon, Alfred Paget, Mack Sennett, Henry Lehrman (Union soldiers); Verner Clarges?, Dell Henderson (Union officers); ? (Sentry); Francis J. Grandon (Surgeon)

THE FACE AT THE WINDOW

D. W. Griffith (d); Stanner E. V. Taylor (au); G. W. Bitzer (c); 10/14 May 1910 (f); Studio (l); 16 June 1910 (r); approx 997 feet (rl); J142395 / 18 June 1910 (copyright)

Verner Clarges (Mr. Bradford); Henry B. Walthall (Ralph Bradford); Joseph Graybill (His son); Vivian Prescott (Mira); Francis J. Grandon (Artist); Dell Henderson (Butler); George O. Nicholls (Bartender); Grace Henderson (Governess); Mack Sennett, James Kirkwood, Charles Craig, Edward Dillon, Dell Henderson (At first club); Charles H. West, Alfred Paget, William A. Quirk, Guy Hedlund, Henry Lehrman (At second club); Clara T. Bracey (Landlady); Edward Dillon (Valet)

NEVER AGAIN

Frank Powell (d); Arthur Marvin (c); 9/10/18 March 1910 (f); Brentwood Park, California (l); 20 June 1910 (r); approx 590 feet (rl); J142450 / 22 June 1910 (copyright)

Mary Pickford (Girl); Mack Sennett, William A. Quirk (Rivals); Anthony O'Sullivan (Sheriff); ? (Friend); Charles Craig (Man in boat)

MAY AND DECEMBER

Frank Powell (d); Mary Pickford (au); Arthur Marvin (c); 12 March 1910 (f); Verdugo, California (l); 20 June 1910 (r); approx 364 feet (rl); J142449 / 22 June 1910 (copyright)

Mary Pickford (May); William A. Quirk (June); Kate Bruce (October); ? (December)

THE MARKED TIME-TABLE

D. W. Griffith (d); Frank E. Woods (au); G. W. Bitzer (c); 17/18/25 May 1910 (f); Studio (l); 23 June 1910 (r); approx 996 feet (rl); J142590 / 25 June 1910 (copyright)

George O. Nicholls (Mr. Powers); Joseph Graybill (Tom Powers); Grace Henderson (Mrs. Powers); ? (Messenger); Clara T. Bracey (Maid); W. Chrystie Miller, Alfred Paget, Charles H. West, Mack Sennett, Dell Henderson, Francis J. Grandon, Edward Dillon (In gambling hall); Verner Clarges (In office); John T. Dillon (Policeman); William J. Butler, Frank Evans (In station); Wilfred Lucas (Office doorman)

A CHILD'S IMPULSE

D. W. Griffith (d); Stanner E. V. Taylor (au); G. W. Bitzer, Arthur Marvin (c); 19/26/27 May 1910 (f); Studio/Westfield, New Jersey (l); 27 June 1910 (r); approx 994 feet (rl); J142715 / 30 June 1910 (copyright)

Vivian Prescott (Mrs. Thurston); Charles H. West (Raymond Hartley); Mary Pickford (Grace); Joseph Graybill (The other man); William J. Butler (Butler); Guy Hedlund (Farmer); Frank Evans (Turk); William J. Butler (Passerby); Frank Evans (Policeman); Robert Harron (Country boy); Mack Sennett (At train); Verner Clarges, Charles Craig, Alfred Paget, Dell Henderson, Edward Dillon (At first party); George O. Nicholls, Clara T. Bracey, Gladys Egan (On farm); Alfred Paget, Henry Lehrman, Dorothy West, Edward Dillon, Dell Henderson, John T. Dillon, Anthony O'Sullivan (At second party)

MUGGSY'S FIRST SWEETHEART

D. W. Griffith (d); Frank E. Woods (au); G. W. Bitzer (c); 20/21/27 May, 3 June 1910 (f); Westfield, New Jersey/Studio (l); 30 June 1910 (r); approx 982 feet (rl); J142787 / 2 July 1910 (copyright)

William A. Quirk (Muggsy); Mary Pickford (Mabel Brown); Edward Dillon, Joseph Graybill (Muggsy's friends); Grace Henderson, George O. Nicholls (Mabel's parents); Clara T. Bracey (Muggsy's mother); Charles Craig (Uplift man)

NOTE: This is the first of the Biograph "Muggsy" films. Although only one other release--MUGGSY BECOMES A HERO--actually contains a character by that name, Biograph produced several stories by Frank E. Woods based on the Muggsy character.

THE PURGATION

D. W. Griffith (d); Stanner E. V. Taylor ["Had It Not So Turned"] (au); G. W. Bitzer (c); 24/27/28 May 1910 (f); Studio/Westerfield, Connecticut (l); 4 July 1910 (r); approx 988 feet (rl); J142946 / 6 July 1910 (copyright)

Gertrude Robinson (The girl); Joseph Graybill, Mack Sennett, Edward Dillon (The misguided youths); Dell Henderson, Grace Henderson (The girl's parents); Francis J. Grandon (The attacker); Charles Craig (In office); ? (Elevator operator); William J. Butler (Inspector); Alfred Paget, George O. Nicholls (Policemen); Clara T. Bracey (Maid)

A MIDNIGHT CUPID

D. W. Griffith (d); Stanner E. V. Taylor (au); G. W. Bitzer (c); 3/4 June 1910 (f); Studio/Coytesville, New Jersey (l); 7 July 1910 (r); approx 997 feet (rl); J143007 / 9 July 1910 (copyright)

Charles H. West (Perry Dudley); Mack Sennett (Nick, the unfortunate); George O. Nicholls (Country father); Florence Barker (Country girl); Verner Clarges (Minister); Frank Evans (Policeman); Alfred Paget, William J. Butler (Butlers); W. Chrystie Miller, William A. Quirk, Charles Craig (At store); Edward Dillon, Dorothy West, Grace Henderson, Vivian Prescott, Gertrude Robinson, Joseph Graybill, John T. Dillon, Francis J. Grandon (At party)

WHAT THE DAISY SAID

D. W. Griffith (d); Stanner E. V. Taylor ["The Loyalty of Martha"] (au); G. W. Bitzer (c); 8/9 June 1910 (f); Delaware Water Gap, New Jersey (l); 11 July 1910 (r); approx 987 feet (rl); J143189 / 13 July 1910 (copyright)

Mary Pickford (Martha); Gertrude Robinson (Milly); Joseph Graybill (Gypsy); Verner Clarges (Father); Charles H. West, Francis J. Grandon (Farmers); Clara T. Bracey, Anthony O'Sullivan (Gypsies); Alfred Paget, Anthony O'Sullivan, Frank Evans, John T. Dillon (Farmhands); ? (Spinster)

A CHILD'S FAITH

D. W. Griffith (d); James Carroll ["A Child's Prayer"] (au); G. W. Bitzer (c); 7/11 June 1910 (f); Studio (l); 14 July 1910 (r); approx 986 feet (rl); J143291 / 16 July 1910 (copyright)

George O. Nicholls (Mr. Paulton); Florence Barker (Alice Paulton);
Alfred Paget (Father's choice); Mack Sennett (Alice's husband);
Gladys Egan (Their child); W. Chrystie Miller (Old man); Gertrude
Robinson (His daughter); William J. Butler (Realtor); ? (Landlord);
Edward Dillon, Frank Evans (Workmen); Charles Craig, Guy Hedlund,
Dorothy West, Edward Dillon, Clara T. Bracey, Jeannie MacPherson,
Henry Lehrman (Well-wishers)

A FLASH OF LIGHT

D. W. Griffith (d); Stanner E. V. Taylor (au); G. W. Bitzer (c);
14/16/17 June 1910 (f); Studio (l); 18 July 1910 (r); approx 998 feet
(rl); J143387 / 20 July 1910 (copyright)

Charles H. West (John Rogers); Vivian Prescott (Belle); Stephanie
Longfellow (Older sister); Verner Clarges (Father); ? (Younger sis-
ter); Joseph Graybill (Horace Dooley); Anthony O'Sullivan, W. C.
Robinson, Kate Toncray (Servants); Charles Craig, Gertrude Robin-
son, Alfred Paget, George Siegmann, Mack Sennett (Wedding guests);
Edward Dillon, Claire McDowell, Dorothy West, John T. Dillon, Guy
Hedlund (At first party); Guy Hedlund, Ruth Hart, John T. Dillon,
Henry Lehrman? (At second party); George O. Nicholls, William J.
Butler (Doctors); Grace Henderson (Visitor); ? (Nurse)

AS THE BELLS RANG OUT!

D. W. Griffith (d); Stanner E. V. Taylor (au); G. W. Bitzer (c) 18
June 1910 (f); Studio (l); 21 July 1910 (r); approx 457 feet (rl);
J143501 / 23 July 1910 (copyright)

George O. Nicholls (Gilbert Allen); Stephanie Longfellow (Grace, his
daughter); Charles H. West (Wilson Breen); Grace Henderson (Mrs.
Allen); Alfred Paget, W. C. Robinson, John T. Dillon (Butlers);
Dorothy West (Maid of honor); Edward Dillon (Best man); Verner
Clarges (Preacher); Charles Craig, ? (Creditors); William J. Butler
(Court officer); Mack Sennett, ? (Policemen); ? (Maid); George Sieg-
mann, Henry Lehrman?, Gladys Egan, Joseph Graybill, Gertrude
Robinson (Wedding guests)

SERIOUS SIXTEEN

D. W. Griffith (d); Stanner E. V. Taylor ["Serious 16"] (au); G. W.
Bitzer, Arthur Marvin (c); 8/9/13 June 1910 (f); Delaware Water Gap,
New Jersey/Studio not noted (l); 21 July 1910 (r); approx 535 feet
(rl); J143502 / 23 July 1910 (copyright)

William J. Butler (Father); William A. Quirk (Tom); Florence Barker
(Adele); Clara T. Bracey (Maid); Mack Sennett, Mabel Van Buren,
Francis J. Grandon (Among friends)

THE CALL TO ARMS

D. W. Griffith (d); Stanner E. V. Taylor (au); G. W. Bitzer (c);
1/6/15/21 June 1910 (f); Studio/Paterson, New Jersey (l); 25 July
1910 (r); approx 994 feet (rl); J143780 / 28 July 1910 (copyright)

Henry B. Walthall (The lord); Marion Leonard (Regina, his wife);
Joseph Graybill (His cousin); Mary Pickford (Messenger); Alfred
Paget (Guard); Dorothy West, Vivian Prescott (Gypsies); Grace Hen-
derson (Lady of the court); William J. Butler, Clara T. Bracey,
Edward Dillon, Guy Hedlund (Servants); W. Chrystie Miller, Alfred
Paget, Francis J. Grandon, Mack Sennett, Verner Clarges (Soldiers)

UNEXPECTED HELP

D. W. Griffith (d); G. W. Bitzer (c); [?] March 1910 (f); California
(l); 28 July 1910 (r); approx 968 feet (rl); J143826 / 30 July 1910
(copyright)

Arthur Johnson (John Bradley); Florence Barker (His wife); Gladys
Egan, ? (Children); Dell Henderson, Alfred Paget (Gamblers); George
O. Nicholls (Marshall); Francis J. Grandon (At Lucky Jim's Place);
W. Chrystie Miller, ? (Priests); ? (Manager); ? (Passersby); Frank
Opperman (On street)

NOTE: Shooting date is unclear and California is the only location
noted in the production records at the Museum of Modern Art.

AN ARCADIAN MAID

D. W. Griffith (d); Stanner E. V. Taylor (au); G. W. Bitzer (c);
22/23/25 June 1910 (f); Studio/Westfield, New Jersey (l); 1 August
1910 (r); approx 984 feet (rl); J143884 / 3 August 1910 (copyright)

Mary Pickford (Priscilla); Mack Sennett (Peddlar); Kate Bruce (Lady
of the house); George O. Nicholls (Man of the house); Edward Dillon,
John T. Dillon, Henry Lehrman, Joseph Graybill, Charles Craig,
Vivian Prescott (In gambling hall); W. Chrystie Miller, Alfred Paget,
Francis J. Grandon, Anthony O'Sullivan, Henry Lehrman? (On train);
Frank Evans, William J. Butler (Two men)

HER FATHER'S PRIDE

D. W. Griffith (d); Stanner E. V. Taylor (au); G. W. Bitzer (c);
28/29/30 June 1910 (f); Studio/Coytesville, New Jersey (l); 4 August
1910 (r); approx 996 feet (rl); J144012 / 6 August 1910 (copyright)

Stephanie Longfellow (Ann Southcomb); W. Chrystie Miller, Kate
Bruce (Her parents); Charles H. West (Allen Edwards); Grace Henderson (His mother); Francis J. Grandon (Father's choice); ? (Maid);

Alfred Paget (Chauffeur); ? (Doctor); Anthony O'Sullivan, Edward
Dillon (Men from bank); George O. Nicholls, Mack Sennett, William
J. Butler, Clara T. Bracey, John T. Dillon (At poor farm)

THE HOUSE WITH CLOSED SHUTTERS

D. W. Griffith (d); Emmett Campbell Hall (au); G. W. Bitzer (c);
25/27 June, 1/2 July 1910 (f); Coytesville, New Jersey/Studio (l); 8
August 1910 (r); approx 998 feet (rl); J144163 / 11 August 1910
(copyright)

Henry B. Walthall (Charles Randolph); Dorothy West (Agnes, his sis-
ter); Grace Henderson (Their mother); Charles H. West, Joseph
Graybill (Agnes' suitors); Gladys Egan, Mabel Van Buren, Alfred
Paget, John T. Dillon (On porch/at farewell); William J. Butler
[blackface] (Servant); Frank Evans, Verner Clarges, John T. Dillon,
Francis J. Grandon (In Lee's tent)

NOTE: Reissued by Biograph 29 May 1916.

A SALUTARY LESSON

D. W. Griffith (d); William J. Butler (au); G. W. Bitzer (c); 6/8/9
July 1910 (f); Studio/Keyport Highlands, New Jersey (l); 11 August
1910 (r); approx 980 feet (rl); J144207 / 12 August 1910 (copyright)

Charles H. West (Mr. Randall); Stephanie Longfellow (Mrs. Randall);
Gladys Egan (Their child); Jeannie MacPherson (Friend); Charles
Craig (Wife's visitor); Vivian Prescott (Woman on beach); Alfred
Paget (Rescuer); Kate Toncray (Maid); Gertrude Robinson, Edward
Dillon, Dell Henderson, W. C. Robinson (On beach)

THE USURER

D. W. Griffith (d); G. W. Bitzer (c); 11-15 July 1910 (f); Studio (l);
15 August 1910 (r); approx 994 feet (rl); J144488 / 18 August 1910
(copyright)

George O. Nicholls (The Usurer); Grace Henderson (His sister); Al-
fred Paget, Anthony O'Sullivan, Edward Dillon (Debt collectors);
Francis J. Grandon (In office); Kate Bruce, ? (First debtors); Henry
B. Walthall, ? (Second debtors); ?, Claire McDowell, Gladys Egan
(Third debtors); Clara T. Bracey (Maid); Frank Evans (Policeman);
William J. Butler (Doctor); Dell Henderson, Guy Hedlund (Movers);
Charles Craig, Dorothy West, Gertrude Robinson, Jeannie MacPher-
son, Mabel Van Buren, Guy Hedlund, W. C. Robinson (At luncheon)

WHEN WE WERE IN OUR 'TEENS

Frank Powell (d); Stanner E. V. Taylor (au); Arthur Marvin (c); 15/16

July 1910 (f); Coytesville, New Jersey/Studio not noted (l); 18 August 1910 (r); approx 475 feet (rl); J144497 / 19 August 1910 (copyright)

Mary Pickford (Mary); William A. Quirk (Tom); Joseph Graybill (Howard); Mack Sennett (Butler)

AN OLD STORY WITH A NEW ENDING

Frank Powell (d); Arthur Marvin (c); 14 July 1910 (f); Coytesville, New Jersey (l); 18 August 1910 (r); approx 512 feet (rl); J144498 / 19 August 1910 (copyright)

Mabel Van Buren (Pauline Smith); Clara T. Bracey (Her mother); Joseph Graybill (Jay Downs); W. Chrystie Miller (Postman); Jeannie MacPherson, ? (In factory); Gertrude Robinson, W. C. Robinson, Charles Craig, William J. Butler (Outside store)

THE SORROWS OF THE UNFAITHFUL

D. W. Griffith (d); Stanner E. V. Taylor ["The Watcher on the Rocks"] (au); G. W. Bitzer (c); 12/13 July 1910 (f); Studio/[Atlantic?] Highlands, New Jersey (l); 22 August 1910 (r); approx 994 feet (rl); J144636 / 23 August 1910 (copyright)

Mary Pickford (Mary); Henry B. Walthall (Bill); Edward Dillon (Joe); Gladys Egan (Mary, as a child); ? (Bill, as a child); W. Chrystie Miller (Fisherman); ? (Messenger); William J. Butler, W. C. Robinson, Gertrude Robinson (On shore)

WILFUL PEGGY

D. W. Griffith (d); G. W. Bitzer (c); 19/22 July 1910 (f); Studio/ Cuddebackville, New York (l); 25 August 1910 (r); approx 997 feet (rl); J144684 / 26 August 1910 (copyright)

Mary Pickford (Peggy); Clara T. Bracey (Her mother); Henry B. Walthall (Lord); ? (Cousin); Claire McDowell (Maid); Alfred Paget, Dell Henderson, William J. Butler (Servants); Kate Bruce, Edward Dillon, ? (At inn); W. Chrystie Miller, Guy Hedlund, Mack Sennett, W. C. Robinson (At wedding); Gertrude Robinson, Grace Henderson, Mabel Van Buren, Charles Craig, William A. Quirk, Edward Dillon, Stephanie Longfellow, Francis J. Grandon (At party); Henry Lehrman? (Bumpkin)

THE MODERN PRODIGAL

D. W. Griffith (d); Dell Henderson ["One Good Turn Deserves Another"] (au); G. W. Bitzer (c); 28/30 July 1910 (f); Cuddebackville, New York (l); 29 August 1910 (r); approx 992 feet (rl); J144748 / 30 August 1910 (copyright)

Guy Hedlund (The Prodigal); Clara T. Bracey (His mother); George O. Nicholls (Sheriff); Kate Bruce (His wife); Jack Pickford (Their son); Alfred Paget, Frank Evans, Edward Dillon (Guards); Robert Harron, Dell Henderson, Francis J. Grandon (At post office); William J. Butler (Farmer); Anthony O'Sullivan (At farewell); Lester Predmore, ? (Boys swimming); ? (Prodigal's sister?)

THE AFFAIR OF AN EGG

Frank Powell (d); Robert F. McGowan ["The Affair of a Cold Storage Egg"] (au); Arthur Marvin (c); 19 July 1910 (f); Fort Lee, New Jersey (l); 1 September 1910 (r); approx 295 feet (rl); J144968 / 6 September 1910 (copyright)

Gertrude Robinson (Young woman); Kate Bruce (Old woman); Edward Dillon (Man); Mack Sennett (Waiter); John T. Dillon? (In restaurant); ? (Man who gives directions)

MUGGSY BECOMES A HERO

Frank Powell (d); Frank E. Woods (au); Arthur Marvin (c); 21/26/29 July, 2/3 August 1910 (f); Cuddebackville, New York/Coytesville, New Jersey/Studio not noted (l); 1 September 1910 (r); approx 693 feet (rl); J144969 / 6 September 1910 (copyright)

William A. Quirk (Muggsy); Mary Pickford (Mabel); Grace Henderson (Her mother); Edward Dillon, ? (Muggsy's friends); Jack Pickford (Brother); Kate Bruce, Claire McDowell (Sisters Frost); William J. Butler (Pastor); Alfred Paget, Dell Henderson (Tramps); William J. Butler, Anthony O'Sullivan, Francis J. Grandon (Bystanders); Charles Craig (Outside church)

A SUMMER IDYL

D. W. Griffith (d); G. W. Bitzer (c); 26/27 July, 1/3 August 1910 (f); Cuddebackville, New York/Studio not noted (l); 5 September 1910 (r); approx 991 feet (rl); J145067 / 7 September 1910 (copyright)

Stephanie Longfellow (Cora); Henry B. Walthall (Albert); Gertrude Robinson (Shepherdess); W. Chrystie Miller (Her father); Charles Craig (Friend); Robert Harron (Country boy); W. C. Robinson, ? (Servants); Guy Hedlund (Farmhand); ? (Foreman); William J. Butler, Claire McDowell, Dorothy West, Charles Hill Mailes, Jeannie MacPherson, Verner Clarges (At party)

LITTLE ANGELS OF LUCK

D. W. Griffith (d); G. W. Bitzer (c); 5/6 August 1910 (f); Studio/Wall Street, New York City (l); 8 September 1910 (r); approx 998 feet (rl); J145184 / 9 September 1910 (copyright)

George O. Nicholls (Mr. Rose); Grace Henderson (Mrs. Rose); Verner Clarges (President of sugar company); Gladys Egan (Alice); Edith Haldeman (Ruth); Clara T. Bracey, Kate Toncray (Maids); Francis J. Grandon (Partner); William J. Butler (Client); Alfred Paget (Butler); Charles Craig, Charles Hill Mailes, W. C. Robinson (In president's office); Anthony O'Sullivan (On street); Jeannie MacPherson, Dell Henderson, Henry Lehrman, Edward Dillon (At work)

NOTE: Wall Street location taken from internal evidence; not noted in production records at the Museum of Modern Art.

A MOHAWK'S WAY

D. W. Griffith (d); Stanner E. V. Taylor (au); Suggested by the works of James Fenimore Cooper (s); G. W. Bitzer (c); 9/12 August 1910 (f); Delaware Water Gap, New Jersey (l); 12 September 1910 (r); approx 991 feet (rl); J145352 / 14 September 1910 (copyright)

George O. Nicholls (Doctor Van Brum); ? (Mrs. Van Brum); Claire McDowell (Indian mother); Edith Haldeman (Indian child); Anthony O'Sullivan, Frank Evans, John T. Dillon (Trappers); William J. Butler (Servant); Alfred Paget, Guy Hedlund, W. C. Robinson, Gertrude Robinson, Charles Hill Mailes, Jeannie MacPherson, Dorothy Davenport (Indians); Francis J. Grandon (Medicine man); Henry Lehrman (Patient); Edward Dillon (Friend); ? (Soldiers)

IN LIFE'S CYCLE

D. W. Griffith (d); Charles Simone ["Posthumous Forgiveness"] (au); G. W. Bitzer (c); 18/21 July, 18 August 1910 (f); Cuddebackville, New York/Fort Lee, New Jersey/Studio (l); 15 September 1910 (r); approx 997 feet (rl); J145612 / 19 September 1910 (copyright)

George O. Nicholls (James Mullen); Stephanie Longfellow (Clara, as an adult); Henry B. Walthall (Vincent, as an adult); ? (Clara, as a child); ? (Vincent, as a child); Charles H. West (Clara's temptor); Edith Haldeman (Their child); W. Chrystie Miller, Anthony O'Sullivan, Francis J. Grandon (In seminary); William J. Butler, Linda Arvidson (James' friends); Alfred Paget, Gertrude Robinson (Young couple); Charles Hill Mailes (Priest in bar); Anthony O'Sullivan (Bartender); Francis J. Grandon, Frank Evans, Edward Dillon, Henry Lehrman, Joseph Graybill, Charles Craig (In bar)

A SUMMER TRAGEDY

Frank Powell (d); John P. Toohey (au); Suggested by "Transients in Arcadia," the story by O. Henry (s); Arthur Marvin (c); 12/18 August 1910 (f); Studio/Greenwich, Connecticut (l); 19 September 1910 (r); approx 987 feet (rl); J145695 / 22 September 1910 (copyright)

Mack Sennett (Clarence Topfloor); Florence Barker (Mabel); Gertrude Robinson (Her friend); Charles Craig, Edward Dillon (At hotel); William Beaudine, ? (Hotel staff); William J. Butler (Manager of soda shop); Gladys Egan (In soda shop); Grace Henderson (Cafe hostess); Mabel Van Buren (Cafe customer)

THE OATH AND THE MAN

D. W. Griffith (d); Stanner E. V. Taylor (au); G. W. Bitzer (c); 16/19 August 1910 (f); Studio/Paterson, New Jersey (l); 22 September 1910 (r); approx 997 feet (rl); J145784 / 26 September 1910 (copyright)

Henry B. Walthall (Henri Prevost); Florence Barker (Madame Prevost); W. Chrystie Miller (Priest); Francis J. Grandon (Nobleman); Charles H. West, William J. Butler, Elmer Booth, Charles Craig, Verner Clarges, Dell Henderson, Gertrude Robinson, Jeannie Mac-Pherson, Charles Hill Mailes, Dorothy West, Dorothy Davenport (Aristocrats); Alfred Paget, Kate Toncray (Servants); Claire McDowell, Guy Hedlund, Frank Evans, Edward Dillon, Anthony O'Sullivan, J. Jiquel Lanoe? (Rebels); Jack Pickford (Messenger); Clara T. Bracey (In parfumerie)

ROSE O' SALEM-TOWN

D. W. Griffith (d); Emmett Campbell Hall (au); G. W. Bitzer (c); 3/20 August 1910 (f); Studio/Delaware Water Gap, New Jersey/Marble Head, New Jersey (l); 26 September 1910 (r); approx 998 feet (rl); J145818 / 27 September 1910 (copyright)

Dorothy West (Sea child); Clara T. Bracey (Her mother); Henry B. Walthall (Trapper); George O. Nicholls (Puritan); Alfred Paget, W. Chrystie Miller, Guy Hedlund, Claire McDowell, Jack Pickford, Charles Hill Mailes, W. C. Robinson (Indians); Gladys Egan (Little child); ? (Her mother); Verner Clarges, William J. Butler, Frank Evans (Judges?); Francis J. Grandon, Henry Lehrman, W. C. Robinson (Captors); Gertrude Robinson, Kate Toncray, Edward Dillon, Claire McDowell, Charles Hill Mailes (Puritans); Frank Evans, Anthony O'Sullivan, Edward Dillon (Extras)

EXAMINATION DAY AT SCHOOL

D. W. Griffith (d); G. W. Bitzer (c); 23/27 August 1910 (f); Westfield, New Jersey/Studio (l); 29 September 1910 (r); approx 991 feet (rl); J145990 / 30 September 1910 (copyright)

W. Chrystie Miller (Old teacher); Kate Bruce (His wife); Mack Sennett, Gladys Egan, Dorothy West, Edith Haldeman, Jack Pickford, Edward Dillon, Gertrude Robinson, Dorothy Davenport (Students); Francis J. Grandon (County examiner); William J. Butler (New teacher); Alfred Paget, Charles Craig?, Verner Clarges, William J. Butler (School board)

THE ICONOCLAST

D. W. Griffith (d); Bernardine R. Leist (au); G. W. Bitzer (c); 25/26 August 1910 (f); Studio (l); 3 October 1910 (r); approx 992 feet (rl); J146130 / 5 October 1910 (copyright)

Henry B. Walthall (Worker); Claire McDowell (His wife); Edith Haldeman, ? (His children); George O. Nicholls (Employer); Gladys Egan (His child); William J. Butler, Grace Henderson, Charles Craig, Dorothy Davenport (Employer's friend); Alfred Paget (Butler); Kate Bruce (Maid); Francis J. Grandon, Verner Clarges (Doctors); Jack Pickford, Frank Evans, Anthony O'Sullivan, W. C. Robinson, J. Jiquel Lanoe, John T. Dillon (In office); Guy Hedlund (Worker's friend)

A GOLD NECKLACE

Frank Powell (d); Grace Duncan (au); Arthur Marvin (c); 26/29/31 August 1910 (f); Cuddebackville, New York/Studio (l); 6 October 1910 (r); approx 576 feet (rl); J146227 / 8 October 1910 (copyright)

Mary Pickford (Mazie); Kate Bruce (Governess); Lottie Pickford (Nellie); Mack Sennett (Sam); Jeannie MacPherson, Dorothy Davenport (Friends); Charles Craig (Sheriff); ? (Messenger); Edward Dillon (Driver); Dell Henderson, ? (In cafe); ? (Waiter)

HOW HUBBY GOT A RAISE

Frank Powell (d); Arthur Marvin (c); 27 August, 2 September 1910 (f); Studio (l); 6 October 1910 (r); approx 416 feet (rl); J146226 / 8 October 1910 (copyright)

Anthony O'Sullivan (Ezra Knowit); Grace Henderson (Mrs. Knowit); Verner Clarges (J. H. Williams, the boss); ? (Secretary); Claire McDowell, Kate Bruce (Neighbors)

THAT CHINK AT GOLDEN GULCH

D. W. Griffith (d); Emmett Campbell Hall (au); G. W. Bitzer (c); 25/31 August, 1 September 1910 (f); Cuddebackville, New York/Studio not noted (l); 10 October 1910 (r); approx 998 feet (rl); J146413 / 12 October 1910 (copyright)

Anthony O'Sullivan (Charley Lee); W. Chrystie Miller, Francis J. Grandon (His friends); Gertrude Robinson (Miss Dean); Charles H.

West (Bud Miller); Dell Henderson (Gentleman Jim Dandy); Edward Dillon (Mail carrier); Frank Evans (Sheriff?); Guy Hedlund, Alfred Paget, George O. Nicholls, W. C. Robinson, John T. Dillon, J. Jiquel Lanoe, William J. Butler (Cowboys); Kate Bruce (Extra)

A LUCKY TOOTHACHE

Frank Powell (d); George W. Terwilliger ["Cure For Toothache"] (au); Arthur Marvin (c); 7 September 1910 (f); Westfield, New Jersey (l); 13 October 1910 (r); approx 570 feet (rl); J146453 / 14 October 1910 (copyright)

Mary Pickford (Bessie); Mack Sennett (Tom); Kate Bruce, W. Chrystie Miller (Parents); Claire McDowell (Cousin); Charles Craig, Charles H. West, Edward Dillon (The "boys"); ? (Farmhand)

THE MASHER

Frank Powell (d); Arthur Marvin (c); 9/10 September 1910 (f); Coytesville, New Jersey/Studio not noted (l); 13 October 1910 (r); approx 415 feet (rl); J146452 / 14 October 1910 (copyright)

Anthony O'Sullivan (Mr. Hiram); Grace Henderson (Mrs. Hiram); Kate Bruce (Old maid); Gertrude Robinson, Charles Craig, William J. Butler, Lily Cahill (Passersby); Edward Dillon (Masher); Alfred Paget (Policeman); Frank Evans (Desk sergeant)

THE BROKEN DOLL

D. W. Griffith (d); Belle Taylor (au); G. W. Bitzer (c); 2/7 September 1910 (f); Coytesville, New Jersey/Cuddebackville, New York (l); 17 October 1910 (r); approx 997 feet (rl); J146623 / 19 October 1910 (copyright)

Gladys Egan (Indian girl); Dark Cloud? (Chief); Jack Pickford, Alfred Paget, Kate Bruce, Dell Henderson, Guy Hedlund, Francis J. Grandon (Indians); Mack Sennett (Joe Stevens); Linda Arvidson (His wife); George O. Nicholls, Gertrude Robinson, W. Chrystie Miller, Frank Evans, John T. Dillon, William J. Butler, J. Jiquel Lanoe, Dorothy Davenport, Lottie Pickford (Townsfolk); Dorothy West, Joseph Graybill, Clara T. Bracey? (Victims of massacre)

THE BANKER'S DAUGHTERS

D. W. Griffith (d); Earl Hodge (au); G. W. Bitzer (c); 8/9 September 1910 (f); Studio (l); 20 October 1910 (r); approx 989 feet (rl); J146849 / 22 October 1910 (copyright)

Verner Clarges (C. W. Bourne); Stephanie Longfellow (Alice Bourne);

Dorothy West (Martha Bourne); ? (Youngest daughter); Anthony O'Sullivan, Henry B. Walthall, Edward Dillon (Criminals); Alfred Paget, ? (Butlers); Clara T. Bracey (Maid); George O. Nicholls (Police sergeant); Frank Evans, John T. Dillon, Dell Henderson, Guy Hedlund (Policemen); ? (Messenger)

THE MESSAGE OF THE VIOLIN

D. W. Griffith (d); G. W. Bitzer (c); 13/14 September 1910 (f); Studio (l); 24 October 1910 (r); approx 997 feet (rl); J147013 / 26 October 1910 (copyright)

Charles H. West (Carl); Clara T. Bracey (His mother); George O. Nicholls (His father); Stephanie Longfellow (The woman); Grace Henderson (Her mother); Verner Clarges (Her father); Dell Henderson (The baron); Lily Cahill (The other woman); Claire McDowell, ? (Her servants); Francis J. Grandon (Doctor); William J. Butler (Music teacher); Alfred Paget (Butler); Charles Craig, Jeannie MacPherson, Edwin August (At reception); Edward Dillon (Accompanist); Henry Lehrman (Music student); W. C. Robinson, Kate Bruce (In hallway); W. C. Robinson, ? (Servants); ? (Dancer)

THE PASSING OF A GROUCH

Frank Powell (d); John P. Toohey (au); Arthur Marvin (c); 21/22 September 1910 (f); Studio/Edgewater, New Jersey (l); 27 October 1910 (r); approx 537 feet (rl); J147353 / 5 November 1910 (copyright)

Mack Sennett (Mr. Nelson); ? (His wife); Lily Cahill (On street); Verner Clarges (Older man); Harry Hyde (In cafe); ? (In office); ? (Policeman); ? (Maid); ? (Boy outside cafe)

THE PROPOSAL

Frank Powell (d); Arthur Marvin (c); 15/17 September 1910 (f); Fort Lee, New Jersey/Studio (l); 27 October 1910 (r); approx 461 feet (rl); J147352 / 5 November 1910 (copyright)

Anthony O'Sullivan (Benjamin Binns); ? (Julia Smith, the widow); ? (Maid); W. C. Robinson, ? (Couple on street); ? (Postman); William J. Butler (Messenger)

TWO LITTLE WAIFS

D. W. Griffith (d); Mrs. James H. Ryan ["Baby Waifs"] (au); G. W. Bitzer (c); 16/21 September 1910 (f); Greenwich, Connecticut/Studio (l); 31 October 1910 (r); approx 997 feet (rl); J147286 / 3 November 1910 (copyright)

Grace Henderson (Mrs. Weston); Verner Clarges (Mr. Weston); Edith Haldeman, ? (Two waifs); Kate Bruce (Mother Ignatius); William J. Butler (Doctor); Alfred Paget, ? (Butlers); Jeannie MacPherson, Lucille Lee Stewart? (Maids); Charles Craig (Man at orphanage); Clara T. Bracey, Claire McDowell, Dorothy Davenport (Nuns); Jack Pickford (Boy on road); Edward Dillon (Workman)

WAITER NO. 5

D. W. Griffith (d); Bernardine R. Leist (au); G. W. Bitzer (c); 19/22 September 1910 (f); Studio (l); 3 November 1910 (r); approx 997 feet (rl); J147562 / 10 November 1910 (copyright)

George O. Nicholls (Chief of police); Claire McDowell (His wife); Jack Pickford (Their son, as a boy); Charles H. West (Their son, as an adult); Mary Pickford (His fiancée); Grace Henderson (Her mother); Kate Bruce, J. Jiquel Lanoe (Wife's friends); Gladys Egan, Dorothy West, Alfred Paget, Clara T. Bracey (The poor); Guy Hedlund (At meeting); William J. Butler (Chief's aide); Alfred Paget, W. C. Robinson (Butlers); Alfred Paget, ? (Policemen); Edward Dillon (A friend); Jeannie MacPherson, ? (Maids); Dell Henderson, William J. Butler, Alfred Paget, Guy Hedlund, Edwin August, Dorothy Davenport, J. Jiquel Lanoe (In restaurant)

THE FUGITIVE

D. W. Griffith (d); John McDonagh (au); G. W. Bitzer (c); 24/29 September 1910 (f); Studio/Fishkill, New York (l); 7 November 1910 (r); approx 996 feet (rl); J147671 / 14 November 1910 (copyright)

Kate Bruce (Confederate mother); Edward Dillon (John, her son); Clara T. Bracey (Union mother); Edwin August (John, her son); Dorothy West (Confederate son's fiancée); Lucy Cotton (Union son's fiancée); W. Chrystie Miller, Dell Henderson, Claire McDowell, Clara T. Bracey, Lily Cahill, Jeannie MacPherson (In farewell crowd); Alfred Paget, Charles H. West, Dell Henderson, Guy Hedlund (Union soldiers); Guy Hedlund, Charles H. West, W. C. Robinson, Francis J. Grandon, J. Jiquel Lanoe, Frank Evans (Confederate soldiers)

NOTE: For the circumstances surrounding the submission of this story to Biograph, see Liam O'Leary, ed., Cinema in Ireland: 1895-1976.

SIMPLE CHARITY

D. W. Griffith (d); Frank E. Woods ["Blood Red Tape of Society"] (au); G. W. Bitzer, Arthur Marvin (c); 23/27 September 1910 (f); Studio/Fort Lee, New Jersey (l); 10 November 1910 (r); approx 993 feet (rl); J147672 / 14 November 1910 (copyright)

Mary Pickford (Miss Wilkins); W. Chrystie Miller, Kate Bruce (Poor couple); Edwin August (Doctor); Francis J. Grandon (In pawn shop); Grace Henderson, Claire McDowell, Verner Clarges (Charity workers); Dell Henderson (Boss in store); Alfred Paget (Behind counter); Edward Dillon, Lottie Pickford (In hallway); Lloyd B. Carleton (Bailiff); William J. Butler (Tradesman)

SUNSHINE SUE

D. W. Griffith (d); Wilfred Lucas ["The Old Piano"] (au); G. W. Bitzer (c); 6/8 October 1910 (f); Studio/Westfield, New Jersey (l); 14 November 1910 (r); approx 998 feet (rl); J147831 / 17 November 1910 (copyright)

Marion Sunshine (Sunshine Sue); W. Chrystie Miller (Her father); Clara T. Bracey (Her mother); Edward Dillon (Tom, her suitor); Charles H. West (Harry, the summer boarder); George O. Nicholls (Head of employment agency); Donald Crisp (Head of sweatshop); Dorothy West, Jeannie MacPherson, Robert Harron (Sweatshop employees); William J. Butler (Piano store owner); Jeannie MacPherson, Jack Mulhall? (Piano store employees); Guy Hedlund, Francis J. Grandon (In piano store); J. Jiquel Lanoe (Waiter); Francis J. Grandon (Yokel); Henry Lehrman (Harry's friend?); ? (Servants)

THE TROUBLESOME BABY

Frank Powell (d); Arthur Marvin (c); 30 September 1910 (f); Highlands, New Jersey (l); 17 November 1910 (r); approx 492 feet (rl); J147936 / 21 November 1910 (copyright)

William J. Butler (Mr. Samuels); ? (Mrs. Samuels); Dorothy Davenport (At station); Gladys Egan (Little girl); ? (Maid); ? (Couple on beach); ? (Busybody); ? (Policeman)

LOVE IN QUARANTINE

Frank Powell (d); Arthur Marvin (c); 28/29 September 1910 (f); Studio/Fort Lee, New Jersey (l); 17 November 1910 (r); approx 505 feet (rl); J147937 / 21 November 1910 (copyright)

Stephanie Longfellow (Edith); Mack Sennett (Harold); Grace Henderson (Mother); Verner Clarges (Doctor); Lucille Lee Stewart? (Maid); Victoria Forde, ? (Two girls)

THE SONG OF THE WILDWOOD FLUTE

D. W. Griffith (d); Mrs. James H. Ryan ["Legend of We-No-Nah"] (au); G. W. Bitzer (c); 1/17 October 1910 (f); Studio/Fishkill, New York/Westfield, New Jersey (l); 21 November 1910 (r); approx 996 feet (rl); J148128 / 25 November 1910 (copyright)

Dark Cloud (Gray Cloud); Mary Pickford (Dove Eyes); Francis J.
Grandon (Her father); Dell Henderson (A suitor); Kate Bruce, Alfred
Paget, J. Jiquel Lanoe (Indians)

HIS NEW LID

Frank Powell (d); S. Walter Bunting ["His Straw Lid"] (au); Arthur
Marvin (c); 4/6/14 October 1910 (f); Studio/Westfield, New Jersey
(l); 24 November 1910 (r); approx 563 feet (rl); J148146 / 26 November 1910 (copyright)

Thomas H. Ince (George); ? (His wife); ? (Messenger); ? (Secretary);
? (In lunch room); W. C. Robinson (Finder of hat); Claire McDowell,
Lucille Lee Stewart (Among mourners); ? (Undertaker); ? (Albert
Simons); ? (Maid)

NOT SO BAD AS IT SEEMED

Frank Powell (d); Stella W. Collart (au); Arthur Marvin (c); 4/14
October 1910 (f); Studio/Fort Lee, New Jersey (l); 24 November 1910
(r); approx 432 feet (rl); J148145 / 26 November 1910 (copyright)

Verner Clarges (Mr. Jones); Grace Henderson (Mrs. Jones); William
J. Butler (Mr. Hall); ? (Mrs. Hall); Mack Sennett (Mr. Young); ?
(Mrs. Young); ? (Messenger); ? (Driver)

A PLAIN SONG

D. W. Griffith (d); Stanner E. V. Taylor (au); G. W. Bitzer (c);
13/17 October 1910 (f); Studio/Westfield, New Jersey (l); 28 November 1910 (r); approx 997 feet (rl); J148441 / 1 December 1910 (copyright)

Mary Pickford (Edith); Kate Bruce (Her mother); W. Chrystie Miller
(Her father); William J. Butler (Her employer); Dell Henderson
(Manager); Jack Pickford, Edward Dillon, W. C. Robinson (On
street); ? (Janitor); Alfred Paget, Lottie Pickford, Robert Harron,
Elmer Booth?, Jeannie MacPherson, Dorothy West, Harry Hyde, J.
Jiquel Lanoe (Storemates and escorts); Lily Cahill, Donald Crisp,
Guy Hedlund (At station)

EFFECTING A CURE

Frank Powell (d); Arthur Marvin (c); 20/22 October 1910 (f); Studio/
Fort Lee, New Jersey (l); 1 December 1910 (r); approx 997 feet (rl);
J148460 / 2 December 1910 (copyright)

Mack Sennett (Wilkens); Stephanie Longfellow (Mrs. Wilkens); Kate
Bruce (Her mother); William J. Butler, Edward Dillon, Donald Crisp

(At club); W. C. Robinson, ? (Servants); ? (At ladies' circle); Florence Barker (Violet, the other woman); ? (Minister); ? (His wife); Joseph Graybill, W. Chrystie Miller (On street)

NOTE: Location not noted in production records at the Museum of Modern Art. Identification of Fort Lee as location is made from internal evidence: the same street and camera angle are used in TURNING THE TABLES, which was filmed in Fort Lee the same week.

A CHILD'S STRATAGEM

D. W. Griffith (d); Belle Taylor (au); G. W. Bitzer (c); 5/26 October 1910 (f); Studio/Westfield, New Jersey (l); 5 December 1910 (r); approx 998 feet (rl); J148630 / 9 December 1910 (copyright)

Edwin August (John Walton); Stephanie Longfellow (Mrs. Walton); Gladys Egan (Their daughter); Claire McDowell (The designing woman); Linda Arvidson, Lily Cahill (Friends); Jeannie MacPherson (Secretary); ? (Maid); Alfred Paget, Jack Mulhall? (In office); Charles Hill Mailes? (Lawyer); Guy Hedlund, Henry Lehrman (Lawyer's aides); William J. Butler, W. C. Robinson, Dell Henderson, Donald Crisp (Policemen); Clara T. Bracey, Jack Pickford (On street); Frank Evans, J. Jiquel Lanoe, ? (Tramps); Harry Hyde, J. Jiquel Lanoe, George O. Nicholls, Donald Crisp? (On trolley)

TURNING THE TABLES

Frank Powell (d); T. P. Bayer (au); Arthur Marvin (c); 25 October, 7 November 1910 (f); Fort Lee, New Jersey/Studio (l); 8 December 1910 (r); approx 416 feet (rl); J148648 / 10 December 1910 (copyright)

Joseph Graybill (Mr. Peck); Stephanie Longfellow (Mrs. Peck); William J. Butler (In bar); ? (Bartender); Edward Dillon (On street)

HAPPY JACK, A HERO

Frank Powell (d); Dell Henderson ["Happy Jack, the Rover"] (au); Arthur Marvin (c); 29 October, 1/3 November 1910 (f); Studio/Fort Lee, New Jersey (l); 8 December 1910 (r); approx 576 feet (rl); J148649 / 10 December 1910 (copyright)

Dell Henderson (Mr. Stamford); Grace Henderson (Mrs. Stamford); Florence Barker (Their daughter); Mack Sennett (Happy Jack); Francis J. Grandon, Edward Dillon (Society crooks); William J. Butler (Butler); Claire McDowell (Maid); W. C. Robinson, Kate Bruce (Servants); Edwin August (Daughter's suitor); Lottie Pickford, Henry Lehrman (At party)

THE GOLDEN SUPPER

D. W. Griffith (d); Dorothy West (au); "A Lover's Story," the poem by Alfred Lord Tennyson (s); G. W. Bitzer (c); 19/29 October 1910 (f); Studio/Greenwich, Connecticut (l); 12 December 1910 (r); approx 998 feet (rl); J148744 / 15 December 1910 (copyright)

Dorothy West (Camilla); Charles H. West (Lionel); Edwin August (Julian); Claire McDowell (Lady-in-waiting); Lottie Pickford, Jeannie MacPherson, Dorothy Davenport (Flower girls); Francis J. Grandon, Donald Crisp, Harry Hyde (Courtiers); Alfred Paget (Messenger); Donald Crisp (Monk); Verner Clarges, Guy Hedlund (Priests); Grace Henderson (Queen); Guy Hedlund (Hermit); W. C. Robinson, J. Jiquel Lanoe (Mourners); Kate Toncray (At feast)

NOTE: Reissued by Biograph 27 March 1916.

HIS SISTER-IN-LAW

D. W. Griffith (d); M. B. Havey (au); G. W. Bitzer (c); 14/18 October 1910 (f); Studio/Westfield, New Jersey (l); 15 December 1910 (r); approx 998 feet (rl); J149038 / 20 December 1910 (copyright)

Lottie Pickford (Eva); Gladys Egan (Blanche); Edward Dillon (John, Eva's sweetheart); Claire McDowell (Maiden aunt); Jeannie MacPherson, Harry Hyde, J. Jiquel Lanoe, Dorothy West, Guy Hedlund, Henry Lehrman (Wedding guests); William J. Butler (Minister); Clara T. Bracey (Nurse)

THE LESSON

D. W. Griffith (d); Dell Henderson ["The Fourth Commandment"] (au); G. W. Bitzer (c); 26/28 October, 2 November 1910 (f); Studio/Fort Lee, New Jersey (l); 19 December 1910 (r); approx 994 feet (rl); J149318 / 22 December 1910 (copyright)

W. Chrystie Miller (Reverend Hollister); Joseph Graybill (James, his son); Stephanie Longfellow (Ruth); Verner Clarges (Doctor); Jeannie MacPherson, ? (Friends); Charles H. West, Edward Dillon (In first bar); Guy Hedlund, W. C. Robinson (In second bar); W. C. Robinson (Bartender on street); Robert Harron (Young boy); Alfred Paget, George O. Nicholls, Dell Henderson (Policemen)

WHITE ROSES

Frank Powell (d); Arthur Marvin (c); 7/9 November 1910 (f); Fort Lee, New Jersey/Studio (l); 22 December 1910 (r); approx 588 feet (rl); J149494 / 24 December 1910 (copyright)

Mary Pickford (Betty); Edward Dillon (Harry); ? (Maid); W. Chrystie

Miller (Florist); Jack Pickford (Delivery boy); ? (Thief); W. C. Robinson (Policeman); William J. Butler (Good Samaritan); Henry Lehrman, Francis J. Grandon (At station); Joseph Graybill, Lottie Pickford (At party); Kate Bruce (Old maid)

THE RECREATION OF AN HEIRESS

Frank Powell (d); Hallie B. Goodman ["The Recreating of an Heiress"] (au); Arthur Marvin (c); 14 November 1910 (f); Studio (l); 22 December 1910 (r); approx 410 feet (rl); J149493 / 24 December 1910 (copyright)

Grace Henderson (Mother); Verner Clarges (Father); Charles H. West (Son); Stephanie Longfellow (Heiress); Claire McDowell (Her maid); W. C. Robinson (Butler)

WINNING BACK HIS LOVE

D. W. Griffith (d); Anthony Donnelly ["Winning Back Her Love"] (au); G. W. Bitzer (c); 1/3 November 1910 (f); Studio/Location not noted (l); 26 December 1910 (r); approx 994 feet (rl); J149495 / 24 December 1910 (copyright)

Wilfred Lucas (Frederick Wallace); Stephanie Longfellow (His wife); Vivian Prescott (Vera Blair); Edwin August (A friend); Alfred Paget, Jeannie MacPherson (Servants); Charles Craig, Adolph Lestina (Waiters); Verner Clarges (Leaving restaurant); Joseph Graybill, Guy Hedlund, Dorothy West, J. Jiquel Lanoe, Frank Evans, Donald Crisp, George O. Nicholls, Robert Harron, W. C. Robinson, Alfred Paget, Harry Hyde (At stage door)

HIS WIFE'S SWEETHEARTS

Frank Powell (d); E. Moulan (au); Arthur Marvin (c); 23/30 November 1910 (f); Studio/Leonia, New Jersey (l); 29 December 1910 (r); approx 682 feet (rl); J150108 / 3 January 1911 (copyright)

Mack Sennett (Mr. Jenkins); Grace Henderson (Mrs. Jenkins); Kate Bruce, ? (Maids); W. Chrystie Miller (Station master); W. C. Robinson (First maid's lover); Frank Evans (Sailor); John T. Dillon [blackface] (Lover); Francis J. Grandon, ? (Policemen)

AFTER THE BALL

Frank Powell (d); Anthony Donnelly (au); Arthur Marvin (c); 25 November 1910 (f); Studio (l); 29 December 1910 (r); approx 311 feet (rl); J150107 / 3 January 1911 (copyright)

Edward Dillon (Mr. Brown); ? (Mrs. Brown); William J. Butler, John T. Dillon (Mr. Brown's friends)

THE TWO PATHS

D. W. Griffith (d); G. W. Bitzer (c); 19/22 November 1910 (f); Studio (l); 2 January 1911 (r); approx 992 feet (rl); J150122 / 4 January 1911 (copyright)

Dorothy Bernard (Florence); ? (Nellie); Wilfred Lucas (Her husband); Adolph Lestina (Temptor); Clara T. Bracey (Mother); Grace Henderson (Temptor's companion); Edith Haldeman, ? (Children); Dell Henderson (Worker); Donald Crisp, Alfred Paget, Frank Evans, W. C. Robinson (Footmen); Harry Hyde, Jeannie MacPherson, John T. Dillon, Vivian Prescott, Lottie Pickford, Henry Lehrman? (At party)

WHEN A MAN LOVES

D. W. Griffith (d); George W. Terwilliger (au); G. W. Bitzer (c); 22/31 October 1910 (f); Studio/Westfield, New Jersey (l); 5 January 1911 (r); approx 998 feet (rl); J150480 / 9 January 1911 (copyright)

Dell Henderson (Mr. Bach); Mary Pickford (Tessie); Charles H. West (John Watson); George O. Nicholls (Tessie's father); ? (First swain); Guy Hedlund (Farmhand); Robert Harron (Young man); Verner Clarges (Preacher); Grace Henderson (Preacher's companion)

THE ITALIAN BARBER

D. W. Griffith (d); G. W. Bitzer (c); 15/16 November 1910 (f); Studio/Fort Lee, New Jersey (l); 9 January 1911 (r); approx 993 feet (rl); J150748 / 11 January 1911 (copyright)

Joseph Graybill (Tony); Mary Pickford (Alice); Marion Sunshine (Florence); Mack Sennett (Bobby Mack); Kate Bruce (Mother); ? (Youth); Robert Harron, Adolph Lestina, Henry Lehrman (Men buying papers); John T. Dillon, W. C. Robinson (In shop); Donald Crisp, Adolph Lestina, Vivian Prescott, Edward Dillon, Jeannie MacPherson, Lottie Pickford, Claire McDowell (At ball)

THE MIDNIGHT MARAUDER

Frank Powell (d); Arthur Marvin (c); 16/18/23 November 1910 (f); Studio/Fort Lee, New Jersey (l); 12 January 1911 (r); approx 392 feet (rl); J150814 / 16 January 1911 (copyright)

Edward Dillon (Mr. Henry Blowhard); Lottie Pickford (Mrs. Blowhard); Kate Bruce (Maid); ? (Burglar); Harry Hyde, Henry Lehrman (Guests); ? (Policeman)

HELP WANTED

Frank Powell (d); Arthur Marvin (c); 7/8 December 1910 (f);

Studio (l); 12 January 1911 (r); approx 605 feet (rl); J150815 / 16
January 1911 (copyright)

Joseph Graybill (Jack); Dell Henderson (Uncle); Marion Sunshine
(Daughter); W. C. Robinson (Butler); Kate Bruce, ? (Maids); ?
(Party guests); Lottie Pickford, Donald Crisp (In corridor); John T.
Dillon? (Driver); William J. Butler (Doctor); ? (Jack's butler)

HIS TRUST

D. W. Griffith (d); Emmett Campbell Hall ["The Trust"] (au); G. W.
Bitzer (c); 5/18 November 1910 (f); Fort Lee, New Jersey/Studio not
noted (l); 16 January 1911 (r); approx 996 feet (rl); J150968 / 19
January 1911 (copyright)

Wilfred Lucas (George); Dell Henderson (Colonel Frazier); Claire
McDowell (His wife); Edith Haldeman (Their child); Guy Hedlund,
Kate Toncray?, Adolph Lestina? (Black servants); Alfred Paget
(Messenger); Alfred Paget, Adolph Lestina, Francis J. Grandon
(Confederate soldiers); Mack Sennett, Joseph Graybill, W. C. Robin-
son (Union soldiers); Jeannie MacPherson, W. Chrystie Miller,
Charles H. West, Vivian Prescott, Lottie Pickford (At farewell)

NOTE: Reissued by Biograph, 4 July 1916, with HIS TRUST FUL-
FILLED.

HIS TRUST FULFILLED

D. W. Griffith (d); Emmett Campbell Hall ["The Trust"] (au); G. W.
Bitzer (c); 5/18 November 1910 (f); Fort Lee, New Jersey/Studio
not noted (l); 19 January 1911 (r); approx 999 feet (rl); J151126 / 24
January 1911 (copyright)

Wilfred Lucas (George); Claire McDowell (Mrs. Frazier); Gladys Egan
(Her daughter, as a child); Dorothy West (Her daughter, as an adult);
Verner Clarges (John Gray, the lawyer); Grace Henderson (Landlady);
Harry Hyde (The English cousin); Jack Pickford[blackface], ?
(Youths); Adolph Lestina, Guy Hedlund, Clara T. Bracey? (Freed
slaves); Marion Sunshine, Guy Hedlund, Clara T. Bracey, Jeannie
MacPherson, John T. Dillon[blackface] (In wedding group)

NOTE: Although released separately, HIS TRUST and HIS TRUST
FULFILLED may be seen as Griffith's first two-reel film. They
were reissued as such on 4 July 1916.

FATE'S TURNING

D. W. Griffith (d); Ashton Crawford ["Her Wedding Gift"] (au); G.
W. Bitzer (c); 3/6 December 1910 (f); Studio (l); 23 January 1911
(r); approx 998 feet (rl); J151150 / 25 January 1911 (copyright)

Charles H. West (John Lawson, Jr.); Stephanie Longfellow (His fian-cée); Grace Henderson (Her mother); Dorothy Bernard (Mary, a waitress); Donald Crisp (Valet); ? (Waitresses); Adolph Lestina (Min-ister); Francis J. Grandon (Doctor); Edward Dillon, J. Jiquel Lanoe (Attorneys?); Kate Toncray, Elmer Booth, Francis J. Grandon (Ser-vants); Claire McDowell, Alfred Paget, Jack Pickford, John T. Dil-lon, Frank Evans (At hotel); Edwin August, Marion Sunshine, Alfred Paget, Claire McDowell, J. Jiquel Lanoe, Guy Hedlund (At wedding)

THE POOR SICK MEN

Frank Powell (d); E. Moulan (au); Arthur Marvin (c); 30 November, 1-9 December 1910 (f); Studio/Fort Lee, New Jersey (l); 26 January 1911 (r); approx 991 feet (rl); J151208 / 27 January 1911 (copyright)

Dell Henderson (Father); Grace Henderson (Mother); ? (Son-in-law); Marion Sunshine (Daughter); William J. Butler, Francis J. Grandon, W. C. Robinson (Gamblers); ? (Hotel detective); Donald Crisp, Al-fred Paget, Frank Evans (Policemen); Jack Pickford (Boy); Kate Bruce, ? (Tenement couple); Edward Dillon, ? (Tramps); John T. Dillon (Gambling hall lookout)

A WREATH OF ORANGE BLOSSOMS

D. W. Griffith (d); Belle Taylor (au); G. W. Bitzer (c); 7/8/10 No-vember 1910 (f); Studio (l); 30 January 1911 (r); approx 993 feet (rl); J151388 / 31 January 1911 (copyright)

Edwin August (Husband); Florence Barker (Wife); Grace Henderson (His mother); Kate Bruce (Her mother); Dell Henderson (The rake); Donald Crisp, Kate Toncray, Guy Hedlund (Servants); ? (English cousin); Jeannie MacPherson, ? (Friends of bride); Francis J. Gran-don (Business associate); William J. Butler, Donald Crisp (In office); W. C. Robinson, Robert Harron, ? (Movers); Adolph Lestina, Harry Hyde, Alfred Paget, Dorothy West (At party)

THREE SISTERS

D. W. Griffith (d); G. W. Bitzer (c); 26/28 November 1910 (f); Studio (l); 2 February 1911 (r); approx 997 feet (rl); J151521 / 4 February 1911 (copyright)

Mary Pickford (Mary); Marion Sunshine (Florence); Vivian Prescott (Adele); Kate Bruce (Mother); Guy Hedlund?, Kate Toncray?, W. C. Robinson, Lottie Pickford (At dancing academy); Charles H. West (Mary's admirer); Harry Hyde (Florence's admirer); Edward Dillon, ? (Customers at Adele's academy); Wilfred Lucas (Curate); Grace Henderson, Claire McDowell (Investigating committee); Alfred Paget (Churchman)

HEART BEATS OF LONG AGO

D. W. Griffith (d); Belle Taylor ["The Missing Key"] (au); G. W.
Bitzer (c); 19/20 December 1910 (f); Studio (l); 6 February 1911 (r);
approx 997 feet (rl); J151842 / 6 February 1911 (copyright)

George O. Nicholls (Father); Dorothy West (Daughter); Wilfred Lucas
(Lover); Francis J. Grandon (Nobleman); Jeannie MacPherson, Kate
Bruce, J. Jiquel Lanoe, ? (At the ball); Alfred Paget, William J.
Butler, Guy Hedlund? (Guards); Adolph Lestina, Donald Crisp (Cour-
tiers); Kate Toncray (Lady-in-waiting); W. C. Robinson (Servant)

PRISCILLA'S ENGAGEMENT KISS

Frank Powell (d); Frank E. Woods (au); Arthur Marvin (c); 13/16
December 1910 (f); Studio (l); 9 February 1911 (r); approx 997 feet
(rl); J151958 / 13 February 1911 (copyright)

Bulletin photograph: Florence Barker (Priscilla); Edward Dillon
(Paul); Mack Sennett (Doctor)

NOTE: This is the first of the Biograph "Priscilla" films. As with
the "Muggsy" films, several of Woods' scenarios involving the Priscilla character were produced under different titles.

WHAT SHALL WE DO WITH OUR OLD

D. W. Griffith (d); G. W. Bitzer (c); 8/16 December 1910 (f); Studio
/Fort Lee, New Jersey (l); 13 February 1911 (r); approx 994 feet
(rl); J152019 / 15 February 1911 (copyright)

W. Chrystie Miller (The old carpenter); Claire McDowell (His wife);
Adolph Lestina (Doctor); George O. Nicholls (Judge); Guy Hedlund,
William J. Butler, Edward Dillon, Alfred Paget, John T. Dillon, W.
C. Robinson (In shop); Francis J. Grandon (Policeman); Frank Evans,
J. Jiquel Lanoe, Donald Crisp, Guy Hedlund, Vivian Prescott (In
court); Wilfred Lucas, Elmer Booth, John T. Dillon (In jail)

FISHER FOLKS

D. W. Griffith (d); Harriet Quimby ["Story of a Fishing Village"]
(au); G. W. Bitzer (c); 5/6/7 January 1911 (f); Fort Lee, New Jer-
sey/Santa Monica, California (l); 16 February 1911 (r); approx 998
feet (rl); J152253 / 18 February 1911 (copyright)

Wilfred Lucas (Steve Hardester); Linda Arvidson (Bertha); Vivian
Prescott (Cora); W. C. Robinson, W. Chrystie Miller, Alfred Paget,
Jeannie MacPherson (At wedding?); Verner Clarges (Minister); Joseph
Graybill, Mack Sennett, Claire McDowell, John T. Dillon, W. C.
Robinson, Alfred Paget, Edward Dillon (At fair); Kate Toncray, Jean-
nie MacPherson (On beach); William J. Butler (Fisherman)

NOTE: The filming dates refer to the California location; no filming date for the New Jersey location is indicated in the production records at the Museum of Modern Art.

THE DIAMOND STAR

D. W. Griffith (d); M. B. Havey (au); G. W. Bitzer (c); 10/12 December 1910 (f); [New York] Studio (l); 20 February 1911 (r); approx 996 feet (rl); J152473 / 21 February 1911 (copyright)

Bulletin photograph: Wilfred Lucas (John Wilson); Florence Barker (His wife)

HIS DAUGHTER

D. W. Griffith (d); Belle Taylor ["Due to Her Trust"?] (au); G. W. Bitzer (c); 11/12 January 1911 (f); Sierra Madre, California (l); 23 February 1911 (r); approx 997 feet (rl); J152549 / 25 February 1911 (copyright)

Bulletin photograph: Edwin August (William Whittier); Florence Barker (Mary)

THE LILY OF THE TENEMENTS

D. W. Griffith (d); G. W. Bitzer (c); 14/22 December 1910 (f); [New York] Studio (l); 27 February 1911 (r); approx 996 feet (rl); J152683 / 1 March 1911 (copyright)

Dorothy West (Tenement girl); Clara T. Bracey, W. Chrystie Miller (Her parents); George O. Nicholls (Tenement owner); ? (His son); William J. Butler, Adolph Lestina (Father's friends); Alfred Paget (Customer); W. C. Robinson (Butler); Francis J. Grandon (Doctor); ? (In office)

THE HEART OF A SAVAGE

D. W. Griffith (d); G. W. Bitzer (c); 17/18 January 1911 (f); Sierra Madre, California (l); 2 March 1911 (r); approx 991 feet (rl); J152909 / 6 March 1911 (copyright)

NOTE: No material survives from which the cast may be determined.

A DECREE OF DESTINY

D. W. Griffith (d); Virginia K. Tucker (au); G. W. Bitzer (c); 2/17 December 1910 (f); [New York] Studio (l); 6 March 1911 (r); approx 995 feet (rl); J152949 / 7 March 1911 (copyright)

Joseph Graybill (Kenneth Marsden); Marion Sunshine (Edith); Mary
Pickford (Mary); Clara T. Bracey (Aunt); Claire McDowell (Nun);
John T. Dillon[blackface] (Servant); George O. Nicholls (Priest);
Adolph Lestina (Doctor); Donald Crisp, Alfred Paget, Edward Dillon,
William J. Butler (At club); Kate Toncray, J. Jiquel Lanoe, Donald
Crisp (At wedding); Grace Henderson (At "taking of the veil")

CONSCIENCE

D. W. Griffith (d); G. W. Bitzer (c); 22/30 November 1910, 19 January 1911 (f); [New York] Studio/Coytesville, New Jersey/Carter
Canyon, California (l); 9 March 1911 (r); approx 995 feet (rl); J153060
/ 10 March 1911 (copyright)

Edwin August (Howard Raymond); Stephanie Longfellow (His wife);
Joseph Graybill (The hunter); Gladys Egan (Child); Dell Henderson,
Alfred Paget (Hunters); Claire McDowell, Kate Toncray, Jeannie
MacPherson (Maids); Guy Hedlund (Doctor); George O. Nicholls,
Adolph Lestina, William J. Butler (Detectives); W. C. Robinson,
Donald Crisp, Frank Evans (Policemen); Henry Lehrman (Stenogra-
pher)

NOTE: Location is listed as "Carter-Carnon" in the production
records at the Museum of Modern Art.

COMRADES

Mack Sennett (d); Mack Sennett (au); Percy Higginson (c); 14/19 January 1911 (f); Studio/Hollywood, California (l); 13 March 1911 (r);
approx 998 feet (rl); J153151 / 14 March 1911 (copyright)

Mack Sennett (Mack); John T. Dillon (Jack); William J. Butler (Mr.
Charles A. Franklin); Grace Henderson (Mrs. Charles A. Franklin);
Vivian Prescott (Their daughter); Henry Lehrman (Butler); Jeannie
MacPherson (Maid); Kate Toncray (Housekeeper); Francis J. Grandon
(Marmaduke Bracegirdle)

NOTE: This is Mack Sennett's first film as a director for the Biograph company.

WAS HE A COWARD?

D. W. Griffith (d); Emmett Campbell Hall ["Hero of the Lost Dog
Ranch"] (au); G. W. Bitzer (c); 23/27 January 1911 (f); Studio/El
Monte, California (l); 16 March 1911 (r); approx 994 feet (rl); J153322
/ 20 March 1911 (copyright)

Wilfred Lucas (Norris Hilton); Joseph Graybill (His friend); W. Chrystie Miller (The rancher); Blanche Sweet (Kate, His daughter); Dell

Henderson (Foreman); Kate Toncray (Maid); Francis J. Grandon
(Doctor); Guy Hedlund (Indian); William J. Butler (At train station);
John T. Dillon, Grace Henderson, Alfred Paget, George O. Nicholls,
Charles H. West, W. C. Robinson (At ranch)

TEACHING DAD TO LIKE HER

D. W. Griffith (d); Emmett Campbell Hall (au); G. W. Bitzer (c);
30/31 January, 1 February 1911 (f); Studio/California (l); 20 March
1911 (r); approx 995 feet (rl); J153364 / 22 March 1911 (copyright)

Joseph Graybill (Harry); Dell Henderson (His father); Vivian Prescott
(Dolly); Verner Clarges (Father's friend); Guy Hedlund (Harry's
friend); Edward Dillon (Footman); Kate Toncray, Francis J. Grandon
(Servants); Alfred Paget, Charles H. West, William J. Butler, Kate
Bruce, Edward Dillon, W. Chrystie Miller, John T. Dillon, Florence
Lee, W. C. Robinson (Outside theater)

THE LONEDALE OPERATOR

D. W. Griffith (d); Mack Sennett (au); G. W. Bitzer (c); 14/16 January, 2/4 February 1911 (f); Studio/Inglewood, California (l); 23
March 1911 (r); approx 998 feet (rl); J153512 / 25 March 1911 (copyright)

Blanche Sweet (Telegrapher); George O. Nicholls (Her father); Fran-
cis J. Grandon (Engineer); Wilfred Lucas (Trainman); Dell Henderson,
Joseph Graybill (Tramps); Verner Clarges, Jeannie MacPherson, W.
C. Robinson (In payroll office); Charles H. West (Company agent);
Guy Hedlund (On train); Edward Dillon (Telegrapher); W. Chrystie
Miller, ? (In station lobby)

NOTE: Reissued by Biograph 19 November 1915.

PRISCILLA'S APRIL FOOL JOKE

Frank Powell (d); Frank E. Woods (au); Percy Higginson (c); 6/7
February 1911 (f); Redondo, California (l); 27 March 1911 (r); approx
686 feet (rl); J153535 / 28 March 1911 (copyright)

Florence Barker (Priscilla); Joseph Graybill (Harry); Edward Dillon
(Paul); Stephanie Longfellow (Alice); Blanche Sweet, William Beaudine
(On lawn)

NOTE: See note for CURED (below).

CURED

Frank Powell (d); Eleanor Hicks (au); Percy Higginson (c); 1/9 Feb-

ruary 1911 (f); Redondo, California (l); 27 March 1911 (r); approx
308 feet (rl); J153534 / 28 March 1911 (copyright)

Mack Sennett (Happy Jack); John T. Dillon (Man with gout); W. C.
Robinson, Alfred Paget (Men at wall); Claire McDowell (Old woman);
Florence Lee, Stephanie Longfellow (Harassed women); Edward Dil-
lon (In crowd at finale)

NOTE: Frank Powell's credit is confirmed by a notice in Moving
Picture World, 25 February 1911, p. 415. In the notice he is re-
ferred to as "Mr. Powers."

THE SPANISH GYPSY

D. W. Griffith (d); G. W. Bitzer (c); 6/8 February 1911 (f); Wentworth Hotel, Santa Monica, California (l); 30 March 1911 (r); approx
996 feet (rl); J153679 / 31 March 1911 (copyright)

Wilfred Lucas (Jose); Vivian Prescott (Pepita); Kate Bruce (Her
mother); William J. Butler (Doctor); Jeannie MacPherson (Mariana);
Claire McDowell (Paula); Dorothy West, Alfred Paget, George O.
Nicholls, Kate Toncray, Florence LaBadie, Mack Sennett, W. C.
Robinson (Gypsies); Alfred Paget, Dell Henderson, John T. Dillon,
Francis J. Grandon, Charles H. West, Guy Hedlund, Verner Clarges
(Spaniards); John T. Dillon (In distant gypsy camp)

PRISCILLA AND THE UMBRELLA

Frank Powell (d); Frank E. Woods (au); Percy Higginson (c); 9/14
February 1911 (f); Studio/Redondo, California (l); 3 April 1911 (r);
997 feet (rl); J153845 / 5 April 1911 (copyright)

Florence Barker (Priscilla); Joseph Graybill (Paul); Edward Dillon
(Harry); Grace Henderson, William J. Butler (Parents); Blanche
Sweet (Sister); Kate Bruce (Maid); Henry Lehrman, Alfred Paget,
Guy Hedlund (At club); W. C. Robinson (Valet)

NOTE: See entry for CURED (above).

THE BROKEN CROSS

D. W. Griffith (d); Harriet Quimby (au); Percy Higginson, G. W.
Bitzer (c); 9/12 February 1911 (f); Studio/Monte Vista, California
(l); 6 April 1911 (r); 996 feet (rl); J153942 / 10 April 1911 (copyright)

Charles H. West (Tom); Florence LaBadie (Kate); Grace Henderson
(Landlady); Dorothy West (Manicurist); Vivian Prescott (Slavey); John
T. Dillon, Jeannie MacPherson, Henry Lehrman (Boarders); Claire
McDowell (Kate's mother); George O. Nicholls (Postman); Dell Hen-
derson (Manicurist's friend)

THE CHIEF'S DAUGHTER

D. W. Griffith (d); G. W. Bitzer (c); 15/16 February 1911 (f); Studio
/San Fernando, California/San Gabriel, California (l); 10 April 1911
(r); 1048 feet (rl); J154077 / 11 April 1911 (copyright)

Francis J. Grandon (Frank, a prospector); John T. Dillon (His
friend); Stephanie Longfellow (Indian woman); Claire McDowell (Susan,
Frank's fiancée); George O. Nicholls (Indian chief); Dorothy West,
Alfred Paget, Florence Lee, Kate Toncray, Jeannie MacPherson?
(Indians); Dell Henderson (At settlement); Grace Henderson (Susan's
companion); Edward Dillon (Servant)

PARADISE LOST

Mack Sennett?/Frank Powell? (d); Percy Higginson (c); 15/16/18
February 1911 (f); Studio/Culver City, California/Wentworth Hotel,
Santa Monica, California (l); 13 April 1911 (r); one reel (rl); J154435
/ 17 April 1911 (copyright)

Verner Clarges (Parson); Mack Sennett (Pete); Vivian Prescott, Florence LaBadie (Angels/Maids); William J. Butler (Parson's friend);
Kate Bruce (Pete's wife); Gladys Egan (Their daughter); Frank Opperman, Charles H. West (Footmen); Kate Toncray, ? (Farm couple);
? (Bartender)

MADAME REX

D. W. Griffith (d); Mary Pickford (au); G. W. Bitzer (c); 21/22
February 1911 (f); Wentworth Hotel and Old Mill, Santa Monica,
California/Studio (l); 17 April 1911 (r); 996 feet (rl); J154546 / 20
April 1911 (copyright)

Edwin August, Stephanie Longfellow, John T. Dillon, Francis J.
Grandon, Joseph Graybill, Edward Dillon, Henry Lehrman, W. C.
Robinson, Vivian Prescott, Alfred Paget, Jeannie MacPherson, Ver-
ner Clarges

NOTE: Cast identifications taken from a still reproduced in Variety,
25 December 1914, p. 6.

A KNIGHT OF THE ROAD

D. W. Griffith (d); Dell Henderson (au); G. W. Bitzer (c); 17/18
February 1911 (f); Studio/Sierra Madre, California (l); 20 April 1911
(r); 996 feet (rl); J154608 / 21 April 1911 (copyright)

Dell Henderson (Hobo); George O. Nicholls (Rancher); Dorothy West
(His daughter); John T. Dillon (Foreman); Edward Dillon (Hobo's
friend); Alfred Paget, Francis J. Grandon, Guy Hedlund, Henry

Lehrman (Dishonest tramps); Kate Toncray, Kate Bruce (Servants);
W. C. Robinson, ? (Rescuers); Jeannie MacPherson, Florence La-
Badie (In kitchen); ? (In orchard)

HIS MOTHER'S SCARF

D. W. Griffith (d); Harriet Quimby (au); G. W. Bitzer (c); 23/28
February 1911 (f); Studio/Santa Monica, California (l); 24 April 1911
(r); 994 feet (rl); J154757 / 26 April 1911 (copyright)

Wilfred Lucas (Will); Charles H. West (Charles); Dorothy West (The
woman); Alfred Paget (Messenger); Kate Bruce, W. Chrystie Miller
(Among pioneers); ? (Renegades)

NOTE: Reissued by Biograph 20 March 1916.

HOW SHE TRIUMPHED

D. W. Griffith (d); Linda Arvidson (au); G. W. Bitzer (c); 1/4 March
1911 (f); Pasadena, California/Studio (l); 27 April 1911 (r); 998 feet
(rl); J154834 / 29 April 1911 (copyright)

Bulletin photograph: Blanche Sweet (Mary); Vivian Prescott (Cousin);
Joseph Graybill (Her sweetheart?)

THE TWO SIDES

D. W. Griffith (d); G. W. Bitzer (c); 12/13 March 1911 (f); Studio/
San Gabriel, California (l); 1 May 1911 (r); one reel (rl); J154897
/ 3 May 1911 (copyright)

Dell Henderson (Mexican laborer); Kate Bruce (His wife); William
J. Butler (Rancher); Gladys Egan (His daughter); Kate Toncray
(Housekeeper); John T. Dillon (Foreman); Alfred Paget, Francis J.
Grandon, Guy Hedlund (Laborers); ? (Child)

MISPLACED JEALOUSY

Mack Sennett (d); Mack Sennett ["A Bit of Suspense"] (au); Percy
Higginson (c); 2 March 1911 (f); Studio (l); 4 May 1911 (r); 503 feet
(rl); J155077 / 8 May 1911 (copyright)

Bulletin photograph: Claire McDowell? (Manicurist); Edward Dillon
(Hairdresser); Mack Sennett (Man); Grace Henderson (His wife)

CUPID'S JOKE

Frank Powell (d); T. P. Bayer (au); Percy Higginson (c); 18 January

1911 (f); Redondo, California (l); 4 May 1911 (r); 493 feet (rl); J155076 / 8 May 1911 (copyright)

NOTE: No material survives from which the cast may be determined. Of the two Biograph comedy units, only Powell's is known to have worked in Redondo during January and February 1911.

IN THE DAYS OF '49

D. W. Griffith (d); Harriet Quimby (au); "Brown of Calaveras," the story by Bret Harte (s); G. W. Bitzer (c); 6/16 March 1911 (f); Studio/Eaton Canyon, California (l); 8 May 1911 (r); 995 feet (rl); J155222 / 10 May 1911 (copyright)

George O. Nicholls (Bill Weston); Claire McDowell (Edith, his wife); Dell Henderson (Handsome Jack); Dorothy West (Edith's friend); Guy Hedlund, John T. Dillon, W. Chrystie Miller (In bar); Alfred Paget (Jack's friend); Wilfred Lucas, Kate Bruce (At stage station); Charles H. West (Fiddler); William J. Butler (Bartender); Frank Opperman, John T. Dillon, Francis J. Grandon (Outside bar)

THE COUNTRY LOVERS

Frank Powell?/Mack Sennett? (d); Frank E. Woods ["Priscilla in the Country"] (au); Percy Higginson (c); 13/14 March 1911 (f); Arcadia, California (l); 11 May 1911 (r); 995 feet (rl); J155412 / 10 May 1911 (copyright)

Bulletin photograph: Blanche Sweet, Charles H. West, Grace Henderson

THE NEW DRESS

D. W. Griffith (d); Grace Henderson ["A Silk Dress"] (au); G. W. Bitzer (c); 17/29 March 1911 (f); Studio/San Gabriel, California (l); 15 May 1911 (r); 998 feet (rl); J155567 / 17 May 1911 (copyright)

Wilfred Lucas (Jose); Dorothy West (Marta); W. Chrystie Miller (Father); Vivian Prescott (The "painted woman"); Guy Hedlund, John T. Dillon, William J. Butler[priest], W. C. Robinson, Florence La-Badie, Charles H. West, Kate Toncray, Joseph Graybill, Jeannie MacPherson, Blanche Sweet, Alfred Paget (At wedding); William J. Butler, Blanche Sweet, Kate Toncray, W. C. Robinson, Joseph Graybill, Jeannie MacPherson (At market); Charles H. West, W. C. Robinson, Joseph Graybill (At cafe); Francis J. Grandon (Doctor); Alfred Paget (Fieldhand); Henry Lehrman (Drinking companion); Kate Bruce (Friend)

THE MANICURE LADY

Mack Sennett (d); Edwin August (au); Percy Higginson (c); 4/7 April 1911 (f); Studio/Pico Street, Glendale, California (l); 18 May 1911 (r); 997 feet (rl); J155661 / 20 May 1911 (copyright)

Mack Sennett (Barber); Vivian Prescott (Manicure lady); Edward Dillon (The rival); Verner Clarges (First customer); Kate Bruce (His wife); W. C. Robinson (Second customer); Kate Toncray (Second manicurist); Guy Hedlund (Third customer); Grace Henderson (Lunchroom hostess); Claire McDowell (Lunchroom waitress); William J. Butler (Maitre d'); Charles H. West (Waiter); Florence LaBadie (Rival's girlfriend); ? (Shoeshine)

THE CROOKED ROAD

D. W. Griffith (d); G. W. Bitzer (c); 4/13 April 1911 (f); Studio/ Lumber company in California (l); 22 May 1911 (r); one reel (rl); J155829 / 25 May 1911 (copyright)

Dell Henderson (Husband); Stephanie Longfellow (Wife); ? (Their child); Joseph Graybill, Charles H. West (Evil companions); Alfred Paget, John T. Dillon (In bar); W. C. Robinson (On street); Kate Toncray, Claire McDowell, Kate Bruce (Neighbors); John T. Dillon, Guy Hedlund, W. Chrystie Miller (In second bar); Gladys Egan, Baden Powell (Children); ? (In lumberyard); Grace Henderson (Landlady); William J. Butler (Pawnbroker); Jeannie MacPherson (In pawnshop)

NOTE: The "lumber company" in California is not specified in the production records at the Museum of Modern Art. Bitzer identifies Baden Powell as a child in this film.

THE WHITE ROSE OF THE WILDS

D. W. Griffith (d); G. W. Bitzer (c); 31 March, 8 April 1911 (f); Rubia Canyon, California (l); 25 May 1911 (r); one reel (rl); J155961 / 27 May 1911 (copyright)

Blanche Sweet (White Rose), Robert Harron (Her brother); W. Chrystie Miller (Her father); Wilfred Lucas, Joseph Graybill (Outlaws)

NOTE: Reissued by Biograph 16 October 1916. Cast taken from Moving Picture World, 21 October 1916, p. 441.

A ROMANY TRAGEDY

D. W. Griffith (d); Stanner E. V. Taylor ["A Romany Vengeance"] (au); G. W. Bitzer (c); 11/12 April 1911 (f); Studio/Lookout Mountain, California (l); 29 May 1911 (r); 996 feet (rl); J156182 / 1 June 1911 (copyright)

Bulletin photograph: W. Christy Cabanne (Eugene); William J. Butler (Carlos' father); Claire McDowell (Elder sister); Gladys Egan (Younger sister)

A DUTCH GOLD MINE

Mack Sennett (d); Charles Inslee (au); Percy Higginson (c); 11/12 April 1911 (f); Studio/Sierra Madre, California (l); 1 June 1911 (r); 769 feet (rl); J156204 / 3 June 1911 (copyright)

Bulletin photograph: Mack Sennett (Hans)

CURIOSITY

Mack Sennett (d); Eleanor Hicks (au); Percy Higginson (c); 29 March 1911 (f); Glendale, California (l); 1 June 1911 (r); 228 feet (rl); J156203 / 3 June 1911 (copyright)

NOTE: No material survives from which the cast may be determined.

A SMILE OF A CHILD

D. W. Griffith (d); Harriet Quimby (au); G. W. Bitzer (c); 17/18 April 1911 (f); Wentworth Hotel, Santa Monica, California/Studio (l); 5 June 1911 (r); 997 feet (rl); J156317 / 7 June 1911 (copyright)

Bulletin photograph: Blanche Sweet (Peasant woman); Baden Powell (Child)

NOTE: Bitzer identifies Baden Powell as the child in this film.

DAVE'S LOVE AFFAIR

Mack Sennett (d); Frank E. Woods ["Reforming Muggsy"] (au); Percy Higginson (c); 14 April 1911 (f); Glendale, California (l); 8 June 1911 (r); 601 feet (rl); J156469 / 10 June 1911 (copyright)

Bulletin photograph: Edward Dillon (Dave); Florence LaBadie (May)

THEIR FATES "SEALED"

Mack Sennett (d); S. R. Simpson ["Fisherman's Luck"] (au); Percy Higginson (c); 20/21 April 1911 (f); Catalina, California (l); 8 June 1911 (r); 396 feet (rl); J156468 / 10 June 1911 (copyright)

NOTE: No material survives from which the cast may be determined.

ENOCH ARDEN (Part One)

D. W. Griffith (d); "Enoch Arden," the poem by Alfred Lord Tennyson (s); G. W. Bitzer (c); 24/28 March 1911 (f); Santa Monica, Cali-
fornia/Studio not noted (l); 12 June 1911 (r); one reel (rl); J156550
/ 13 June 1911 [Parts 1-3]; J156633 / 17 June 1911 [Part 2] (copyright)

Wilfred Lucas (Enoch Arden); Linda Arvidson (Annie Lee); Francis
J. Grandon (Philip Ray); George O. Nicholls (Captain); Alfred Paget,
Jeannie MacPherson, Florence Lee, Blanche Sweet (On beach); Al-
fred Paget, Joseph Graybill (Shipwrecked sailors); ? (Children)

NOTE: Reissued by Biograph 29 August 1916 with ENOCH ARDEN
(Part Two), as a two-reeler.

ENOCH ARDEN (Part Two)

D. W. Griffith (d); "Enoch Arden," the poem by Alfred Lord Tennyson (s); G. W. Bitzer (c); 24/28 March 1911 (f); Santa Monica, Cali-
fornia/Studio not noted (l); 15 June 1911 (r); one reel (rl); J156550
/ 13 June 1911 [Parts 1-3]; J156633 / 17 June 1911 [Part 2] (copyright)

Wilfred Lucas (Enoch Arden); Linda Arvidson (Annie Lee); Francis
J. Grandon (Philip Ray); Robert Harron, Florence LaBadie (Children
as teenagers); Joseph Graybill (Dead shipmate); Dell Henderson, Edward Dillon, W. C. Robinson (Rescuers); Guy Hedlund, Henry Lehrman (On rescue ship); Jeannie MacPherson (Servant); Grace Henderson (Gossip); William J. Butler, Charles H. West, ? (In bar)

NOTE: Reissued by Biograph 29 August 1916 with ENOCH ARDEN
(Part One), as a two-reeler.

THE DELAYED PROPOSAL

Mack Sennett (d); Francis J. Grandon (au); Percy Higginson (c); 1/2
May 1911 (f); Glendale, California (l); 19 June 1911 (r); 511 feet (rl);
J156842 / 21 June 1911 (copyright)

Bulletin photograph: Vivian Prescott (Flossie); Edward Dillon (Zeke)

BEARDED YOUTH

Mack Sennett (d); Edwin August ["Letters"] (au); Percy Higginson (c);
27/28 April 1911 (f); Arcadia, California (l); 19 June 1911 (r); 484
feet (rl); J156841 / 21 June 1911 (copyright)

NOTE: No material survives from which the cast may be determined.

THE PRIMAL CALL

D. W. Griffith (d); Emmett Campbell Hall (au); G. W. Bitzer (c); 19/21 April 1911 (f); Redondo, California/Studio (l); 22 June 1911 (r); 997 feet (rl); J156920 / 24 June 1911 (copyright)

Wilfred Lucas (Fisherman); Claire McDowell (Woman); Grace Henderson (Her mother); Dell Henderson (Creditor); Joseph Graybill (Millionaire); John T. Dillon (His friend); Vivian Prescott (His girlfriend); Alfred Paget, Francis J. Grandon, Marguerite Marsh? (At party); Frank Opperman, Florence LaBadie (Servants); Kate Toncray (Woman's maid); Alfred Paget (On beach); W. Chrystie Miller (Minister); W. C. Robinson, Alfred Paget, John T. Dillon, Francis J. Grandon (At club); George O. Nicholls, Frank Opperman, W. C. Robinson, Robert Harron (On ship)

HER SACRIFICE

D. W. Griffith (d); G. W. Bitzer (c); 4/5 May 1911 (f); Wentworth, Santa Monica, California (l); 26 June 1911 (r); one reel (rl); J157124 / 28 June 1911 (copyright)

Vivian Prescott (Barmaid); Grace Henderson (Widow); Charles H. West (Her son); Florence LaBadie (His sweetheart)

NOTE: Reissued by Biograph 11 December 1916. Cast taken from Moving Picture World, 9 December 1916, p. 1543, except for Grace Henderson, who is identified from the Bulletin photograph.

FIGHTING BLOOD

D. W. Griffith (d); G. W. Bitzer (c); 11/17 May 1911 (f); San Fernando, California/Lookout Mountain, California/Studio not noted (l); 29 June 1911 (r); one reel (rl); J157258 / 1 July 1911 (copyright)

George O. Nicholls (Old soldier); Kate Bruce (His wife); Robert Harron (His son); Gladys Egan, ? (Children); Florence LaBadie (Son's friend); Kate Toncray, Francis J. Grandon (Her parents); William J. Butler, W. C. Robinson (Settlers); Alfred Paget, Dell Henderson (Soldiers); Edward Dillon (Wagon driver); Alfred Paget (Among Indians)

NOTE: Reissued by Biograph 25 June 1915.

STUBBS' NEW SERVANTS

Mack Sennett (d); Frank E. Woods (au); Percy Higginson (c); 3 May 1911 (f); Studio/Glendale, California (l); 3 July 1911 (r); 501 feet (rl); J157385 / 8 July 1911 (copyright)

Bulletin photograph: William J. Butler (Mr. Stubbs); Stephanie Long-fellow

THE WONDERFUL EYE

Mack Sennett (d); Captain Leslie T. Peacocke (au); Percy Higginson (c); 28/29 April, 1/6 May 1911 (f); Studio/Sierra Madre, California (l); 3 July 1911 (r); 495 feet (rl); J157386 / 8 July 1911 (copyright)

NOTE: No material survives from which the cast may be determined.

THE THIEF AND THE GIRL

D. W. Griffith (d); G. W. Bitzer (c); 1/6 May 1911 (f); Studio/Pasadena, California (l); 6 July 1911 (r); one reel (rl); J157384 / 8 July 1911 (copyright)

Bulletin photograph: Wilfred Lucas (Thief); Florence LaBadie (The girl); Baden Powell (Child)

NOTE: Bitzer identifies Baden Powell as the child in this film.

THE JEALOUS HUSBAND

D. W. Griffith?/Mack Sennett? (d); Isobel M. Reynolds (au); G. W. Bitzer (c); 22/24 April 1911 (f); Studio/Santa Monica, California (l); 10 July 1911 (r); 998 feet (rl); J157529 / 12 July 1911 (copyright)

Bulletin photograph: John T. Dillon (Hubby); Vivian Prescott (Wifey); Dell Henderson (Doctor)

BOBBY, THE COWARD

D. W. Griffith (d); Dell Henderson ["The Coward"] (au); G. W. Bitzer (c); 1/5/9 June 1911 (f); Fort Lee, New Jersey/Studio (l); 13 July 1911 (r); 998 feet (rl); J157652 / 15 July 1911 (copyright)

Robert Harron (Bobby); W. Chrystie Miller (Grandfather); Gladys Egan (Sister); Florence LaBadie (The girl next door); William J. Butler (Her father); Joseph Graybill, Guy Hedlund (Thugs); Verner Clarges, Grace Henderson (Rich couple); Francis J. Grandon, Alfred Paget, John T. Dillon (Policemen); Edward Dillon, Edna Foster, Kate Toncray, Jeannie MacPherson, William J. Butler, J. Jiquel Lanoe, W. C. Robinson (On street)

THE INDIAN BROTHERS

D. W. Griffith (d); G. W. Bitzer (c); 28/29 April 1911 (f); Lookout

Mountain, California (l); 17 July 1911 (r); one reel (rl); J157874 /
20 July 1911 (copyright)

Frank Opperman (Chief); Wilfred Lucas (His brother); Guy Hedlund
(The renegade); Blanche Sweet, Kate Toncray, Francis J. Grandon
(Indians); Alfred Paget, W. C. Robinson (In second tribe); Charles
H. West, Alfred Paget, John T. Dillon (At funeral)

THE GHOST

Mack Sennett (d); Mack Sennett ["The White Man's Ghost"] (au); Percy
Higginson (c); 2/3 June 1911 (f); Studio/Fort Lee, New Jersey (l); 20
July 1911 (r); 481 feet (rl); J158071 / 24 July 1911 (copyright)

Bulletin photograph: Mack Sennett, Dell Henderson, Charles H.
West? (Crooks); Charles Hill Mailes (Policeman)

JINKS JOINS THE TEMPERANCE CLUB

Mack Sennett (d); Frank E. Woods (au); Percy Higginson (c); 6/8
May 1911 (f); Venice, California/Studio (l); 20 July 1911 (r); 516 feet
(rl); J158070 / 24 July 1911 (copyright)

NOTE: No material survives from which the cast may be determined.

A COUNTRY CUPID

D. W. Griffith (d); G. W. Bitzer (c); 5/10 June 1911 (f); Studio/
Westfield, New Jersey (l); 24 July 1911 (r); one reel (rl); J158240
/ 29 July 1911 (copyright)

Blanche Sweet (Edith); Edwin August (Jack); Edna Foster (Billy);
Joseph Graybill (The half-wit); Robert Harron, Edward Dillon (Among
students); Kate Bruce (Edith's mother); Claire McDowell (Half-wit's
mother); Frank Evans (Jack's father); Alfred Paget (Farmer)

THE LAST DROP OF WATER

D. W. Griffith (d); G. W. Bitzer (c); 14/20 May 1911 (f); San Fernando, California/Lookout Mountain, California (l); 27 July 1911 (r);
one reel (rl); J158241 / 29 July 1911 (copyright)

Blanche Sweet (Mary); Joseph Graybill (John); Charles H. West (Jim);
Alfred Paget (Indian); Francis J. Grandon (John's friend); Frank Opperman, Kate Bruce, Guy Hedlund, W. C. Robinson, Kate Toncray,
Francis J. Grandon, Gladys Egan, Jeannie MacPherson, Alfred Paget, Robert Harron (In wagon train); John T. Dillon (Cavalry soldier)

NOTE: Reissued by Biograph 13 August 1915. Source supplied by intertitle--"Suggested by the lines to Sir Philip Sydney who, upon the field of blood, dying, gave the drop of water for the sake of brotherhood."--may be from the reissue print.

MR. PECK GOES CALLING

Mack Sennett (d); Frank E. Woods (au); Percy Higginson (c); 9/14 May 1911 (f); Glendale, California/Studio (l); 31 July 1911 (r); 748 feet (rl); J158428 / 3 August 1911 (copyright)

Bulletin photograph: Mack Sennett (Mr. Peck); Vivian Prescott (Mrs. Peck)

THE BEAUTIFUL VOICE

Mack Sennett (d); George W. Terwilliger (au); Percy Higginson (c); 17/19 June 1911 (f); [New York] Studio (l); 31 July 1911 (r); 247 feet (rl); J158429 / 3 August 1911 (copyright)

NOTE: No material survives from which the cast may be determined.

OUT FROM THE SHADOW

D. W. Griffith (d); Emmett Campbell Hall (au); G. W. Bitzer (c); 15/20 June 1911 (f); Studio/Bayonne, New Jersey (l); 3 August 1911 (r); 998 feet (rl); J158553 / 5 August 1911 (copyright)

Bulletin photograph: Blanche Sweet (Mrs. Vane); Edwin August (Mr. Vane); Jeannie MacPherson (Young widow); Marion Sunshine, John T. Dillon, Donald Crisp, Alfred Paget, Charles Hill Mailes, Charles H. West (At dance)

THE RULING PASSION

D. W. Griffith (d); Wilfred Lucas (au); G. W. Bitzer, Percy Higginson (c); 10/23 June, 10 July 1911 (f); Bayonne, New Jersey/Studio (l); 7 August 1911 (r); 997 feet (rl); J158615 / 8 August 1911 (copyright)

Edna Foster (Billy); Wilfred Lucas (His father); Claire McDowell (His mother); Marie Newton, ? (His siblings); Kate Bruce, Kate Toncray, ? (Servants); Gladys Egan, ? (Children); John T. Dillon, W. C. Robinson, Frank Evans, Jeannie MacPherson, Guy Hedlund (At dock); George O. Nicholls (Extra)

NOTE: Although announced for reissue in The Biograph, 19 June 1915, this film apparently did not have a second release.

THAT DARE DEVIL

Mack Sennett (d); Percy Higginson (c); 14/19 June, 1 July 1911 (f);
Edgewater, New Jersey/Fort Lee, New Jersey/Studio (l); 10 August
1911 (r); one-half reel (rl); J158882 / 15 August 1911 (copyright)

Bulletin photograph: Mack Sennett (Dan); Vivian Prescott (His sweetheart)

AN INTERRUPTED GAME

Mack Sennett (d); George Hennessy (au); Percy Higginson (c); 21/22
June 1911 (f); Studio/Edgewater, New Jersey (l); 10 August 1911 (r);
392 feet (rl); J158881 / 15 August 1911 (copyright)

NOTE: No material survives from which the cast may be determined.

THE SORROWFUL EXAMPLE

D. W. Griffith (d); G. W. Bitzer (c); 23/24 June 1911 (f); Studio/Fort
Lee, New Jersey (l); 14 August 1911 (r); one reel (rl); J158883 / 15
August 1911 (copyright)

Bulletin photograph: Wilfred Lucas (Husband); Claire McDowell (Wife)

THE BLIND PRINCESS AND THE POET

D. W. Griffith (d); Harriet Quimby ["The Happy Princess"] (au); G.
W. Bitzer (c); 8/9 May 1911 (f); Hollywood, California (l); 17 August
1911 (r); 1000 feet (rl); J159032 / 19 August 1911 (copyright)

Bulletin photograph: Blanche Sweet (Princess); Charles H. West
(Poet); Grace Henderson, Guy Hedlund, Jeannie MacPherson, Charles
Gorman

NOTE: Reissued by Biograph 24 April 1916.

THE DIVING GIRL

Mack Sennett (d); Percy Higginson (c); 6/8 July 1911 (f); Huntington,
Long Island [New York]/Studio (l); 21 August 1911 (r); one-half reel
(rl); J159204 / 23 August 1911 (copyright)

Fred Mace (Uncle); Mabel Normand (Niece); William J. Butler
(Uncle's friend); Verner Clarges (Doctor); Robert Harron (Bellboy);
Donald Crisp, Edward Dillon, Joseph Graybill, Dell Henderson,
Florence Lee, Guy Hedlund, W. C. Robinson, J. Waltham (Bathers)

$500 REWARD

Mack Sennett (d); Percy Higginson (c); 29/30 June, 3 July 1911 (f); Studio/Fort Lee, New Jersey (l); 21 August 1911 (r); one-half reel (rl); J159203 / 23 August 1911 (copyright)

NOTE: No material survives from which the cast may be determined.

THE ROSE OF KENTUCKY

D. W. Griffith (d); G. W. Bitzer (c); 13/14/29 June, 5 /15 July 1911 (f); Hartford, Connecticut/Coytesville, New Jersey/Studio (l); 24 August 1911 (r); one reel (rl); J159452 / 26 August 1911 (copyright)

Wilfred Lucas (Planter); Marion Sunshine (Orphan); Charles H. West (Partner); Kate Bruce (Housekeeper); William J. Butler[blackface] (Servant); Kate Toncray (Mother); Alfred Paget (Among nightriders)

SWORDS AND HEARTS

D. W. Griffith (d); Emmett Campbell Hall (au); G. W. Bitzer (c); 27 June, 7/18 July 1911 (f); Coytesville, New Jersey/Studio (l); 28 August 1911 (r); 1000 feet (rl); J159606 / 30 August 1911 (copyright)

Wilfred Lucas (Hugh Frazier); Claire McDowell (Irene Lambert); Dorothy West (Jennie Baker); William J. Butler (Old Ben); Charles H. West (Suitor); Francis J. Grandon (Jennie's father); Verner Clarges (Hugh's father); Kate Bruce (At Lambert house); Guy Hedlund, Donald Crisp (At Frazier house); Alfred Paget, Guy Hedlund, J. Jiquel Lanoe (Union soldiers); Frank Evans, Charles Hill Mailes, W. C. Robinson, Donald Crisp, J. Jiquel Lanoe (Bushwackers)

NOTE: Reissued by Biograph 1 May 1916.

THE BARON

Mack Sennett (d); Edwin August ["Just Too Late"] (au); Percy Higginson (c); 24/28 July 1911 (f); Fort Lee, New Jersey/Studio (l); 31 August 1911 (r); 587 feet (rl); J159734 / 5 September 1911 (copyright)

Bulletin photograph: Dell Henderson (Baron/Waiter); Joseph Graybill (His friend); Mabel Normand (Heiress); Grace Henderson

THE VILLAIN FOILED

Mack Sennett (d); David Morrison ["Almost a Tragedy"] (au); Percy Higginson (c); 14/18 July 1911 (f); Fort Lee, New Jersey/Studio (l); 31 August 1911 (r); 411 feet (rl); J159733 / 5 September 1911 (copyright)

NOTE: No material survives from which the cast may be determined.

THE STUFF HEROES ARE MADE OF

D. W. Griffith (d); G. W. Bitzer (c); 28 June, 1/17 July 1911 (f);
Studio/Lynbrook, New York (l); 4 September 1911 (r); one reel (rl);
J159747 / 6 September 1911 (copyright)

Bulletin photograph: Blanche Sweet (Alice); Marion Sunshine (Jennie);
Edwin August (Young author)

THE OLD CONFECTIONER'S MISTAKE

D. W. Griffith (d); Edward Acker ["The Lawn Party"] (au); G. W.
Bitzer (c); 10/20 July, 12 August 1911 (f); Studio/Fort Lee, New
Jersey (l); 7 September 1911 (r); 999 feet (rl); J159947 / 12 Septem-
ber 1911 (copyright)

Bulletin photograph: Wilfred Lucas (Old Daddy Dodson); Grace Henderson (Lady Bountiful); Edna Foster, ? (Children)

THE VILLAGE HERO

Mack Sennett (d); Percy Higginson (c); 31 July, 4 August 1911 (f);
Cuddebackville, New York (l); 11 September 1911 (r); one-half reel
(rl); J159946 / 12 September 1911 (copyright)

Bulletin photograph: Fred Mace (Eugene); Mack Sennett (Max); Jeannie MacPherson, W. Chrystie Miller, Gladys Egan, Frank Evans
(Villagers)

THE LUCKY HORSESHOE

Mack Sennett (d); Percy Higginson (c); 26 July, 3 August 1911 (f);
Cuddebackville, New York/Fort Lee, New Jersey (l); 11 September
1911 (r); one-half reel (rl); J159945 / 12 September 1911 (copyright)

NOTE: No material survives from which the cast may be determined.

THE SQUAW'S LOVE

D. W. Griffith (d); Stanner E. V. Taylor (au); G. W. Bitzer, Percy
Higginson, John Mahr (c); 31 July, 1/3 August 1911 (f); Cuddebackville, New York (l); 14 September 1911 (r); 998 feet (rl); J160195 /
18 September 1911 (copyright)

Mabel Normand (Wildflower); Dark Cloud (White Eagle); Alfred Paget
(Gray Fox); Claire McDowell (Silver Fawn); William J. Butler, Kate
Bruce (Parents); Donald Crisp (Extra)

NOTE: Reissued by Biograph 10 July 1916.

DAN, THE DANDY

D. W. Griffith (d); Bernardine R. Leist (au); G. W. Bitzer (c); 24/
27 July 1911 (f); Fort Lee, New Jersey/Studio (l); 18 September 1911
(r); 998 feet (rl); J160241 / 20 September 1911 (copyright)

Bulletin photograph: William J. Butler (Father); Charles H. West
(Son); Wilfred Lucas (Tramp/Clubman); Marion Sunshine (Heiress)

A CONVENIENT BURGLAR

Mack Sennett (d); George Hennessy (au); Percy Higginson (c); 5/8
August 1911 (f); Studio/New York City roof/Fort Lee, New Jersey
(l); 21 September 1911 (r); 534 feet (rl); J160416 / 25 September
1911 (copyright)

Bulletin photograph: Grace Henderson (Mrs. Gay); Fred Mace (Mr.
Gay); Edward Dillon (His friend); Guy Hedlund, J. Jiquel Lanoe

WHEN WIFEY HOLDS THE PURSE-STRINGS

Mack Sennett (d); Hallie B. Goodman (au); Percy Higginson (c); 11/12
August 1911 (f); Fort Lee, New Jersey/Studio (l); 21 September 1911
(r); 463 feet (rl); J160415 / 25 September 1911 (copyright)

NOTE: No material survives from which the cast may be determined.

THE REVENUE MAN AND THE GIRL

D. W. Griffith (d); G. W. Bitzer (c); 29 July, 5 August 1911 (f);
Studio/Fort Lee, New Jersey/Cuddebackville, New York (l); 25 September 1911 (r); one reel (rl); J160517 / 27 September 1911 (copyright)

Bulletin photograph: Edwin August (Revenue man); Dorothy West
(Moonshiner's daughter)

HER AWAKENING

D. W. Griffith (d); G. W. Bitzer (c); 21/22 August 1911 (f); Fort
Lee, New Jersey/Studio (l); 28 September 1911 (r); one reel (rl);
J160853 / 28 September 1911 (copyright)

Mabel Normand (Daughter); Kate Bruce (Mother); Harry Hyde (Sweetheart); Vivian Prescott, ? (Laundry employees); Fred Mace, ? (Laundry customers); Robert Harron (On street); Kate Toncray (Old wo-

man); William J. Butler, J. Jiquel Lanoe (Doctors); J. Jiquel Lanoe, Robert Harron, Frank Evans, Charles Hill Mailes, W. C. Robinson, Donald Crisp, Kate Toncray (Accident witnesses)

TOO MANY BURGLARS

Mack Sennett (d); Thornton Cole (au); Percy Higginson (c); 26/29 August 1911 (f); Studio/Fort Lee, New Jersey (l); 2 October 1911 (r); 499 feet (rl); J161094 / 4 October 1911 (copyright)

Edward Dillon (Mr. Brown); ? (Mrs. Brown); Mack Sennett (The actor friend); Fred Mace (The burglar); ? (Policemen); ? (Messenger)

MR. BRAGG, A FUGITIVE

Mack Sennett (d); Frank E. Woods ["Stubbs a Fugitive"] (au); Percy Higginson (c); 20/22 July 1911 (f); Fort Lee, New Jersey/Studio (l); 2 October 1911 (r); 497 feet (rl); J161095 / 4 October 1911 (copyright)

NOTE: No material survives from which the cast may be determined.

THE MAKING OF A MAN

D. W. Griffith (d); R. L. Bond (au); G. W. Bitzer (c); 14/17 August 1911 (f); Studio/Fort Lee, New Jersey (l); 5 October 1911 (r); 1000 feet (rl); J161219 / 7 October 1911 (copyright)

Dell Henderson (Leading man); Blanche Sweet (Young woman); William J. Butler, J. Jiquel Lanoe, ? (Her family); Frank Evans (Sheriff); Kate Toncray (Landlady); Gladys Egan, Charles Hill Mailes, Frank Evans, W. Chrystie Miller (In first audience); Guy Hedlund (Boyfriend); Edward Dillon (Usher); Joseph Graybill, Claire McDowell, Donald Crisp (Actors); Edward Dillon, Frank Evans, W. Chrystie Miller, Kate Toncray (At dance); W. C. Robinson, Charles Hill Mailes (At first stage door); Vivian Prescott, Mabel Normand, Harry Hyde, Frank Evans, Wilfred Lucas, Kate Toncray, Grace Henderson (In second audience); Harry Hyde (At second stage door); Donald Crisp, Charles Hill Mailes, Joseph Graybill (Backstage); J. Waltham (Desk clerk)

ITALIAN BLOOD

D. W. Griffith (d); Bernardine R. Leist (au); G. W. Bitzer (c); 8/11 August 1911 (f); Coytesville, New Jersey/Studio (l); 9 October 1911 (r); 999 feet (rl); J161479 / 11 October 1911 (copyright)

Bulletin photograph: Vivian Prescott (Wife); Charles H. West, Joseph Graybill

TRAILING THE COUNTERFEITER

Mack Sennett (d); Percy Higginson (c); 16/18 August 1911 (f); Studio /Fort Lee, New Jersey (l); 12 October 1911 (r); one-half reel (rl); J161681 / 16 October 1911 (copyright)

Mack Sennett, Fred Mace (The Biograph Sleuths); Alfred Paget, ? (Policemen); J. Jiquel Lanoe, ? (Counterfeiters); J. Jiquel Lanoe (Mustachioed man); W. C. Robinson, ? (In front of tonsorial parlor); Eddie Lyons, ? (Detectives); ? (Two station sergeants); ? (Two bricklayers); ? (Shopkeeper)

NOTE: This is the first of the "Biograph Sleuths" comedies.

JOSH'S SUICIDE

Mack Sennett (d); J. Harry Cannon ["The Dead Return"] (au); Percy Higginson (c); 23/24 August 1911 (f); Leonia, New Jersey/Studio/New York City location? (l); 12 October 1911 (r); 469 feet (rl); J161682 / 16 October 1911 (copyright)

NOTE: No material survives from which the cast may be determined. New York City notation is unclear in the production records at the Museum of Modern Art.

THE UNVEILING

D. W. Griffith (d); T. P. Bayer (au); G. W. Bitzer (c); 13 July, 26/28 August 1911 (f); Studio (l); 16 October 1911 (r); 998 feet (rl); J161771 / 17 October 1911 (copyright)

Bulletin photograph: Robert Harron (Boy); Grace Henderson (Mother); Mabel Normand (Showgirl); William J. Butler

NOTE: Reissued by Biograph 18 September 1916.

THE ADVENTURES OF BILLY

D. W. Griffith (d); James Carroll ["An American Boy"] (au); G. W. Bitzer (c); 23/24 August, 2/3 September 1911 (f); Studio/Fort Lee, New Jersey/Westfield, New Jersey (l); 19 October 1911 (r); 999 feet (rl); J161914 / 21 October 1911 (copyright)

Edna Foster (Billy); Joseph Graybill, Donald Crisp (Tramps); Dell Henderson, Claire McDowell (Rich couple); Kate Bruce (Maid); Frank Evans (Farmer); W. Chrystie Miller (Robbery victim); Alfred Paget, Charles Hill Mailes (Farmhands/Rescuers); Grace Henderson (Woman on porch); Harry Hyde (On lawn); D. W. Griffith (On bench)

THROUGH HIS WIFE'S PICTURE

Mack Sennett (d); George Hennessy ["The Masqueraders"] (au); Percy Higginson (c); 10/17 September 1911 (f); Studio (l); 23 October 1911 (r); 530 feet (rl); J162081 / 25 October 1911 (copyright)

Bulletin photograph: Mabel Normand (Wifey); Fred Mace? (Friend); Edward Dillon

THE INVENTOR'S SECRET

Mack Sennett (d); George Hennessy ["The Professor's Secret"] (au); Percy Higginson (c); 14/18 September 1911 (f); Fort Lee, New Jersey/Studio (l); 23 October 1911 (r); 468 feet (rl); J162080 / 25 October 1911 (copyright)

NOTE: No material survives from which the cast may be determined.

THE LONG ROAD

D. W. Griffith (d); Bernardine R. Leist ["The Swinging Door"] (au); G. W. Bitzer (c); 30/31 August, 1/5 September 1911 (f); Studio/Fort Lee, New Jersey (l); 26 October 1911 (r); 1000 feet (rl); J162358 / 30 October 1911 (copyright)

Blanche Sweet (Edith); Grace Henderson (Her mother); Charles H. West (Ned); Claire McDowell (His wife); Edna Foster (Their son); Kate Bruce (Mother Superior); Kate Toncray (Nun); Donald Crisp, ? (Servants); Donald Crisp (Landlord); Charles Hill Mailes (Priest); Dell Henderson, Frank Evans, Harry Hyde, J. Jiquel Lanoe, Alfred Paget (Wedding guests); Robert Harron (Family friend); J. Jiquel Lanoe (On street); Edwin August, Alfred Paget, Harry Hyde, William J. Butler, Kate Toncray (At party); Wilfred Lucas, ? (Policemen); Frank Evans, Charles Hill Mailes, Joseph Graybill, Fred Mace, W. C. Robinson, Alfred Paget, Edward Dillon (In bar); ? (Bartender); J. Jiquel Lanoe (Doctor); ? (Old man); Guy Hedlund? (Butler)

LOVE IN THE HILLS

D. W. Griffith (d); Dell Henderson (au); G. W. Bitzer (c); 21/23 September 1911 (f); Suffern, New York (l); 30 October 1911 (r); 998 feet (rl); J162396 / 31 October 1911 (copyright)

Blanche Sweet (The girl); Wilfred Lucas (The manly suitor); Charles H. West (The shiftless suitor); Joseph Graybill (The city suitor); Kate Toncray, ? (Girl's parents)

A VICTIM OF CIRCUMSTANCES

Mack Sennett (d); Mrs. Montayne Perry (au); Percy Higginson (c);

23/30 September, 2 October 1911 (f); Studio/Fort Lee, New Jersey
(l); 2 November 1911 (r); 382 feet (rl); J162531 / 4 November 1911
(copyright)

Bulletin photograph: Dell Henderson (Hubby); Lily Cahill (Wife); Fred
Mace (Jewelry clerk)

THEIR FIRST DIVORCE CASE

Mack Sennett (d); George Hennessy (au); Percy Higginson (c); 2/11/13
September 1911 (f); Studio/Edgewater, New Jersey (l); 2 November
1911 (r); 616 feet (rl); J162530 / 4 November 1911 (copyright)

Mack Sennett, Fred Mace (The Biograph Sleuths)

NOTE: No material survives from which other cast members may
be determined.

THE BATTLE

D. W. Griffith (d); G. W. Bitzer (c); 8/19 September 1911 (f); Coytesville, New Jersey/Studio (l); 6 November 1911 (r); one reel (rl);
J162613 / 7 November 1911 (copyright)

Blanche Sweet (Woman); Charles H. West (Her sweetheart); Charles
Hill Mailes (Union commander); Robert Harron, Harry Hyde, Donald
Crisp, W. Christy Cabanne, Guy Hedlund, W. C. Robinson (Union
soldiers); Dell Henderson, J. Jiquel Lanoe, Edwin August, William
J. Butler, Joseph Graybill (Union officers); Kate Toncray, Edna
Foster, W. Chrystie Miller (At dance); William J. Butler, Kate Ton-
cray (At farewell); Lionel Barrymore (Wagon driver); Alfred Paget
(Confederate officer); Kate Bruce (In the town)

NOTE: Reissued by Biograph 11 June 1915.

THE TRAIL OF BOOKS

D. W. Griffith (d); Jerome J. Olson (au); G. W. Bitzer (c); 26/30
September 1911 (f); Studio/Fort Lee, New Jersey (l); 9 November
1911 (r); 997 feet (rl); J162883 / 13 November 1911 (copyright)

Bulletin photograph: Edwin August (Husband)

DOOLEY'S SCHEME

Mack Sennett (d); George Hennessy ["In Search of Dooley"] (au); Percy Higginson (c); 20/22 September 1911 (f); Fort Lee, New Jersey/
Studio (l); 13 November 1911 (r); 530 feet (rl); J162974 / 15 November 1911 (copyright)

Bulletin photograph: Fred Mace (Officer Dooley); Vivian Prescott (Maid); Frank Evans (A guest); W. Chrystie Miller (Minister?)

WON THROUGH A MEDIUM

Mack Sennett (d); George Hennessy ["The Medium"] (au); Percy Higginson (c); 27 September, 3 October 1911 (f); Studio (l); 13 November 1911 (r); 467 feet (rl); J162973 / 15 November 1911 (copyright)

NOTE: No material survives from which the cast may be determined.

THROUGH DARKENED VALES

D. W. Griffith (d); Stanner E. V. Taylor (au); G. W. Bitzer (c); 28/30 September, 2/5 October 1911 (f); Studio/Fort Lee, New Jersey (l); 16 November 1911 (r); 999 feet (rl); J163014 / 18 November 1911 (copyright)

Blanche Sweet (Grace); Grace Henderson (Her mother); Charles H. West (Dave); Joseph Graybill (Howard); J. Jiquel Lanoe (Among party guests); Dell Henderson (First doctor); Kate Toncray (Nurse); Charles Hill Mailes (Oculist); Fred Mace (Dave's employer); Jackie Saunders (Howard's next girlfriend); Kate Bruce (Cleaning woman); William J. Butler (Second doctor); William Bechtel (Office technician?); Adolph Lestina (Oculist's assistant); J. Jiquel Lanoe (Office worker); W. Christy Cabanne, Harry Hyde (In oculist's office)

THE MISER'S HEART

D. W. Griffith (d); George Hennessy (au); G. W. Bitzer (c); 9/14 October 1911 (f); Fort Lee, New Jersey/Studio (l); 20 November 1911 (r); 998 feet (rl); J163115 / 22 November 1911 (copyright)

Adolph Lestina (The Miser); Wilfred Lucas, Charles Hill Mailes (Crooks); Edith Haldeman (Little child); Edward Dillon (Down-and-out young man); Kate Toncray (Woman); ? (Young girls); Robert Harron, J. Waltham (On street); W. C. Robinson (In front of clothing store); William J. Butler, Frank Evans, Alfred Paget, Donald Crisp (Policemen)

NOTE: Reissued by Biograph 17 January 1916.

RESOURCEFUL LOVERS

Mack Sennett (d); Elmer Booth (au); Percy Higginson (c); 13/14 October 1911 (f); Fort Lee, New Jersey/Studio (l); 23 November 1911 (r); 423 feet (rl); J163175 / 25 November 1911 (copyright)

Bulletin photograph: William Bechtel (Old chemist); Vivian Prescott (His daughter); Charles H. West (Her sweetheart)

HER MOTHER INTERFERES

Mack Sennett (d); Elmer Booth ["His Mother-in-law"] (au); Percy Higginson (c); 10/13 October 1911 (f); Riverside Drive, New York City/Fort Lee, New Jersey/Studio (l); 23 November 1911 (r); 574 feet (rl); J163176 / 25 November 1911 (copyright)

NOTE: No material survives from which the cast may be determined.

SUNSHINE THROUGH THE DARK

D. W. Griffith (d); Harriet Quimby (au); G. W. Bitzer (c); 16/24 October 1911 (f); Studio/Fort Lee, New Jersey (l); 27 November 1911 (r); 999 feet (rl); J163271 / 29 November 1911 (copyright)

Bulletin photograph: Dorothy Bernard (Maid); Grace Henderson (Her employer); Edward Dillon (Stable boy)

A WOMAN SCORNED

D. W. Griffith (d); George Hennessy (au); G. W. Bitzer (c); 4/10 October 1911 (f); Fort Lee, New Jersey/Studio (l); 30 November 1911 (r); 998 feet (rl); J163355 / 2 December 1911 (copyright)

Wilfred Lucas (Doctor); Claire McDowell (His wife); ? (Their child); Adolph Lestina (Sneak thief); Vivian Prescott (His sweetheart); Alfred Paget (Thief's companion); Charles Hill Mailes, Frank Evans (Policemen)

NOTE: This film contains narrative elements that are derived from THE LONELY VILLA.

WHY HE GAVE UP

Mack Sennett (d); George Hennessy ["Two of a Kind"] (au); Percy Higginson (c); 1/8/28 September 1911 (f); Studio/Huntington, New York (l); 4 December 1911 (r); 695 feet (rl); J163420 / 5 December 1911 (copyright)

Fred Mace (Hubby); Mabel Normand (Wife); Edward Dillon, William J. Butler (His chums); ? (Mother-in-law); ? (Bellboy); W. C. Robinson (Cafe employee); J. Waltham, William Beaudine, W. C. Robinson, Kathleen Butler (At club)

ABE GETS EVEN WITH FATHER

Mack Sennett (d); Elmer Booth ["Abe Got Even with His Father"] (au); Percy Higginson (c); 25/26 October 1911 (f); Studio/Fort Lee, New Jersey (l); 4 December 1911 (r); 303 feet (rl); J163419 / 5 December 1911 (copyright)

? (Abe); William Bechtel (Cohen, his father); Fred Mace (Murphy, the janitor); Mrs. William Bechtel? (Mrs. Cohen); ? (Mrs. Murphy); Gus Pixley (A visitor)

THE FAILURE

D. W. Griffith (d); M. B. Havey (au); G. W. Bitzer (c); 13/24 October 1911 (f); Studio/Englewood, New Jersey (l); 7 December 1911 (r); 998 feet (rl); J163469 / 8 December 1911 (copyright)

Wilfred Lucas (The man); Dorothy Bernard (The woman); Adolph Lestina (Bank manager); J. Jiquel Lanoe, Donald Crisp (Bank employees); Lily Cahill (Fiancée); Grace Henderson (Her mother); Joseph Graybill, Robert Harron, W. Christy Cabanne (At fiancée's house); J. Waltham (Tavern owner); Alfred Paget, Charles Hill Mailes, W. Christy Cabanne, Kate Toncray, Edward Dillon, W. C. Robinson, Adolph Lestina, J. Jiquel Lanoe, Robert Harron, Harry Hyde, Frank Evans, Edwin August, Dell Henderson (In tavern)

NOTE: Reissued by Biograph 20 December 1915.

SAVED FROM HIMSELF

D. W. Griffith (d); George Hennessy (au); G. W. Bitzer (c); 12/16 September, 23/26 October 1911 (f); Studio (l); 11 December 1911 (r); 999 feet (rl); J163617 / 13 December 1911 (copyright)

Joseph Graybill (Young clerk); Mabel Normand (Stenographer); Charles Hill Mailes (Proprietor); William J. Butler (Guest)

NOTE: Reissued by Biograph 14 August 1916. Cast taken from Moving Picture World, 19 August 1916, p. 1296.

TAKING HIS MEDICINE

Mack Sennett (d); Percy Higginson (c); 21/30 March 1911 (f); Studio/ Glendale, California/Arcadia, California (l); 14 December 1911 (r); one-half reel (rl); J163668 / 15 December 1911 (copyright)

Bulletin photograph: Edward Dillon (Lazy Lou); Ford Sterling (Doctor)

HER PET

Mack Sennett (d); Percy Higginson (c); 3/6 March 1911 (f); Studio/7-Hill Streets, California (l); 14 December 1911 (r); one-half reel (rl); J163667 / 15 December 1911 (copyright)

NOTE: No material survives from which the cast may be determined.

In the production records at the Museum of Modern Art, the location appears as follows: 7-Hill Sts.

AS IN A LOOKING GLASS

D. W. Griffith (d); George Hennessy (au); G. W. Bitzer (c); 20/25 October 1911 (f); Studio (l); 18 December 1911 (r); 999 feet (rl); J163801 / 20 December 1911 (copyright)

Bulletin photograph: Wilfred Lucas (Husband); Claire McDowell (Wife)

A TERRIBLE DISCOVERY

D. W. Griffith (d); Edward Acker (au); G. W. Bitzer (c); 1/2/3/4/6 November 1911 (f); Studio/Fort Lee, New Jersey (l); 21 December 1911 (r); 998 feet (rl); J163846 / 22 December 1911 (copyright)

Wilfred Lucas (District attorney); Edna Foster (His son); Charles Hill Mailes (Dick); Kate Bruce (Housekeeper); Adolph Lestina, W. C. Robinson, Charles H. West (Thugs); Frank Evans, Adolph Lestina (D. A.'s friends); Alfred Paget, Charles Gorman (Policemen); J. Jiquel Lanoe (Rescuer)

CAUGHT WITH THE GOODS

Mack Sennett (d); George Hennessy (au); G. W. Bitzer (c); 21/23/25/ 26 October 1911 (f); Studio/Fort Lee, New Jersey (l); 25 December 1911 (r); 517 feet (rl); J163911 / 26 December 1911 (copyright)

Bulletin photograph: Mack Sennett, Fred Mace (The Biograph Sleuths); John T. Dillon, William Bechtel, Kate Toncray (In vice committee)

A MIX-UP IN RAIN COATS

Mack Sennett (d); Isobel M. Reynolds (au); Percy Higginson (c); 2/3 November 1911 (f); Fort Lee, New Jersey/Studio (l); 25 December 1911 (r); 482 feet (rl); J163910 / 26 December 1911 (copyright)

NOTE: No material survives from which the cast may be determined.

THE VOICE OF THE CHILD

D. W. Griffith (d); George Hennessy ["The Turning Point"] (au); G. W. Bitzer (c); 9/28 November 1911 (f); Studio/Fort Lee, New Jersey (l); 28 December 1911 (r); 998 feet (rl); J164068 / 29 December 1911 (copyright)

Bulletin photograph: Edwin August? (Husband); Blanche Sweet (Wife); Joseph Graybill (False friend)

THE BABY AND THE STORK

D. W. Griffith (d); George Hennessy (au); G. W. Bitzer (c); 9/22 November 1911 (f); Studio/Westfield, New Jersey (l); 1 January 1912 (r); 999 feet (rl); J164467 / 8 January 1912 (copyright)

Edna Foster (Bobby); Charles Hill Mailes, Claire McDowell (His parents); Kate Bruce (Nurse); William J. Butler (Doctor); Grace Henderson (Maid); Edward Dillon (Workman); Dorothy Bernard (His wife); Edith Haldeman, ? (Their children); Alfred Paget (At zoo); Frank Evans, J. Jiquel Lanoe (On street); Charles H. West, W. C. Robinson (Policemen); William Bechtel (Assisting doctor)

WHO GOT THE REWARD?

Mack Sennett (d); Isobel M. Reynolds ["How Hubby Paid the Reward"] (au); Percy Higginson (c); 10/16 November 1911 (f); Studio/Fort Lee, New Jersey/New York City (l); 4 January 1912 (r); 515 feet (rl); J164468 / 8 January 1912 (copyright)

Bulletin photograph: Dell Henderson (Husband); Vivian Prescott (Wife); William Bechtel

THE JOKE ON THE JOKER

Mack Sennett (d); Julian Lamothe ["The Tables Turned, or The Joke on Mr. Jollot"] (au); Percy Higginson (c); 5/10 October 1911 (f); Studio/Fort Lee, New Jersey (l); 4 January 1912 (r); 483 feet (rl); J164469 / 8 January 1912 (copyright)

NOTE: No material survives from which the cast may be determined.

A TALE OF THE WILDERNESS

D. W. Griffith (d); G. W. Bitzer (c); 8/13/14/20 November 1911 (f); Coytesville, New Jersey (l); 8 January 1912 (r); one reel (rl); J164534 / 11 January 1912 (copyright)

Dorothy Bernard (Young woman); Charles Hill Mailes (The outlaw); Edwin August (His younger brother); William J. Butler (Pioneer leader); Dark Cloud (Indian chief)

NOTE: Reissued by Biograph 9 October 1916. Cast taken from Moving Picture World, 21 October 1916, p. 441.

THE ETERNAL MOTHER

D. W. Griffith (d); G. W. Bitzer (c); 19/22/25 July, 11 August 1911
(f); Coytesville, New Jersey/Studio (l); 11 January 1912 (r); one reel
(rl); J164577 / 13 January 1911 (copyright)

Edwin August (John, the husband); Blanche Sweet (Martha, the wife);
Mabel Normand (Mary, the woman); Kate Bruce (Old woman); J.
Jiquel Lanoe, Guy Hedlund (Friends); Donald Crisp, Jeannie Mac-
Pherson (In field); Charles Hill Mailes (Mary's father)

BRAVE AND BOLD

Mack Sennett (d); Dell Henderson (au); Percy Higginson (c); finished
November 1911 (f); Studio (l); 15 January 1912 (r); 422 feet (rl);
J164602 / 15 January 1912 (copyright)

Bulletin photograph: Fred Mace (Mr. Blowhard); Kate Toncray (Mrs.
Blowhard)

DID MOTHER GET HER WISH?

Mack Sennett (d); Dell Henderson (au); Percy Higginson (c); finished
October 1911 (f); 15 January 1912 (r); 575 feet (rl); J164603 / 15
January 1912 (copyright)

NOTE: No material survives from which the cast and/or location
may be determined.

THE OLD BOOKKEEPER

D. W. Griffith (d); Belle Taylor (au); G. W. Bitzer (c); finished
November 1911 (f); Studio (l); 18 January 1912 (r); 998 feet (rl);
J165052 / 20 January 1912 (copyright)

W. Chrystie Miller (The old bookkeeper); Edwin August (Employer);
Blanche Sweet (His wife); Alfred Paget, ? (Thieves); Jackie Saunders
(Maid); Joseph McDermott (Police sergeant); Edward Dillon (Office
visitor); Kate Toncray (Landlady?); W. C. Robinson, ? (Policemen);
Charles Gorman, Harry Hyde, Adolph Lestina, Charles H. West,
J. Jiquel Lanoe, Vivian Prescott (In office); ? (Newsboy); ? (Visitor)

FOR HIS SON

D. W. Griffith (d); Emmett Campbell Hall ["His Only Son"] (au); G.
W. Bitzer (c); finished November 1911 (f); Studio/New Jersey location? (l); 22 January 1912 (r); 999 feet (rl); J165127 / 22 January
1912 (copyright)

Charles Hill Mailes (Physician); Charles H. West (His son); Blanche Sweet (Son's fiancée); Dorothy Bernard (Secretary); Dell Henderson, Alfred Paget, William Bechtel (In office); Harry Hyde, W. Christy Cabanne, ? (Son's friends); Grace Henderson (Landlady); Robert Harron, W. Christy Cabanne, Gus Pixley, Kate Toncray, Edna Foster, Edward Dillon, J. Jiquel Lanoe, W. C. Robinson, Inez Seabury (At soda fountain); ? (On loading dock)

WITH A KODAK

Mack Sennett (d); George E. Glaser ["Two of a Kind"] (au); Percy Higginson (c); finished November 1911 (f); Studio/New Jersey location (l); 25 January 1912 (r); 511 feet (rl); J165155 / 24 January 1912 (copyright)

Edward Dillon (Secretary); Vivian Prescott (Maid); Fred Mace (Mr. Hobbs); Kate Bruce (Mrs. Hobbs); William Beaudine, ? (Couple in park)

PANTS AND PANSIES

Mack Sennett (d); Thornton Cole (au); Percy Higginson (c); finished November 1911 (f); 25 January 1912 (r); 487 feet (rl); J165156 / 24 January 1912 (copyright)

NOTE: No material survives from which the cast and/or location may be determined.

A BLOT IN THE 'SCUTCHEON

D. W. Griffith (d); Linda Arvidson ["A Blot on the Escutcheon"] (au); "A Blot in the 'Scutcheon," the poem by Robert Browning (s); G. W. Bitzer (c); finished December 1911 (f); Studio/New Jersey location (l); 29 January 1912 (r); 1500 feet (rl); J165263 / 29 January 1912 (copyright)

Charles Hill Mailes (Thorold, Earl Tresham); Dorothy Bernard (Mildred, his sister); Edwin August (Henry, Earl Mertoun); Claire McDowell (A lady); William J. Butler (Hunter); Charles H. West, ? (Footmen); Edna Foster (Courtier); Edward Dillon, Charles H. West, Harry Hyde, W. Christy Cabanne, Joseph Graybill, J. Jiquel Lanoe (Nobles)

NOTE: Reissued by Biograph 12 September 1916.

THE TRANSFORMATION OF MIKE

D. W. Griffith (d); Wilfred Lucas (au); G. W. Bitzer (c); finished December 1911 (f); Studio (l); 1 February 1912 (r); one reel (rl); J165425 / 31 January 1912 (copyright)

Wilfred Lucas (Mike); Blanche Sweet (Tenement girl); Edna Foster (Her brother); William J. Butler (Their father); John T. Dillon, Frank Evans (Policemen); Kate Bruce (Neighbor); W. Christy Cabanne, J. Jiquel Lanoe, W. C. Robinson, Joseph McDermott (In bar); ? (Girl's friend); ? (Bartender); Grace Henderson, Gus Pixley, W. C. Robinson, Joseph McDermott, Robert Harron, John T. Dillon, J. Jiquel Lanoe (At dance)

A NEAR-TRAGEDY

Mack Sennett (d); Edna Alexander ["A Make Believe Tragedy"] (au); Percy Higginson (c); finished December 1911 (f); Studio/New Jersey location? (l); 5 February 1912 (r); 415 feet (rl); J165553 / 3 February 1912 (copyright)

Bulletin photograph: Fred Mace (Sheriff)

LILY'S LOVERS

Mack Sennett (d); Isobel M. Reynolds (au); Percy Higginson (c); finished November 1911 (f); 5 February 1912 (r); 582 feet (rl); J165554 / 3 February 1912 (copyright)

NOTE: No material survives from which the cast and/or location may be determined.

A SISTER'S LOVE

D. W. Griffith (d); Mrs. E. C. Pierson ["Her Awakening"] (au); G. W. Bitzer (c); finished November 1911 (f); Studio (l); 8 February 1912 (r); 999 feet (rl); J166053 / 7 February 1912 (copyright)

Bulletin photograph: Wilfred Lucas, Dorothy Bernard

BILLY'S STRATAGEM

D. W. Griffith (d); George Hennessy (au); G. W. Bitzer (c); finished December 1911 (f); New Jersey location? (l); 12 February 1912 (r); 998 feet (rl); J166224 / 12 February 1912 (copyright)

Edna Foster (Billy); Wilfred Lucas, Claire McDowell (His parents); Edith Haldeman (Little girl); ? (Grandfather); ? (Indian trader); Harry Hyde, Robert Harron, Frank Evans (Settlers); Alfred Paget, Charles Hill Mailes, W. Christy Cabanne, J. Jiquel Lanoe, W. C. Robinson (Indians)

NOTE: Reissued by Biograph 8 October 1915.

THE MENDER OF NETS

D. W. Griffith (d); G. W. Bitzer (c); January 1912 (f); Santa Monica, California (l); 15 February 1912 (r); one reel (rl); J166369 / 15 February 1912 (copyright)

Bulletin photograph: Mary Pickford (The Little Mender); Charles H. West

NOTE: Santa Monica location taken from handwritten notation on the Bulletin.

THE FATAL CHOCOLATE

Mack Sennett (d); Edna Alexander ["The Fatal Pill"] (au); Percy Higginson (c); finished December 1911 (f); New York (l); 19 February 1912 (r); 574 feet (rl); J166565 / 20 February 1912 (copyright)

Bulletin photograph: Mabel Normand (City girl); Dell Henderson (Her city beau); Mack Sennett, Charles H. West (Zeke and Jake)

"GOT A MATCH?"

Mack Sennett (d); George Hennessy ["Nan's Double"] (au); Percy Higginson (c); finished December 1911 (f); New York (l); 19 February 1912 (r); 424 feet (rl); J166564 / 20 February 1912 (copyright)

NOTE: No material survives from which the cast may be determined.

UNDER BURNING SKIES

D. W. Griffith (d); G. W. Bitzer (c); January 1912 (f); California (l); 22 February 1912 (r); one reel (rl); J166557 / 20 February 1912 (copyright)

Wilfred Lucas (Joe); Blanche Sweet (Emily); W. Christy Cabanne (Her husband); Alfred Paget (His friend); Kate Toncray (Mother?); Claire McDowell (Friend); Charles H. West (Bartender); Charles Hill Mailes, Frank Evans, Charles Gorman (In bar); Robert Harron, W. C. Robinson, Edwin August (On street); W. Chrystie Miller, Charles Hill Mailes, Robert Harron, Marguerite Marsh (At farewell party)

THE SUNBEAM

D. W. Griffith (d); George Hennessy ["Little Sunbeam"] (au); G. W. Bitzer (c); finished December 1911 (f); New York (l); 26 February 1912 (r); 1000 feet (rl); J166712 / 27 February 1912 (copyright)

Inez Seabury (The Sunbeam); Kate Bruce (Her mother); Claire Mc-
Dowell (Spinster); Dell Henderson (Bachelor); Edna Foster, Gladys
Egan, ? (Children); Adolph Lestina, Joseph McDermott, John T.
Dillon (Policemen); W. Chrystie Miller, W. Christy Cabanne (In
hallway); Charles Hill Mailes (Janitor)

NOTE: Reissued by Biograph 25 September 1916.

A MESSAGE FROM THE MOON

Mack Sennett (d); M. Shannon Fife ["A Message from Mars"] (au);
Percy Higginson (c); December 1911, January 1912 (f); New York/
California (l); 29 February 1912 (r); 411 feet (rl); J166795 / 1 March
1912 (copyright)

Bulletin photograph: Dell Henderson (Old astronomer); Vivian Prescott (His daughter); Mack Sennett (Her sweetheart)

PRISCILLA'S CAPTURE

Frank Powell (d); Florence Barker ["A Queer Mishap"] (au); Percy
Higginson (c); finished February 1911 (f); California (l); 29 February
1912 (r); 587 feet (rl); J166794 / 1 March 1912 (copyright)

NOTE: No material survives from which the cast and/or location
may be determined.

A SIREN OF IMPULSE

D. W. Griffith (d); G. W. Bitzer (c); January 1912 (f); California
(l); 4 March 1912 (r); one reel (rl); J167013 / 6 March 1912 (copyright)

Bulletin photograph: Dorothy Bernard, Charles H. West

A STRING OF PEARLS

D. W. Griffith (d); Bernardine R. Leist (au); G. W. Bitzer (c); finished December 1911 (f); New York (l); 7 March 1912 (r); 998 feet
(rl); J167062 / 8 March 1912 (copyright)

Dorothy Bernard (Poor Woman); Charles H. West (Her brother); Kate
Bruce (Her mother); Blanche Sweet (Second woman); William J. Butler
(Her father); Adolph Lestina (Doctor); Mack Sennett (Musician);
Charles Hill Mailes (Rich doctor); Dell Henderson (Millionaire); Grace
Henderson (His wife); J. Jiquel Lanoe, Claire McDowell, Robert Har-
ron, Edward Dillon, Kate Toncray (In tenement); Edna Foster, W.
Chrystie Miller (In hallway); W. Christy Cabanne, Harry Hyde, Ed-
ward Dillon, Alfred Paget, John T. Dillon (In restaurant)

A SPANISH DILEMMA

Mack Sennett (d); Percy Higginson (c); c. January 1912 (f); California (l); 11 March 1912 (r); one-half reel (rl); J167111 / 11 March 1912 (copyright)

Fred Mace (Jose); Mack Sennett (Carlos, his brother); Mabel Normand (The Señorita); Dell Henderson (Friend); W. C. Robinson (At party); J. Jiquel Lanoe (At duel)

THE ENGAGEMENT RING

Mack Sennett (d); Mabel Normand (au); Percy Higginson (c); finished January 1912 (f); California (l); 11 March 1912 (r); 497 feet (rl); J167110 / 11 March 1912 (copyright)

Mabel Normand (Alice); Edward Dillon (Harry); Dell Henderson (Redmond); Kate Bruce (Alice's mother); Fred Mace (Jeweler); J. Jiquel Lanoe (Jeweler's assistant); William J. Butler (Benefactor); Charles H. West (Waiter); Harry Hyde (In restaurant); William Beaudine (In park)

IOLA'S PROMISE

D. W. Griffith (d); Belle Taylor (au); G. W. Bitzer (c); finished January 1912 (f); California (l); 14 March 1912 (r); 1056 feet (rl); J167112 / 11 March 1912 (copyright)

Mary Pickford (Iola); Alfred Paget (Jack Harper); Frank Evans (His partner); Dorothy Bernard (Jack's sweetheart); Frank Opperman, Kate Toncray (Her parents); William Carroll, Henry Lehrman?, Charles Hill Mailes (Mexican cutthroats); William J. Butler, Antonio Moreno, Charles Gorman, Kate Bruce (Indians); J. Jiquel Lanoe (Medicine man); Charles H. West, Charles Hill Mailes, Harry Hyde, Robert Harron (Settlers)

NOTE: Reissued by Biograph 4 September 1916.

THE ROOT OF EVIL

D. W. Griffith (d); George Hennessy (au); G. W. Bitzer (c); finished December 1911 (f); New York (l); 18 March 1912 (r); 999 feet (rl); J167176 / 15 March 1912 (copyright)

William J. Butler (Wealthy man); Dorothy Bernard (His daughter); Edward Dillon (Secretary); J. Jiquel Lanoe (Confidential secretary); ? (Child); Alfred Paget (Bailiff); Harry Hyde (Faithful servant); Charles Hill Mailes (Doctor); John T. Dillon (Lawyer)

A VOICE FROM THE DEEP

Mack Sennett (d); Dell Henderson ["It Served Him Right"] (au); Percy Higginson (c); finished January 1912 (f); California (l); 21 March 1912 (r); 509 feet (rl); J167394 / 21 March 1912 (copyright)

Edward Dillon (Percy); Fred Mace (Harold); Marguerite Marsh (The girl); William J. Butler (Fisherman); ? (Policeman); Dell Henderson, Harry Hyde, Florence Lee (On roller coaster); J. Jiquel Lanoe, Mae Marsh, Harry Hyde (On beach)

HOT STUFF

Mack Sennett (d); Dell Henderson (au); Percy Higginson (c); finished January 1912 (f); California (l); 21 March 1912 (r); 488 feet (rl); J167393 / 21 March 1912 (copyright)

Mack Sennett (Hank Hawkins); Mabel Normand (His sweetheart); Dell Henderson (Cigar drummer); William Beaudine (Cigar store owner); ? (Assistant); William J. Butler, Kate Bruce (Sweetheart's parents); Fred Mace (Sweetheart's uncle?); Kate Toncray, Harry Hyde, Edward Dillon, Grace Henderson, Ella Hall? (Party guests)

THE GODDESS OF SAGEBRUSH GULCH

D. W. Griffith (d); G. W. Bitzer (c); c. January 1912 (f); California (l); 25 March 1912 (r); one reel (rl); J167455 / 23 March 1912 (copyright)

Blanche Sweet (The Goddess); Charles H. West (Blue-Grass Pete); Dorothy Bernard (The sister); Harry Hyde (Prospector); Charles Hill Mailes, W. Christy Cabanne, William Carroll (Villains); Alfred Paget, Charles Gorman, W. C. Robinson, Frank Opperman, Frank Evans (Cowboys); W. Chrystie Miller (Old man)

NOTE: Reissued by Biograph 30 October 1916.

THE GIRL AND HER TRUST

D. W. Griffith (d); George Hennessy ["The Silent Call"] (au); THE LONEDALE OPERATOR, released by Biograph 23 March 1911 (s); G. W. Bitzer (c); c. January-February 1912 (f); California (l); 28 March 1911 (r); 998 feet (rl); J167566 / 28 March 1912 (copyright)

Dorothy Bernard (Grace); Wilfred Lucas (Jack); Alfred Paget, Charles Hill Mailes (Tramps); Charles H. West (Telegrapher); Robert Harron (His companion); W. C. Robinson (Simple suitor); W. Christy Cabanne (Baggage handler); William Carroll (Engineer); Charles Gorman (Next to train)

NOTE: Reissued by Biograph 17 September 1915.

OH, THOSE EYES!

Mack Sennett (d); Juanita Bennett ["Three To One"] (au); Percy Higginson (c); finished January 1912 (f); California (l); 1 April 1912 (r); 506 feet (rl); J167693 / 1 April 1912 (copyright)

Mabel Normand (Gladys); Dell Henderson (Her father); Edward Dillon (Henrico); J. Jiquel Lanoe (Jose); William J. Butler (Butler); Frank Evans (Policeman); Kate Toncray (On bench); Edwin August, Harry Hyde, W. C. Robinson, W. Christy Cabanne (Gladys' admirers)

THOSE HICKSVILLE BOYS

Mack Sennett (d); Dell Henderson ["An Exciting Moment"] (au); Percy Higginson (c); finished February 1912 (f); California (l); 1 April 1912 (r); 492 feet (rl); J167692 / 1 April 1912 (copyright)

Dell Henderson (Hank); Fred Mace (Zeb); Grace Henderson (Mother); Mack Sennett (Stage manager); Edward Dillon (Farmer); Frank Evans (Policeman); W. C. Robinson, Kate Toncray, Mae Marsh? (At party); William Beaudine (At stage door); Edwin August, Charles Hill Mailes (Picnickers)

THE PUNISHMENT

D. W. Griffith (d); George Hennessy (au); G. W. Bitzer (c); finished February 1912 (f); California (l); 4 April 1912 (r); 999 feet (rl); J167862 / 5 April 1912 (copyright)

Blanche Sweet (The fruit grower's daughter); J. Jiquel Lanoe, Kate Bruce (Her parents); William J. Butler (The landowner); W. Christy Cabanne (His son); Harry Hyde (Lucien, the sweetheart); Frank Opperman (Old gardener); ? (Servants)

FATE'S INTERCEPTION

D. W. Griffith (d); George Hennessy ["It's Time to Say Goodbye"] (au); G. W. Bitzer (c); finished February 1912 (f); California (l); 8 April 1912 (r); 998 feet (rl); J167954 / 8 April 1912 (copyright)

Mary Pickford (Mexican girl); Wilfred Lucas (American); Charles Hill Mailes (Mexican sweetheart); Charles H. West (Mexican); Frank Opperman (Old man); Robert Harron (Errand boy); William J. Butler, Harry Hyde, Edwin August (Americans); William Carroll (In hotel)

THEIR FIRST KIDNAPPING CASE

Mack Sennett (d); George E. Johnson (au); Percy Higginson (c); finished February 1912 (f); California (l); 11 April 1912 (r); 501 feet (rl); J168045 / 10 April 1912 (copyright)

Mack Sennett, Fred Mace (The Biograph Sleuths); Edward Dillon (The Boob Admirer); ? (Sheriff); William J. Butler, Frank Evans, ? (Health officers); Harry Hyde (In office); Dell Henderson (Guard); William Beaudine, Marguerite Marsh? (In crowd)

HELP! HELP!

Mack Sennett (d); Percy Higginson (c); c. February 1912 (f); California (l); 11 April 1912 (r); one-half reel (rl); J168044 / 10 April 1912 (copyright)

Fred Mace (Mr. Suburbanite); Mabel Normand (Mrs. Suburbanite); Edward Dillon, Dell Henderson (Office workers); Alfred Paget, W. C. Robinson ("Burglars"); Frank Evans (Wagon owner)

THE FEMALE OF THE SPECIES

D. W. Griffith (d); G. W. Bitzer (c); c. February 1912 (f); California desert location (l); 15 April 1912 (r); one reel (rl); J168165 / 13 April 1912 (copyright)

Charles H. West (The miner); Claire McDowell (His wife); Mary Pickford (Her sister); Dorothy Bernard (The young woman)

JUST LIKE A WOMAN

D. W. Griffith (d); George Hennessy (au); G. W. Bitzer (c); finished February 1912 (f); California (l); 18 April 1912 (r); 998 feet (rl); J168396 / 20 April 1912 (copyright)

Mary Pickford (Young woman); Grace Henderson (Her mother); Harry Hyde (Fortune hunter); J. Jiquel Lanoe (Broker); Wilfred Lucas (Wealthy friend); Charles Hill Mailes, Frank Opperman, Hector Dion (Oil men); W. Christy Cabanne, Marguerite Marsh, Mae Marsh (In club); Robert Harron (Stableboy); Kathleen Butler, ? (Servants); ? (Butcher); ? (Assistant to broker); Mae Marsh (Friend); Kate Bruce (Maid); ? (Messenger); ? (Bill collector)

THE BRAVE HUNTER

Mack Sennett (d); Percy Higginson (c); c. January-February 1912 (f); California (l); 22 April 1912 (r); one-half reel (rl); J168476 / 22 April 1912 (copyright)

Mack Sennett (The hunter); Dell Henderson (His rival); Mabel Normand (The woman); William J. Butler, Kate Bruce, Charles Avery, J. Jiquel Lanoe (In lodge)

WON BY A FISH

Mack Sennett (d); George Hennessy ["Father's Day Off"] (au); Percy Higginson (c); finished February 1912 (f); Santa Monica, California (l); 22 April 1912 (r); 533 feet (rl); J168477 / 22 April 1912 (copyright)

Edward Dillon (Harry); Mary Pickford (The woman); Dell Henderson (Her father); ? (Fish store owner); ? (Photo store owner); Kate Bruce (Maid); Grace Henderson, William J. Butler, Kate Toncray, Charles Hill Mailes, Frank Evans, Florence Lee, W. C. Robinson (At dinner)

NOTE: Santa Monica location taken from internal evidence.

ONE IS BUSINESS; THE OTHER CRIME

D. W. Griffith (d); George Hennessy ["The Greater Evil"] (au); G. W. Bitzer (c); finished February 1912 (f); California (l); 25 April 1912 (r); 998 feet (rl); J168597 / 24 April 1912 (copyright)

Charles H. West, Dorothy Bernard (Poor couple); Edwin August, Blanche Sweet (Rich couple); Frank Evans (Landlord); William Carroll, ? (Foremen); Kate Bruce, Kate Toncray (Maids); ? (Briber); Robert Harron (Delivery boy); W. C. Robinson (Brickyard worker); Frank Opperman (Rich man's foreman)

THE LESSER EVIL

D. W. Griffith (d); George Hennessy (au); G. W. Bitzer (c); begun February, finished March 1912 (f); California (l); 29 April 1912 (r); 1009 feet (rl); J168738 / 27 April 1912 (copyright)

Blanche Sweet (Young woman); Edwin August (Her sweetheart); Mae Marsh (Her companion); Alfred Paget (Smuggler leader); Charles Hill Mailes (Revenue officer); Charles H. West (Go-between); Frank Opperman, Robert Harron?, William Carroll, J. Jiquel Lanoe, Charles Gorman, W. C. Robinson (In smuggler band); Harry Hyde, Charles Hill Mailes, Frank Evans (Policemen); W. Christy Cabanne (In rescue boat)

NOTE: Reissued by Biograph 3 January 1916.

THE LEADING MAN

Mack Sennett (d); Edward Dillon ["The Vacation"] (au); Percy Higginson (c); finished March 1912 (f); California (l); 2 May 1912 (r); 542 feet (rl); J168888 / 3 May 1912 (copyright)

Dell Henderson (Hector La Grand); Fred Mace (Landlord); Kate Bruce (Landlady); Edward Dillon (Ringmaster); Claire McDowell, Marguerite Marsh, Frank Evans, Grace Henderson, Kate Toncray (Boarders)

THE FICKLE SPANIARD

Mack Sennett (d); Dell Henderson ["A Close Shave"] (au); Percy Higginson (c); finished February 1912 (f); California (l); 2 May 1912 (r); 456 feet (rl); J168889 / 3 May 1912 (copyright)

Mabel Normand (Marcel); William J. Butler (Her father); Fred Mace (The Spaniard); Claire McDowell (Margot); Edward Dillon (Jose, the barber); Dell Henderson (Padre); J. Jiquel Lanoe, Harry Hyde, Kate Bruce, Kate Toncray, Edward Dillon (In chase); William Beaudine (In barber shop)

THE OLD ACTOR

D. W. Griffith (d); George Hennessy ["The Eyesore"] (au); G. W. Bitzer (c); finished February 1912 (f); California (l); 6 May 1912 (r); 998 feet (rl); J168900 / 4 May 1912 (copyright)

W. Chrystie Miller (The Old Actor); Kate Bruce (His wife); Mary Pickford (His daughter); Edwin August (Her sweetheart); Frank Opperman (Old beggar); Charles Hill Mailes (Replacement actor); Alfred Paget (Policeman); Frank Opperman (Stage manager); William Carroll (His assistant); Grace Henderson (Old woman); Robert Harron (Messenger); Claire McDowell, J. Jiquel Lanoe, Marguerite Marsh, W. C. Robinson, Vivian Prescott, W. Christy Cabanne (At audition)

A LODGING FOR THE NIGHT

D. W. Griffith (d); George Hennessy (au); G. W. Bitzer (c); finished March 1912 (f); California (l); 9 May 1912 (r); 999 feet (rl); J169195 / 13 May 1912 (copyright)

Charles H. West (Dick Logan); Mary Pickford (Mexican girl); Charles Hill Mailes (Her father); William Carroll, ? (Tramps); Frank Opperman (Gambling hall owner); Frank Evans (Gambler); W. C. Robinson (Bartender); W. Christy Cabanne, Robert Harron (In gambling hall); Robert Harron (Victim); Mae Marsh, W. Christy Cabanne (First Mexican couple); ? (Second Mexican couple); Alfred Paget (Sheriff); W. C. Robinson, Adolph Lestina (Deputies); Hector Dion (Porter)

WHEN THE FIRE-BELLS RANG

Mack Sennett (d); Morris H. Black ["When the Bell Rang Out"] (au);

Percy Higginson (c); finished March 1912 (f); California (l); 13 May 1912 (r); 555 feet (rl); J169194 / 13 May 1912 (copyright)

Edward Dillon (The Fireman); Fred Mace (His brother); Frank Evans, Frank Opperman (Among firemen); Dell Henderson, William J. Butler, Claire McDowell, Marshall Neilan, J. Jiquel Lanoe, Vivian Prescott, Grace Henderson (Actors); ? (Homeowner); Kate Bruce, Kate Toncray, Harry Hyde, Edwin August (In audience)

THE FURS

Mack Sennett (d); Percy Higginson (c); March 1912 (f); California (l); 13 May 1912 (r); one-half reel (rl); J169193 / 13 May 1912 (copyright)

Dell Henderson (Husband); Mabel Normand (Wife); Kate Bruce (Her mother); Mack Sennett (Salesman); ? (Husband's friend); William J. Butler (Moneylender); ? (Messenger); William Beaudine (In office)

NOTE: Filming date taken from internal evidence.

HIS LESSON

D. W. Griffith (d); George Hennessy (au); G. W. Bitzer (c); finished March 1912 (f); California (l); 16 May 1912 (r); 999 feet (rl); J169289 / 16 May 1912 (copyright)

Edwin August (Bob, the husband); Dorothy Bernard (Mary, the wife); Charles H. West (Young man); Harry Hyde (His friend); W. C. Robinson (Hired hand); Charles Gorman (Porter); Grace Henderson (Cleaning woman); Kate Toncray, Mae Marsh (Visitors)

WHEN KINGS WERE THE LAW

D. W. Griffith (d); Wilfred Lucas ["The Necklace"] (au); G. W. Bitzer (c); finished March 1912 (f); California (l); 20 May 1912 (r); 1049 feet (rl); J169418 / 20 May 1912 (copyright)

Wilfred Lucas (King of Romanda); Harry Hyde (His cousin); Dorothy Bernard (The king's favorite); J. Jiquel Lanoe (Cardinal); Claire McDowell, Kate Toncray (Ladies-in-waiting); W. Christy Cabanne (Courtier); Frank Opperman (Bishop); Alfred Paget, Charles Gorman (Soldiers); Frank Evans, Charles Hill Mailes (Serfs); William J. Butler, Kate Bruce, Mabel Normand, Mae Marsh, Charles Hill Mailes (At court)

NOTE: Reissued by Biograph 31 January 1916.

A CLOSE CALL

Mack Sennett (d); Florence Lee (au); Percy Higginson (c); finished
March 1912 (f); California (l); 23 May 1912 (r); 573 feet (rl); J169460
/ 22 May 1912 (copyright)

Fred Mace, Dell Henderson (Street fakers); Kate Bruce (Nurse);
Grace Henderson (Mother); Frank Opperman (Father); Edward Dillon
[blackface] (Jasper); Frank Evans, William Beaudine, Charles Hill
Mailes (In crowd); Florence Lee, J. Jiquel Lanoe, Charles H. West,
Harry Hyde (In "lynch mob")

HELEN'S MARRIAGE

Mack Sennett (d); Earl Hodge (au); Percy Higginson (c); finished
March 1912 (f); California (l); 23 May 1912 (r); 425 feet (rl); J169461
/ 22 May 1912 (copyright)

Mabel Normand (Helen); Edward Dillon (Tom); Frank Opperman,
Grace Henderson (Parents); Fred Mace, Charles H. West, Dell Henderson, Frank Evans, William J. Butler, J. Jiquel Lanoe (Club
friends); Mack Sennett (Film director); William Beaudine (Cameraman); ? (Actors); ? (Chaplain)

A BEAST AT BAY

D. W. Griffith (d); George Hennessy (au); G. W. Bitzer (c); finished
March 1912 (f); California (l); 27 May 1912 (r); 998 feet (rl); J169785
/ 29 May 1912 (copyright)

Mary Pickford (Young woman); Edwin August (Her ideal); Alfred Paget
(Convict); Mae Marsh (Young woman's friend); Charles Hill Mailes,
William Carroll, Henry Lehrman, W. C. Robinson (Guards); ?
(Rowdy bum); Charles H. West (Engineer); Robert Harron (Farmer);
J. Jiquel Lanoe (At station); W. Christy Cabanne (Station master);
W. Christy Cabanne (In sports car)

AN OUTCAST AMONG OUTCASTS

Wilfred Lucas (d); George Hennessy (au); G. W. Bitzer (c); finished
March 1912 (f); California (l); 30 May 1912 (r); 985 feet (rl); J169786
/ 29 May 1912 (copyright)

Frank Opperman (Blanket tramp); Blanche Sweet (Young woman); W.
Chrystie Miller (Postmaster); Kate Toncray (Homemaker); J. Jiquel
Lanoe, ? (Factory managers); William Carroll, W. C. Robinson
(Tramps); Charles H. West (Station master)

NOTE: This is Wilfred Lucas' first film as a director for Biograph.
Director's credit taken from the Biograph Company Story Register
(1910-1916) at the Museum of Modern Art.

TOMBOY BESSIE

Mack Sennett (d); William E. Wing ["Busy Bessie and the New Hired Man"] (au); Percy Higginson (c); finished April 1912 (f); California (l); 3 June 1912 (r); 521 feet (rl); J170132 / 8 June 1912 (copyright)

Mabel Normand (Bessie); Mack Sennett (Andrew); Kate Toncray (Aunt Cissie); William J. Butler (Father); W. C. Robinson, ? (Children); Frank Opperman (Chicken farmer); Charles Gorman? (Policeman)

ALGY, THE WATCHMAN

Mack Sennett (d); H. F. Hughes ["Bughouse Billy, Detective"] (au); Percy Higginson (c); finished March 1912 (f); California (l); 3 June 1912 (r); 476 feet (rl); J170133 / 8 June 1912 (copyright)

Grace Henderson (Mrs. Johnson); Fred Mace (Algy); Dell Henderson (Steve); Edward Dillon (Bank manager); Frank Evans (In bank); William J. Butler (Bank president); Charles Hill Mailes, William Carroll (His assistants); Alfred Paget, W. Christy Cabanne (Clerks); ? (Tramp); Charles Gorman, ? (Policemen)

HOME FOLKS

D. W. Griffith? (d); G. W. Bitzer (c); c. March 1912 (f); California (l); 6 June 1912 (r); one reel (rl); J170147 / 10 June 1912 (copyright)

Mary Pickford (Young woman); Charles Hill Mailes, Kate Bruce (Her parents); Robert Harron (Her brother); Wilfred Lucas (Blacksmith); W. Christy Cabanne (His assistant); Charles Gorman, ? (Movers); Mae Marsh, William Carroll, Frank Opperman, Charles H. West, W. C. Robinson, Charles Avery, W. Christy Cabanne, Kate Toncray (At barn dance); Alfred Paget, Frank Evans (Outside dance)

A TEMPORARY TRUCE

D. W. Griffith (d); George Hennessy (au); G. W. Bitzer (c); finished April 1912 (f); California (l); 10 June 1912 (r); 1507 feet (rl); J170148 / 10 June 1912 (copyright)

Charles Hill Mailes (Mexican Jim); Claire McDowell (His wife); Charles Gorman (Jack, the prospector); Blanche Sweet (Alice, his wife); Alfred Paget, Frank Opperman, ? (Drunken cutthroats); W. Chrystie Miller (Murdered Indian); Robert Harron (His son?); Frank Opperman (Indian chief); Wilfred Lucas, J. Jiquel Lanoe, W. Christy Cabanne, Alfred Paget, Jack Pickford, W. C. Robinson (Indians); Mae Marsh, ? (Murdered settlers); Frank Opperman (Bartender); Frank Evans, W. C. Robinson, William Carroll, Bert Hendler? (In bar); J. Jiquel Lanoe, Harry Hyde, Alfred Paget, W. C. Robinson,

Frank Evans, William Carroll (Among rescuers); Harry Hyde (Outside Pony Express office); W. Chrystie Miller (Indian on street)

NOTE: Reissued by Biograph 15 August 1916.

NEIGHBORS

Mack Sennett (d); Dell Henderson (au); Percy Higginson (c); finished April 1912 (f); California (l); 13 June 1912 (r); 363 feet (rl); J170617 / 25 June 1912 (copyright)

Fred Mace, Mabel Normand (First French family); ? (Second French family); Frank Evans, ? (Seconds at duel); William J. Butler, J. Jiquel Lanoe, Frank Opperman (At duel); Kate Toncray (On street)

KATCHEM KATE

Mack Sennett (d); Dell Henderson ["Cunning Kate"] (au); Percy Higginson (c); finished April 1912 (f); California (l); 13 June 1912 (r); 636 feet (rl); J170618 / 25 June 1912 (copyright)

NOTE: No material survives from which the cast may be determined.

LENA AND THE GEESE

D. W. Griffith (d); Mary Pickford ["The Goose Girl"] (au); G. W. Bitzer (c); finished April 1912 (f); California (l); 17 June 1912 (r); 1012 feet (rl); J170619 / 25 June 1912 (copyright)

Mary Pickford (Lena); J. Jiquel Lanoe (Her sweetheart); Kate Bruce (Gretchen); Mae Marsh ("Adopted" daughter); Edwin August, Claire McDowell (Her noble parents); W. Chrystie Miller (Courtier); Charles Hill Mailes, Harry Hyde, Frank Opperman, William Carroll, Grace Henderson, Alfred Paget, W. Christy Cabanne (Nobles); W. C. Robinson, Frank Opperman, Charles H. West (Servants)

THE SPIRIT AWAKENED

D. W. Griffith (d); G. W. Bitzer (c); c. April 1912 (f); California (l); 20 June 1912 (r); one reel (rl); J170667 / 28 June 1912 (copyright)

Blanche Sweet (Young woman); W. Chrystie Miller, Kate Bruce (Her parents); Edward Dillon (Christian farmhand); Alfred Paget (Renegade farmhand); Mae Marsh (His girlfriend)

NOTE: Reissued by Biograph 12 June 1916.

A DASH THROUGH THE CLOUDS

Mack Sennett (d); Dell Henderson (au); Percy Higginson (c); finished
April 1912 (f); California (l); 24 June 1912 (r); 742 feet (rl); J170666
/ 28 June 1912 (copyright)

Fred Mace (Arthur); Mabel Normand (Martha); Philip Parmalee (Avi-
ator); Kate Bruce, Jack Pickford, Edward Dillon, William J. Butler,
Harry Hyde, Charles Gorman, J. Jiquel Lanoe, Alfred Paget, Sylvia
Ashton (Townsfolk)

NOTE: Identification of Philip Parmalee from Kemp Niver's The
First Twenty Years.

THE NEW BABY

Mack Sennett (d); M. Shannon Fife ["Oh! Papa"] (au); Percy Higginson (c); finished April 1912 (f); California (l); 24 June 1912 (r); 258
feet (rl); J170665 / 28 June 1912 (copyright)

NOTE: No material survives from which the cast may be determined.

THE SCHOOL TEACHER AND THE WAIF

D. W. Griffith (d); "MLiss," the short story by Bret Harte (s); G.
W. Bitzer (c); c. April 1912 (f); California (l); 27 June 1912 (r); one
reel (rl); J170957 / 10 July 1912 (copyright)

Edwin August (The school teacher); Mary Pickford (Nora, the waif);
Charles Hill Mailes (Her father); Bert Hendler? (Street faker); Claire
McDowell (His girlfriend); William Carroll[blackface] (His assistant);
Robert Harron, Mae Marsh, Ella Hall? (School children); Alfred
Paget, Frank Opperman (At bee); Grace Henderson (A mother); Jack
Pickford (Extra)

MAN'S LUST FOR GOLD

D. W. Griffith (d); George Hennessy (au); G. W. Bitzer (c); finished
May 1912 (f); California (l); 1 July 1912 (r); 1000 feet (rl); J170958
/ 10 July 1912 (copyright)

William J. Butler (Prospector); Blanche Sweet, Robert Harron (His
children); Frank Opperman (Claim jumper); Charles Hill Mailes
(Mexican); William Carroll, Jack Pickford (Among Indians)

ONE-ROUND O'BRIEN

Mack Sennett (d); Richard Daly ["Getting the Money"] (au); "The
Supreme Bumper's Degree," the short story by Charles Van Loan

(s); Percy Higginson (c); finished May 1912 (f); California (l); 4 July 1912 (r); 454 feet (rl); J171148 / 12 July 1912 (copyright)

Fred Mace (O'Brien); ? (Duffy); William J. Butler (Fight manager); Edward Dillon, Frank Evans, ? (Contestants); Alfred Paget, William Beaudine, J. Jiquel Lanoe (In crowd)

NOTE: This film was reissued by Biograph in January 1917 on a states' rights basis, after a lengthy litigation involving Van Loan, the Popular magazine, and its publisher Street and Smith (Moving Picture World, 2 December 1916, p. 1347). In March 1916 an unspecified group of Sennett Biograph split-reel comedies was made available to exhibitors for reissue, though not in the general service.

TRYING TO FOOL UNCLE

Mack Sennett (d); William E. Wing ["Greasing the Skids for Uncle"] (au); Percy Higginson (c); finished April 1912 (f); California (l); 4 July 1912 (r); 544 feet (rl); J171147 / 12 July 1912 (copyright)

Dell Henderson (Dick); William J. Butler (His uncle); Claire McDowell (His wife); ? (Waitress); Frank Opperman (Employer); Grace Henderson (His wife); Kate Toncray, ? (Servants); W. C. Robinson (In cafe)

AN INDIAN SUMMER

D. W. Griffith (d); George Hennessy (au); G. W. Bitzer (c); finished April 1912 (f); California (l); 8 July 1912 (r); 1000 feet (rl); J171149 / 12 July 1912 (copyright)

W. Chrystie Miller (Widower); Kate Bruce (Widow); Mary Pickford, Mae Marsh (Her daughters); Harry Hyde (Young man); Jack Pickford, Kate Toncray, Frank Opperman, Bert Hendler? (Among boarders)

MAN'S GENESIS

D. W. Griffith (d); G. W. Bitzer (c); c. May 1912 (f); California (l); 11 July 1912 (r); one reel (rl); J171534 / 23 July 1912 (copyright)

Robert Harron (Weak Hands); Mae Marsh (Lilywhite); Wilfred Lucas (Brute Force); Charles Hill Mailes, W. C. Robinson, Claire McDowell? (Tribe members); W. Chrystie Miller (Storyteller); ? (Children)

NOTE: Reissued by Biograph 23 July 1915.

THE SPEED DEMON

Mack Sennett (d); Dell Henderson (au); Percy Higginson (c); finished

May 1912 (f); Santa Monica, California (l); 15 July 1912 (r); 451 feet (rl); J171532 / 23 July 1912 (copyright)

Fred Mace (The Demon); Kate Toncray (His wife); ? (His mother); Jack Pickford (His son); ? (Driver); Charles H. West, William J. Butler (In crowd); Charles Hill Mailes, Harry Hyde, ? (Judges); Dell Henderson (Friend)

NOTE: Santa Monica location taken from Bulletin.

HIS OWN FAULT

Mack Sennett (d); Terry Myers ["One Queen Seats Four Kings"] (au); Percy Higginson (c); finished May 1912 (f); California (l); 15 July 1912 (r); 549 feet (rl); J171533 / 23 July 1912 (copyright)

Fred Mace, Kate Bruce (Mr. and Mrs. Brown); William J. Butler, ? (Mr. and Mrs. Jenks); Harry Hyde (Salesman); Frank Evans (Gambler); ? (Friend); J. Jiquel Lanoe (Policeman); Kate Toncray, Marguerite Marsh (In purity league); Henry Lehrman, Antonio Moreno (In gambling hall)

HEAVEN AVENGES

D. W. Griffith (d); George Hennessy ["I Will Repay"] (au); G. W. Bitzer (c); finished May 1912 (f); California (l); 18 July 1912 (r); 994 feet (rl); J171535 / 23 July 1912 (copyright)

Dorothy Bernard (Ynez); William J. Butler (Her father); W. Christy Cabanne (Her sweetheart); Charles H. West (Owner of grove); Grace Henderson (His mother); W. Chrystie Miller (Doctor); Frank Evans (Sheriff); Kate Toncray (Maid); W. C. Robinson (Servant)

THE SANDS OF DEE

D. W. Griffith (d); "The Sands O' Dee," the poem by Charles Kingsley (s); G. W. Bitzer (c); c. May 1912 (f); California (l); 22 July 1912 (r); one reel (rl); J171536 / 23 July 1912 (copyright)

Mae Marsh (Mary); Charles Hill Mailes, Grace Henderson (Her parents); Robert Harron (Bobby); Kate Toncray (His mother); Edwin August (Artist); Claire McDowell (His fiancée); Frank Opperman, W. Chrystie Miller, ? (Fishermen)

NOTE: Reissued by Biograph 2 July 1915.

THE WOULD-BE SHRINER

Mack Sennett (d); Percy Higginson (c); c. January 1912 (f); Los Angeles, California (l); 25 July 1912 (r); one-half reel (rl); J171805 / 30 July 1912 (copyright)

Mack Sennett (Hank Hopkins); Kate Bruce (His wife); ? (Her friend); William J. Butler, Fred Mace (On street); Charles H. West, Frank Opperman (Club members); Edward Dillon, Alfred Paget (Policemen); J. Jiquel Lanoe (Asylum director); Charles Avery, ? (Inmates); Jack Pickford, W. Christy Cabanne, W. C. Robinson, Frank Opperman, Harry Hyde (Parade bystanders)

NOTE: Filming date determined from internal evidence of a Tournament of Roses Parade float.

WILLIE BECOMES AN ARTIST

Mack Sennett (d); William E. Wing ["Willie, He Learns to Paint"] (au); Percy Higginson (c); finished May 1912 (r); California (l); 25 July 1912 (r); 482 feet (rl); J171804 / 30 July 1912 (copyright)

Edward Dillon (Willie); William J. Butler, Kate Toncray (His parents); ? (His girlfriend); ? (Artist); Florence Lee (His girlfriend); J. Jiquel Lanoe (Waiter); Harry Hyde (In restaurant); Frank Opperman (Art dealer); ? (Friend of family)

BLACK SHEEP

Wilfred Lucas (d); George Hennessy ["Two Black Sheep"] (au); J. C. Bitzer (c); finished May 1912 (f); California (l); 29 July 1912 (r); 1000 feet (rl); J171872 / 1 August 1912 (copyright)

Charles H. West (The son); Alfred Paget, ? (His parents); Charles Gorman (Sheriff); William Carroll (Mexican); Dorothy Bernard (Young woman); Jack Pickford (Kid brother); Frank Evans (Gambler); W. Christy Cabanne, W. C. Robinson (Cowboys); J. Jiquel Lanoe (In bar)

THE NARROW ROAD

D. W. Griffith (d); George Hennessy (au); G. W. Bitzer (c); finished June 1912 (f); New York (l); 1 August 1912 (r); 999 feet (rl); J171930 / 5 August 1912 (copyright)

Elmer Booth (Jim Holcomb); Mary Pickford (His wife); Charles Hill Mailes (Counterfeiter); Alfred Paget, Charles Gorman (Detectives); J. Jiquel Lanoe (Prisoner); W. Christy Cabanne, Max Davidson? (Tramps); Frank Evans, W. C. Robinson (Prison guards); Adolph Lestina (Bartender); J. Jiquel Lanoe (Foreman)

THE TOURISTS

Mack Sennett (d); Percy Higginson (c); late May-early June 1912 (f);
Albuquerque, New Mexico (l); 5 August 1912 (r); one-half reel (rl);
J172002 / 7 August 1912 (copyright)

Charles H. West, Mabel Normand, William J. Butler, Grace Henderson (Tourists); Frank Evans (Big Chief); Kate Toncray (His wife);
Harry Hyde, Alfred Paget? (On train platform); ? (Indians)

NOTE: Location taken from "Photoplay People in Albuquerque Until
Tuesday," a news item in the Albuquerque Evening Herald, 29 May
1912.

WHAT THE DOCTOR ORDERED

Mack Sennett (d); Dell Henderson ["The Rest Cure"] (au); Percy
Higginson (c); finished April 1912 (f); Rubio Canyon, California/Mount
Lowe, California (l); 5 August 1912 (r); 617 feet (rl); J172003 / 7
August 1912 (copyright)

Mack Sennett (Jenks); Kate Toncray (His wife); Mabel Normand, Jack
Pickford (Their children); Edward Dillon (Daughter's suitor); J. Jiquel
Lanoe (Doctor); William J. Butler (Wife's friend); ? (Rescuer)

NOTE: Locations taken from internal evidence.

A CHILD'S REMORSE

D. W. Griffith (d); George Hennessy (au); G. W. Bitzer (c); finished
June 1912 (f); Greenwich, Connecticut (l); 8 August 1912 (r); 998
feet (rl); J172322 / 17 August 1912 (copyright)

Gladys Egan (The girl); Edwin August, Claire McDowell (Her parents);
George Hennessy (Her brother); Charles Hill Mailes (Father's friend);
? (His children); Kate Toncray (Nursemaid); Edith Haldeman, Jack
Pickford (Among children); Grace Henderson (At tea); Robert Harron,
W. Christy Cabanne (Boatmen); Kate Bruce (Governess); Alfred Paget
(On deck)

NOTE: Bitzer identifies Hennessy as the brother.

THE INNER CIRCLE

D. W. Griffith (d); George Hennessy (au); G. W. Bitzer (c); finished
June 1912 (f); New York (l); 12 August 1912 (r); 1000 feet (rl);
J172323 / 17 August 1912 (copyright)

Adolph Lestina (Widower); ? (Child); Jack Pickford (Messenger); J.
Jiquel Lanoe (Rich Italian); Mary Pickford (His daughter); Charles

Hill Mailes, ? (Gangsters); Alfred Paget, Joseph McDermott (Police agents); Frank Evans, W. C. Robinson (In police station); Kate Toncray, Robert Harron (In crowd); W. Christy Cabanne (In gang); Charles Gorman, Robert Harron (Accident witnesses)

AN INTERRUPTED ELOPEMENT

Mack Sennett (d); S. Walter Bunting ["Kidnapping Papa"] (au); Percy Higginson (c); finished June 1912 (f); New York (l); 15 August 1912 (r); 477 feet (rl); J172320 / 17 August 1912 (copyright)

Edward Dillon (Bob); Mabel Normand (Alice, his sweetheart); William J. Butler (Papa); Elmer Booth, Ford Sterling (Bob's friends); ? (Maid); Charles Gorman (Reverend Brown)

THE TRAGEDY OF A DRESS SUIT

Mack Sennett (d); Mabel Normand ["Before and After"] (au); Percy Higginson (c); finished June 1912 (f); New York (l); 15 August 1912 (r); 520 feet (rl); J172321 / 17 August 1912 (copyright)

Dell Henderson (Dick); Mabel Normand (Heiress); Edward Dillon (Her friend); Ford Sterling (Boardinghouse keeper); W. Christy Cabanne, William J. Butler, Kate Bruce, Grace Henderson, Harry Hyde, Charles Avery (At party); Frank Evans (Accosted man); William Beaudine (Dick's friend)

WITH THE ENEMY'S HELP

Wilfred Lucas (d); J. C. Bitzer (c); c. May 1912 (f); California (l); 19 August 1912 (r); one reel (rl); J172418 / 22 August 1912 (copyright)

Charles H. West (Prospector); Blanche Sweet (His wife); Edna Foster, ? (Their children); Mary Pickford (Faro Kate); Charles Hill Mailes (Her husband); Charles Gorman (Sheriff); J. Jiquel Lanoe (Claim assessor)

A CHANGE OF SPIRIT

D. W. Griffith (d); D. W. Griffith (au); G. W. Bitzer (c); c. June 1912 (f); New York (l); 22 August 1912 (r); one reel (rl); LU24 / 11 October 1912 (copyright)

Blanche Sweet (Young woman); William J. Butler, Kate Toncray (Her parents); Henry B. Walthall, Charles Hill Mailes (Gentlemen thieves); Walter Miller (Robbery victim); Robert Harron (Young man on street); W. C. Robinson, Joseph McDermott, ? (Policemen)

NOTE: Reissued by Biograph 28 August 1916.

MR. GROUCH AT THE SEASHORE

Dell Henderson? (d); Frank E. Woods (au); Percy Higginson (c); c.
July 1912 (f); New York (l); 26 August 1912 (r); one-half reel (rl);
LU26 / 11 October 1912 (copyright)

Fragment: Edward Dillon (Mr. Grouch); J. Jiquel Lanoe (French-
man); Jack Pickford (His son); ? (Mrs. Grouch); Florence Lee, William Beaudine (Friends of the Grouches); Charles Murray (Old friend);
William Beaudine (Outside hotel)

THROUGH DUMB LUCK

Dell Henderson (d); Dell Henderson ["While the City Sleeps"] (au);
Percy Higginson (c); finished July 1912 (f); New York (l); 26 August
1912 (r); 564 feet (rl); LU27 / 11 October 1912 (copyright)

Fragment: Edward Dillon (Boob detective); Grace Henderson (Crime
victim); J. Jiquel Lanoe, ? (Thieves); ? (Rube); J. Waltham (Police
sergeant); ? (Policemen); William Beaudine, Charles Murray? (Among
bystanders)

A PUEBLO LEGEND

D. W. Griffith (d); D. W. Griffith (au); G. W. Bitzer (c); late May-
early June 1912 (f); Albuquerque, New Mexico (l); 29 August 1912
(r); one reel (rl); LU30 / 11 October 1912 (copyright)

Mary Pickford (Indian girl); Wilfred Lucas (Great Brother); Robert
Harron (His friend); J. Jiquel Lanoe (Sun priest); Charles Hill Mailes
(Old man); Jack Pickford (Young brave); ? (Captain); Alfred Paget,
W. C. Robinson (Apaches); W. Christy Cabanne, Harry Hyde, Charles
Hill Mailes (Pueblos)

NOTE: Reissued by Biograph 10 October 1916. Location and filming
date taken from "Photoplay People in Albuquerque Until Tuesday,"
a news item in the Albuquerque Evening Herald, 29 May 1912.

IN THE NORTH WOODS

Wilfred Lucas (d); Stanner E. V. Taylor (au); J. C. Bitzer (c); c.
June-July 1912 (f); New York (l); 2 September 1912 (r); one reel (rl);
LU25 / 11 October 1912 (copyright)

Fragment: Charles H. West (Trapper); Claire McDowell (His wife);
Gladys Egan (Their child); Elmer Booth (The adventurer); ? (Guide);
Wilfred Lucas (Extra)

NOTE: A remake of THE INGRATE, released by Biograph 20 November 1908.

GETTING RID OF TROUBLE

Dell Henderson (d); Edward Acker (au); Percy Higginson (c); finished
July 1912 (f); New York (l); 5 September 1912 (r); 569 feet (rl); LU29
/ 11 October 1912 (copyright)

Charles Murray (The Cook); Edward Dillon (Husband); ? (Wife); William J. Butler (Dad); Kathleen Butler, W. Chrystie Miller (In employment agency); J. Waltham (Policeman); ? (Bill collector)

HE MUST HAVE A WIFE

Mack Sennett? (d); John A. Walsh ["The Genius"] (au); Percy Higginson (c); finished June 1912 (f); New York (l); 5 September 1912 (r);
430 feet (rl); LU28 / 11 October 1912 (copyright)

Fragment: Gus Pixley (Harry); William J. Butler (Uncle William);
Mabel Normand (The girl); Ford Sterling (Rival); Kathleen Butler
(Maid); ? (Friend)

AN UNSEEN ENEMY

D. W. Griffith (d); Edward Acker (au); G. W. Bitzer (c); finished
July 1912 (f); New York (l); 9 September 1912 (r); 999 feet (rl); LU38
/ 16 October 1912 (copyright)

Dorothy Gish, Lillian Gish (The Sisters); Elmer Booth (Their brother);
Grace Henderson (Maid); Harry Carey (Her accomplice); Robert Harron (A friend); Walter Miller (Car owner); Adolph Lestina (In boardinghouse); ? (Telegraph man); Antonio Moreno (On bridge)

NOTE: Reissued by Biograph 24 September 1915.

BLIND LOVE

Wilfred Lucas (d); M. B. Havey ["When Pride Goes"] (au); J. C.
Bitzer (c); finished July 1912 (f); New York (l); 12 September 1912
(r); 1000 feet (rl); LU39 / 16 October 1912 (copyright)

Blanche Sweet (Young woman); Harry Hyde (Her husband); Edward
Dillon (Young man); Hector V. Sarno, ? (Gypsies); ? (Young woman's
parents); W. Chrystie Miller (Young man's father); ? (Young man's
sister); ? (Minister); Kate Toncray (His wife); William J. Butler
(Landlord); Joseph McDermott (Doctor); Alfred Paget (Policeman);
John T. Dillon, Kathleen Butler, W. C. Robinson, Walter P. Lewis
(At the social); Frank Evans (On road); ? (Justice of the peace)

STERN PAPA

Mack Sennett (d); Edward Acker (au); Percy Higginson (c); finished

June 1912 (f); New York (l); 16 September 1912 (r); 506 feet (rl);
LU40 / 16 October 1912 (copyright)

Ford Sterling (Papa); ? (His daughter); Edward Dillon (Her suitor);
Gus Pixley (Papa's friend); Dell Henderson, William Beaudine (In
outdoor cafe); ? (Innkeeper); ? (Priest); ? (Waiter)

LOVE'S MESSENGER

Dell Henderson (d); Belle Taylor ["Jasper's Love Note"] (au); Percy
Higginson (c); c. July 1912 (f); New York (l); 16 September 1912 (r);
492 feet (rl); LU37 / 16 October 1912 (copyright)

Charles Murray (Husband); ? (Wife); J. Jiquel Lanoe (Lucian, the
cook); Kate Toncray (Maid); Edward Dillon, ? (Visitors); W. C.
Robinson (Delivery man)

TWO DAUGHTERS OF EVE

D. W. Griffith (d); George Hennessy (au); G. W. Bitzer (c); finished
July 1912 (f); New York (l); 19 September 1912 (r); 1057 feet (rl);
LU50 / 21 October 1912 (copyright)

Fragment: Claire McDowell (Mother); Henry B. Walthall (Father); ?
(Daughter); Florence Geneva (Actress); Antonio Moreno, Robert Har-
ron, D. W. Griffith (At stage door); Antonio Moreno, Elmer Booth,
Gertrude Bambrick, Walter Miller, Kathleen Butler, W. C. Robinson
(Backstage); W. Christy Cabanne (Driver); Harry Hyde, Harry Carey,
Alfred Paget (In audience)

NOTE: Reissued by Biograph 26 November 1915. Identification of
Griffith at stage door taken from Moving Picture World, 12 October
1912, p. 130.

FRIENDS

D. W. Griffith (d); D. W. Griffith (au); G. W. Bitzer (c); c. July
1912 (f); New York (l); 23 September 1912 (r); one reel (rl); LU51
/ 21 October 1912 (copyright)

Mary Pickford (The Orphan); Henry B. Walthall (Dandy Jack); Lionel
Barrymore (His friend); Charles Hill Mailes (Bartender); Harry Carey
(Prospector); Robert Harron (Outside saloon); Elmer Booth, Walter
Miller, Frank Evans, W. C. Robinson, Adolph Lestina (In saloon)

NOTE: Reissued by Biograph 23 October 1916.

A DISAPPOINTED MAMMA

Dell Henderson (d); Dell Henderson (au); Percy Higginson (c); c. July

1912 (f); New York (l); 26 September 1912 (r); one-half reel (rl); LU53
/ 23 October 1912 (copyright)

Charles Murray (Traveling salesman); Madge Kirby (Alice Maxwell,
the daughter); ? (The adventurer); Charles H. West (A suitor); ?
(Mamma); ? (Minister); Florence Lee, William Beaudine, John T.
Dillon, Grace Henderson (In front of hotel); John T. Dillon (Second
at duel); Kathleen Butler (Maid); Dell Henderson (A "down-and-out")

A MIXED AFFAIR

Dell Henderson (d); Ruth M. Elmer (au); Percy Higginson (c); finished
July 1912 (f); New York (l); 26 September 1912 (r); 492 feet (rl); LU55
/ 23 October 1912 (copyright)

Fragment: Dell Henderson (Jenkins); Grace Henderson (Mrs. Jenkins); Florence Lee (Nursemaid); Charles Murray (Policeman); Madge
Kirby (Stenographer); William J. Butler (Jewelry store owner); William Beaudine, ? (Jewelry store customers); ? (In office)

SO NEAR, YET SO FAR

D. W. Griffith (d); George Hennessy ["Their First Meeting"] (au);
G. W. Bitzer (c); finished July 1912 (f); New York (l); 30 September
1912 (r); 999 feet (rl); LU54 / 23 October 1912 (copyright)

Walter Miller (Howard); Mary Pickford (Young woman); L. M. Wells?
(Her father); Robert Harron (The rival); ? (Brother); Charles Hill
Mailes, Claire McDowell (Rich friends in other town); ? (Maid);
Lionel Barrymore, Antonio Moreno, Courtenay Foote, Adolph Lestina,
Robert Harron, W. Christy Cabanne, Gus Pixley, W. C. Robinson,
J. Waltham (In club); Elmer Booth, Harry Carey (Thieves); Dorothy
Gish, Lillian Gish (Friends); W. Christy Cabanne, Florence Geneva
(On street)

A FEUD IN THE KENTUCKY HILLS

D. W. Griffith (d); D. W. Griffith (au); G. W. Bitzer (c); c. July
1912 (f); Milford, Pennsylvania (l); 3 October 1912 (r); one reel (rl);
LU65 / 30 October 1912 (copyright)

Mary Pickford (Daughter); Charles Hill Mailes, Kate Bruce (Her
parents); Walter Miller, Robert Harron, Jack Pickford (Her brothers);
Henry B. Walthall (Psalm singer); William J. Butler, Harry Hyde
(Clan members); Elmer Booth, Harry Carey, Frank Opperman, W.
C. Robinson, Frank Evans, J. Jiquel Lanoe, Adolph Lestina (In
second clan)

THE LINE AT HOGAN'S

Dell Henderson (d); Stanner E. V. Taylor (au); finished August 1912 (f); New York (l); 7 October 1912 (r); 643 feet (rl); LU66 / 30 October 1912 (copyright)

Fragment: Charles Murray (Hogan); ? (McNabb); ? (Widow O'Shaghnessy); Kathleen Butler (Nora, Hogan's daughter); Madge Kirby (Among wedding guests)

A TEN-KARAT HERO

Dell Henderson (d); Edward Acker (au); c. August 1912 (f); New York (l); 7 October 1912 (r); 356 feet (rl); LU64 / 30 October 1912 (copyright)

Edward Dillon (Zeke Thompson); ? (His sweetheart); Charles Murray (Town bully); ? (Farmer); John T. Dillon, Jack Pickford, Florence Lee (In crowd)

THE CHIEF'S BLANKET

Wilfred Lucas? (d); Wilfred Lucas (au); J. C. Bitzer (c); c. May-June 1912 (f); California? (l); 10 October 1912 (r); one reel (rl); LU67 / 30 October 1912 (copyright)

Blanche Sweet, Lionel Barrymore (Young couple); W. Chrystie Miller (The father); Charles H. West (The outlaw); Alfred Paget (Unfaithful sentinel); Adolph Lestina (Doctor); Walter P. Lewis (Indian chief); Charles Gorman, W. C. Robinson, Hector V. Sarno, Jack Pickford (Indians); Joseph McDermott (Among settlers)

IN THE AISLES OF THE WILD

D. W. Griffith (d); Stanner E. V. Taylor (au); G. W. Bitzer (c); c. July 1912 (f); New York (l); 14 October 1912 (r); one reel (rl); LU68 / 30 October 1912 (copyright)

Fragment: Claire McDowell (Elder daughter); Lillian Gish (Younger daughter); William J. Butler (Widower); Henry B. Walthall (Jim Watson); Harry Carey (Bob Cole); Alfred Paget (Indian); Elmer Booth, Charles Hill Mailes (Woodsmen)

NOTE: Reissued by Biograph 10 January 1916.

A LIMITED DIVORCE

Dell Henderson (d); Dell Henderson (au); Percy Higginson (c); c.

August 1912 (f); New York (l); 17 October 1912 (r); one-half reel
(rl); LU73 / 30 October 1912 (copyright)

Fragment: Charles Murray (Mr. Peck); Kate Toncray (Mrs. Peck);
Edward Dillon (Her brother); Harry Hyde, Florence Lee, J. Jiquel
Lanoe, William Beaudine (At resort); Gertrude Bambrick, Kathleen
Butler (Among bathers)

LIKE THE CAT, THEY CAME BACK

Dell Henderson (d); Royal A. Baker ["Passing It Up"] (au); finished
August 1912 (f); New York (l); 17 October 1912 (r); 536 feet (rl);
LU69 / 30 October 1912 (copyright)

Fragment: Charles Murray (Police commissioner); ? (Maid); ? (Her
sweetheart); ? (Lieutenant); ? (Police board); John T. Dillon (Police
sergeant); Joseph McDermott (Desk sergeant); Florence Lee (On
street)

THE ONE SHE LOVED

D. W. Griffith (d); George Hennessy (au); G. W. Bitzer (c); finished
August 1912 (f); New York (l); 21 October 1912 (r); 999 feet (rl); LU74
/ 30 October 1912 (copyright)

Henry B. Walthall (Husband); Mary Pickford (Wife); Lionel Barrymore
(Neighbor); Kate Bruce (His wife); Gertrude Bambrick (Stenographer);
Madge Kirby (Nurse); ? (Friend); Harry Carey (Neighbor's friend);
Eldean Stewart (Baby)

NOTE: Identification of Eldean Stewart as Baby taken from New
York Dramatic Mirror, 15 October 1913, p. 34.

THE PAINTED LADY

D. W. Griffith (d); D. W. Griffith (au); G. W. Bitzer (c); c. August
1912 (f); New York (l); 24 October 1912 (r); one reel (rl); LU72 / 30
October 1912 (copyright)

Blanche Sweet (Elder sister); Madge Kirby (Younger sister); Charles
Hill Mailes (Father); Kate Bruce (Maid); Joseph Graybill (The Stran-
ger); William J. Butler (Minister); Harry Carey, Lionel Barrymore,
Walter Miller, W. Christy Cabanne, Henry B. Walthall, Robert Har-
ron, Lillian Gish, Dorothy Gish, Elmer Booth, Jack Pickford, Walter
P. Lewis (At ice cream festival); ? (Stranger's accomplice); Gladys
Egan, ? (Girls); Harry Carey, Charles Gorman (Hired hands)

NOTE: Reissued by Biograph 10 December 1915.

AT THE BASKET PICNIC

Dell Henderson (d); Frank E. Woods ["Muggsy At the Picnic"] (au); Percy Higginson (c); finished August 1912 (f); New York (l); 28 October 1912 (r); 436 feet (rl); LU70 / 30 October 1912 (copyright)

Fragment: Edward Dillon (Dave); Madge Kirby (His sweetheart); W. Christy Cabanne (His rival); Charles Murray (Pastor); ? (Dave's mother); ? (Tramps); ? (At picnic)

A REAL ESTATE DEAL

Dell Henderson (d); S. R. Osborn ["The House that Jack Bought"] (au); Percy Higginson (c); finished August 1912 (f); New York (l); 28 October 1912 (r); 563 feet (rl); LU71 / 20 October 1912 (copyright)

Fragment: Dell Henderson, Edward Dillon (Real estate clerks); ? (Their employer); ? (His daughter); Gertrude Bambrick, ? (Daughter's friends); Charles Murray (Fisherman client); ? (Other clients)

THE MUSKETEERS OF PIG ALLEY

D. W. Griffith (d); D. W. Griffith (au); G. W. Bitzer (c); c. September 1912 (f); New York (l); 31 October 1912 (r); one reel (rl); LU90 / 4 November 1912 (copyright)

Elmer Booth (Snapper Kid); Lillian Gish (The Little Lady); Clara T. Bracey (Her mother); Walter Miller (Musician); Alfred Paget (Rival gang leader); John T. Dillon (Policeman); Madge Kirby (Little Lady's friend); Harry Carey (In Snapper Kid's gang); Robert Harron, W. C. Robinson (In rival gang); Adolph Lestina (Bartender); Jack Pickford (A gang member); Dorothy Gish, Adolph Lestina, Kathleen Butler (On street); Madge Kirby, Robert Harron, Walter P. Lewis, J. Waltham (In alley); Jack Pickford, Antonio Moreno, Gertrude Bambrick, W. Christy Cabanne, Robert Harron, Kathleen Butler, Frank Evans, Walter P. Lewis, Marie Newton (At dance); ? (Musician's friend)

NOTE: Reissued by Biograph 5 November 1915.

HEREDITY

D. W. Griffith (d); George Hennessy (au); G. W. Bitzer (c); finished September 1912 (f); New York (l); 4 November 1912 (r); 1015 feet (rl); LU89 / 4 November 1912 (copyright)

Fragment: Harry Carey (White renegade father); Madge Kirby (Indian mother); Jack Pickford (Their son); Walter P. Lewis (Indian chief); Kate Bruce (Indian woman); W. Christy Cabanne, Alfred Paget, Robert Harron, W. C. Robinson, Hector V. Sarno (Indians); Alfred Paget, Lionel Barrymore (Woodsmen)

NOTE: Reissued by Biograph 27 December 1915. Partial cast due to fragment deterioration.

THE MASSACRE

D. W. Griffith (d); D. W. Griffith (au); G. W. Bitzer (c); finished 21 May 1912 (f); California (l); 7 November 1912 [Europe] / 26 February 1914 [U. S. A.] (r); 2097 feet (rl); LP104 / 20 September 1912 & LU75 / 30 October 1912 (copyright)

Wilfred Lucas (Stephen); Blanche Sweet (His ward); Charles H. West (Her husband); Alfred Paget (Indian chief); Harry Hyde, W. Chrystie Miller, Dell Henderson, J. Jiquel Lanoe, Charles Hill Mailes (In wagon train); Frank Opperman (Old settler); Jack Pickford (Young boy); W. C. Robinson (Among Indians); Charles Gorman, Edward Dillon, Robert Harron (In cavalry); Prologue: Claire McDowell (Stephen's belle); Edward Dillon (John Randolph); Kate Toncray (Maid)

HIS AUTO'S MAIDEN TRIP

Dell Henderson (d); Elmer Booth ["Ambition of His Life"] (au); finished August 1912 (f); New York (l); 7 November 1912 (r); 599 feet (rl); LU95 / 7 November 1912 (copyright)

Fragment: Edward Dillon (Jinx); Florence Lee (His wife); Charles Murray, ? (Tramps); John T. Dillon (Policeman); ? (Maid); ? (Doctor)

THE CLUB-MAN AND THE CROOK

Dell Henderson (d); Dell Henderson (au); c. August-September 1912 (f); New York (l); 7 November 1912 (r); one-half reel (rl); LU96 / 7 November 1912 (copyright)

Fragment: Charles Murray (Mr. Billings); ? (His wife); W. Christy Cabanne, William J. Butler, Edward Dillon (Friends); ? (Cook); ? (Policeman); ? (Valet); ? (Crook)

GOLD AND GLITTER

D. W. Griffith (d); George Hennessy ["True Gold That Glitters"] (au); G. W. Bitzer (c); finished October 1912 (f); New York (l); 11 November 1912 (r); 999 feet (rl); LU109 / 13 November 1912 (copyright)

Fragment: Elmer Booth (Husband); Grace Lewis (Wife); Lionel Barrymore (Lover); Lillian Gish (Young woman); William J. Butler, Walter P. Lewis (Her older brothers); John T. Dillon, Harry Carey, Joseph Graybill, W. C. Robinson (Lumbermen); Dorothy Gish (On street); Alfred Paget (In canoe); ? (Young mother)

NOTE: Reissued by Biograph 31 July 1916.

MY BABY

D. W. Griffith (d); D. W. Griffith (au); G. W. Bitzer (c); c. October
1912 (f); New York (l); 14 November 1912 (r); one reel (rl); LU119
/ 16 November 1912 (copyright)

Mary Pickford (The wife); Henry B. Walthall (Her husband); Eldean
Stewart (Their baby); W. Chrystie Miller (Grandfather); ? (Married
sister); Alfred Paget (Her husband); Madge Kirby (Wife's friend);
John T. Dillon, Walter Miller, Jack Pickford, Dorothy Gish, Walter
P. Lewis (Wedding guests); W. C. Robinson, John T. Dillon, Adolph
Lestina, Clara T. Bracey, Elmer Booth, Lionel Barrymore (At table)

NOTE: Reissued by Biograph 4 December 1916.

THEIR IDOLS

Dell Henderson (d); Josephine T. Gregory ["Over the Garden Wall"]
(au); finished August 1912 (f); New York (l); 18 November 1912 (r);
593 feet (rl); LU124 / 21 November 1912 (copyright)

Fragment: Charles Murray (Schmaltz); Edward Dillon (Heinie, his
son); Madge Kirby (Irene Labrun); ? (Labrun); John T. Dillon,
Florence Lee, William Beaudine (On street); ? (Crooks)

HOIST ON HIS OWN PETARD

Dell Henderson (d); C. A. Griffin (au); finished September 1912 (f);
New York (l); 18 November 1912 (r); 406 feet (rl); LU125 / 21
November 1912 (copyright)

Fragment: ? (Husband); ? (Wife); Charles Murray (Henrico); ?
(Maid); ? (Wife's mother); Kathleen Butler, Gus Pixley, Edward
Dillon (At dancing academy)

THE INFORMER

D. W. Griffith (d); George Hennessy (au); G. W. Bitzer (c); finished
October 1912 (f); Milford, Pennsylvania (l); 21 November 1912 (r);
1080 feet (rl); LU131 / 23 November 1912 (copyright)

Walter Miller (Confederate captain); Mary Pickford (His sweetheart);
Henry B. Walthall (False brother); Kate Bruce (Mother); Harry Carey
(Union corporal); Lionel Barrymore, John T. Dillon, Elmer Booth,
Joseph Graybill, W. C. Robinson (Union soldiers); Alfred Paget
(Confederate general); Edward Dillon (Confederate soldier); Clara T.
Bracey[blackface] (Servant); Jack Pickford[blackface] (Boy); W. Christy
Cabanne, Robert Harron, Dorothy Gish, Lillian Gish (Other couples)

NOTE: Reissued by Biograph 17 July 1916.

A SAILOR'S HEART

Wilfred Lucas (d); Wilfred Lucas (au); finished October 1912 (f); Canada (l); 25 November 1912 (r); 999 feet (rl); LU134 / 25 November 1912 (copyright)

Fragment: Wilfred Lucas (False husband); Blanche Sweet (The wife); Charles Gorman (Suitor); Claire McDowell (Second wife); Charles Hill Mailes, J. Jiquel Lanoe, Bess Meredyth, Robert Harron? (On porch); Charles H. West (On street); ? (Minister)

NOTE: Reissued by Biograph 24 July 1916.

AN ABSENT-MINDED BURGLAR

Dell Henderson (d); Isobel M. Reynolds (au); finished August 1912 (f); New York (l); 28 November 1912 (r); 457 feet (rl); LU136 / 27 November 1912 (copyright)

Fragment: Edward Dillon, Madge Kirby (Mr. and Mrs. Hardluck); Charles Murray, John T. Dillon, ? (Crooks); ? (Amateur crook); ? (Mrs. Hardluck's friend); ? (Neighbors)

AFTER THE HONEYMOON

Dell Henderson (d); V. Fulton (au); finished September 1912 (f); New York (l); 28 November 1912 (r); 542 feet (rl); LU135 / 27 November 1912 (copyright)

Fragment: Edward Dillon (Mr. Gooddresser); ? (His wife); ? (Friends); ? (Secretary); ? (Maid); Gus Pixley, ? (Croquet players); ? (In office)

BRUTALITY

D. W. Griffith (d); George Hennessy ["The Brute"] (au); G. W. Bitzer (c); finished October 1912 (f); New York (l); 2 December 1912 (r); two reels (rl); LU144 / 29 November 1912 (copyright)

Walter Miller (Young man); Mae Marsh (Young woman); Joseph Graybill (Victim of anger); Lionel Barrymore, John T. Dillon, Clara T. Bracey, Walter P. Lewis (At wedding); ? (Bouncer); John T. Dillon, Alfred Paget, Frank Evans (Outside bar); Harry Carey, Clara T. Bracey, Madge Kirby, W. C. Robinson, Charles Hill Mailes, Jack Pickford, Gus Pixley, William J. Butler, J. Waltham, Lillian Gish (At theater); Elmer Booth, Henry B. Walthall (In play)

NOTE: Reissued by Biograph 1 October 1915.

THE NEW YORK HAT

D. W. Griffith (d); Anita Loos (au); G. W. Bitzer (c); finished November 1912 (f); New York (l); 5 December 1912 (r); 999 feet (rl);
LU151 / 5 December 1912 (copyright)

Mary Pickford (Young woman); Charles Hill Mailes (Her father); Kate
Bruce (Her mother); Lionel Barrymore (Minister); Alfred Paget
(Doctor); Claire McDowell, Mae Marsh, Clara T. Bracey (Gossips);
Madge Kirby (Shopkeeper); Lillian Gish, Gertrude Bambrick, W. C.
Robinson (In shop); Jack Pickford, Lillian Gish, Robert Harron,
Gertrude Bambrick (Outside church); Walter P. Lewis, John T. Dil-
lon, Adolph Lestina (Church board); Madge Kirby (At mother's death-
bed); Kathleen Butler, Marguerite Marsh (Windowshoppers)

NOTE: Reissued by Biograph 6 November 1916.

JINX'S BIRTHDAY PARTY

Dell Henderson (d); George Terwilliger ["Inbad's Birthday Dinner"]
(au); finished September 1912 (f); New York (l); 9 December 1912 (r);
513 feet (rl); LU153 / 7 December 1912 (copyright)

Fragment: ? (Mr. Jinx); Grace Lewis (Mrs. Jinx); Gus Pixley, ?
(Housecleaners); Edward Dillon, ? (Visiting friends); Madge Kirby
(At party); J. Waltham, ? (Policemen)

"SHE IS A PIPPIN"

Dell Henderson (d); E. E. Clyde ["The Jealous Wife and the Cat"]
(au); finished September 1912 (f); New York (l); 9 December 1912
(r); 486 feet (rl); LU154 / 7 December 1912 (copyright)

Fragment: Edward Dillon (Husband); Peggy Reid (Wife); Gus Pixley
(In office); ? (Stenographer); ? (Maid); J. Waltham (Policeman)

MY HERO

D. W. Griffith (d); D. W. Griffith (au); G. W. Bitzer (c); c. November 1912 (f); New York (l); 12 December 1912 (r); one reel (rl);
LU162 / 10 December 1912 (copyright)

Fragment: Dorothy Gish (Young woman); Walter P. Lewis, ? (Her
parents); Robert Harron (Young man); Henry B. Walthall (Indian
Charlie); Alfred Paget, W. C. Robinson, Hector V. Sarno, Jack
Pickford?, Charles Hill Mailes, Harry Carey, Frank Lanning (In-
dians); W. Christy Cabanne, J. Jiquel Lanoe, Frank Evans, Charles
H. West, Adolph Lestina (Settlers); John T. Dillon, Gus Pixley?,
W. C. Robinson (Men in room)

NOTE: Reissued by Biograph 3 December 1915. Identification of Frank Lanning as an Indian taken from Moving Picture World, 28 December 1912, "Comments on the Films" column.

THE BURGLAR'S DILEMMA

D. W. Griffith (d); Lionel Barrymore ["The Brothers"] (au); G. W. Bitzer (c); finished November 1912 (f); New York (l); 16 December 1912 (r); 998 feet (rl); LU169 / 13 December 1912 (copyright)

Lionel Barrymore (Householder); Henry B. Walthall (The weakling brother); Adolph Lestina (Butler); Lillian Gish, Madge Kirby, Gertrude Bambrick, J. Jiquel Lanoe (Householder's friends); Harry Carey, Robert Harron (Thieves); W. C. Robinson, ? (Policemen); Alfred Paget, John T. Dillon (Detectives); Charles H. West (Medic); Frank Evans (Policeman)

NOTE: Reissued by Biograph 28 February 1916.

THE DIVORCEE

Dell Henderson (d); Edward Dillon (au); finished September 1912 (f); New York (l); 19 December 1912 (r); 502 feet (rl); LU181 / 16 December 1912 (copyright)

Dell Henderson (Divorced husband)

NOTE: Identification taken from advertisement in New York Dramatic Mirror, 18 December 1912. No material survives from which other cast members may be determined.

PAPERING THE DEN

Dell Henderson (d); Mrs. J. W. Stacey (au); finished September 1912 (f); New York (l); 19 December 1912 (r); 496 feet (rl); LU179 / 16 December 1912 (copyright)

NOTE: No material survives from which the cast may be determined.

A CRY FOR HELP

D. W. Griffith (d); Edward Acker (au); G. W. Bitzer (c); finished November 1912 (f); New York (l); 23 December 1912 (r); 1000 feet (rl); LU185 / 18 December 1912 (copyright)

Lionel Barrymore (The Bum); Walter Miller (Doctor); Lillian Gish (Maid); Harry Carey (Thief); Alfred Paget, John T. Dillon, ? (Policemen); Robert Harron, W. Christy Cabanne, John T. Dillon (Witnesses to accident); Claire McDowell (Charity patient)

NOTE: Reissued by Biograph 17 April 1916.

THE GOD WITHIN

D. W. Griffith (d); T. P. Bayer (au); G. W. Bitzer (c); finished
November 1912 (f); New York (l); 26 December 1912 (r); 1000 feet
(rl); LU191 / 21 December 1912 (copyright)

Henry B. Walthall (Woodsman); Claire McDowell (His wife); Blanche
Sweet (Woman of the camp); Lionel Barrymore (Her lover); Charles
Hill Mailes (Doctor); John T. Dillon, W. Christy Cabanne (On street);
Clara T. Bracey (Madam); Frank Evans, Charles Gorman, Joseph
Graybill, W. C. Robinson, Gertrude Bambrick (In bar); J. Jiquel
Lanoe, Charles Gorman, Charles H. West, Adolph Lestina, William
J. Butler (In other town)

NOTE: Reissued by Biograph 12 November 1915.

A DAY'S OUTING

Dell Henderson (d); Stanner E. V. Taylor (au); c. October 1912 (f);
California (l); 30 December 1912 (r); one-half reel (rl); LU212 / 26
December 1912 (copyright)

Fragment: Clarence L. Barr, Gux Pixley, Charles Avery (The Men);
Sylvia Ashton, Grace Lewis (The Women); William Beaudine (On
beach)

BILL BOGG'S WINDFALL

Dell Henderson (d); Paul West ["Bill Blunder"] (au); finished October
1912 (f); California (l); 30 December 1912 (r); 599 feet (rl); LU213
/ 26 December 1912 (copyright)

Edward Dillon (Bill Bogg); Florence Lee (His wife); Clarence L. Barr
(Butler); ? (Maid); William J. Butler (Lawyer); Kate Toncray (His
wife?); Frank Opperman, William Carroll, Gus Pixley, "Bud" Duncan
(Bill's old gang)

THREE FRIENDS

D. W. Griffith (d); M. S. Reardon ["Baby's Future"] (au); G. W.
Bitzer (c); finished November 1912 (f); New York (l); 2 January 1913
(r); 999 feet (rl); LP218 / 27 December 1912 (copyright)

Fragment: Henry B. Walthall (Husband); Blanche Sweet (Wife); John
T. Dillon, Lionel Barrymore, Joseph McDermott (Three friends);
Mae Marsh (Wife's friend?); Harry Carey, W. C. Robinson (In sa-
loon); Harry Carey, Kathleen Butler, J. Jiquel Lanoe, Frank Evans,

Clara T. Bracey (In first factory); Walter P. Lewis (Foreman); Wilfred Lucas, J. Waltham (In second factory)

NOTE: Reissued by Biograph 3 April 1916.

THE TELEPHONE GIRL AND THE LADY

D. W. Griffith (d); Edward Acker ["The Heroine at Central Office"] (au); G. W. Bitzer (c); finished November 1912 (f); New York (1); 6 January 1913 (r); 1000 feet (rl); LU240 / 3 January 1913 (copyright)

Mae Marsh (Telephone girl); Alfred Paget (Her sweetheart); Claire McDowell (The lady); Walter P. Lewis (Father); Harry Carey (Thief); John T. Dillon (Grocery man); Madge Kirby (Telephone operator); Joseph McDermott (Jewelry salesman); Kate Bruce (The lady's friend); Gertrude Bambrick (Maid); Lionel Barrymore (Desk sergeant); ? (Girl's sister)

NOTE: Reissued by Biograph 7 August 1916.

THE BEST MAN WINS

Dell Henderson (d); George Terwilliger (au); finished November 1912 (f); California (1); 9 January 1913 (r); 446 feet (rl); LU242 / 4 January 1913 (copyright)

Fragment: Grace Lewis (Bride); William Carroll (Groom); Gus Pixley (Best man); ? (Baby); Florence Lee, Victoria Forde? (Bridesmaids); Frank Opperman, Kate Toncray (Parents); ? (Kidnappers); ? (Preacher); Clarence L. Barr (Policeman)

THE BITE OF A SNAKE

Dell Henderson (d); Fred Mace (au); finished November 1912 (f); California (1); 9 January 1913 (r); 553 feet (rl); LU243 / 4 January 1913 (copyright)

Fragment: Gus Pixley (Zeke); Kate Toncray, Sylvia Ashton?, Victoria Forde? (WCTU members); William Carroll, Clarence L. Barr, Frank Opperman (Zeke's friends); ? (Prospector); Edward Dillon (Druggist); William J. Butler (Sheriff)

PIRATE GOLD

D. W. Griffith? (d); George Hennessy (au); G. W. Bitzer (c); finished October 1912 (f); New York (1); 13 January 1913 (r); 1000 feet (rl); LU252 / 9 January 1913 (copyright)

Fragment: Blanche Sweet (Daughter); Charles Hill Mailes (Father);

J. Jiquel Lanoe (Successful suitor); Hector V. Sarno (Miscreant sailor); W. Chrystie Miller (The old mate); Joseph McDermott (In crew)

AN ADVENTURE IN THE AUTUMN WOODS

D. W. Griffith (d); W. Christy Cabanne (au); G. W. Bitzer (c); finished November 1912 (f); New York (l); 16 January 1913 (r); 999 feet (rl); LU256 / 10 January 1913 (copyright)

Fragment: Mae Marsh (Girl); W. Chrystie Miller (Grandad); Lionel Barrymore (Father); Walter Miller (Boy); Alfred Paget (Woodsman); Frank Opperman, Charles Hill Mailes, Harry Carey (Thieves); Joseph McDermott, Adolph Lestina (At trading post); Walter P. Lewis (In posse)

NOTE: Reissued by Biograph 24 January 1916.

KISSING KATE

Dell Henderson (d); Carl K. Coolidge (au); finished November 1912 (f); California (l); 20 January 1913 (r); 441 feet (rl); LU265 / 15 January 1913 (copyright)

Fragment: Grace Lewis (Kate); Dell Henderson (Bob); William Carroll (Preacher); William J. Butler, Frank Opperman, William Beaudine, Sylvia Ashton, Florence Lee, Gus Pixley, Vivian Prescott? (At church fair); Edward Dillon (Among men)

THE HIGH COST OF REDUCTION

Dell Henderson (d); Dell Henderson (au); c. December 1912 (f); California (l); 20 January 1913 (r); one-half reel (rl); LU264 / 15 January 1913 (copyright)

Fragment: Sylvia Ashton, Kathleen Butler (Members of the "Fly-By-Nights" theatrical troupe); ? (Physical culture teacher); Clarence L. Barr, Kate Toncray, Gus Pixley, Grace Lewis, Frank Opperman (In school); Florence Lee (On street); Billy Horne (In front of theater)

NOTE: Billy Horne is identified in Motography, 1 February 1913, p. 73.

THE TENDER-HEARTED BOY

D. W. Griffith (d); Lionel Barrymore (au); G. W. Bitzer (c); finished November 1912 (f); New York (l); 23 January 1913 (r); 1008 feet (rl); LU285 / 18 January 1913 (copyright)

Fragment: Robert Harron (Tender-hearted boy); Kate Bruce (His mother); Mae Marsh (His sister); John T. Dillon (Butcher); W. C. Robinson (On street); Clara T. Bracey (Old woman); Alfred Paget, J. Waltham (Policemen); Walter P. Lewis (Rent collector); W. Chrystie Miller (Extra)

NOTE: Reissued by Biograph 10 April 1916. Partial cast due to fragment deterioration.

A MISAPPROPRIATED TURKEY

D. W. Griffith? (d); Edward Acker (au); G. W. Bitzer (c); c. December 1912 (f); New York (l); 27 January 1913 (r); one reel (rl); LU294 / 24 January 1913 (copyright)

Fragment: Charles H. West (Striker); Claire McDowell (Mrs. Fallon); Edna Foster (His son); Charles Hill Mailes, John T. Dillon, Robert Harron, W. Chrystie Miller, Frank Evans, Joseph McDermott, Walter P. Lewis (Union members); Harry Carey (Bartender); Joseph McDermott (In bar); Jack Pickford (On street); ? (Children)

THE MASHER COP

Dell Henderson (d); S. Walter Bunting ["Brown Booms Business"] (au); finished November 1912 (f); California (l); 30 January 1913 (r); 471 feet (rl); LU296 / 25 January 1913 (copyright)

Fragment: Florence Lee (Girl); Dell Henderson (Her sweetheart); Sylvia Ashton (Mother); Frank Opperman (Justice of the Peace); William Carroll (Constable Brown)

WHAT IS THE USE OF REPINING?

Dell Henderson (d); Dell Henderson (au); c. December 1912 (f); California (l); 30 January 1913 (r); approx. 527 feet (rl); LU297 / 25 January 1913 (copyright)

Fragment: Kate Toncray (Widow); Grace Lewis (Her daughter); Edward Dillon (Sweetheart); William Carroll (Widow's suitor); ? (Maid); Clarence L. Barr (Minister)

BROTHERS

D. W. Griffith (d); H. M. L. Nolte (au); G. W. Bitzer (c); finished December 1912 (f); New York (l); 3 February 1913 (r); 999 feet (rl); LU308 / 29 January 1913 (copyright)

Fragment: Charles Hill Mailes (Father); Robert Harron (His favorite); Clara T. Bracey (Mother); Harry Carey (Her favorite); Adolph

Lestina (Doctor); Gertrude Bambrick (Non-committal woman); Walter P. Lewis (Neighbor)

OIL AND WATER

D. W. Griffith (d); E. J. Montagne ["The Better Way"] (au); G. W. Bitzer (c); finished November 1912 (f); New York (l); 6 February 1913 (r); 1513 feet (rl); LU329 / 31 January 1913 (copyright)

Fragment: Blanche Sweet (Mlle. Genova); Henry B. Walthall (The Idealist); Walter Miller (His brother, a minister); Clara T. Bracey (Nurse); ? (Child); Lionel Barrymore, Lillian Gish, Kathleen Butler, Dorothy Gish, W. Chrystie Miller, J. Jiquel Lanoe, Charles H. West, Frank Evans, Matt B. Snyder (In theater audience); J. Jiquel Lanoe, Alfred Paget, William J. Butler?, Gertrude Bambrick, Kathleen Butler (Among dancers); Charles H. West, Lionel Barrymore, John T. Dillon, Adolph Lestina, Frank Evans (In second audience); Joseph McDermott, Antonio Moreno, L. Willis (Actors in play); Harry Carey (Stage manager); Joseph McDermott, Harry Carey, John T. Dillon (At dinner); ? (Maid); ? (Governess); Lionel Barrymore (Visitor); ? (Father Time)

NOTE: Reissued by Biograph 10 September 1915 and 21 November 1916.

THE PRESS GANG

Dell Henderson (d); George F. Payne (au); finished October 1912 (f); California (l); 10 February 1913 (r); 545 feet (rl); LU351 / 7 February 1913 (copyright)

Fragment: William Carroll (Herbert); Grace Lewis (Caroline); Frank Opperman, Kate Toncray (Herbert's parents); Gus Pixley (Brother); ? (Tramps)

OH, WHAT A BOOB!

Dell Henderson (d); Austin F. Roberts ["A Hopeless Case"] (au); finished October 1912 (f); California (l); 10 February 1913 (r); 453 feet (rl); LU350 / 7 February 1913 (copyright)

Fragment: Grace Lewis (Miss Lavinia Binks); Edward Dillon (Boy); Gus Pixley (Tramp); Florence Lee (Lavinia's sister); William Carroll, William Beaudine (Bystanders)

A FATHER'S LESSON

Dell Henderson (d); W. Christy Cabanne (au); finished November 1912 (f); New York (l); 13 February 1913 (r); 997 feet (rl); LU360 / 8 February 1913 (copyright)

Fragment: Hector Dion (Husband); Claire McDowell (Wife); ? (Children); ? (Sick neighbor); Kathleen Butler (Friend of neighbor); ? (Policeman); ? (Man on street)

DRINK'S LURE

D. W. Griffith? (d); George Hennessy ["The Struggle"] (au); G. W. Bitzer (c); finished December 1912 (f); New York (l); 17 February 1913 (r); 1005 feet (rl); LU378 / 12 February 1913 (copyright)

Fragment: Claire McDowell (Neglected wife); Hector Dion (Husband); Kate Bruce (Salvation Anne); Matt B. Snyder (Mr. Edwards); Elmer Booth (Burglar); Alfred Paget, ? (Policemen); ? (Child); ? (Desk sergeant)

THERE WERE HOBOES THREE

Dell Henderson (d); William Beaudine ["Up Against It"] (au); finished November 1912 (f); California (l); 20 February 1913 (r); 529 feet (rl); LU385 / 14 February 1913 (copyright)

Fragment: Clarence L. Barr, Edward Dillon, Gus Pixley (Hoboes); William J. Butler (Employer); Grace Lewis (His assistant); Gus Pixley (Hill climber); Florence Lee (At mountain); Kate Toncray, William Beaudine, William Carroll (At resort); Sylvia Ashton (Rescued from lake); ? (Bellhop)

AN UP-TO-DATE LOCHINVAR

Dell Henderson (d); Leona Radnor ["A Love that Came C. O. D."] (au); finished 9 November 1912 (f); California (l); 20 February 1913 (r); 470 feet (rl); LU384 / 14 February 1913 (copyright)

Fragment: Florence Lee (Dora); William J. Butler, Sylvia Ashton (Her parents); Edward Dillon ("C. O. D."); Gus Pixley, William Carroll (Suitors); Kate Toncray ("C. O. D."'s mother); ? (Maid); ? (Messenger)

A CHANCE DECEPTION

D. W. Griffith (d); W. Christy Cabanne (au); G. W. Bitzer (c); finished November 1912 (f); New York (l); 24 February 1913 (r); 998 feet (rl); LU390 / 18 February 1913 (copyright)

Fragment: Blanche Sweet (Wife); Charles Hill Mailes (Jealous husband); Harry Carey (Raffles); Mildred Manning (His woman); John T. Dillon (Waiter); ? (Maid); Joseph McDermott, Lionel Barrymore (Policemen); Adolph Lestina (Visitor); ? (In restaurant)

NOTE: Reissued by Biograph 7 February 1916.

LOVE IN AN APARTMENT HOTEL

D. W. Griffith (d); William M. Marston ["The Thief"] (au); G. W. Bitzer (c); begun December 1912, finished January 1913 (f); New York/California (l); 27 February 1913 (r); 1000 feet (rl); LU398 / 21 February 1913 (copyright)

Blanche Sweet (Young woman); Adolph Lestina (Her father); Henry B. Walthall (Her fiancé); Harry Carey (Thief); Mae Marsh (Angelina Millingford, a maid); Edward Dillon (Pinky Doolan, a bellboy); John T. Dillon, Walter Miller (Fiancé's friends); Frank Evans, W. C. Robinson (Hotel detectives); Kathleen Butler (Young woman's maid); Kate Toncray (Head chambermaid); Robert Harron (Desk clerk); Joseph McDermott (Fiancé's valet); Clara T. Bracey (Maid); Jack Pickford (Bellhop); Matt B. Snyder, Harry Hyde, Gertrude Bambrick, Lionel Barrymore, Hattie Delaro?, J. Jiquel Lanoe, Walter P. Lewis (In hotel lobby)

NOTE: Reissued by Biograph 18 June 1915.

A QUEER ELOPEMENT

Dell Henderson (d); George A. Posner ["A Near Tragedy"] (au); finished December 1912 (f); California (l); 3 March 1913 (r); 487 feet (rl); LU411 / 25 February 1913 (copyright)

Fragment: Edward Dillon (Deputy); William J. Butler (Sheriff); Grace Lewis (His daughter); Sylvia Ashton (His wife); "Bud" Duncan (Convict); Frank Opperman, Clarence L. Barr (Outside sheriff's office)

LOOK NOT UPON THE WINE

Dell Henderson (d); Ralph E. Hellawell (au); finished November 1912 (f); California (l); 3 March 1913 (r); 522 feet (rl); LU410 / 25 February 1913 (copyright)

Fragment: Charles Murray (Mr. Tucker, League president); Kate Toncray (His wife); Frank Opperman (Neighbor); Gus Pixley, Florence Lee, William Carroll, Edward Dillon, Sylvia Ashton, Grace Lewis (In cabaret)

THE WRONG BOTTLE

Anthony O'Sullivan (d); Leon J. Suckert (au); begun November, finished December 1912 (f); New York (l); 6 March 1913 (r); 998 feet (rl); LU418 / 28 February 1913 (copyright)

Fragment: Claire McDowell (Blind sister); Charles Hill Mailes (Husband?/Friend?); Pearl Sindelear (Younger sister); Charles H. West (Her faithless lover); Hector Dion (The faithful lover); Lionel

Barrymore (Father); Clara T. Bracey (Neighbor?); W. C. Robinson, Walter Miller (In road house); Harry Carey (Extra)

BROKEN WAYS

D. W. Griffith (d); T. P. Bayer ["Heart Throbs"] (au); G. W. Bitzer (c); finished 13 January 1913 (f); California (l); 8 March 1913 (r); 1045 feet (rl); LU434 / 3 March 1913 (copyright)

Henry B. Walthall (The road agent); Blanche Sweet (His wife); Harry Carey (Sheriff); Frank Opperman, Joseph McDermott (Road agent's gang); Charles Gorman (Hold-up victim); Walter Miller (In town); Alfred Paget, William Carroll (In posse); Robert Harron, Dorothy Gish, Adolph Lestina, Gertrude Bambrick (In telegraph office); Gertrude Bambrick (On street)

NOTE: Reissued by Biograph 16 July 1915.

A GIRL'S STRATAGEM

D. W. Griffith? (d); George Hennessy ["The Midnight Hour"] (au); G. W. Bitzer (c); finished January 1913 (f); California (l); 10 March 1913 (r); 998 feet (rl); LU437 / 5 March 1913 (copyright)

New York Dramatic Mirror advertisement: Mae Marsh, Charles H. West

THE SPRING OF LIFE

Dell Henderson (d); Florence Lee (au); finished January 1913 (f); California (l); 13 March 1913 (r); 476 feet (rl); LU445 / 7 March 1913 (copyright)

Fragment: Grace Lewis (Innkeeper's daughter); Edward Dillon (Her suitor); William J. Butler (Cruel papa); William Carroll, Frank Opperman ("Spring of Life" patients); Gus Pixley, "Bud" Duncan ("Spring of Life" employees)

TIGHTWAD'S PREDICAMENT

Dell Henderson (d); Dell Henderson (au); c. January 1913 (f); California (l); 13 March 1913 (r); one-half reel (rl); LU446 / 7 March 1913 (copyright)

Fragment: Charles Murray (Tightwad); Kate Toncray (His wife); ? (Maid); Gus Pixley (Tramp); Clarence L. Barr, Sylvia Ashton (Wife's friends); William J. Butler (Cleaner); Edward Dillon (Policeman)

THE UNWELCOME GUEST

D. W. Griffith (d); George Hennessy (au); G. W. Bitzer (c); c. October 1912 (f); New York (l); 15 March 1913 (r); 1004 feet (rl);
LU456 / 10 March 1913 (copyright)

Mary Pickford (The Slavey); W. Chrystie Miller (The old father);
Charles Hill Mailes (The son); Claire McDowell (His wife); Jack
Pickford, ? (Their children); Elmer Booth (Hired hand); Kate Bruce
(Old wife); Harry Carey (Sheriff?); J. Jiquel Lanoe (Doctor); Lillian
Gish, Frank Evans, Adolph Lestina, W. C. Robinson, Lionel Barry-
more (At auction)

NOTE: Reissued by Biograph 26 June 1916.

THE POWER OF THE CAMERA

Dell Henderson (d); Anita Loos (au); finished January 1913 (f); California (l); 17 March 1913 (r); 453 feet (rl); LU462 / 11 March 1913
(copyright)

Fragment: Charles Murray, Dell Henderson (Convicts); Edward Dillon,
? (Guards); Clarence L. Barr? (Tramp); ? (Constable); Gus Pixley,
(Sheriff); Frank Opperman (Bartender); Sylvia Ashton, William J.
Butler, Kate Toncray, Florence Lee (Townsfolk)

A DELIVERY PACKAGE

Dell Henderson (d); Albert "Bud" Duncan (au); finished December 1912
(f); California (l); 17 March 1913 (r); 545 feet (rl); LU463 / 11 March
1913 (copyright)

Fragment: Clarence L. Barr (Groom); Sylvia Ashton (Bride); Charles
Murray (Rival); William Carroll (Best man?); William J. Butler,
Frank Opperman (In wedding party); William Beaudine (In cafe); Ed-
ward Dillon (Waiter); Gus Pixley (Delivery boy)

NEAR TO EARTH

D. W. Griffith (d); James Orr (au); G. W. Bitzer (c); finished January 1913 (f); California (l); 20 March 1913 (r); 999 feet (rl); LU484
/ 15 March 1913 (copyright)

Lionel Barrymore (Gato); Robert Harron (His brother); Gertrude
Bambrick (Gato's sweetheart); Mae Marsh, Kathleen Butler (Her
friends); Frank Opperman (Friend); Walter Miller (Stranger); Joseph
McDermott, W. Christy Cabanne (Businessmen)

NOTE: Reissued by Biograph 13 November 1916.

FATE

D. W. Griffith (d); Mrs. William L. Honkers (au); G. W. Bitzer (c); finished November 1912 (f); New York (l); 22 March 1913 (r); 1038 feet (rl); LP490 / 18 March 1913 (copyright)

Charles Hill Mailes (Sim); Robert Harron (Beloved son); John T. Dillon (Friend); Lionel Barrymore, Mae Marsh (Loving family); Adolph Lestina, Frank Evans, W. C. Robinson, Walter P. Lewis, J. Waltham (In bar); Jack Pickford, Gladys Egan (At school); Joseph McDermott, ? (Two hunters); ? (Teacher); Charles Gorman, Walter P. Lewis (Villagers)

NOTE: Reissued by Biograph 17 December 1915.

A WELCOME INTRUDER

D. W. Griffith? (d); Belle Taylor (au); G. W. Bitzer (c); c. January 1913 (f); California (l); 24 March 1913 (r); one reel (rl); LU506 / 22 March 1913 (copyright)

? (Child); Kate Toncray (Neighbor); Charles Hill Mailes (Father); Charles H. West (Workman); W. Chrystie Miller (Shopkeeper); Joseph McDermott (Policeman); Frank Opperman (Hurdy-gurdy man); John T. Dillon (On street); William Carroll, ? (Wagon drivers); Claire McDowell (Their sister, a widow); Adolph Lestina (Construction boss); Frank Opperman (At second site); ? (Desk sergeant)

THE OLD GRAY MARE

Dell Henderson (d); Dell Henderson (au); c. January 1913 (f); California (l); 27 March 1913 (r); 424 feet (rl); LU519 / 27 March 1913 (copyright)

Fragment: Charles Murray (Zeke); Kate Toncray (Matilda, his wife); William J. Butler, Clarence L. Barr, J. Jiquel Lanoe (Inside saloon); William Beaudine, Edward Dillon, Gus Pixley (Outside saloon)

ALL HAIL TO THE KING

Dell Henderson (d); William E. Wing ["A King for $1,000 a Minute"] (au); finished January 1913 (f); California (l); 27 March 1913 (r); 569 feet (rl); LU518 / 27 March 1913 (copyright)

Fragment: Gus Pixley (King); Charles Murray (Tramp); Edward Dillon (Jester); Sylvia Ashton (Queen); Gertrude Bambrick (Dancer); William J. Butler, ? (Assassins); Harry Hyde, Kathleen Butler, Clarence L. Barr (At court); Clarence L. Barr (Policeman)

NOTE: Gertrude Bambrick is identified as the dancer in Moving Picture World, 14 June 1913, "Inquiries" column.

THE SHERIFF'S BABY

D. W. Griffith (d); Edward Bell ["The 3 Bad Men of the Desert"] (au); G. W. Bitzer (c); finished February 1913 (f); California (l); 29 March 1913 (r); 1004 feet (rl); LU531 / 31 March 1913 (copyright)

Fragment: Alfred Paget (Sheriff); Henry B. Walthall, Harry Carey, Lionel Barrymore (Bandits); John T. Dillon, Kate Bruce (Settlers); Robert Harron (Deputy); ? (Baby)

NOTE: Reissued by Biograph 27 August 1915.

EDWIN MASQUERADES

Dell Henderson (d); Isobel M. Reynolds ["A Losing Wager"] (au); finished January 1913 (f); California (l); 31 March 1913 (r); 446 feet (rl); LU532 / 31 March 1913 (copyright)

Fragment: Grace Lewis (Bessie); Edward Dillon (Jack); Charles Murray (Edwin, a prisoner); Gus Pixley, Clarence L. Barr, ? (Guards); Florence Lee, J. Jiquel Lanoe, Harry Hyde, Sylvia Ashton (At ball)

THEIR ONE GOOD SUIT

Dell Henderson (d); Helen Combes (au); finished January 1913 (f); California (l); 31 March 1913 (r); 556 feet (rl); LU530 / 31 March 1913 (copyright)

Fragment: Clarence L. Barr (Paul); Charles Murray (Harry); ? (First young woman); ? (Second young woman); Edward Dillon (Guard?); William J. Butler (Policeman); Gus Pixley (Extra)

THE HERO OF LITTLE ITALY

D. W. Griffith? (d); Grace D. de Sellen (au); G. W. Bitzer (c); c. February 1913 (f); California (l); 3 April 1913 (r); one reel (rl); LU546 / 3 April 1913 (copyright)

Fragment: Charles H. West (Joe); Blanche Sweet (Maria); Harry Carey (Tony); Kate Toncray, Charles Hill Mailes (Parents); ? (Boy); Kathleen Butler, John T. Dillon, J. Jiquel Lanoe (At ball); William J. Butler, Frank Opperman, Frank Evans, Walter Miller (In bar)

THE PERFIDY OF MARY

D. W. Griffith (d); George Hennessy (au); G. W. Bitzer (c); finished February 1913 (f); California (l); 5 April 1913 (r); 1004 feet (rl); LU562 / 5 April 1913 (copyright)

Dorothy Gish (Rose); Mae Marsh (Mary); Walter Miller (Rose's suitor); Harry Hyde (Mary's suitor); Lionel Barrymore (Mary's father); Kate Bruce (Mother); Henry B. Walthall, Gertrude Bambrick, J. Jiquel Lanoe, Viola Barry (Storybook lovers); W. C. Robinson (Porter); Robert Harron (Boy who gives directions); Olive Fuller Golden? (Maid); ? ("Lothario")

NOTE: Reissued by Biograph 15 May 1916.

THE STOLEN BRIDE

Anthony O'Sullivan (d); Kate McCabe ["The Trail of Orange Blossoms"] (au); finished February 1913 (f); California (l); 7 April 1913 (r); 1000 feet (rl); LU579 / 8 April 1913 (copyright)

Fragment: Harry Carey (Husband); Claire McDowell (Wife); ? (Baby); Charles H. West (Overseer); Blanche Sweet (Grower's daughter); Harry Hyde, Hector V. Sarno (In posse)

AN "UNCLE TOM'S CABIN" TROUPE

Dell Henderson (d); Dell Henderson ["Where Alfalfa Grows"] (au); finished February 1913 (f); California (l); 10 April 1913 (r); 679 feet (rl); LU583 / 10 April 1913 (copyright)

Fragment: Gus Pixley (Uncle Tom); Grace Lewis (Little Eva); William Beaudine, Edward Dillon, J. Jiquel Lanoe, Charles Murray (The troupe); W. Chrystie Miller, Frank Opperman (In audience); Clarence L. Barr (Hotel owner); Kate Bruce (In second audience)

NOTE: Grace Lewis is identified as Little Eva in Moving Picture World, 26 April 1913, "Comments on the Films" column.

A LESSON TO MASHERS

Dell Henderson (d); Paul West (au); c. January 1913 (f); California (l); 10 April 1913 (r); one-half reel (rl); LU584 / 10 April 1913 (copyright)

Fragment: William Carroll (Fastidious Ferdinand); William J. Butler, Gus Pixley, Florence Lee, Kate Toncray, Edward Dillon, Grace Lewis (In laundry); Frank Opperman (Foreman)

THE LITTLE TEASE

D. W. Griffith (d); D. W. Griffith (au); G. W. Bitzer (c); c. March 1913 (f); California (l); 12 April 1913 (r); 1500 feet (rl); LU587 / 12 April 1913 (copyright)

Fragment: Mae Marsh (The Little Tease, grown); ? (The Little Tease, as a child); W. Chrystie Miller, Kate Bruce (Her parents); Robert Harron (Jim); Henry B. Walthall (The valley man); Viola Barry (The other woman); Lionel Barrymore (In bar); Frank Opperman, Walter Miller? (On street); Edward Dillon, Frank Opperman (In lunchroom); Frank Opperman, ? (Prospectors)

HE HAD A GUESS COMING

Dell Henderson (d); William E. Wing (au); finished February 1913 (f); California (l); 14 April 1913 (r); 439 feet (rl); LU595 / 14 April 1913 (copyright)

Fragment: Edward Dillon (Dick); Charles Murray (Uncle Bill); Gus Pixley, John T. Dillon, ? (Poker players); ? (Two women); Charles Hill Mailes, Kate Toncray (At temperance lecture); Grace Lewis (Extra)

NOTE: Grace Lewis is identified in Moving Picture World, 26 April 1913, "Comments on the Films" column.

A HORSE ON BILL

Dell Henderson (d); Anita Loos (au); finished February 1913 (f); California (l); 14 April 1913 (r); 560 feet (rl); LU596 / 14 April 1913 (copyright)

Fragment: John T. Dillon (Bill); Gertrude Bambrick (Leading lady); Charles Murray, Edward Dillon, J. Jiquel Lanoe, Gus Pixley, Clarence L. Barr (Town band); William Elmer (At rehearsal); Henry B. Walthall, William Beaudine, William J. Butler (In audience); Charles H. West (Extra)

NOTE: Charles H. West is identified in Moving Picture World, 26 April 1913, "Comments on the Films" column.

A FRIGHTFUL BLUNDER

Anthony O'Sullivan (d); Edward Acker (au); finished February 1913 (f); California (l); 17 April 1913 (r); 998 feet (rl); LU610 / 16 April 1913 (copyright)

Fragment: Viola Barry (Young woman); Charles H. West (Young businessman); Walter Miller (Pharmacist); Kate Bruce (Young woman's mother); William Carroll (Customer); ? (Clerk); Harry Carey (Superintendent); ? (Messenger)

A MISUNDERSTOOD BOY

D. W. Griffith (d); W. Christy Cabanne (au); G. W. Bitzer (c); finished February 1913 (f); California (l); 19 April 1913 (r); 998 feet (rl); LU620 / 18 April 1913 (copyright)

Fragment: Kate Bruce, Lionel Barrymore (Parents); Lillian Gish, Robert Harron (Children); W. Christy Cabanne (On street); Alfred Paget (Vigilante leader); William Carroll, Antonio Moreno, Joseph McDermott, W. C. Robinson? (Vigilantes); Charles Hill Mailes, Viola Barry (Thieving merchants); Frank Opperman (In next town); ? (Girl)

NOTE: Reissued by Biograph 19 June 1916.

THE LEFT-HANDED MAN

D. W. Griffith?/Anthony O'Sullivan? (d); Frank E. Woods (au); G. W. Bitzer? (c); c. February 1913 (f); California (l); 21 April 1913 (r); one reel (rl); LU621 / 19 April 1913 (copyright)

Fragment: ? (Old soldier); Lillian Gish (His daughter); Charles H. West (Her sweetheart); Harry Carey (Thief); ? (Desk clerk); Charles Gorman (In bar); Frank Evans, Joseph McDermott, William Elmer, Alfred Paget (Policemen); William J. Butler, Kathleen Butler (In court); William Carroll (Extra)

A RAGTIME ROMANCE

Dell Henderson (d); Dell Henderson (au); finished February 1913 (f); California (l); 24 April 1913 (r); one-half reel (rl); LU634 / 22 April 1913 (copyright)

Fragment: Charles Murray (Groom); Gertrude Bambrick (Bride); Gus Pixley (Groom's friend); Clarence L. Barr (Razor Jim); John T. Dillon (At wedding)

THE CURE

Dell Henderson (d); Laura B. Chandler (au); c. February 1913 (f); California (l); 24 April 1913 (r); one-half reel (rl); LU633 / 22 April 1913 (copyright)

Fragment: William J. Butler (Father); Grace Lewis (Daughter); Gus Pixley (Suitor); Clarence L. Barr (Gardener); Kate Toncray, ? (His family); Frank Opperman (Neighbor)

THE LADY AND THE MOUSE

D. W. Griffith (d); D. W. Griffith (au); G. W. Bitzer (c); c. March 1913 (f); California (l); 26 April 1913 (r); 999 feet (rl); LU636 / 23 April 1913 (copyright)

Lillian Gish (Young woman); Lionel Barrymore (Her father); Harry
Hyde (Rich man/tramp); Dorothy Gish (Sick sister); Kate Toncray
(The aunt); Robert Harron (Young friend); Adolph Lestina (Doctor);
Henry B. Walthall, Viola Barry, J. Jiquel Lanoe (At garden party);
W. C. Robinson, Frank Opperman, Joseph McDermott (Creditors)

NOTE: Reissued by Biograph 13 March 1916.

BLAME THE WIFE

Dell Henderson (d); Eleanor Hicks (au); finished February 1913 (f);
California (l); 28 April 1913 (r); 513 feet (rl); LU641 / 24 April 1913
(copyright)

Fragment: Dell Henderson (Husband); Kate Toncray (Wife); ? (Children); ? (At magazine stand)

THE DAYLIGHT BURGLAR

Dell Henderson (d); C. B. Loomis (au); c. February 1913 (f); California (l); 28 April 1913 (r); one-half reel (rl); LU642 / 24 April
1913 (copyright)

Fragment: Charles Murray (Burglar); Dell Henderson (Victim); Clarence L. Barr (Policeman); Gus Pixley, William J. Butler, William
Beaudine (In club); ? (In store)

IF WE ONLY KNEW

D. W. Griffith? (d); George Hennessy (au); G. W. Bitzer? (c); c.
March 1913 (f); California (l); 1 May 1913 (r); one reel (rl); LU643
/ 25 April 1913 (copyright)

Fragment: Henry B. Walthall (Father); Blanche Sweet (Mother); ?
(Child); ? (Gardener); ? (Nurse); Harry Carey (Sailor); ? (Fisherman's
wife); William Courtwright (Minister)

THE WANDERER

D. W. Griffith (d); D. W. Griffith (au); "Pippa Passes," the poem
by Robert Browning (s); G. W. Bitzer (c); c. March 1913 (f); California (l); 3 May 1913 (r); 1003 feet (rl); LU651 / 26 April 1913
(copyright)

Henry B. Walthall (The Wanderer); Charles Hill Mailes (The father);
W. Christy Cabanne (The brother); Kate Bruce (The old woman);
Lionel Barrymore, Claire McDowell (Lovers); Kate Toncray, Frank
Opperman (Parents); Mae Marsh (Their child, grown); John T. Dillon
(Crafty merchant); Adolph Lestina (Customer); Joseph McDermott, ?
(Soldiers); Walter Miller (The "other man"); Charles H. West (Friar)

NOTE: Reissued by Biograph 3 September 1915. This film is a remake of PIPPA PASSES or, THE SONG OF CONSCIENCE, originally released by Biograph 4 October 1909.

THE TENDERFOOT'S MONEY

Anthony O'Sullivan (d); Stanner E. V. Taylor ["The Salted Mine"] (au); c. March 1913 (f); California (l); 5 May 1913 (r); 998 feet (rl); LU660 / 29 April 1913 (copyright)

Fragment: Harry Carey (Gambler); William Carroll (Tenderfoot); Henry B. Walthall, Claire McDowell (Prospecting couple); William Beaudine, William J. Butler (In bar)

FRAPPE LOVE

Dell Henderson (d); William E. Wing ["Bessie Makes A Match"] (au); finished March 1913 (f); California (l); 8 May 1913 (r); one-half reel (rl); LU665 / 30 April 1913 (copyright)

Fragment: Gertrude Bambrick (Bessie); Kate Toncray (Her mother); Charles Murray (Her suitor); Gus Pixley, ? (Farmers); "Bud" Duncan (In barn)

THE COVETED PRIZE

Dell Henderson (d); P. W. Stockton (au); c. March 1913 (f); California (l); 8 May 1913 (r); 423 feet (rl); LU664 / 30 April 1913 (copyright)

Fragment: ? (Father); ? (Girl); ? (Brothers); Gus Pixley, J. Waltham (Friends)

THE HOUSE OF DARKNESS

D. W. Griffith (d); J. F. Looney ["Saved by Music"] (au); G. W. Bitzer (c); finished March 1913 (f); California (l); 10 May 1913 (r); one reel (rl); LU670 / 3 May 1913 (copyright)

Lionel Barrymore (The doctor); Claire McDowell (His wife); Charles Hill Mailes (The "unfortunate" patient); Lillian Gish (Nurse); Kate Bruce, Adolph Lestina, Frank Opperman (Patients); Walter Miller, J. Jiquel Lanoe, Frank Opperman (Clerks); Alfred Paget, W. C. Robinson, William Elmer (Guards); Robert Harron, Joseph McDermott (Searchers); W. Christy Cabanne, ? (Attack victims); Mrs. Adelaide Bronti (In tenement apartment); William J. Butler (Extra)

NOTE: Reissued by Biograph 6 March 1916.

THE KING AND THE COPPER

Dell Henderson (d); Dell Henderson (au); c. March 1913 (f); California
(l); 12 May 1913 (r); 669 feet (rl); LU688 / 6 May 1913 (copyright)

Fragment: ? (King); Charles Murray (Jonah, the substitute king);
Gertrude Bambrick (Queen); William J. Butler (King's aide); ?
(Copper); ? (Women); ? (Extras in blackface)

A RAINY DAY

Dell Henderson (d); Florence Lee (au); finished February 1913 (f);
California (l); 12 May 1913 (r); 329 feet (rl); LU687 / 6 May 1913
(copyright)

Fragment: Edward Dillon (Clubman); Alfred Paget, William Beaudine, Walter Miller, Charles Murray, "Bud" Duncan[blackface] (At
the club); ? (Blind man)

THE STOLEN LOAF

Anthony O'Sullivan?/D. W. Griffith? (d); Grace Barton (au); c. March
1913 (f); California (l); 15 May 1913 (r); one reel (rl); LU696 / 8
May 1913 (copyright)

Fragment: Charles Hill Mailes, William Carroll (At dinner)

NOTE: Partial cast due to fragment deterioration.

THE YAQUI CUR

D. W. Griffith (d); Stanner E. V. Taylor (au); G. W. Bitzer (c);
c. April 1913 (f); California (l); 17 May 1913 (r); two reels (rl);
LU717 / 10 May 1913 (copyright)

Robert Harron (Yaqui youth); Kate Bruce (His mother); Walter Miller
(Ocallo, his friend); Lionel Barrymore (The Easterner); Frank Opper-
man (The preacher); Charles Hill Mailes (The chief); Victoria Forde
(His daughter); Alfred Paget, J. Jiquel Lanoe, Charles Gorman, Wil-
liam J. Butler (In tribe); Joseph McDermott, Charles Hill Mailes,
Frank Evans, William J. Butler, Harry Hyde (Goldseekers)

NOTE: Reissued by Biograph 6 June 1916.

OLAF - AN ATOM

Anthony O'Sullivan (d); William E. Wing (au); finished March 1913
(f); California (l); 19 May 1913 (r); 1003 feet (rl); LU732 / 13 May
1913 (copyright)

Harry Carey (Olaf, an atom); Kate Bruce (His mother); Charles Hill Mailes, Claire McDowell (Parents); ? (Their child); Donald Crisp (Beggar); Frank Evans (Blacksmith); ? (Tramps); Thomas Jefferson? (Doctor); John T. Dillon (Claim jumper); ? (Assistant); ? (In claim office)

CINDERELLA AND THE BOOB

Dell Henderson (d); Florence Lee ["The Golden Slipper"] (au); finished March 1913 (f); California (l); 22 May 1913 (r); 557 feet (rl); LU752 / 15 May 1913 (copyright)

Fragment: Grace Lewis (Cinderella); Edward Dillon (The Boob); Kate Toncray (Stepmother); Charles Murray, Gertrude Bambrick (Cruel stepsisters); Clarence L. Barr (Prince Charming); Gus Pixley (A party guest); ? (Page); ? (Witch); ? (Ladies-in-waiting)

THE HICKSVILLE EPICURE

Dell Henderson (d); Anita Loos (au); finished March 1913 (f); California (l); 22 May 1913 (r); 433 feet (rl); LU751 / 14 May 1913 (copyright)

Fragment: Clarence L. Barr (Constable, the epicure); Gus Pixley (Cook); Kate Toncray, Gertrude Bambrick (In purity league)

JUST GOLD

D. W. Griffith (d); D. W. Griffith (au); G. W. Bitzer (c); March 1913 (f); California (l); 24 May 1913 (r); 999 feet (rl); LU756 / 17 May 1913 (copyright)

Lionel Barrymore, Alfred Paget, Charles H. West, Joseph McDermott (The brothers); Kate Bruce, Charles Hill Mailes (Their parents); Lillian Gish (The sweetheart); Dorothy Gish (Her friend); Adolph Lestina, Frank Opperman, Kathleen Butler (At farewell); Adolph Lestina, Frank Opperman (In town); ? (Indians)

NOTE: Reissued by Biograph 14 February 1916.

HIGHBROW LOVE

Dell Henderson (d); Anita Loos (au); finished March 1913 (f); California (l); 26 May 1913 (r); one-half reel (rl); LU762 / 20 May 1913 (copyright)

Fragment: Clarence L. Barr (Fred); Kate Toncray (Miss Highbrow); Charles Murray ("Samuel Johnson"); Gus Pixley, Gertrude Bambrick, Sylvia Ashton (Extras)

THE TRIMMERS TRIMMED

Dell Henderson (d); Albert "Bud" Duncan ["Trimming the Trimmers"] (au); finished March 1913 (f); California (l); 26 May 1913 (r); one-half reel (rl); LU763 / 20 May 1913 (copyright)

Fragment: Edward Dillon ("Wise Guy"); "Bud" Duncan (His side-kick); Clarence L. Barr (Sheriff); Kate Toncray (His wife); Florence Lee, ? ("Fair Speeders"); Gus Pixley (Speeder)

A DANGEROUS FOE

Anthony O'Sullivan (d); Edward Acker (au); finished April 1913 (f); California (l); 29 May 1913 (r); one reel (rl); LU772 / 22 May 1913 (copyright)

Fragment: Charles Hill Mailes (The judge); ? (His daughter); Harry Carey ("The Bull"); John T. Dillon (His friend); ? (Maid); ? (Ching Fow); ? (Policemen)

HIS MOTHER'S SON

D. W. Griffith (d); W. Christy Cabanne (au); G. W. Bitzer (c); begun February, finished March 1913 (f); California (l); 31 May 1913 (r); one reel (rl); LU776 / 23 May 1913 (copyright)

W. Chrystie Miller, Jennie Lee (The parents); Walter Miller, Mae Marsh (Their children); Robert Harron (Orphan); William Carroll (Steamer captain); Frank Opperman, Adolph Lestina, W. Christy Cabanne, Mrs. Adelaide Bronti (Neighbors); W. Christy Cabanne (Among revelers); Frank Opperman, Joseph McDermott, Adolph Lestina (In restaurant); Dorothy Gish, Viola Barry (Women at docks); W. C. Robinson, Kathleen Butler (In kitchen)

NOTE: Reissued by Biograph 21 February 1916. February filming date taken from internal evidence.

THE RANCHERO'S REVENGE

D. W. Griffith? (d); Charles Inslee (au); G. W. Bitzer (c); c. April 1913 (f); California (l); 2 June 1913 (r); one reel (rl); LU785 / 27 May 1913 (copyright)

Fragment: Lionel Barrymore (Ranchero); Claire McDowell, Harry Carey (Two schemers); Clarence L. Barr (Chinese cook); Charles Hill Mailes, Viola Barry (At party); William Courtwright (At wedding)

SLIPPERY SLIM REPENTS

Dell Henderson (d); Walter S. Fredericks (au); c. April 1913 (f);

California (l); 5 June 1913 (r); one-half reel (rl); LU790 / 29 May 1913 (copyright)

Fragment: Charles H. West (Slippery Slim); Clarence L. Barr (Parson); J. Jiquel Lanoe (Rattlesnake Joe); Harry Hyde, Gus Pixley, William Beaudine (In crowd); ? (Wild Cat Fred); Kate Toncray (Bashful Belinda); Charles Murray (Her suitor); William J. Butler (Minister)

JUST KIDS

Dell Henderson (d); Kathleen Butler, Olive Fuller Golden (au); c. April 1913 (f); California (l); 5 June 1913 (r); one-half reel (rl); LU789 / 29 May 1913 (copyright)

Fragment: Edward Dillon (Half-back Harold); Charles Murray (Professor); Gertrude Bambrick (His daughter); Sylvia Ashton (His wife); Florence Lee, ? (Academy pupils); "Bud" Duncan, Charles H. West (Bold Bad Boys)

A TIMELY INTERCEPTION

D. W. Griffith (d); W. Christy Cabanne (au); G. W. Bitzer (c); finished 31 March 1913 (f); California (l); 7 June 1913 (r); 998 feet (rl); LU801 / 2 June 1913 (copyright)

W. Chrystie Miller (Farmer); Lillian Gish (His daughter); Robert Harron (His adopted son); Lionel Barrymore (His brother); Joseph McDermott, William J. Butler, Alfred Paget (The oil syndicate); Frank Evans, Frank Opperman (Foremen); Adolph Lestina (Brother's friend); Charles Gorman (Policeman); ? (Brother's daughter); ? (Two creditors)

NOTE: Reissued by Biograph 9 July 1915.

JENKS BECOMES A DESPERATE CHARACTER

Dell Henderson (d); William E. Wing (au); finished April 1913 (f); California (l); 9 June 1913 (r); one-half reel (rl); LU805 / 3 June 1913 (copyright)

Fragment: Dell Henderson (Jenks); Florence Lee (His wife); Kate Toncray, Sylvia Ashton (Visitors); Charles Murray (Chief of police); Edward Dillon, William J. Butler, Gus Pixley, W. C. Robinson, William Beaudine (In club); Dave Morris (Valet); Clarence L. Barr, "Bud" Duncan, Charles Gorman, ? (Policemen); Gertrude Bambrick (On street)

RED HICKS DEFIES THE WORLD

Dell Henderson (d); William E. Wing ["Cupid Dons the Gloves"] (au); finished April 1913 (f); California (l); 9 June 1913 (r); one-half reel (rl); LU806 / 3 June 1913 (copyright)

Fragment: Charles Murray (Red Hicks); Edward Dillon (O'Shea, the fighting Irishman); Dorothy Gish (His girlfriend); Kate Toncray (His mother); "Bud" Duncan (His trainer); William J. Butler, Adolph Lestina (Creditors); Lionel Barrymore (Referee); William Beaudine (In ring); John T. Dillon, Harry Carey, Charles H. West, Frank Evans, Harry Hyde, J. Jiquel Lanoe, Walter Miller, Frank Opperman, Henry B. Walthall, Joseph McDermott, Charles Gorman, Gertrude Bambrick, Charles Hill Mailes, Alfred Paget (In crowd)

THE WELL

Anthony O'Sullivan (d); Minnie Meyer ["On the Way to Town*] (au); finished 23 April 1913 (f); California (l); 12 June 1913 (r); one reel (rl); LU809 / 6 June 1913 (copyright)

Fragment: Lionel Barrymore (Farmer); Claire McDowell (His wife); Harry Carey (Giuseppe, the farmhand); ? (Daughter); George Beranger? (The accomplice)

DEATH'S MARATHON

D. W. Griffith (d); William E. Wing (au); G. W. Bitzer (c); finished 5 April 1913 (f); California (l); 14 June 1913 (r); 1027 feet (rl); LU825 / 9 June 1913 (copyright)

Blanche Sweet (The wife); Henry B. Walthall (Her husband); Walter Miller (His partner); Lionel Barrymore (Their backer); Kate Bruce (Nurse); Robert Harron (Messenger); ? (Maid); Harry Hyde (A friend); William J. Butler, Alfred Paget, Harry Hyde, J. Jiquel Lanoe, Adolph Lestina, W. C. Robinson (At club)

NOTE: Reissued by Biograph 20 August 1915.

THE SWITCH-TOWER

Anthony O'Sullivan (d); George Hennessy ["Between Love And Duty"] (au); finished 29 April 1913 (f); California (l); 16 June 1913 (r); 998 feet (rl); LU827 / 10 June 1913 (copyright)

Henry B. Walthall (Switchman); Claire McDowell (His wife); ? (Their son); Lionel Barrymore, Charles H. West, John T. Dillon (Counterfeiters); William Carroll, Frank Evans (Federal agents); George Beranger, ? (Tramps); Anthony O'Sullivan (Storekeeper)

THE RISE AND FALL OF McDOO

Dell Henderson (d); Dolly Ohnet ["A Mixture of College Love"] (au); finished 11 April 1913 (f); California (l); 19 June 1913 (r); one-half reel (rl); LU830 / 13 June 1913 (copyright)

Fragment: Charles Murray (Knock-out McDoo); ? (His wife); Edward Dillon, Clarence L. Barr (The Nilly Boys); Florence Lee, ? (The Misses McNeil); Dave Morris (Muscle-bound Joe); ? (Lawn party reps); William Beaudine, Gus Pixley (At lawn party)

ALMOST A WILD MAN

Dell Henderson (d); William Beaudine (au); finished 10 April 1913 (f); California (l); 19 June 1913 (r); 576 feet (rl); LU831 / 13 June 1913 (copyright)

Fragment: Charles Murray, Gus Pixley, Edward Dillon (Rooly, Pooly, Dooly); Gertrude Bambrick, Nan Christy?, ? (Lizzy and Her Dancing Dolls); Clarence L. Barr, "Bud" Duncan (Guppy and Fugg); Dorothy Gish (Miss Smart); Charles Gorman (At stage door); William J. Butler (Policeman); Charles Gorman, Dorothy Gish, "Bud" Duncan, Gertrude Bambrick[blackface] (Sideshow patrons); John T. Dillon, Harry Hyde, Viola Barry, Charles Hill Mailes, Jennie Lee, Mrs. Adelaide Bronti, George Beranger, J. Jiquel Lanoe, Alfred Paget, W. Christy Cabanne, Lionel Barrymore, William J. Butler, William Carroll, Adolph Lestina, W. C. Robinson (In audience); Kate Toncray (Extra)

THE MOTHERING HEART

D. W. Griffith (d); Hazel H. Hubbard ["Mother Love"] (au); G. W. Bitzer (c); begun March, finished April 1913 (f); California (l); 21 June 1913 (r); 1525 feet (rl); LU835 / 14 June 1913 (copyright)

Walter Miller (Husband); Lillian Gish (Wife); Kate Bruce (Her mother); Peggy Pearce (The "Idle Woman"); Charles H. West (Her "New Light"); Adolph Lestina (Doctor); Jennie Lee (Wash customer); Charles Murray, Gertrude Bambrick (Lead dancers); Joseph McDermott, Charles H. West (Among waiters); Harry Hyde, J. Jiquel Lanoe, W. Christy Cabanne, Viola Barry (Outside club); William Elmer (Doorman); Adolph Lestina, John T. Dillon, Henry B. Walthall, Edward Dillon, W. C. Robinson, Charles Hill Mailes, Alfred Paget, William J. Butler, Dell Henderson, J. Jiquel Lanoe, Gus Pixley (Club patrons)

NOTE: According to Moving Picture World, 17 May 1913, p. 690, this took five weeks to film and the club scenes cost $1800 exclusive of salaries. This news item announced that the film would be released at the "odd length" of 1700 feet.

A COMPROMISING COMPLICATION

Dell Henderson (d); William E. Wing ["Busy Bessie"] (au); finished
19 April 1913 (f); California (l); 23 June 1913 (r); one-half reel (rl);
LU839 / 17 June 1913 (copyright)

Fragment: "Bud" Duncan (Bud); William J. Butler (Mayor); Gertrude
Bambrick (Bessie, his daughter); Dave Morris (Sprigly Jones); Ed-
ward Dillon (Bully Boy); Clarence L. Barr, ? (Flirting couple); Gus
Pixley, ? (Second couple)

MR. JEFFERSON GREEN

Dell Henderson (d); Florence Lee (au); finished 17 April 1913 (f);
California (l); 23 June 1913 (r); one-half reel (rl); LU840 / 17 June
1913 (copyright)

Fragment: Charles Murray (Jefferson Green); ? (Mrs. Green); Dave
Morris, Gus Pixley, "Bud" Duncan, Clarence L. Barr, Edward Dillon (Doctors of Dr. White's Sanitarium); Gertrude Bambrick (Among
nurses); ? (Patient)

NOTE: All performers appear in blackface.

IN DIPLOMATIC CIRCLES

Anthony O'Sullivan (d); Frank E. Woods ["Diana Dash, Journalist"]
(au); finished 6 May 1913 (f); California (l); 26 June 1913 (r); 999
feet (rl); LU846 / 19 June 1913 (copyright)

Fragment: Walter Miller (Reporter); William J. Butler (Father);
Nan Christy? (Daughter); Charles H. West (Lover); Lionel Barrymore
(Japanese ambassador); William Courtwright (Secretary of State?);
Harry Hyde (Foreign agent); Harry Carey (Butler); John T. Dillon
(Detective)

HER MOTHER'S OATH

D. W. Griffith (d); D. W. Griffith (au); G. W. Bitzer (c); finished
22 April 1913 (f); California (l); 28 June 1913 (r); 1049 feet (rl);
LU851 / 21 June 1913 (copyright)

Jennie Lee (Mother); Dorothy Gish (Daughter); Henry B. Walthall
(The actor); Frank Opperman (In medicine show); John T. Dillon,
Robert Harron, Charles H. West, Charles Hill Mailes, W. C. Robinson (Medicine show patrons); Charles Hill Mailes (Minister); Robert Harron, Mae Marsh, Alfred Paget, Frank Evans, Charles Gorman, Mrs. Adelaide Bronti, Charles H. West, Adolph Lestina,
Kathleen Butler, John T. Dillon, W. Chrystie Miller, W. C. Robinson (Church congregation); Robert Harron (Messenger); Adolph Les-

tina (Justice of the Peace); Joseph McDermott (Delivery man); Kathleen Butler (Nursemaid); W. Christy Cabanne, Frank Opperman, Charles Gorman (In second crowd); ? (Porter)

NOTE: Reissued by Biograph 6 August 1915.

A GAMBLE WITH DEATH

Anthony O'Sullivan (d); F. W. Randolph (au); finished 10 May 1913 (f); California (l); 30 June 1913 (r); one reel (rl); LU858 / 24 June 1913 (copyright)

Fragment: Walter Miller (Reed); Claire McDowell (Kate); Charles H. West (Gambler); Lionel Barrymore (Jim Benton, the bartender); Harry Carey (Cowpuncher); ? (Other player)

FAUST AND THE LILY

Dell Henderson (d); Florence Lee ["Faust"] (au); finished April 1913 (f); California (l); 3 July 1913 (r); 531 feet (rl); LU862 / 25 June 1913 (copyright)

Fragment: Edward Dillon (Faust); Charles Murray (Margharita); Charles Hill Mailes (Devil); Clarence L. Barr, W. C. Robinson (Among nobles); Gertrude Bambrick (Among maidens)

NOTE: Intertitle: "With apologies to Goethe and Gounod."

AN OLD MAID'S DECEPTION

Dell Henderson (d); Ralph E. Hellawell (au); finished April 1913 (f); California (l); 3 July 1913 (r); 465 feet (rl); LU863 / 25 June 1913 (copyright)

Fragment: Kate Toncray (Beauty); Dave Morris (Sim); Charles Murray (Sam); Clarence L. Barr (Constable Jim Gorman); Edward Dillon, Sylvia Ashton, Gertrude Bambrick, Gus Pixley, Florence Lee (At picnic)

THE SORROWFUL SHORE

D. W. Griffith (d); W. Christy Cabanne ["Sands by the Sea"] (au); G. W. Bitzer (c); finished 29 April 1913 (f); California (l); 5 July 1913 (r); one reel (rl); LU865 / 27 June 1913 (copyright)

Harry Carey (Widowed father); W. Christy Cabanne (His son); Olive Fuller Golden (Orphan); Frank Opperman (Her father); Robert Harron, ? (Son's friends); Mae Marsh, Jennie Lee, Adolph Lestina, J. Jiquel Lanoe, William Courtwright (On shore)

A SEA DOG'S LOVE

Dell Henderson (d); H. C. Bohlander ["A Sailor's Love Affair"] (au); finished 30 April 1913 (f); California (l); 7 July 1913 (r); one-half reel (rl); LU895 / 1 July 1913 (copyright)

Fragment: Dave Morris (Slivers); William Carroll (Mate); Sylvia Ashton? (Widow McManus); Edward Dillon (Panty Smart, the would-be protector); Charles Murray (In bar)

NOTE: Partial cast due to fragment deterioration.

THE NOISY SUITORS

Dell Henderson (d); Edward Acker ["A Boxing Duel"] (au); finished 3 May 1913 (f); California (l); 7 July 1913 (r); one-half reel (rl); LU894 / 1 July 1913 (copyright)

Fragment: Grace Lewis (Bella Donna); Charles Murray (Musician); ? (Maid); Dave Morris (Flutist); Gus Pixley (Jew's harpist); Edward Dillon (Jealous suitor); Clarence L. Barr (At duel)

THE ENEMY'S BABY

Anthony O'Sullivan? (d); B. F. Clinton (au); c. May 1913 (f); California (l); 10 July 1913 (r); one reel (rl); LU900 / 5 July 1913 (copyright)

Fragment: Lionel Barrymore (Ben Brown); ? (His wife); William J. Butler (Sam Miller, the granddad); Kate Bruce (His wife); Harry Carey (Miller); Claire McDowell (His wife); ? (Their baby); William Courtwright, John T. Dillon (Extras)

THE MISTAKE

D. W. Griffith (d); D. W. Griffith (au); G. W. Bitzer (c); finished 12 May 1913 (f); California (l); 12 July 1913 (r); 1031 feet (rl); LU901 / 5 July 1913 (copyright)

Fragment: Blanche Sweet (Young woman); Henry B. Walthall, Charles Hill Mailes (Prospectors); J. Jiquel Lanoe, Charles Gorman, Hector V. Sarno, Harry Hyde (Indians)

NOTE: Reissued by Biograph 22 May 1916.

A GAMBLER'S HONOR

Anthony O'Sullivan (d); Harry Carey ["Brother and Sister"] (au); finished 24 May 1913 (f); California (l); 14 July 1913 (r); 999 feet (rl); LU906 / 8 July 1913 (copyright)

Fragment: Harry Carey (Gambler); Claire McDowell (Beth); Henry B. Walthall (Her brother); John T. Dillon, William Carroll, Charles H. West (In bar); ? (Sheriff); John T. Dillon (Extra)

THE SWEAT-BOX

Dell Henderson (d); Richard Daly ["The Sweat Bath"] (au); finished 10 May 1913 (f); California (l); 17 July 1913 (r); one-half reel (rl); LU919 / 10 July 1913 (copyright)

Fragment: ? (Bridget); Gus Pixley (Isidore); Dave Morris (Dr. Sweatum); Edward Dillon (Ricco); ? (Women); Clarence L. Barr, ? (Policemen)

A CHINESE PUZZLE

Dell Henderson (d); Miss C. Johnson ["The Phoney Chink"] (au); finished 14 May 1913 (f); California (l); 17 July 1913 (r); one-half reel (rl); LU918 / 10 July 1913 (copyright)

Fragment: Gus Pixley, Sylvia Ashton (Parents); Grace Lewis (Daughter); Dave Morris (Her own true love); ? (Chinese cook); ? (Gossipers); ? (Preacher); ? (Neighbors)

DURING THE ROUND-UP

W. Christy Cabanne (d); W. Christy Cabanne (au); finished 31 May 1913 (f); California (l); 19 July 1913 (r); 997 feet (rl); LU922 / 11 July 1913 (copyright)

Fragment: Frank Opperman (The ranchero); Lillian Gish (His daughter); Henry B. Walthall (The stranger); ? (His accomplice); William Carroll (The Mexican); Fred Burns (Foreman); Bob Burns (His brother)

NOTE: Reissued by Biograph 8 May 1916. According to Moving Picture World, 26 July 1913, pp. 415-416, this was the first film Cabanet [sic] directed for Biograph. It was especially noted that he was no longer a Griffith assistant.

PA SAYS

Dell Henderson (d); Anita Loos ["The Queen of the Carnival"] (au); finished 15 May 1913 (f); California (l); 21 July 1913 (r); 465 feet (rl); LU948 / 15 July 1913 (copyright)

NOTE: Cast unidentifiable due to fragment deterioration.

WHILE THE COUNT GOES BATHING

Dell Henderson (d); William Beaudine ["More to be Pitied than Scorned"] (au); finished 19 May 1913 (f); California (l); 21 July 1913 (r); 535 feet (rl); LU947 / 15 July 1913 (copyright)

Fragment: Dell Henderson (The count); Florence Lee (Young woman); Gus Pixley, Sylvia Ashton (Her parents); William Beaudine (The count's friend); ? (Preacher); Edward Dillon, Clarence L. Barr (Family friends)

THE MIRROR

Anthony O'Sullivan (d); Frank E. Woods (au); finished 31 May 1913 (f); California (l); 24 July 1913 (r); 977 feet (rl); LU951 / 17 July 1913 (copyright)

Fragment: Henry B. Walthall (Station agent); Claire McDowell (Daisy); Lionel Barrymore (Her father); Harry Carey, Charles H. West, John T. Dillon (Tramps); ? (Debtor)

THE COMING OF ANGELO

D. W. Griffith (d); D. W. Griffith (au); G. W. Bitzer (c); finished 28 May 1913 (f); California (l); 26 July 1913 (r); 1000 feet (rl); LU965 / 19 July 1913 (copyright)

Fragment: Blanche Sweet (Theresa); Charles Hill Mailes (Gudio); Adolph Lestina, Jennie Lee (Theresa's parents); Walter Miller (Angelo); Kathleen Butler, ? (Theresa's friends)

NOTE: Reissued by Biograph 29 October 1915.

THE VENGEANCE OF GALORA

Anthony O'Sullivan (d); Lionel Barrymore ["Nick of Time"] (au); finished 7 June 1913 (f); California (l); 28 July 1913 (r); 1011 feet (rl); LU990 / 24 July 1913 (copyright)

Fragment: Claire McDowell (Galora); Charles H. West (The express agent); Nan Christy? (His fiancée); Harry Carey, ? (Prospectors); John T. Dillon (Sheriff); ? (In town)

THOSE LITTLE FLOWERS

Dell Henderson (d); Marion Leonard (au); c. May 1913 (f); California (l); 31 July 1913 (r); one-half reel (rl); LU997 / 25 July 1913 (copyright)

Fragment: Gus Pixley (Mr. Ronald G. Saunders); Kate Toncray (Mrs. Saunders); Clarence L. Barr (Music grinder); Gertrude Bambrick (Marguerite Fleischer); ? (Maid); Dorothy Gish (Messenger); ? (Woman); ? (In flower shop)

MR. SPRIGGS BUYS A DOG

Dell Henderson (d); Frank B. Gribbin ["Jones Buys a Dog"] (au); finished 23 May 1913 (f); California (l); 31 July 1913 (r); 448 feet (rl); LU998 / 25 July 1913 (copyright)

Fragment: Clarence L. Barr (Mr. Spriggs); ? (His wife); ? (Their two daughters); ? (Policemen); Gertrude Bambrick, William Beaudine, John T. Dillon (On street); Edward Dillon, Kate Toncray (In police station)

WHEN LOVE FORGIVES

Anthony O'Sullivan? (d); Lulu S. Vollmer (au); finished December 1912 (f); New York (l); 2 August 1913 (r); 680 feet (rl); LU1001 / 26 July 1913 (copyright)

Fragment: Charles H. West (Man); ? (Woman); George Beranger (Bartender); Charles Gorman, Harry Carey (Criminals); Charles Hill Mailes (Employer)

THE MONUMENT

Anthony O'Sullivan (d); Anthony O'Sullivan (au); c. June 1913 (f); California (l); 2 August 1913 (r); one-quarter reel (rl); LU1000 / 26 July 1913 (copyright)

Fragment: ? (Son); W. Chrystie Miller, ? (Gravediggers); John T. Dillon (At gravesite)

THE WIDOW'S KIDS

Dell Henderson (d); Anita Loos ["A Hicksville Romance"] (au); finished 29 May 1913 (f); California (l); 4 August 1913 (r); 439 feet (rl); LU1046 / 31 July 1913 (copyright)

Fragment: Kate Toncray (Mary Ann, the widow); Dave Morris (Soon-to-be father); Dell Henderson (The traveling man); ? (Women on street); Gertrude Bambrick, Dorothy Gish (The kids); ? (Arabella); "Bud" Duncan (Minister)

CUPID AND THE COOK

Dell Henderson (d); Edward Dillon ["Love Finds a Way"] (au); finished

30 May 1913 (f); California (l); 4 August 1913 (r); 558 feet (rl); LU1045 / 31 July 1913 (copyright)

Fragment: Clarence L. Barr (Policeman); Kate Toncray (Cook); Gertrude Bambrick (Young woman); Edward Dillon (Suitor); Sylvia Ashton, William J. Butler (Her parents)

UNDER THE SHADOW OF THE LAW

Anthony O'Sullivan (d); Harry Carey ["Jimmy's Finish"] (au); finished 17 June 1913 (f); California (l); 7 August 1913 (r); 999 feet (rl); LU1060 / 1 August 1913 (copyright)

Fragment: Harry Carey (Convict); Charles H. West (John Haywood, a clerk); Claire McDowell (His sister); Lionel Barrymore (Charles Darnton, employer); Walter Miller (Bookkeeper); Kate Toncray (Mother); John T. Dillon (Doctor); Nan Christy?, ? (Nurses); ? (Police commissioner)

THE REFORMERS, or THE LOST ART OF MINDING ONE'S BUSINESS

D. W. Griffith (d); Frank E. Woods ["The Awakening of Modeltown"] (au); G. W. Bitzer (c); finished 6 July 1913 (f); California/New York (l); 9 August 1913 (r); 1553 feet (rl); LU1074 / 7 August 1913 (copyright)

Charles Hill Mailes, Jennie Lee (Parents); Robert Harron, Mae Marsh (Children); Kate Bruce (Maid); Walter Miller (The Bad Influence); Kate Toncray, Adolph Lestina, J. Jiquel Lanoe, Kathleen Butler, Gertrude Bambrick (League of Civic Purity); William Courtwright (Indigent man); Harry Hyde (At rally); Harry Hyde, Alfred Paget (In campaign audience); ? (Streetwalkers); William J. Butler (Man with pipe); ? (Maid's beau); Frank Evans, ? (Policemen); W. C. Robinson, Dave Morris (In bar); Charles H. West, William J. Butler, Joseph McDermott, W. C. Robinson, Harry Hyde, William Elmer, Charles Gorman (At dance); Charles Murray (Among musicians); Charles Murray, W. Chrystie Miller, Elmo Lincoln, Joseph McDermott (In theater audience); Gus Pixley, Dave Morris (Minstrels); Alfred Paget (In Othello scene); Dorothy Gish, Gertrude Bambrick (Terpsichore); ? (Vaudeville manager); Alfred Paget (Movie theater manager); William Courtwright, Elmo Lincoln (Bootleggers); William J. Butler (On street)

NOTE: Reissued by Biograph 20 June 1916.

I WAS MEANT FOR YOU

Anthony O'Sullivan (d); Harvey H. Gates (au); finished 21 June 1913 (f); California (l); 11 August 1913 (r); 999 feet (rl); LU1076 / 8 August 1913 (copyright)

Fragment: Charles H. West (Theron); Claire McDowell (Lavina); Harry Carey (Luke); ? (Susan); Lionel Barrymore (Lavina's father); John T. Dillon (In town)

COME SEBEN, LEBEN

Dell Henderson (d); Edward Dillon (au); finished 4 June 1913 (f); California (l); 14 August 1913 (r); 641 feet (rl); LU1078 / 9 August 1913 (copyright)

Fragment: Dave Morris (Mr. Toot Williams); Gus Pixley (Rufus); ? (Wife); ? (Dice thrower); Clarence L. Barr (The Law); ? (Women); ? (Other players)

PAPA'S BABY

Dell Henderson (d); Walter B. Hay ["At High Tide"] (au); finished 12 June 1913 (f); California (l); 14 August 1913 (r); 353 feet (rl); LU1077 / 9 August 1913 (copyright)

Fragment: Dell Henderson (Papa Binks); Sylvia Ashton (Ma Binks); Dave Morris, ? (Policemen); ? (Nurse); William Beaudine, Dorothy Gish (Young parents); Clarence L. Barr (Rescuer)

AN INDIAN'S LOYALTY

W. Christy Cabanne? (d); Fred Burns ["The Loyal Indian"] (au); finished 5 June 1913 (f); California (l); 16 August 1913 (r); 1000 feet (rl); LU1085 / 11 August 1913 (copyright)

Fragment: Frank Opperman (Ranchero); Lillian Gish (His daughter); Edward Dillon (Young foreman); Eagle Eye (Indian); Fred Burns (Ranchhand); Lionel Barrymore (Cattle buyer); William Carroll (Accomplice)

NOTE: Reissued by Biograph 2 October 1916.

THE SUFFRAGETTE MINSTRELS

Dell Henderson (d); Dorothy Gish ["A Lesson in Burlesque"] (au); finished 7 June 1913 (f); California (l); 18 August 1913 (r); 466 feet (rl); LU1097 / 13 August 1913 (copyright)

Fragment: Dorothy Gish, Gertrude Bambrick (Among suffragette minstrels); William J. Butler, Charles Murray, William Beaudine, Dave Morris, Gus Pixley, Frank Evans, William Courtwright, Elmo Lincoln, Edward Dillon, William Elmer (In audience); Dell Henderson (At theater); ? (Old man); Kate Toncray, Sylvia Ashton (Old women)

FATHER'S CHICKEN DINNER

Dell Henderson (d); Beatrice Prucha ["A Deacon Keen"] (au); finished 11 June 1913 (f); California (l); 18 August 1913 (r); 531 feet (rl); LU1095 / 13 August 1913 (copyright)

Fragment: Clarence L. Barr (Ferdinand Fiction, author); Dave Morris (His father); ? (Police sergeant); ? (Maid); ? (Mrs. Fiction); Charles Murray, Gus Pixley (Policemen); Charles H. West (Butcher)

THE WORK HABIT

Anthony O'Sullivan (d); O. A. Nelson (au); finished 11 July 1913 (f); New York (l); 21 August 1913 (r); 999 feet (rl); LU1096 / 13 August 1913 (copyright)

Fragment: Lionel Barrymore (Father); Kathleen Butler (Mother); ? (Daughter on farm); Claire McDowell (Daughter in the city); W. Chrystie Miller (Street sweeper); Kate Bruce (His wife); Charles Hill Mailes (Street commissioner); John T. Dillon (Among street sweepers); ? (At party); William J. Butler (Visitor)

TWO MEN OF THE DESERT

D. W. Griffith (d); D. W. Griffith (au); G. W. Bitzer (c); finished 8 June 1913 (f); California (l); 23 August 1913 (r); 1037 feet (rl); LU1106 / 14 August 1913 (copyright)

Fragment: Blanche Sweet (Authoress); ? (Her mother); Henry B. Walthall, Walter Miller (The partners); Alfred Paget (Indian); Jennie Lee (Old Indian woman); ? (Baby)

NOTE: Reissued by Biograph 25 December 1916.

THE CROOK AND THE GIRL

Anthony O'Sullivan (d); Emil Kruschke (au); finished 21 July 1913 (f); New York (l); 25 August 1913 (r); 1000 feet (rl); LU1107 / 14 August 1913 (copyright)

Fragment: ? (Uncle); Lionel Barrymore (Nephew); ? (Maid); Hector Dion (Butler); Claire McDowell (Uncle's adopted daughter); William J. Butler (Lawyer); Harry Carey (Crook)

OBJECTIONS OVERRULED

Dell Henderson (d); George Hennessy ["A Guilty Conscience"] (au); finished 20 June 1913 (f); California (l); 28 August 1913 (r); 472 feet (rl); LU1125 / 18 August 1913 (copyright)

Fragment: Clarence L. Barr (Paul); Gertrude Bambrick (Young woman); Kate Toncray (Mother); Charles Murray (Father); Dave Morris (Lawyer); ? (Policeman); Florence Lee, Sylvia Ashton (Extras)

BLACK AND WHITE

Dell Henderson (d); William Beaudine (au); finished 14 June 1913 (f); California (l); 28 August 1913 (r); 524 feet (rl); LU1195 / 18 August 1913 (copyright)

Fragment: Dave Morris (Tramp); ? (Black man); ? (Black woman); Clarence L. Barr (Gardener); ? (Sheriff)

THE ADOPTED BROTHER

D. W. Griffith, W. Christy Cabanne (co-d); W. Christy Cabanne (au); finished 15 July 1913 (f); California/New York? (l); 30 August 1913 (r); 998 feet (rl); LU1124 / 18 August 1913 (copyright)

Fragment: Robert Harron (Adopted brother); W. Chrystie Miller (Father); Dorothy Gish (Daughter); Elmer Booth (Son); Charles Gorman (His friend); William Carroll (Drunk); ? (In bar); W. C. Robinson (Outside bar); George Beranger (Employer); ? (Workmen); Fred Burns?, Adolph Lestina (Outside sheriff's office); ? (Guards)

NOTE: Reissued by Biograph 21 August 1916.

AMONG CLUB FELLOWS

Dell Henderson (d); William E. Wing ["Harold, the Desperado"] (au); finished November 1912 (f); California (l); 1 September 1913 (r); 442 feet (rl); LU1207 / 5 September 1913 (copyright)

Fragment: William Carroll (Reggie); Edward Dillon ("The Heartbreaker"); Grace Lewis (Reggie's sweetheart); William J. Butler, Gus Pixley, Clarence L. Barr, Frank Opperman (In club); "Bud" Duncan (Club porter); Kate Toncray (Woman with policeman)

EDWIN'S BADGE OF HONOR

Dell Henderson (d); Laura B. Chandler? ["The Cure"]/Paul West? (au); finished 7 December 1912 (f); California (l); 1 September 1913 (r); 554 feet (rl); LU1206 / 5 September 1913 (copyright)

Fragment: Charles Murray (Edwin); Gus Pixley (A prisoner); Edward Dillon, ? (Guards); Clarence L. Barr (Third prisoner)

NOTE: Laura B. Chandler is identified as the author in the production records at the Museum of Modern Art. Paul West is identified as the author in the Catalogue of Copyright Entries: 1912-1939.

A WOMAN IN THE ULTIMATE

Dell Henderson (d); William E. Wing (au); finished 16 July 1913 (f); New York (l); 4 September 1913 (r); 999 feet (rl); LU1211 / 6 September 1913 (copyright)

Fragment: Lillian Gish (Verda); Charles Hill Mailes (Her stepfather); Henry B. Walthall, Alfred Paget, John T. Dillon, Joseph McDermott (Badger Gang); ? (Dancers); ? (Policeman)

THE STRONG MAN'S BURDEN

Anthony O'Sullivan (d); George Hennessy (au); finished 25 July 1913 (f); New York (l); 6 September 1913 (r); 1000 feet (rl); LU1215 / 8 September 1913 (copyright)

Fragment: Kate Bruce (Mother); Harry Carey (Bob, her son); Lionel Barrymore (John, her son); William J. Butler (Doctor); Claire McDowell (Nurse); ? (In bar); ? (Woman)

NOTE: Partial cast due to fragment deterioration.

A MODEST HERO

Dell Henderson (d); George Hennessy (au); finished 22 July 1913 (f); New York (l); 8 September 1913 (r); 1000 feet (rl); LU1216 / 8 September 1913 (copyright)

Fragment: Walter Miller (Husband); Lillian Gish (Wife); ? (Mother); Charles Hill Mailes, John T. Dillon (Thieves); Charles H. West (Crook/Cleaning man); Alfred Paget, ? (Policemen)

NOTE: Partial cast due to fragment deterioration.

BABY INDISPOSED

Dell Henderson (d); Charles S. Wheaton ["Mr. Smith's Baby"] (au); finished 17 June 1913 (f); California (l); 11 September 1913 (r); 406 feet (rl); LU1222 / 10 September 1913 (copyright)

Fragment: Charles Murray (Papa); Florence Lee (Mama); ? (Nurse); Sylvia Ashton (In office); Gus Pixley (Messenger); Clarence L. Barr, Gertrude Bambrick (On street); Kate Toncray (In sidecar); Dave Morris (Powder-puff thief)

THE LADY IN BLACK

Dell Henderson (d); Anita Loos ["The Mayor Elect"] (au); finished
24 June 1913 (f); California (l); 11 September 1913 (r); 592 feet (rl);
LU1227 / 10 September 1913 (copyright)

Fragment: Charles Murray (The villain); Gertrude Bambrick (His
che-eld); Dorothy Gish (The girl); Edward Dillon (Her sweetheart);
Dave Morris (Her father)

AN UNJUST SUSPICION

W. Christy Cabanne (d); Harry O. Hoyt (au); finished 29 July 1913
(f); New York (l); 13 September 1913 (r); 998 feet (rl); LU1233 / 11
September 1913 (copyright)

Fragment: Alfred Paget (Ex-convict); Elmer Booth (Detective); ?
(His wife); ? (Their child); Robert Harron (On beach); Fred Burns
(Policeman); ? (Thieves)

NOTE: Partial cast due to fragment deterioration.

HIS HOODOO

Edward Dillon (d); Anita Loos ["The Making of a Masher"] (au);
finished 11 July 1913 (f); New York (l); 15 September 1913 (r); 513
feet (rl); LU1247 / 13 September 1913 (copyright)

Fragment: Charles Murray (Floorwalker); ? (His Hoodoo); Gertrude
Bambrick, Gus Pixley (Couple); William J. Butler (In club); ? (In
store); J. Waltham (Policeman); Dave Morris, ? (Tough couple)

DAN GREEGAN'S GHOST

Dell Henderson (d); Stanner E. V. Taylor (au); finished 23 June 1913
(f); California (l); 15 September 1913 (r); 407 feet (rl); LU1248 / 13
September 1913 (copyright)

Fragment: Gus Pixley (Dan Greegan); ? (His wife); Clarence L.
Barr (In work crew); Dave Morris (A Dago)

THE STOLEN TREATY

Anthony O'Sullivan (d); Julia M. Purdy (au); finished 2 August 1913
(f); New York (l); 18 September 1913 (r); 999 feet (rl); LU1246 / 13
September 1913 (copyright)

Fragment: Lionel Barrymore (Japanese diplomat); Claire McDowell

(Olga); Reggie Morris (Her friend); William J. Butler (Diplomat); Harry Carey (Detective); ? (Maid); ? (Treaty signatories)

NOTE: Shot number two contains an insert of The Washington Post, 28 July 1913.

FOR THE SON OF THE HOUSE

Dell Henderson (d); T. P. Bayer ["The Acid Test"] (au); finished 16 July 1913 (f); New York (l); 20 September 1913 (r); 1000 feet (rl); LU1260 / 17 September 1913 (copyright)

Fragment: Mae Marsh (The girl); Charles H. West (The son); ? (The mother); John T. Dillon, ? (The temptors); Charles Hill Mailes (Minister); Clara T. Bracey (In mission); Kate Bruce, Gertrude Bambrick, Florence Lee (In garment factory); Charles Murray, Jack Pickford (In gambling hall); ? (Valet); Frank M. Norcross, ? (Policemen)

NOTE: Reissued by Biograph 11 September 1916.

THE LAW AND HIS SON

Anthony O'Sullivan (d); George A. Posner ["The Law and the Man"] (au); finished 13 August 1913 (f); New York (l); 22 September 1913 (r); 999 feet (rl); LU1265 / 19 September 1913 (copyright)

Fragment: Harry Carey (Manning); Claire McDowell (Marguerite, his sister); Reggie Morris (The outcast son); William J. Butler (His father); ? (Manning's parents); Hector V. Sarno (In club); Frank Evans (Prison official); ? (At reception)

A SATURDAY HOLIDAY

Edward Dillon (d); Pearson Barrows (au); finished 21 July 1913 (f); New York (l); 25 September 1913 (r); 550 feet (rl); LU1271 / 20 September 1913 (copyright)

Fragment: Gus Pixley (Harry Hurry-up); Gertrude Bambrick (His sweetheart); Hector V. Sarno, W. C. Robinson, ? (Policemen); Kathleen Butler (In office); Walter P. Lewis (Sheriff?); Dave Morris (Pawnbroker); Kate Toncray (Landlady)

THE END OF THE WORLD

Edward Dillon (d); Ralph E. Hellawell (au); finished 15 July 1913 (f); New York (l); 25 September 1913 (r); 450 feet (rl); LU1272 / 20 September 1913 (copyright)

Fragment: Charles Murray, Dave Morris, Gus Pixley (Tramps);
Walter P. Lewis (The Prophet); Kathleen Butler, Gertrude Bambrick
(Among the Holy Groaners)

THE INFLUENCE OF THE UNKNOWN

W. Christy Cabanne (d); Frank B. Gribbin (au); finished 30 July 1913
(f); New York (l); 27 September 1913 (r); 1057 feet (rl); LU1288 /
24 September 1913 (copyright)

Fragment: Mae Marsh (Young woman); Robert Harron (Her sweetheart); Henry B. Walthall, Fred Burns, ? (Revenue officers); Dark
Cloud? (Old Moonshiner)

NOTE: Reissued by Biograph 27 November 1916.

DYED BUT NOT DEAD

Edward Dillon (d); F. Schliebitz ["They Dye But Are Not Dead"]
(au); finished 26 July 1913 (f); New York (l); 29 September 1913 (r);
449 feet (rl); LU1311 / 27 September 1913 (copyright)

Fragment: Charles Murray (Tramp); Gus Pixley (Dad Binks); Kate
Toncray (Mom Binks); Edna Foster, ? (Daughters); ? (Maid); ?
(Her caller); Walter P. Lewis, Dave Morris (Policemen)

WITH THE AID OF PHRENOLOGY

Edward Dillon (d); Donald D. Garcelon ["The Triumph of Phrenology"]
(au); finished 5 August 1913 (f); New York (l); 29 September 1913
(r); 551 feet (rl); LU1312 / 27 September 1913 (copyright)

Fragment: Charles Murray (Husband); ? (Wife); Dave Morris (Strong-
man); ? (Professor of phrenology); Kathleen Butler (Suffragette)

A TENDER-HEARTED CROOK

Anthony O'Sullivan (d); James G. Steven? ["A Man's a Man"]/I. P.
Dodge? (au); finished 16 August 1913 (f); New York (l); 2 October
1913 (r); 998 feet (rl); LU1318 / 29 September 1913 (copyright)

Fragment: Charles H. West (James); Claire McDowell (Edith); Harry
Carey (Thief); Hector Dion (Minister); ? (At party)

NOTE: James G. Steven is identified as the author in the production
records at the Museum of Modern Art. I. P. Dodge is identified as
the author in the Catalogue of Copyright Entries: 1912-1939.

THE CHIEFTAIN'S SONS

W. Christy Cabanne (d); W. Christy Cabanne (au); finished 7 August 1913 (f); New York (l); 4 October 1913 (r); 998 feet (rl); LU1337 / 2 October 1913 (copyright)

Fragment: ? (Old chief); Alfred Paget, Dark Cloud, ? (His three sons); ? (Indian girl); W. C. Robinson, Charles Gorman, Hector V. Sarno, Eagle Eye? (In tribe)

HIS SECRET

Lionel Barrymore? (d); Paul L. Feltus ["Two Ways"] (au); finished 22 August 1913 (f); New York (l); 6 October 1913 (r); 999 feet (rl); LU1340 / 4 October 1913 (copyright)

NOTE: Cast unidentifiable due to fragment deterioration.

NEVER KNOWN TO SMILE

Edward Dillon (d); Frank H. Clark ["Why Don't You Laugh?"] (au); finished 12 August 1913 (f); New York (l); 9 October 1913 (r); 450 feet (rl); LU1345 / 7 October 1913 (copyright)

Fragment: Charles Murray (O'Brien); ? (Mrs. O'Brien); ? (Miss Allen); Kathleen Butler, Gus Pixley (At picnic)

NOTE: Partial cast due to fragment deterioration.

SCENTING A TERRIBLE CRIME

Edward Dillon (d); E. Lynn Summers (au); finished 1 August 1913 (f); New York (l); 9 October 1913 (r); 549 feet (rl); LU1346 / 7 October 1913 (copyright)

Dave Morris (Husband); Kate Toncray (Wife); Charles Murray, ? (Policemen); Kathleen Butler, ? (Women); Gus Pixley (Coroner); ? (His assistants); Max Davidson (Superintendent)

SO RUNS THE WAY

W. Christy Cabanne (d); W. Christy Cabanne (au); finished 18 August 1913 (f); New York (l); 11 October 1913 (r); 998 feet (rl); LU1356 / 9 October 1913 (copyright)

Fragment: Reggie Morris (Frederick A. Paulson); ? (His popular sister); Lillian Gish (Young woman); ? (Aspiring mother); W. C. Robinson (Butler); Kate Toncray (At party); Joseph McDermott (Detective)

McGANN AND HIS OCTETTE

Edward Dillon (d); Jane Norton ["Retaliation"] (au); finished 16 August 1913 (f); New York (l); 13 October 1913 (r); 494 feet (rl); LU1381 / 11 October 1913 (copyright)

Fragment: Gus Pixley (Ikey Goldstein); Charles Murray (Dan Mc-Gann); ? (Mrs. McGann); Gertrude Bambrick, Gladys Egan (Their children); ? (Judge Denis J. O'Reilly); ? (Policemen)

AUNTS, TOO MANY

Edward Dillon (d); Frank B. Gribbin ["Suffragettic Ma"] (au); finished 20 August 1913 (f); New York (l); 13 October 1913 (r); 505 feet (rl); LU1382 / 11 October 1913 (copyright)

Fragment: Edward Dillon (Peter Jay, a newlywed); Gertrude Bambrick (Mrs. Jay); ? (Auntie Jane); Gus Pixley (Krazy-Nutt); Joseph Schrode (Front of horse); James Harris (Back of horse); ? (Maid); ? (Policemen)

NOTE: Schrode and Harris are identified as the horse in New York Dramatic Mirror, 29 October 1913, p. 39.

RED AND PETE, PARTNERS

Anthony O'Sullivan (d); George Hennessy ["Honor of Thieves"] (au); finished 23 October 1913 (f); New York (l); 16 October 1913 (r); 997 feet (rl); LU1396 / 13 October 1913 (copyright)

Fragment: Franklin B. Ritchie, ? (Red and Pete); Charles H. West (Husband); ? (Wife); ? (Maid); ? (Hogan); Gladys Egan (His daughter); ? (In office); ? (Neighbors); ? (Policemen)

THE GIRL ACROSS THE WAY

W. Christy Cabanne (d); W. Christy Cabanne (au); finished 26 August 1913 (f); New York (l); 18 October 1913 (r); 996 feet (rl); LU1418 / 17 October 1913 (copyright)

Fragment: Mae Marsh (Girl); W. Chrystie Miller (Her father); Robert Harron (Boy); Lillian Langdon (His mother); Mildred Manning (Visiting cousin); Joseph McDermott, William Carroll (At inn)

NOTE: Reissued by Biograph 5 June 1916.

THE VAN NOSTRAND TIARA

Anthony O'Sullivan? (d); Clarence A. Frambers (au); finished 1

September 1913 (f); New York (1); 20 October 1913 (r); 1014 feet (rl);
LU1435 / 21 October 1913 (copyright)

Fragment: Reggie Morris (Raffles); Claire McDowell (Kate); Harry
Carey (Society detective); ? (Mrs. Van Nostrand); ? (Her friends);
? (Servants)

A FALLEN HERO

Edward Dillon (d); Anita Loos (au); finished 28 August 1913 (f); New
York (1); 23 October 1913 (r); 595 feet (rl); LU1442 / 23 October
1913 (copyright)

Gus Pixley (Sammy Getup); Charles Murray (Arnold, the judge); ?
(Mathilda); ? (Wiggins); John T. Dillon, ? (Friends); ? (In band); ?
(In audience)

THE WINNING PUNCH

Edward Dillon (d); D. B. John ["The Silver Tea"] (au); finished 23
August 1913 (f); New York (1); 23 October 1913 (r); 400 feet (rl);
LU1441 / 23 October 1913 (copyright)

Fragment: Charles Murray (Deacon Hicks); Gertrude Bambrick
(Gertie); Reggie Morris (Bud); Kate Toncray (Neighbor); Walter P.
Lewis, ? (Creditors); ? (At social)

THE MADONNA OF THE STORM

Alfred Paget? (d); M. B. Havey ["Out of the Storm"] (au); finished
28 August 1913 (f); New York (1); 25 October 1913 (r); 999 feet (rl);
LU1456 / 25 October 1913 (copyright)

Fragment: Lillian Gish (Mother); Charles Hill Mailes (Father); J.
Jiquel Lanoe (Club-man); ? (The demi-monde); W. C. Robinson
(Waiter); ? (At club)

AN EVENING WITH WILDER SPENDER

? (d); Irma Skinner ["Aunt Hannah Arrives"] (au); finished 8 September
1913 (f); New York (1); 27 October 1913 (r); 993 feet (rl); LU1463 /
27 October 1913 (copyright)

Fragment: Edward Dillon (Wilder Spender); ? (Dottie Dewdrop);
Charles Murray (Her uncle); ? (Aunt Alice); ? (Spender's friends)

A BARBER CURE

Edward Dillon (d); Robert A. Donaldson ["The Count and the Barber"] (au); finished 11 September 1913 (f); New York (l); 30 October 1913 (r); 570 feet (rl); LU1500 / 30 October 1913 (copyright)

Fragment: Gus Pixley (The barber); ? (Flossie Fluff); Charles Murray (The count); ? (Flossie's father); ? (Barber's assistant); ? (Customer); ? (Maid)

BOARDERS AND BOMBS

Edward Dillon (d); Fred Hayn ["The Anarchist Plot"] (au); finished 16 September 1913 (f); New York (l); 30 October 1913 (r); 428 feet (rl); LU1499 / 30 October 1913 (copyright)

Fragment: Charles Murray, Gus Pixley (Members of "The Hamfats," an acting company); ? (Landlord); ? (Landlady); ? (Good citizens)

THE STOPPED CLOCK

Anthony O'Sullivan (d); Frank E. Woods (au); finished 8 September 1913 (f); New York (l); 1 November 1913 (r); 1003 feet (rl); LU1517 / 3 November 1913 (copyright)

Fragment: ? (Antique dealer); Claire McDowell (His daughter); Charles H. West (Senior clerk); Reggie Morris (Junior clerk); Kate Bruce (Mother); Frank Evans, Joseph McDermott (Policemen); Hector Dion (Doctor); Harry Carey (Detective?); W. Chrystie Miller (Extra)

DIVERSION

Anthony O'Sullivan (d); M. Shannon Fife (au); finished 15 September 1913 (f); New York (l); 3 November 1913 (r); 1000 feet (rl); LU1533 / 6 November 1913 (copyright)

Fragment: Henry B. Walthall (Mr. Wilson); Claire McDowell (Mrs. Wilson); ? (Child); Reggie Morris, ? (Rich couple); Joseph McDermott (In office)

IN THE HANDS OF THE BLACK HANDS

Edward Dillon (d); Will S. Gidley ["A Black Hand Affair"] (au); finished 2 September 1913 (f); New York (l); 6 November 1913 (r); 598 feet (rl); LU1540 / 8 November 1913 (copyright)

New York Dramatic Mirror advertisement: Charles Murray [blackface] (Servant); ? (Woman)

NOTE: Partial cast due to fragment deterioration.

WHERE'S THE BABY?

Lionel Barrymore? (d); Beatrice Buch (au);/ finished 4 September 1913 (f); New York (l); 6 November 1913 (r); 417 feet (rl); LU1542 / 8 November 1913 (copyright)

NOTE: Cast unidentifiable due to fragment deterioration.

"OLD COUPONS"

Anthony O'Sullivan (d); Edward McWade (au); finished 23 September 1913 (f); New York (l); 8 November 1913 (r); 1005 feet (rl); LU1556 / 10 November 1913 (copyright)

Fragment: ? (Thomas Edsall, "Old Coupons"); ? (Thomas Tracey); Charles H. West, Joseph McDermott (Gang members); Edna Foster, Marie Newton (Newsboys); Reggie Morris (At counter); ? (Workmen); Frank Evans (Policeman)

NO PLACE FOR FATHER

Lionel Barrymore? (d); H. L. Johnson (au); finished 23 September 1913 (f); New York (l); 10 November 1913 (r); 1004 feet (rl); LU1564 / 12 November 1913 (copyright)

Fragment: Antonio Moreno (Son); ? (Father); J. Jiquel Lanoe, Hector Dion, ? (Son's friends); ? (Young woman); Walter P. Lewis, ? (Father's friends); Kathleen Butler, ? (Nurses)

MRS. CASEY'S GORILLA

Edward Dillon (d); William J. Rackham ["Casey's Gorilla"] (au); finished 27 September 1913 (f); New York (l); 13 November 1913 (r); 662 feet (rl); LU1588 / 14 November 1913 (copyright)

New York Dramatic Mirror advertisement: Kate Toncray?

NOTE: Cast unidentifiable due to fragment deterioration.

"MIXED NUTS"

Edward Dillon (d); Edward Dillon (au); finished 23 September 1913 (f); New York (l); 13 November 1913 (r); 337 feet (rl); LU1589 / 14 November 1913 (copyright)

Charles Murray (Hamlet/Romeo)

NOTE: Charles Murray identified in Moving Picture World, 29 November 1913, "Comments on the Films" column. Remainder of cast unidentifiable due to fragment deterioration.

206 / D. W. Griffith

HIS INSPIRATION

W. Christy Cabanne (d); W. Christy Cabanne (au); finished 2 October
1913 (f); New York (l); 15 November 1913 (r); 1001 feet (rl); LU1590
/ 17 November 1913 (copyright)

Fragment: Alan Hale (Artist); Irene Howley (His inspiration); ?
(The girl); Alfred Paget (Her husband); Charles Gorman, Hector
Dion (At party)

A CURE FOR SUFFRAGETTES

Edward Dillon? (d); Anita Loos (au); finished 24 September 1913
(f); New York (l); 17 November 1913 (r); 405 feet (rl); LU1630 / 20
November 1913 (copyright)

Fragment: Kathleen Butler (Among suffragettes)

HE'S A LAWYER

Edward Dillon? (d); Alta M. Coultas ["Pull Down the Curtain"] (au);
finished 3 October 1913 (f); New York (l); 17 November 1913 (r);
595 feet (rl); LU1631 / 20 November 1913 (copyright)

Fragment: Charles Murray (U. R. Dunn, lawyer); Walter V. Coyle
(G. M. Barker, broker); ? (His wife); Louise Orth (Dunn's secretary)

THE DETECTIVE'S STRATAGEM

Anthony O'Sullivan (d); John J. A. Gibney ["A Desperate Capture"]
(au); finished 3 October 1913 (f); New York (l); 20 November 1913
(r); 1000 feet (rl); LU1632 / 20 November 1913 (copyright)

Fragment: Reggie Morris (Bank clerk); Claire McDowell (Kate, his
sweetheart); Harry Carey (Keene, the detective); ? (Bank president);
Charles H. West, Joseph McDermott (Plotters); Raoul Walsh?
(Gang's driver); Hector V. Sarno (Bartender); Frank Evans (Policeman); Frank M. Norcross (In detective agency)

BY MAN'S LAW

W. Christy Cabanne (d); William E. Wing ["Souls Adrift"] (au);
finished 5 October 1913 (f); New York (l); 22 November 1913 (r);
1600 feet (rl); LU1644 / 22 November 1913 (copyright)

Charles Hill Mailes (Oil magnate); Alfred Paget (His son); Mildred
Manning (His daughter); Donald Crisp, Mae Marsh, Alan Hale
(Brother and sister owners); Frank Evans, Guy Hedlund (Magnate's

aides); Robert Harron (Young boy); Antonio Moreno (Procurer); ?
(Streetwalker); ? (Members of reform society); Frank M. Norcross?
(Judge); J. Jiquel Lanoe (In court); Edward N. Hoyt, ? (Magnate's
servants); Dorothy Gish, Kathleen Butler, Clara T. Bracey (At
league meeting); Charles Gorman (Driver); ? (Old man turned away);
? (Man posting sign); ? (At reform school)

NOTE: Reissued by Biograph 18 July 1916.

ALL FOR SCIENCE

Anthony O'Sullivan (d); Albert Glassmire ["The Eternal Woman"] (au);
finished 15 October 1913 (f); New York (l); 24 November 1913 (r);
1070 feet (rl); LU1665 / 26 November 1913 (copyright)

Fragment: Reggie Morris (Chemist); Harry Carey (Young man); ?
(Old man); Joseph McDermott (Detective); Claire McDowell, Lionel
Barrymore (In detective agency); Charles H. West (In restaurant)

NOTE: Partial cast due to fragment deterioration.

A CIRCUMSTANTIAL HERO

Edward Dillon (d); H. S. Thompson ["Mr. No Courage"] (au); finished 8 August 1913 (f); New York (l); 27 November 1913 (r); 390
feet (rl); LU1683 / 29 November 1913 (copyright)

Fragment: Gertrude Bambrick (Woman); ? (Man); ? (On porch)

THE SOMNAMBULISTS

Edward Dillon (d); Aaron E. Bishop (au); finished 10 October 1913
(f); New York (l); 27 November 1913 (r); 638 feet (rl); LU1682 /
29 November 1913 (copyright)

Fragment: Charles Murray (Mr. Hennessy); ? (His wife); ? (Von
Meyer); ? (His wife); ? (Policemen)

THE BLUE OR THE GRAY

W. Christy Cabanne (d); W. Christy Cabanne (au); finished 15 October
1913 (f); New York (l); 29 November 1913 (r); 1009 feet (rl); LU1681
/ 29 November 1913 (copyright)

Fragment: Robert Harron (Southern boy); Irene Howley (Northern
girl); W. Chrystie Miller (Her uncle); Donald Crisp, Bob Burns (The
rivals); Clara T. Bracey (The girl's aunt); Frank M. Norcross,
Charles Gorman (Northerners); ? (Cousins)

NOTE: Reissued by Biograph 3 July 1916. Partial cast due to fragment deterioration.

HOW THE DAY WAS SAVED

Edward Dillon (d); Anita Loos (au); finished 16 October 1913 (f); New York (l); 1 December 1913 (r); 407 feet (rl); LU1687 / 1 December 1913 (copyright)

Fragment: Charles Murray (Police inspector); ? (Policemen)

BINK'S VACATION

Edward Dillon (d); Anita Loos ["Binks Runs Away"] (au); finished 13 October 1913 (f); New York (l); 1 December 1913 (r); 603 feet (rl); LU1686 / 1 December 1913 (copyright)

Fragment: Charles Murray (Mr. Binks); ? (His wife); ? (Hair goods dealer); ? (In detective agency); ? (In bar)

THE BIRTHDAY RING

Alfred Paget? (d); Isobel M. Reynolds ["Baby Fingers"] (au); finished 10 September 1913 (f); New York (l); 4 December 1913 (r); 982 feet (rl); LU1707 / 3 December 1913 (copyright)

NOTE: Cast unidentifiable due to fragment deterioration.

IN THE ELEMENTAL WORLD

W. Christy Cabanne? (d); Stanner E. V. Taylor (au); c. October 1913 (f); New York (l); 6 December 1913 (r); one reel (rl); LU1706 / 3 December 1913 (copyright)

Fragment: Donald Crisp (Husband); Irene Howley (Wife); Robert Harron (Young hunter)

* * * * *

NOTE: The following selected titles, although produced during the Griffith period, were not released until well after his departure from Biograph.

HER WEDDING BELL

Anthony O'Sullivan (d); Edward Acker ["An Unsuspected Peril"] (au);

finished January 1913 (f); California (l); 25 December 1913 (r); 1001
feet (rl); LU1818 / 19 December 1913 (copyright)

Fragment: Henry B. Walthall (Pedro); Blanche Sweet (Young woman);
Charles H. West (Her fiancé); Kate Bruce (Mrs. Thayer, her mother); William Carroll (Jack, her brother); Charles Hill Mailes (Florist); ? (Servants); Harry Hyde, Alfred Paget, William J. Butler,
Adolph Lestina, J. Jiquel Lanoe, Grace Lewis, Kathleen Butler
(Wedding guests); Charles Gorman (On stagecoach); William Courtwright (Minister)

A MOTORCYCLE ELOPEMENT

Dell Henderson (d); Byron C. Wainwright (au); finished 24 December
1912 (f); California (l); 1 January 1914 (r); 371 feet (rl); LU1894
/ 3 January 1914 (copyright)

NOTE: No material survives from which the cast may be determined.

THE MYSTERY OF THE MILK

Mack Sennett (d); William E. Wing ["The Widow and the Maid"] (au);
finished April 1912 (f); California (l); 5 January 1914 (r); 274 feet
(rl); LU1908 / 6 January 1914 (copyright)

Fragment: Edward Dillon (Policeman); Charles Avery, Kate Bruce,
Clara T. Bracey (Extras); ? (Two children)

HOW THEY STRUCK OIL

Dell Henderson (d); Richard Ridgely ["Joey and Tilly"] (au); finished
January 1913 (f); California (l); 15 January 1914 (r); 437 feet (rl);
LU1957 / 14 January 1914 (copyright)

Fragment: Charles Murray (Farmer); Harry Hyde, J. Jiquel Lanoe,
? (City people); Gus Pixley (Rube); ? (His girlfriend); ? (Farmer's
daughter?); William J. Butler (Extra)

JUST BOYS

Lionel Barrymore? (d); Ralph E. Hellawell ["Bold Ben"] (au); finished 10 September 1913 (f); New York (l); 19 January 1914 (r); 373
feet (rl); LU1980 / 19 January 1914 (copyright)

Fragment: ? (The Town Terrors); Clarence L. Barr, ? (Their
constable fathers); ? (Outside store); Clara T. Bracey (In crowd)

CHOCOLATE DYNAMITE

Lionel Barrymore? (d); Helen Combes ["Captured by Dynamite"] (au);
finished 28 August 1913 (f); New York (l); 28 February 1914 (r); 435
feet (rl); LU2233 / 27 February 1914 (copyright)

NOTE: No material survives from which the cast may be determined.

JUDITH OF BETHULIA

D. W. Griffith (d); Grace A. Pierce ["Judith and Holofernes"] (au);
Judith of Bethulia, the play and "Judith and Holofernes," the poem
by Thomas Bailey Aldrich, from the Book of Judith in the Apocrypha
of the Old Testament (s); G. W. Bitzer (c); June–July 1913 (f);
California/New York (l); 8 March 1914 (r); four reels (rl); LP1660
/ 31 October 1913 and LU1591 / 17 November 1913 (copyright)

Blanche Sweet (Judith); Henry B. Walthall (Holofernes); Mae Marsh
(Naomi); Robert Harron (Nathan, son of Eliah); Kate Bruce (Marah,
Judith's servant); Lillian Gish (Young mother); J. Jiquel Lanoe (Holo-
fernes' eunuch); Dorothy Gish (Crippled beggar); Kate Toncray, ?
(Judith's servants); Frank Opperman, Adolph Lestina, W. Chrystie
Miller, Jennie Lee, J. Jiquel Lanoe, Kathleen Butler, William J.
Butler, Alfred Paget, Harry Hyde, Clara T. Bracey (Inhabitants
of Bethulia); Harry Hyde, W. C. Robinson, Frank Evans, Charles
Hill Mailes (Soldiers of Bethulia); Gertrude Bambrick (Lead Assyrian
dancer); Harry Carey (Assyrian traitor); Harry Hyde, William Carroll, Alfred Paget (Assyrian soldiers)

NOTE: Reissued by Biograph in January 1917 as HER CONDONED
SIN [LP10278 / 12 January 1917 (copyright)]. Expanded to six reels
and new titles added, this version was offered to exhibitors on a
states' rights basis. Reviews of the time noted that the extra footage
was taken from 150,000 feet of original negative. Thomas Bailey
Aldrich is identified as the author in Catalogue of Copyright Entries:
1912-1939.

THE BATTLE AT ELDERBUSH GULCH

D. W. Griffith (d); G. W. Bitzer (c); finished 8 May 1913 (f); California (l); 28 March 1914 (r); 2021 feet (rl); LU893 / 1 July 1913
and LP1807 / 15 July 1913 (copyright)

Mae Marsh, Leslie Loveridge (The waifs); Alfred Paget (Their
uncle); Robert Harron, Lillian Gish (Young couple); Charles Hill
Mailes (Ranch boss); William Carroll (The Mexican); Frank Opperman
(Indian chief); Henry B. Walthall (His son); Joseph McDermott, Jennie
Lee (Waifs' guardians); Charles Gorman, W. C. Robinson, Alfred
Paget (Among Indians); W. Chrystie Miller, Frank Opperman, Kate
Bruce (Among settlers); Joseph McDermott, Henry B. Walthall, Elmo
Lincoln (In cavalry); Frank Opperman (In wagon); ? (Wagon driver)

NOTE: Reissued by Biograph 30 July 1915 and 24 October 1916.

BRUTE FORCE

D. W. Griffith (d); D. W. Griffith (au); Dell Henderson, W. Christy
Cabanne (production assistants); G. W. Bitzer (c); finished 2 June
1913 (f); California (l); 25 April 1914 (r); 2053 feet (rl); LU1629 /
20 November 1913 [as IN PREHISTORIC DAYS, two reels], LP1806
/ 14 November 1913 and LU1651 / 24 November 1913 [as THE
PRIMITIVE MAN, three reels] (copyright)

[Prologue]: Robert Harron (Harry Falkner); Mae Marsh (Priscilla
Mayhew); William J. Butler (Her father); Alfred Paget, Harry Hyde,
J. Jiquel Lanoe, Frank Evans, Joseph McDermott, John T. Dillon,
Elmo Lincoln (In club); Charles Hill Mailes, W. C. Robinson (Valets)

[The Old Days]: Robert Harron (Weakhands); Mae Marsh, Charles
Hill Mailes, Kate Toncray, W. C. Robinson, Joseph McDermott, J.
Jiquel Lanoe (In his tribe); Alfred Paget, J. Jiquel Lanoe, Elmo
Lincoln, Frank Evans, Harry Carey (In womanless tribe); Jennie
Lee (Rejected mate)

NOTE: Reissued by Biograph 22 October 1915. This film was also
advertised in its original release as WARS OF THE PRIMAL TRIBES.
It was a sequel to MAN'S GENESIS, released by Biograph 11 July
1912.

* * * * *

In 1913, theatrical producers Marc Klaw, Abraham Erlanger
and Al H. Woods formed the Protective Amusement Company for the
purpose of adapting their large holding of stage plays to the screen.
An agreement was concluded with Biograph, which made available
to the new concern its Bronx stages, as well as its creative personnel.

All of the legal arrangements for this partnership were made
while Griffith and his company were still in California. Upon his
return to New York, it became clear to Griffith that he would not
be allowed to produce his own longer films--Biograph had balked at
the production costs for JUDITH OF BETHULIA--but would have to
act as supervisor of the Klaw and Erlanger "Famous Plays in
Pictures" series. This fact, as much as any other, forced Griffith
to break with Biograph.

Just how closely Griffith was involved with these films is
difficult to say. These four have been listed because they are the
only ones mentioned by G. W. Bitzer as having been supervised by
Griffith (D. W. Griffith Papers, MOMA). Even so, it would seem
clear that such supervision was nominal at best; by Bitzer's own

testimony, Griffith rarely appeared at the Bronx studio in September of 1913, choosing instead to pursue negotiations with Harry Aitken's Mutual organization. We have included them so that the reader may have a complete picture of Griffith's activities at Biograph during his last weeks with the company.

CLASSMATES

James Kirkwood (d); Tony Gaudio (c); Classmates, the play by William C. de Mille and Margaret Turnbull (s); c. August-September 1913 (f); Bronx Studio/New York and New Jersey? locations/Jacksonville, Florida (l); four reels (rl); LP 2468 / 23 February 1914 (copyright)

Blanche Sweet (Sylvia Randolph); Henry B. Walthall (Duncan Irving); Marshall Neilan (Bert Stafford); Gertrude Robinson (Phyllis Stafford); Augusta Anderson (Mrs. Stafford); Lionel Barrymore ("Bubby" Dumble); Thomas Jefferson (Mr. Irving)

NOTE: The scenes of the Amazon expedition were filmed at Atlantic Beach in Jacksonville, Florida (New York Dramatic Mirror, 3 September 1913, p. 27).

STRONGHEART

James Kirkwood (d); Tony Gaudio (c); Strongheart, the play by William C. de Mille (s); c. August-September 1913 (f); Bronx Studio/ New York and New Jersey? locations/Cambridge, Massachusetts (l); 9 March 1914 (r); three reels (rl); LP 2488 / 9 March 1914 (copyright)

Antonio Moreno (Frank Nelson); Blanche Sweet (Dorothy, his sister); Henry B. Walthall (Soangataha/Strongheart); Gertrude Robinson (Molly Livingston); Tom McEvoy (Dick, her brother); Lionel Barrymore (Billy Saunders); Alan Hale (Ralph Thorne); William J. Butler (Manager of the opposing team); W. C. Robinson (Team assistant); Jack Mulhall (In stadium crowd)

NOTE: The football game footage was taken at the Harvard-Cornell game in Cambridge, Massachusetts (Motion Picture News, 15 November 1913, p. 20).

MEN AND WOMEN

James Kirkwood (d); Tony Gaudio (c); Men and Women, the play by Henry C. de Mille and David Belasco (s); c. September 1913 (f); Bronx Studio/New York? locations (l); August 1914 (r); three reels (rl); LP 3035 / 23 April 1914 (copyright)

Lionel Barrymore (Stephen Rodman, aka Robert Stevens); ? (His wife); Blanche Sweet (Agnes, their daughter); F. Hearn (D. A. Stedman); Gertrude Robinson (Dora Prescott); Marshall Neilan (Will Prescott); Frank Crane (Ned Seabury); F. Kerzog (Kirke, the broker); Edna Foster, Gladys Egan (Among orphans); Antonio Moreno (In Kirke's office); Alan Hale, ? (Kirke's creditors); Frank M. Norcross (Cohen); Hattie Delaro (Will and Dora's mother)

NOTE: Cast taken from film and review in Moving Picture World, 15 August 1914, p. 969.

THE WIFE

David Miles (d); ? (c); The Wife, the play by David Belasco and Henry C. de Mille (s); c. October-November 1913 (f); Bronx Studio (l); three reels (rl); no official release; LP 3032 / 28 May 1914 (copyright)

Linda Arvidson, Clara T. Bracey, Charles Perley, Charles H. West, Robert Druet, Dorothy Gish, Jack J. Brammall, William J. Butler, Charles Fleming, Mrs. La Varnie

NOTE: Miles' directorial credit is confirmed in New York Dramatic Mirror, 5 November 1913, p. 27.

(Including creative and technical personnel;
film titles are listed in order of production)

ACKER, EDWARD: Author

  1909: What Drink Did

  1911: The Old Confectioner's Mistake; A Terrible Discovery

  1912: Stern Papa; An Unseen Enemy; Getting Rid of Trouble; A
  Ten-Karat Hero; A Cry for Help; The Telephone Girl and the
  Lady; A Misappropriated Turkey

  1913: Her Wedding Bell; A Frightful Blunder; A Dangerous Foe;
  The Noisy Suitors

ALDRICH, THOMAS BAILEY: Poet (1836-1907)

  1913: Judith of Bethulia

ALEXANDER, EDNA: Author

  1912: A Near Tragedy; The Fatal Chocolate

ALLER, JOSEPH: Assistant cutter with Scott, 1907-1908

ANDERSON, MR.: Biograph Company "manager" in 1911. Noted in
  Moving Picture World, 18 March 1911, p. 587.

ANDERSON, AUGUSTA: Actress

  1913: Classmates

ARVIDSON, LINDA: Actress, Author (1884-1949) (aka Linda Griffith,
  Mrs. D. W. Griffith) (b. Linda Johnson)

  1907: Mr. Gay and Mrs.

  1908: Classmates; The Princess in the Vase; King of the Cannibal
  Islands; The King's Messenger; The Stage Rustler; The Adventures
  of Dollie; The Redman and the Child; The Bandit's Waterloo; A
  Calamitous Elopement; The Greaser's Gauntlet; The Man and the
  Woman; The Fatal Hour; For a Wife's Honor; Balked at the Altar;
  The Red Girl; Betrayed by a Handprint; Where the Breakers Roar;
  The Stolen Jewels; A Smoked Husband; Taming of the Shrew; A

Woman's Way; The Pirate's Gold; The Curtain Pole; The Song of
the Shirt; The Clubman and the Tramp; The Feud and the Turkey;
The Test of Friendship; One Touch of Nature; An Awful Moment;
The Helping Hand; A Wreath in Time; The Criminal Hypnotist;
The Sacrifice; The Welcome Burglar; A Rural Elopement; Mr.
Jones Has a Card Party; The Joneses Have Amateur Theatricals;
Edgar Allen Poe; The Roue's Heart; The Salvation Army Lass;
Love Finds a Way; Tragic Love

1909: Those Boys; The Cord of Life; Those Awful Hats; The
Drive for a Life; Politician's Love Story; His Wife's Mother; The
Golden Louis; His Ward's Love; The Medicine Bottle; The Lure
of the Gown; A Fool's Revenge; I Did It, Mamma; The Voice of
the Violin; Jones and His New Neighbors; A Drunkard's Reforma-
tion; The Winning Coat; The Eavesdropper; Twin Brothers; Con-
fidence; Lucky Jim; 'Tis an Ill Wind That Blows No Good; Resur-
rection; A Baby's Shoe; The Cricket on the Hearth; The Peach-
basket Hat; The Heart of An Outlaw; The Mills of the Gods;
Pranks; The Sealed Room; "1776" or, The Hessian Renegades; In
Old Kentucky; The Children's Friend; Comata, the Sioux; Leather
Stocking; Pippa Passes or, The Song of Conscience; Lines of
White on a Sullen Sea; A Corner in Wheat; To Save Her Soul; The
Day After; The Honor of His Family; The Woman from Mellon's;
The Englishman and the Girl

1910: The Thread of Destiny; The Converts; Gold is Not All;
Thou Shalt Not; The Way of the World; The Unchanging Sea; The
Two Brothers; In Life's Cycle; The Broken Doll; A Child's Strata-
gem

1911: Fisher Folks; How She Triumphed (au only); Enoch Arden,
Parts One and Two; A Blot in the 'Scutcheon (au only)

1913: The Wife

ASHTON, SYLVIA: Actress (1880-1940)

1912: A Dash Through the Clouds; A Day's Outing; The Bite of
a Snake; Kissing Kate; The Masher Cop; There Were Hoboes
Three; An Up-to-Date Lochinvar; Look Not Upon the Wine; The
High Cost of Reduction; A Queer Elopement; A Delivery Package

1913: Tightwad's Predicament; The Power of the Camera; All
Hail to the King; Edwin Masquerades; Highbrow Love; Just Kids;
Jenks Becomes a Desperate Character; An Old Maid's Deception;
A Sea Dog's Love; While the Count Goes Bathing; Cupid and the
Cook; The Suffragette Minstrels; Papa's Baby; Baby Indisposed;
Objections Overruled

AUER, FLORENCE: Actress (1880-1962)

1908: The Sculptor's Nightmare; Over the Hills to the Poorhouse;
At the Crossroads of Life; The Kentuckian; The Fight for Freedom;
The Tavern-Keeper's Daughter; The Fatal Hour

AUGUST, EDWIN: Actor, Author (1883-1964)

1910: The Message of the Violin; Waiter No. 5; Simple Charity; The Fugitive; A Child's Stratagem; The Golden Supper; Happy Jack, a Hero; Winning Back His Love; A Wreath of Orange Blossoms; Conscience; Fate's Turning

1911: His Daughter; Madame Rex; The Manicure Lady (au only); Bearded Youth; A Country Cupid; Out From the Shadow; The Stuff Heroes Are Made Of; The Eternal Mother; The Baron (au only); The Revenue Man and the Girl; The Long Road; The Battle; The Trail of Books; The Failure; The Voice of the Child; A Tale of the Wilderness; The Old Bookkeeper; A Blot in the 'Scutcheon

1912: Fate's Interception; One is Business, The Other Crime; The Old Actor; The Lesser Evil; Those Hicksville Boys; His Lesson; A Beast at Bay; When the Fire-Bells Rang; Lena and the Geese; The School Teacher and the Waif; The Sands of Dee; A Child's Remorse

AVERY, CHARLES: Actor (1873-1926) (b. Charles Bradford Avery)

1908: Father Gets in the Game; Taming of the Shrew; The Valet's Wife; The Helping Hand; Love Finds a Way; A Wreath in Time; Tragic Love; The Salvation Army Lass

1909: Jones and His New Neighbors; A Drunkard's Reformation; Confidence; Twin Brothers; 'Tis An Ill Wind That Blows No Good; The Suicide Club; One Busy Hour; The French Duel; The Jilt; Resurrection; Two Memories; Eradicating Aunty; What Drink Did; The Violin Maker of Cremona; The Lonely Villa; The Son's Return; The Peachbasket Hat; Her First Biscuits; Was Justice Served?; The Necklace; The Cardinal's Conspiracy; A Strange Meeting; With Her Card; The Seventh Day; The Little Darling

1912: The Would-Be Shriner; The Brave Hunter; Home Folks; The Mystery of the Milk; The Tragedy of a Dress Suit; A Day's Outing

BAKER, ROYAL A.: Author

1912: Like The Cat, They Came Back

BALZAC, HONORE DE: Writer (1799-1850)

1909: The Sealed Room

BAMBRICK, GERTRUDE: Actress

1912: Two Daughters of Eve; A Limited Divorce; The One She Loved; A Real Estate Deal; The New York Hat; The Burglar's Dilemma; The God Within; The Telephone Girl and the Lady; Oil and Water; Brothers

1913:   Broken Ways; Near to Earth; All Hail to the King; The
Perfidy of Mary; A Horse on Bill; A Ragtime Romance; Frappe
Love; The King and the Copper; Cinderella and the Boob; The
Hicksville Epicure; Highbrow Love; Just Kids; Red Hicks Defies
the World; Jenks Becomes a Desperate Character; Almost a Wild
Man; The Mothering Heart; Mister Jefferson Green; A Compromis-
ing Complication; Faust and the Lily; An Old Maid's Deception;
Mr. Spriggs Buys a Dog; The Widow's Kids; Cupid and the Cook;
Those Little Flowers; The Suffragette Minstrels; Baby Indisposed;
Objections Overruled; The Lady in Black; The Reformers, or The
Lost Art of Minding One's Business; Judith of Bethulia; His Hoo-
doo; The End of the World; For the Son of the House; A Saturday
Holiday; A Circumstantial Hero; McGann and His Octette; Aunts,
Too Many; The Winning Punch

BARKER, FLORENCE: Actress, Author (1891-1913)

1909:   Choosing a Husband; The Dancing Girl of Butte; Her Terrible Ordeal; The Call; The Course of True Love; One Night, and
Then---

1910:   The Love of Lady Irma; The Newlyweds; The Man; Faith-
ful; The Kid; The Tenderfoot's Triumph; Up a Tree; The Way of
the World; An Affair of Hearts; The Gold-Seekers; The Two
Brothers; Unexpected Help; A Knot in the Plot; The Impalement;
A Victim of Jealousy; A Midnight Cupid; A Child's Faith; Serious
Sixteen; A Summer Tragedy; The Oath and the Man; Effecting a
Cure; Happy Jack, a Hero; A Wreath of Orange Blossoms; The
Diamond Star; Priscilla's Engagement Kiss

1911:   His Daughter; Priscilla's April Fool Joke; Priscilla and the
Umbrella; Priscilla's Capture (au only)

BARR, CLARENCE L.: Actor (b. 1876)

1912:   Bill Bogg's Windfall; A Day's Outing; The Bite of a Snake;
The Best Man Wins; There Were Hoboes Three; Among Club Fel-
lows; The High Cost of Reduction; What is the Use of Repining?;
A Queer Elopement; A Delivery Package; Edwin's Badge of Honor

1913:   Tightwad's Predicament; The Power of the Camera; The
Old Gray Mare; All Hail to the King; Edwin Masquerades; Their
One Good Suit; An "Uncle Tom's Cabin" Troupe; A Horse on Bill;
A Ragtime Romance; The Cure; The Daylight Burglar; Cinderella
and the Boob; The Hicksville Epicure; The Trimmers Trimmed;
Highbrow Love; The Ranchero's Revenge; Slippery Slim Repents;
Jenks Becomes a Desperate Character; Almost a Wild Man; The
Rise and Fall of McDoo; Mister Jefferson Green; A Compromising
Complication; Faust and the Lily; An Old Maid's Deception; The
Noisy Suitors; The Sweat-Box; While the Count Goes Bathing; Mr.
Spriggs Buys a Dog; Cupid and the Cook; Those Little Flowers;
Come Seben, Leben; Father's Chicken Dinner; Papa's Baby; Black
and White; Baby Indisposed; Objections Overruled; Dan Greegan's
Ghost; Just Boys

BARROWS, PEARSON: Author

1913: A Saturday Holiday

BARRY, MR.: Actor

1908: Cupid's Pranks

BARRY, VIOLA: Actress (1894-1964)

1913: The Perfidy of Mary; A Frightful Blunder; A Misunderstood Boy; The Little Tease; The Lady and the Mouse; His Mother's Son; The Ranchero's Revenge; Almost A Wild Man; The Mothering Heart

BARRYMORE, LIONEL: Actor, Author, Director (1878-1954)

1911: The Battle

1912: Friends; So Near, Yet So Far; The One She Loved; The Painted Lady; Heredity; Gold and Glitter; My Baby; The Informer; Brutality; The Unwelcome Guest; The New York Hat; The Burglar's Dilemma (also au); A Cry For Help; The God Within; Three Friends; The Telephone Girl and the Lady; An Adventure in the Autumn Woods; The Tender-Hearted Boy (au); Oil and Water; A Chance Deception; Fate; The Wrong Bottle

1913: Near to Earth; The Sheriff's Baby; The Perfidy of Mary; A Misunderstood Boy; The Little Tease; The Lady and the Mouse; The Wanderer; The House of Darkness; Just Gold; A Timely Interception; Death's Marathon; The Yaqui Cur; The Ranchero's Revenge; Red Hicks Defies the World; Almost a Wild Man; The Well; The Switch-Tower; In Diplomatic Circles; A Gamble With Death; The Enemy's Baby; The Mirror; An Indian's Loyalty; The Vengeance of Galora (au only); Under the Shadow of the Law; I Was Meant For You; The Work Habit; The Crook and the Girl; The Strong Man's Burden; The Stolen Treaty; His Secret (d only); Chocolate Dynamite (d only); Where's the Baby? (d only); Just Boys (d only); No Place For Father (d only); All for Science; Classmates; Strongheart; Men and Women

BARTON, GRACE: Author

1913: The Stolen Loaf

BAYER, T. P.: Author

1910: Turning the Tables

1911: Cupid's Joke; The Unveiling

1912: The God Within

1913: Broken Ways; For the Son of the House

BEAUDINE, WILLIAM: Actor, Author (1892-1970)

1910: A Summer Tragedy

1911: Priscilla's April Fool Joke; Why He Gave Up; With A Kodak

1912: The Engagement Ring; Hot Stuff; Those Hicksville Boys; Their First Kidnapping Case; The Fickle Spaniard; The Furs; A Close Call; Helen's Marriage; One-Round O'Brien; The Tragedy of a Dress Suit; Stern Papa; Mr. Grouch at the Seashore; Through Dumb Luck; A Disappointed Mamma; A Mixed Affair; A Limited Divorce; Their Idols; A Day's Outing; Oh, What A Boob!; Kissing Kate; There Were Hoboes Three (also au); A Delivery Package

1913: The Old Gray Mare; An "Uncle Tom's Cabin" Troupe; A Horse on Bill; The Daylight Burglar; A Rainy Day; The Tender-foot's Money; Slippery Slim Repents; Red Hicks Defies the World; Jenks Becomes a Desperate Character; Almost a Wild Man (au only); The Rise and Fall of McDoo; While the Count Goes Bathing (also au); Mr. Spriggs Buys a Dog; The Suffragette Minstrels; Papa's Baby; Black and White (au only)

BECHTEL, WILLIAM: Actor (1867-1930) (aka William A. "Billy" Bechtel)

1911: Through Darkened Vales; Resourceful Lovers; Caught with the Goods; Abe Gets Even With Father; The Baby and the Stork; Who Got the Reward?; For His Son

BECHTEL, MRS. WILLIAM: Actress

1911: Abe Gets Even With Father

BELASCO, DAVID: Producer, Playwright (1853-1931)

1908: The Heart of O Yama

1913: Men and Women; The Wife

BELL, EDWARD: Author

1913: The Sheriff's Baby

BERANGER, GEORGE ANDRE: Actor (1895-1973) (aka Andre Beranger; George Andre)

1912: When Love Forgives

1913: Almost A Wild Man; The Well; The Switch-Tower; The Adopted Brother

BERNARD, DOROTHY: Actress (1890-1955) (aka Dorothy Bernard Van Buren)

1910: The Final Settlement; His Last Burglary; Taming a Husband; The Two Paths; Fate's Turning

1911: The Failure; Sunshine Through the Dark; The Baby and the Stork; A Tale of the Wilderness; A Sister's Love; For His Son; A Blot in the 'Scutcheon; A String of Pearls; The Root of Evil

1912: A Siren of Impulse; Iola's Promise; The Goddess of Sagebrush Gulch; The Girl and Her Trust; The Female of the Species; One is Business, The Other Crime; His Lesson; When Kings Were The Law; Heaven Avenges; Black Sheep

BISHOP, AARON E.: Author

1913: The Somnambulists

BITZER, G. W. (Johann Gottlob Wilhelm); Cameraman; Author (1872-1944) (aka Billy Bitzer)

1907: Yale Laundry; Dr. Skinum; Mr. Gay and Mrs.; Professional Jealousy; Falsely Accused!

1908: Lonesome Junction; Classmates; Bobby's Kodak; The Snowman; The Princess in the Vase; The Yellow Peril; The Boy Detective; Her First Adventure; Caught By Wireless; Old Isaacs, the Pawnbroker; A Famous Escape; King of the Cannibal Islands; The Music Master; Hulda's Lovers; The King's Messenger; The Sculptor's Nightmare; His Day of Rest; When Knights Were Bold; Mixed Babies; The Romance of an Egg; Thompson's Night Out; 'Ostler Joe; A Night of Terror; Over the Hills to the Poorhouse; The Invisible Fluid; The Outlaw; The Man in the Box; Deceived Slumming Party; At the French Ball; At the Crossroads of Life; The Black Viper; The Kentuckian; The Stage Rustler; The Fight for Freedom; A Calamitous Elopement; The Man and the Woman; Betrayed By A Handprint; Monday Morning in a Coney Island Police Court; Behind the Scenes; The Heart of O Yama; Where the Breakers Roar; The Stolen Jewels; A Smoked Husband; The Zulu's Heart; The Vaquero's Vow; Father Gets in the Game; The Barbarian, Ingomar; The Planter's Wife; The Devil; The Romance of a Jewess; The Call of the Wild; After Many Years; Mr. Jones at the Ball; Concealing a Burglar; Taming of the Shrew; The Ingrate; The Pirate's Gold; The Guerrilla; The Curtain Pole (also au); The Song of the Shirt; The Clubman and the Tramp; Money Mad; Mrs. Jones Entertains; The Feud and the Turkey; The Test of Friendship; The Reckoning; The Valet's Wife; One Touch of Nature; The Maniac Cook; The Christmas Burglars; A Wreath in Time; The Honor of Thieves; The Criminal Hypnotist; The Sacrifice; The Welcome Burglar; A Rural Elopement; Mr. Jones Has A Card Party; The

Joneses Have Amateur Theatricals; Edgar Allen Poe; The Roue's
Heart; The Hindoo Dagger; The Salvation Army Lass; Love Finds
a Way; Tragic Love; The Girls and Daddy

1909; Those Boys; The Cord of Life; The Fascinating Mrs. Fran-
cis; Those Awful Hats; Jones and the Lady Book Agent; Trying to
Get Arrested; The Brahma Diamond; The Drive for a Life; Politician's Love Story; His Wife's Mother; The Golden Louis; His
Ward's Love; At the Altar; The Prussian Spy; The Medicine Bottle; The Deception; The Lure of the Gown; Lady Helen's Escapade;
A Fool's Revenge; The Wooden Leg; I Did It, Mamma; A Burglar's
Mistake; The Voice of the Violin; "And A Little Child Shall Lead
Them"; The French Duel; Jones and His New Neighbors; A Drunk-
ard's Reformation; The Winning Coat; A Rude Hostess; The Eaves-
dropper; Schneider's Anti-Noise Crusade; Confidence; The Note in
the Shoe; Lucky Jim; A Sound Sleeper; A Troublesome Satchel;
'Tis An Ill Wind That Blows No Good; The Suicide Club; Resur-
rection; One Busy Hour; A Baby's Shoe; Eloping With Aunty; The
Cricket on the Hearth; The Jilt; Eradicating Aunty; What Drink
Did; Her First Biscuits; The Violin Maker of Cremona; Two
Memories; The Lonely Villa; The Peachbasket Hat; The Son's Re-
turn; His Duty; A New Trick; The Necklace; The Way of Man; The
Faded Lilies; The Message; The Friend of the Family; Was Justice
Served?; Mrs. Jones' Lover or, "I Want My Hat"; The Mexican
Sweethearts; The Country Doctor; Jealousy and the Man; The Re-
nunciation; The Cardinal's Conspiracy; The Seventh Day; Tender
Hearts; A Convict's Sacrifice; A Strange Meeting; Sweet and Twen-
ty; The Slave; They Would Elope; Jones' Burglar; The Mended
Lute; The Indian Runner's Romance; With Her Card; The Better
Way; His Wife's Visitor; The Heart of an Outlaw; The Mills of
the Gods; "Oh, Uncle"; The Sealed Room; "1776" or, The Hessian
Renegades; The Little Darling; In Old Kentucky; The Children's
Friend; Comata, the Sioux; Leather Stocking; Getting Even; The
Broken Locket; A Fair Exchange; The Awakening; Pippa Passes or,
the Song of Conscience; Fools of Fate; Wanted, A Child; The Little
Teacher; A Change of Heart; His Lost Love; Lines of White on a
Sullen Sea; The Gibson Goddess; In the Watches of the Night; The
Expiation; What's Your Hurry?; The Restoration; Nursing a Viper;
Two Women and a Man; The Light That Came; A Midnight Adven-
ture; The Open Gate; Sweet Revenge; The Mountaineer's Honor;
In the Window Recess; The Trick That Failed; The Death Disc;
Through the Breakers; A Corner in Wheat; In A Hempen Bag; The
Redman's View; The Test; A Trap for Santa Claus; In Little Italy;
To Save Her Soul; The Day After; Choosing a Husband; The Rocky
Road; The Dancing Girl of Butte; Her Terrible Ordeal; The Call;
The Honor of His Family; On the Reef; The Last Deal; The Clois-
ter's Touch; The Woman From Mellon's; The Duke's Plan; One
Night, and Then---; The Englishman and the Girl

1910: The Final Settlement; His Last Burglary; Taming a Husband;
The Newlyweds; The Thread of Destiny; In Old California; The Man;
The Converts; Faithful; The Twisted Trail; Gold Is Not All; As It
Is In Life; A Rich Revenge; A Romance of the Western Hills; Thou

Shalt Not; The Way of the World; The Unchanging Sea; The Gold-
Seekers; Love Among the Roses; The Two Brothers; Unexpected
Help; Ramona; Over Silent Paths; The Impalement; In the Season
of Buds; A Child of the Ghetto; In the Border States; A Victim
of Jealousy; The Face at the Window; The Marked Time-Table;
A Child's Impulse; Muggsy's First Sweetheart; The Purgation; The
Call to Arms; A Midnight Cupid; A Child's Faith; What the Daisy
Said; Serious Sixteen; A Flash of Light; As the Bells Rang Out!;
An Arcadian Maid; The House with Closed Shutters; Her Father's
Pride; A Salutary Lesson; The Usurer; The Sorrows of the Un-
faithful; In Life's Cycle; Wilful Peggy; A Summer Idyl; The Modern
Prodigal; Rose O'Salem-Town; Little Angels of Luck; A Mohawk's
Way; The Oath and the Man; Examination Day at School; The Icono-
clast; That Chink at Golden Gulch; The Broken Doll; The Banker's
Daughters; The Message of the Violin; Two Little Waifs; Waiter
No. 5; Simple Charity; The Fugitive; The Song of the Wildwood
Flute; A Child's Stratagem; Sunshine Sue; A Plain Song; His Sister-
In-Law; The Golden Supper; When a Man Loves; The Lesson;
Winning Back His Love; His Trust; His Trust Fulfilled; A Wreath
of Orange Blossoms; The Italian Barber; The Two Paths; Con-
science; Three Sisters; A Decree of Destiny; Fate's Turning; What
Shall We Do With Our Old; The Diamond Star; The Lily of the
Tenements; Heart Beats of Long Ago

1911: Fisher Folks; His Daughter; The Lonedale Operator; The
Heart of a Savage; Was He a Coward?; Teaching Dad to Like Her;
The Spanish Gypsy; The Chief's Daughter; A Knight of the Road;
Madame Rex; His Mother's Scarf; How She Triumphed; In the Days
of '49; The Two Sides; The New Dress; Enoch Arden, Parts One
and Two; The White Rose of the Wilds; The Crooked Road; A
Romany Tragedy; A Smile of a Child; The Primal Call; The Jeal-
ous Husband; The Indian Brothers; The Thief and the Girl; Her
Sacrifice; The Blind Princess and the Poet; Fighting Blood; The
Last Drop of Water; Bobby, the Coward; A Country Cupid; The
Ruling Passion; The Rose of Kentucky; Out from the Shadow; The
Sorrowful Example; Swords and Hearts; The Stuff Heroes Are
Made Of; The Old Confectioner's Mistake; The Unveiling; The
Eternal Mother; Dan, the Dandy; The Revenue Man and the Girl;
The Squaw's Love; Italian Blood; The Making of a Man; Her
Awakening; The Adventures of Billy; The Long Road; The Battle;
Saved From Himself; Love in the Hills; The Trail of the Books;
Through Darkened Vales; A Woman Scorned; The Miser's Heart;
The Failure; Sunshine Through the Dark; As In a Looking Glass;
Caught with the Goods; A Terrible Discovery; A Tale of the
Wilderness; The Baby and the Stork; The Voice of a Child; The
Old Bookkeeper; A Sister's Love; For His Son; The Transformation
of Mike; A Blot in the 'Scutcheon; Billy's Stratagem; The Sunbeam;
A String of Pearls; The Root of Evil

1912: Under Burning Skies; A Siren of Impulse; Iola's Promise;
The Goddess of Sagebrush Gulch; The Girl and Her Trust; The
Punishment; Fate's Interception; The Female of the Species; Just
Like a Woman; One is Business, the Other Crime; The Old Actor;

The Lesser Evil; A Lodging for the Night; His Lesson; When Kings Were the Law; A Beast at Bay; Home Folks; An Outcast Among Outcasts; A Temporary Truce; Lena and the Geese; The Spirit Awakened; The School Teacher and the Waif; An Indian Summer; Man's Lust for Gold; Man's Genesis; Heaven Avenges; The Sands of Dee; A Pueblo Legend; The Massacre; The Narrow Road; A Child's Remorse; The Inner Circle; A Change of Spirit; An Unseen Enemy; Two Daughters of Eve; Friends; So Near, Yet So Far; A Feud in the Kentucky Hills; In the Aisles of the Wild; The One She Loved; The Painted Lady; The Musketeers of Pig Alley; Heredity; Gold and Glitter; My Baby; The Informer; Brutality; Pirate Gold; The Unwelcome Guest; The New York Hat; My Hero; The Burglar's Dilemma; A Cry for Help; The God Within; Three Friends; The Telephone Girl and the Lady; An Adventure in the Autumn Woods; The Tender-Hearted Boy; Oil and Water; A Chance Deception; Fate; A Misappropriated Turkey; Brothers; Drink's Lure; Love in an Apartment Hotel

1913: Broken Ways; A Girl's Stratagem; Near to Earth; A Welcome Intruder; The Sheriff's Baby; The Hero of Little Italy; The Perfidy of Mary; A Misunderstood Boy; The Left-Handed Man; The Little Tease; The Lady and the Mouse; If We Only Knew; The Wanderer; The House of Darkness; Just Gold; His Mother's Son; A Timely Interception; Death's Marathon; The Yaqui Cur; The Ranchero's Revenge; The Mothering Heart; Her Mother's Oath; The Sorrowful Shore; The Battle at Elderbush Gulch; The Mistake; The Coming of Angelo; Brute Force; Two Men of the Desert; The Reformers, or The Lost Art of Minding One's Business; Judith of Bethulia

BITZER, J. C.: Cameraman

1912: Black Sheep; With the Enemy's Help; The Chief's Blanket; In the North Woods; Blind Love

BLACK, MORRIS H.: Author

1912: When the Fire-Bells Rang

BOHLANDER, H. C.: Author

1913: A Sea Dog's Life

BOND, R. L.: Author

1911: The Making of a Man

BOOTH, ELMER: Actor (1882-1915)

1910: The Oath and the Man; A Plain Song; Fate's Turning; What Shall We Do With Our Old

1911: Her Mother Interferes; Resourceful Lovers; Abe Gets Even With Father

1912: The Narrow Road; An Interrupted Elopement; An Unseen Enemy; In the North Woods; Two Daughters of Eve; Friends; So Near, Yet So Far; A Feud in the Kentucky Hills; In the Aisles of the Wild; The Painted Lady; The Musketeers of Pig Alley; His Auto's Maiden Trip; Gold and Glitter; My Baby; The Informer; Brutality; The Unwelcome Guest; Drink's Lure

1913: The Adopted Brother; An Unjust Suspicion

BRACEY, CLARA T.: Actress (1847-1941) (aka Clara T. Bracy)

1910: A Child of the Ghetto; The Face at the Window; The Marked Time-Table; A Child's Impulse; Muggsy's First Sweetheart; The Purgation; The Call to Arms; A Child's Faith; What the Daisy Said; Serious Sixteen; Her Father's Pride; The Usurer; An Old Story With A New Ending; Wilful Peggy; The Modern Prodigal; Rose O'Salem-Town; Little Angels of Luck; The Oath and the Man; The Broken Doll; The Banker's Daughters; The Message of the Violin; Two Little Waifs; Waiter No. 5; The Fugitive; A Child's Stratagem; Sunshine Sue; His Sister-in-Law; His Trust Fulfilled; The Two Paths; A Decree of Destiny; The Lily of the Tenements

1912: The Mystery of the Milk; The Musketeers of Pig Alley; My Baby; The Informer; Brutality; The New York Hat; The God Within; Three Friends; The Tender-Hearted Boy; Oil and Water; Brothers; The Wrong Bottle; Love in an Apartment Hotel

1913: Judith of Bethulia; For the Son of the House; Just Boys; By Man's Law; The Blue or the Gray; The Wife

BRADY, PHIL: Stuntman

BRAMMALL, JACK J.: Actor

1913: The Wife

BRONTI, MRS. ADELAIDE: Actress

1913: The House of Darkness; His Mother's Son; Almost a Wild Man; Her Mother's Oath

BROWN, BILL: Carpenter, Grip

BROWNING, ROBERT: Poet (1812-1889)

1909: Pippa Passes

BRUCE, KATE: Actress (c. 1858-1946)

1909: His Duty; The Country Doctor; A Strange Meeting; The

Slave; They Would Elope; The Better Way; "1776" or, The Hessian
Renegades; In Old Kentucky; Getting Even; The Broken Locket; A
Fair Exchange; The Awakening; Wanted, A Child; The Little
Teacher; A Change of Heart; His Lost Love; Lines of White on a
Sullen Sea; The Gibson Goddess; In the Watches of the Night;
What's Your Hurry?; The Restoration; Two Women and a Man;
The Light That Came; A Midnight Adventure; The Open Gate; The
Mountaineer's Honor; The Trick That Failed; Through the Break-
ers; A Corner in Wheat; In a Hempen Bag; The Redman's View;
A Trap for Santa Claus; In Little Italy; To Save Her Soul; Choos-
ing a Husband; The Rocky Road; The Call; All on Account of the
Milk; The Honor of His Family; The Cloister's Touch; The Woman
From Mellon's; The Duke's Plan; One Night, and Then---; The
Englishman and the Girl

1910: His Last Burglary; The Newlyweds; The Converts; Faithful;
The Twisted Trail; Gold Is Not All; As It Is In Life; A Romance
of the Western Hills; May and December; The Unchanging Sea; The
Gold-Seekers; Love Among the Roses; The Two Brothers; Ramona;
A Knot in the Plot; The Impalement; In the Season of Buds; A
Child of the Ghetto; An Arcadian Maid; Her Father's Pride; The
Usurer; The Affair of An Egg; Wilful Peggy; Muggsy Becomes a
Hero; The Modern Prodigal; Examination Day at School; The Icono-
clast; That Chink at Golden Gulch; A Gold Necklace; How Hubby
Got a Raise; The Broken Doll; A Lucky Toothache; The Masher;
The Message of the Violin; Two Little Waifs; Waiter No. 5;
Simple Charity; The Fugitive; The Song of the Wildwood Flute; A
Plain Song; Effecting a Cure; Happy Jack, a Hero; A Wreath of
Orange Blossoms; White Roses; The Italian Barber; The Midnight
Marauder; His Wife's Sweethearts; Three Sisters; The Poor Sick
Men; Help Wanted; Heart Beats of Long Ago

1911: Teaching Dad to Like Her; The Spanish Gypsy; Priscilla
and the Umbrella; Paradise Lost; A Knight of the Road; His
Mother's Scarf; In the Days of '49; The Two Sides; The New Dress;
The Manicure Lady; The Crooked Road; Fighting Blood; The Last
Drop of Water; A Country Cupid; The Ruling Passion; The Rose of
Kentucky; Swords and Hearts; The Eternal Mother; The Squaw's
Love; Her Awakening; The Adventures of Billy; The Long Road;
The Battle; Through Darkened Vales; A Terrible Discovery; The
Baby and the Stork; With a Kodak; The Transformation of Mike;
The Sunbeam; A String of Pearls

1912: Iola's Promise; The Engagement Ring; Hot Stuff; The Would-
Be Shriner; The Punishment; One is Business, the Other Crime;
Just Like a Woman; The Brave Hunter; The Old Actor; Won By a
Fish; The Fickle Spaniard; When Kings Were the Law; Home Folks;
The Leading Man; When the Fire-Bells Rang; The Furs; A Close
Call; Lena and the Geese; The Spirit Awakened; An Indian Summer;
A Dash Through the Clouds; The Mystery of the Milk; His Own
Fault; A Child's Remorse; The Tragedy of a Dress Suit; A Feud
in the Kentucky Hills; The One She Loved; The Painted Lady;

Heredity; The Informer; The Unwelcome Guest; The New York
Hat; The Telephone Girl and the Lady; The Tender-Hearted Boy;
Drink's Lure

1913: Her Wedding Bell; The Sheriff's Baby; The Perfidy of Mary;
An "Uncle Tom's Cabin" Troupe; A Frightful Blunder; A Misunder-
stood Boy; The Little Tease; The Wanderer; The House of Dark-
ness; Olaf - An Atom; Just Gold; Death's Marathon; The Yaqui
Cur; The Mothering Heart; The Battle at Elderbush Gulch; The
Enemy's Baby; The Reformers, or The Lost Art of Minding One's
Business; Judith of Bethulia; The Work Habit; For the Son of the
House; The Strong Man's Burden; The Stopped Clock

BUCH, BEATRICE: Author

1913: Where's the Baby?

BUNTING, S. WALTER: Author

1910: His New Lid

1912: An Interrupted Elopement; The Masher Cop

BURNS, BOB: Actor (1892-1956)

1913: During the Round-Up; The Blue or the Gray

BURNS, FRED: Actor, Author (1878-1955)

1913: During the Round-Up; An Indian's Loyalty (also au); The
Adopted Brother; An Unjust Suspicion; The Influence of the Unknown

BUTLER, KATHLEEN: Actress, Author (b. 1890) (aka Kathleen
Butler Pemberton)

1911: Why He Gave Up

1912: Just Like a Woman; He Must Have A Wife; Two Daughters
of Eve; Getting Rid of Trouble; Blind Love; A Limited Divorce;
The Musketeers of Pig Alley; The Line at Hogan's; Hoist on His
Own Petard; The New York Hat; Three Friends; Oil and Water;
A Father's Lesson; The High Cost of Reduction; Love in an Apart-
ment Hotel

1913: Near to Earth; All Hail to the King; Her Wedding Bell; The
Hero of Little Italy; The Left-Handed Man; Just Gold; His Mother's
Son; Just Kids (au only); Her Mother's Oath; The Coming of Angelo;
The Reformers, or The Lost Art of Minding One's Business;
Judith of Bethulia; The Work Habit; The End of the World; A
Saturday Holiday; Scenting a Terrible Crime; With the Aid of
Phrenology; Never Known to Smile; No Place for Father; A Cure
for Suffragettes; By Man's Law

228 / D. W. Griffith

BUTLER, WILLIAM J.: Actor, Author (1860-1927) (aka "Daddy" Butler)

1909: The Slave; They Would Elope; Jones' Burglar; With Her Card; The Better Way; His Wife's Visitor; The Mills of the Gods; The Sealed Room; "1776" or, The Hessian Renegades; In Old Kentucky; A Corner in Wheat; The Test; A Trap for Santa Claus; In Little Italy

1910: A Child of the Ghetto; In The Border States; A Victim of Jealousy; The Marked Time-Table; A Child's Impulse; The Purgation; The Call to Arms; A Midnight Cupid; A Child's Faith; Serious Sixteen; A Flash of Light; As the Bells Rang Out!; An Arcadian Maid; The House With Closed Shutters; Her Father's Pride; A Salutary Lesson (au only); The Usurer; The Sorrows of the Unfaithful; An Old Story With A New Ending; In Life's Cycle; Wilful Peggy; Muggsy Becomes A Hero; A Summer Idyl; The Modern Prodigal; Rose O'Salem-Town; Little Angels of Luck; A Mohawk's Way; A Summer Tragedy; The Oath and the Man; Examination Day at School; The Iconoclast; That Chink At Golden Gulch; The Broken Doll; The Masher; The Message of the Violin; The Proposal; Two Little Waifs; Waiter No. 5; Simple Charity; A Troublesome Baby; Not So Bad As It Seemed; A Child's Stratagem; Sunshine Sue; A Plain Song; His Sister-In-Law; Effecting a Cure; Turning The Tables; Happy Jack, a Hero; A Wreath of Orange Blossoms; White Roses; Conscience; After the Ball; The Poor Sick Men; A Decree of Destiny; Help Wanted; What Shall We Do With Our Old; The Lily of the Tenements; Heart Beats of Long Ago

1911: Fisher Folks; Comrades; Was He a Coward?; Teaching Dad To Like Her; The Spanish Gypsy; Priscilla and the Umbrella; Paradise Lost; In the Days of '49; The Two Sides; The New Dress; Enoch Arden, Part Two; The Manicure Lady; The Crooked Road; A Romany Tragedy; Stubbs' New Servants; Fighting Blood; Bobby, the Coward; The Rose of Kentucky; Swords and Hearts; The Diving Girl; The Unveiling; Dan, the Dandy; The Squaw's Love; The Making of a Man; Her Awakening; The Long Road; Why He Gave Up; The Battle; Through Darkened Vales; The Miser's Heart; Saved From Himself; The Baby and the Stork; A Tale of the Wilderness; The Transformation of Mike; A Blot in the 'Scutcheon; A String of Pearls; The Root of Evil

1912: Iola's Promise; The Engagement Ring; A Voice from the Deep; Hot Stuff; The Would-Be Shriner; The Punishment; Fate's Interception; The Brave Hunter; Their First Kidnapping Case; Won by a Fish; The Fickle Spaniard; When Kings Were The Law; When the Fire-Bells Rang; The Furs; Helen's Marriage; Algy, the Watchman; Tomboy Bessie; Neighbors; A Dash Through the Clouds; Trying to Fool Uncle; What the Doctor Ordered; Man's Lust For Gold; Heaven Avenges; The Tourists; One-Round O'Brien; The Speed Demon; His Own Fault; Willie Becomes an Artist; A Change of Spirit; An Interrupted Elopement; The Tragedy of a Dress Suit;

He Must Have A Wife; A Feud in the Kentucky Hills; In the Aisles of the Wild; Getting Rid of Trouble; Blind Love; A Mixed Affair; The Painted Lady; The Club-Man and the Crook; Gold and Glitter; Brutality; Bill Bogg's Windfall; The God Within; Oil and Water; The Bite of a Snake; Kissing Kate; There Were Hoboes Three; An Up-to-Date Lochinvar; Among Club Fellows; A Queer Elopement; A Delivery Package

1913: The Spring of Life; Tightwad's Predicament; The Power of the Camera; The Old Gray Mare; All Hail to the King; Their One Good Suit; A Lesson to Mashers; Her Wedding Bell; How They Struck Oil; The Hero of Little Italy; A Horse on Bill; The Left-Handed Man; The Cure; The Daylight Burglar; The Tenderfoot's Money; The House of Darkness; The King and the Copper; A Time-ly Interception; Death's Marathon; The Yaqui Cur; Slippery Slim Repents; Red Hicks Defies the World; Jenks Becomes a Desperate Character; Almost a Wild Man; The Mothering Heart; A Compro-mising Complication; In Diplomatic Circles; The Enemy's Baby; Cupid and the Cook; Brute Force; The Suffragette Minstrels; The Reformers, or The Lost Art of Minding One's Business; Judith of Bethulia; His Hoodoo; The Work Habit; The Crook and the Girl; The Strong Man's Burden; The Stolen Treaty; The Law and His Son; Strongheart; The Wife

CABANNE, W. CHRISTY: Actor, Director, Author (1888-1950) (aka Walter Chrystie Cabanne; Christy Cabanne)

1911: (as actor) Was He a Coward?; Teaching Dad to Like Her; A Romany Tragedy; The Battle; Through Darkened Vales; The Failure; For His Son; The Transformation of Mike; A Blot in the 'Scutcheon; Billy's Stratagem; The Sunbeam; A String of Pearls

1912: (as actor) Under Burning Skies; The Goddess of Sagebrush Gulch; The Girl and Her Trust; The Would-Be Shriner; The Punish-ment; Just Like a Woman; The Old Actor; The Lesser Evil; A Lodging for the Night; When Kings Were the Law; A Beast at Bay; Home Folks; Algy, the Watchman; A Temporary Truce; Lena and the Geese; Heaven Avenges; Black Sheep; A Pueblo Legend; The Narrow Road; A Child's Remorse; The Inner Circle; The Tragedy of a Dress Suit; Two Daughters of Eve; So Near, Yet So Far; The Painted Lady; The Musketeers of Pig Alley; At the Basket Picnic; Heredity; The Club-Man and the Crook; The Informer; My Hero; A Cry for Help; The God Within; An Adventure in the Autumn Woods (au only); A Chance Deception (au only); A Father's Lesson (au only)

1913: (as director) Near to Earth (a only); A Misunderstood Boy (a and au only); The Wanderer (a only); The House of Darkness (a only); His Mother's Son (a and au only); A Timely Interception (au only); Almost a Wild Man (a only); The Mothering Heart (a only); The Sorrowful Shore (a and au only); During the Round-Up (also au); An Indian's Loyalty; The Adopted Brother (co-d and au); An Unjust Suspicion; The Influence of the Unknown; The Chieftain's

Sons (also au); So Runs the Way (also au); The Girl Across the
Way (also au); His Inspiration (also au); By Man's Law; The Blue
or the Gray (also au); In the Elemental World

CAHILL, LILY: Actress (1886-1955)

1910: The Masher; The Message of the Violin; The Passing of a
Grouch; The Fugitive; A Child's Stratagem; A Plain Song

1911: A Victim of Circumstances; The Failure

CANNON, J. HARRY: Author

1911: Josh's Suicide

CAREY, HARRY: Actor, Author (1878-1947)

1912: An Unseen Enemy; Two Daughters of Eve; Friends; So Near,
Yet So Far; A Feud in the Kentucky Hills; In the Aisles of the
Wild; The One She Loved; The Painted Lady; The Musketeers of
Pig Alley; Heredity; Gold and Glitter; The Informer; Brutality; The
Unwelcome Guest; My Hero; The Burglar's Dilemma; A Cry for
Help; Three Friends; The Telephone Girl and the Lady; An Adven-
ture in the Autumn Woods; Oil and Water; A Chance Deception; A
Misappropriated Turkey; Brothers; The Wrong Bottle; When Love
Forgives; Love in an Apartment Hotel

1913: Broken Ways; The Sheriff's Baby; The Hero of Little Italy;
The Stolen Bride; A Frightful Blunder; The Left-Handed Man; If
We Only Knew; The Tenderfoot's Money; Olaf - An Atom; A Dan-
gerous Foe; The Ranchero's Revenge; Red Hicks Defies the World;
The Well; The Sorrowful Shore; In Diplomatic Circles; A Gamble
with Death; The Enemy's Baby; A Gambler's Honor (also au); The
Mirror; Brute Force; The Vengeance of Galora; Under the Shadow
of the Law (also au); I Was Meant for You; Judith of Bethulia;
The Crook and the Girl; The Strong Man's Burden; The Stolen
Treaty; The Law and His Son; A Tender-Hearted Crook; The Van
Nostrand Tiara; The Stopped Clock; The Detective's Stratagem; All
for Science

CARLETON, LLOYD B.: Actor (1872-1933)

1910: Simple Charity

CARLETON, WILL: Poet (1845-1912)

1908: Over the Hills to the Poorhouse

CARLYLE, THOMAS: Writer (1795-1881)

1909: The Death Disc

CARNEGIE, ANDREW: Industrialist (1835-1919)

1908: Classmates

CARROLL, JAMES: Author

1910: A Child's Faith

1911: The Adventures of Billy

CARROLL, WILLIAM: Actor (1875-1928)

1912: Iola's Promise; The Goddess of Sagebrush Gulch; The Girl and Her Trust; Fate's Interception; One is Business, The Other Crime; The Old Actor; The Lesser Evil; A Lodging for the Night; A Beast at Bay; Home Folks; An Outcast Among Outcasts; Algy, the Watchman; A Temporary Truce; Lena and the Geese; The School Teacher and the Waif; Man's Lust for Gold; Black Sheep; Bill Bogg's Windfall; Oh, What a Boob!; The Press Gang; The Bite of a Snake; The Best Man Wins; Kissing Kate; The Masher Cop; There Were Hoboes Three; An Up-to-Date Lochinvar; Look Not Upon the Wine; Among Club Fellows; What is the Use of Repining?; A Delivery Package

1913: Broken Ways; The Spring of Life; A Welcome Intruder; A Lesson to Mashers; Her Wedding Bell; A Frightful Blunder; A Misunderstood Boy; The Left-Handed Man; The Tenderfoot's Money; The Stolen Loaf; His Mother's Son; Almost a Wild Man; The Switch-Tower; A Sea Dog's Life; The Battle at Elderbush Gulch; A Gambler's Honor; During the Round-up; An Indian's Loyalty; Judith of Bethulia; The Adopted Brother; The Girl Across the Way

CHANDLER, LAURA B.: Author

1912: Edwin's Badge of Honor

1913: The Cure

CHRISTY, NAN: Actress (b. 1894)

1913: Almost a Wild Man; In Diplomatic Circles; The Vengeance of Galora; Under the Shadow of the Law

CLAIRE, GERTRUDE: Actress (1852-1928)

1910: The Way of the World; The Two Brothers; Ramona

CLAPP, CHESTER BLINN: Joined scenario staff in October 1912

CLARGES, VERNER: Actor (1848-1911)

1909: With Her Card; The Better Way; The Mills of the Gods;
The Sealed Room; "1776" or, The Hessian Renegades; The Little
Darling; In Old Kentucky; The Children's Friend; Comata, the
Sioux; Getting Even; A Fair Exchange; Two Women and a Man;
The Honor of His Family; On the Reef; The Impalement

1910: In the Border States; A Victim of Jealousy; The Face at
the Window; The Marked Time-Table; A Child's Impulse; The Call
to Arms; A Midnight Cupid; What the Daisy Said; A Flash of
Light; As the Bells Rang Out!; The House With Closed Shutters;
A Summer Idyl; Rose O'Salem-Town; Little Angels of Luck; The
Oath and the Man; Examination Day at School; The Iconoclast;
How Hubby Got a Raise; The Banker's Daughters; The Message
of the Violin; Two Little Waifs; The Passing of a Grouch; Simple
Charity; Love in Quarantine; Not So Bad As It Seemed; The Golden
Supper; When A Man Loves; The Lesson; Winning Back His Love;
His Trust Fulfilled; The Recreation of an Heiress

1911: Fisher Folks; The Lonedale Operator; Teaching Dad to Like
Her; The Spanish Gypsy; Paradise Lost; Madame Rex; The Mani-
cure Lady; Bobby, The Coward; Swords and Hearts; The Diving
Girl

CLARK, FRANK H.: Author

1913: Never Known to Smile

CLINTON, B. F.: Author

1913: The Enemy's Baby

CLYDE, E. E.: Author

1912: "She Is a Pippin"

COLE, THORNTON: Author

1911: Too Many Burglars; Pants and Pansies

COLLART, STELLA W.: Author

1910: Not So Bad As It Seemed

COMBS, MRS. HELEN: Author

1913: Their One Good Suit; Chocolate Dynamite

COMPSON, JOHN (See Cumpson, John R.)

COOGAN, LAWRENCE: Assistant to Henry Marvin

COOLIDGE, CARL K.: Author

1912: Kissing Kate

COOPER, JAMES FENIMORE: Writer (1789-1851)

1909: Leather Stocking

1910: A Mohawk's Way

COPPEE, FRANÇOIS: Author

1909: The Violin Maker of Cremona

COTTON, LUCY: Actress (1891-1948) (b. Lucy Cotton Magraw)

1910: The Fugitive

COULTAS, ALTA M.: Author

1913: He's a Lawyer

COURTWRIGHT, WILLIAM: Actor (1848-1933) (aka William Court-right)

1913: Her Wedding Bell; If We Only Knew; The Ranchero's Revenge; The Sorrowful Shore; In Diplomatic Circles; The Enemy's Baby; The Suffragette Minstrels; The Reformers, or The Lost Art of Minding One's Business

COYLE, WALTER V.: Actor (1888-1948)

1913: He's A Lawyer

CRAIG, CHARLES: Actor

1909: The Death Disc; Through the Breakers; A Corner in Wheat; The Redman's View; The Test; A Trap For Santa Claus; In Little Italy; To Save Her Soul; Choosing a Husband; The Rocky Road; The Dancing Girl of Butte; Her Terrible Ordeal; The Call; The Honor of His Family; On the Reef; The Last Deal; The Cloister's Touch; The Woman from Mellon's; One Night, and Then---; The English-man and the Girl; The Newlyweds

1910: The Thread of Destiny; In Old California; The Converts; His Last Dollar; Gold Is Not All; The Tenderfoot's Triumph; Up a Tree; Never Again; The Way of the World; The Gold-Seekers; The Impalement; A Child of the Ghetto; A Victim of Jealousy; The Face at the Window; A Child's Impulse; Muggsy's First Sweet-heart; The Purgation; A Midnight Cupid; A Child's Faith; A Flash of Light; As The Bells Rang Out!; An Arcadian Maid; A Salutary Lesson; The Usurer; An Old Story With a New Ending; In Life's Cycle; Wilful Peggy; Muggsy Becomes a Hero; A Summer Idyl;

Little Angels of Luck; A Summer Tragedy; The Oath and the Man; Examination Day at School; The Iconoclast; A Gold Necklace; A Lucky Toothache; The Masher; The Message of the Violin; Two Little Waifs; Winning Back His Love

CRANE, FRANK: Actor

1913: Men and Women

CRAWFORD, ASHTON: Author

1910: Fate's Turning

CRISP, DONALD: Actor (1880-1974)

1909: Through the Breakers

1910: A Child's Stratagem; Sunshine Sue; A Plain Song; The Golden Supper; Effecting a Cure; Winning Back His Love; A Wreath of Orange Blossoms; The Italian Barber; The Two Paths; Conscience; The Poor Sick Men; A Decree of Destiny; Fate's Turning; Help Wanted; What Shall We Do With Our Old; Heart Beats of Long Ago

1911: Out from the Shadow; Swords and Hearts; The Diving Girl; The Eternal Mother; The Squaw's Love; The Making of a Man; Her Awakening; The Adventures of Billy; The Long Road; The Battle; The Miser's Heart; The Failure

1913: Olaf - An Atom; By Man's Law; The Blue or the Gray; In the Elemental World

CROMWELL, OLIVER: Lord Protector of England (1599-1658)

1909: The Death Disc

CUMPSON, JOHN R.: Actor (1868-1913) (aka John Compson)

1908: Monday Morning in a Coney Island Police Court; The Stolen Jewels; A Smoked Husband; The Zulu's Heart; Romance of a Jewess; The Call of the Wild; Mr. Jones at the Ball; Mrs. Jones Entertains; The Sacrifice; A Rural Elopement; Mr. Jones Has a Card Party; The Joneses Have Amateur Theatricals; The Roue's Heart; The Hindoo Dagger; The Salvation Army Lass; Love Finds a Way; Tragic Love; The Girls and Daddy

1909: The Cord of Life; The Fascinating Mrs. Francis; Those Awful Hats; Jones and the Lady Book Agent; Trying to Get Arrested; The Brahma Diamond; His Wife's Mother; At the Altar; The Lure of the Gown; Lady Helen's Escapade; A Fool's Revenge; The Wooden Leg; The Voice of the Violin; "And A Little Child Shall Lead Them"; The French Duel; Jones And His New Neighbors; A Drunkard's Reformation; The Winning Coat; The Road to the Heart; Schneider's Anti-Noise Crusade; Twin Brothers; Confidence; The Note in the Shoe; Lucky Jim; A Troublesome Satchel; 'Tis An Ill Wind That Blows No Good; The Suicide Club; Resurrection; One Busy Hour; The Cricket on the Hearth; What Drink Did; Her First Biscuits; The Violin Maker of Cremona; Two Memories; The Lonely Villa; The Peachbasket Hat; Was Justice Served?; Mrs. Jones' Lover or, "I Want My Hat"; The Cardinal's Conspiracy; A Strange Meeting; They Would Elope; Jones' Burglar; With Her Card; The Mills of the Gods; The Little Darling; In Old Kentucky; Getting Even; A Fair Exchange

DALY, RICHARD: Author, Property Man

1912: One-Round O'Brien

1913: The Sweat Box

DARK CLOUD: Actor

1910: The Broken Doll; The Song of the Wildwood Flute

1911: The Squaw's Love; A Tale of the Wilderness

1913: The Influence of the Unknown; The Chieftain's Sons

DAVENPORT, DOROTHY: Actress (1895-1977) (aka Mrs. Wallace Reid)

1910: A Mohawk's Way; The Oath and the Man; Examination Day at School; The Iconoclast; A Gold Necklace; The Broken Doll; Two Little Waifs; Waiter No. 5; A Troublesome Baby; The Golden Supper

DAVIDSON, MAX: Actor (1875-1950)

1912: The Narrow Road

1913: Scenting a Terrible Crime

DAWLEY, J. SEARLE: Director (1878-1949)

1908: Rescued from an Eagle's Nest; Cupid's Pranks

DE GARDE, ADELE: Actress

1908: The Christmas Burglars; The Roue's Heart; The Salvation Army Lass

1909: The Golden Louis; The Medicine Bottle; The Deception; The Lure of the Gown; I Did It, Mamma; A Burglar's Mistake; The Voice of the Violin; "And A Little Child Shall Lead Them"; A Drunkard's Reformation; Twin Brothers; 'Tis An Ill Wind That Blows No Good; What Drink Did; The Lonely Villa; The Country Doctor; In the Window Recess; The Death Disc; Through the Breakers; In A Hempen Bag

DE LORDE, ANDRE: Author

  1909: The Lonely Villa

DE MILLE, HENRY C.: Playwright (1850-1893)

  1913: Men and Women; The Wife

DE MILLE, WILLIAM C.: Playwright (1878-1955)

  1913: Classmates; Strongheart

DE SELLEN, GRACE: Author

  1913: The Hero of Little Italy

DELARO, HATTIE: Actress (1860?-1941)

  1913: Men and Women

DICKENS, CHARLES: Author (1812-1870)

  1909: The Cricket on the Hearth

DILLON, EDWARD: Actor, Director, Author (1880-1933) (aka Eddie
  Dillon)

  1907: (as actor) Falsely Accused!

  1908: (as actor) Lonesome Junction; Classmates; Bobby's Kodak;
  The Princess in the Vase; The Boy Detective -or- The Abductors
  Foiled; Caught by Wireless; Old Isaacs, the Pawnbroker; The
  Sculptor's Nightmare; His Day of Rest; Mixed Babies; The Romance
  of an Egg; Thompson's Night Out; 'Ostler Joe; Over the Hills to
  the Poorhouse; The Invisible Fluid; The Outlaw; The Man in the
  Box; Deceived Slumming Party; At The French Ball; At The Cross-
  roads of Life; The Black Viper; The Kentuckian; The Stage Rustler;
  The Fight for Freedom; The Tavern-Keeper's Daughter; Where
  the Breakers Roar

  1909: (as actor) The Little Teacher; A Change of Heart

  1910: (as actor) In the Border States; A Victim of Jealousy; The
  Face at the Window; The Marked Time-Table; A Child's Impulse;
  Muggsy's First Sweetheart; The Purgation; The Call to Arms; A
  Midnight Cupid; A Child's Faith; A Flash of Light; As The Bells
  Rang Out!; An Arcadian Maid; Her Father's Pride; A Salutary
  Lesson; The Usurer; The Sorrows of the Unfaithful; In Life's
  Cycle; The Affair of an Egg; Wilful Peggy; Muggsy Becomes A
  Hero; The Modern Prodigal; Rose O'Salem-Town; Little Angels of
  Luck; A Mohawk's Way; A Summer Tragedy; The Oath and the
  Man; Examination Day at School; That Chink At Golden Gulch; A
  Gold Necklace; A Lucky Toothache; The Banker's Daughters; The

Masher; The Message of the Violin; Two Little Waifs; Waiter No.
5; Simple Charity; The Fugitive; Sunshine Sue; A Plain Song; His
Sister-In-Law; Effecting A Cure; Turning the Tables; The Lesson;
Happy Jack, a Hero; White Roses; The Italian Barber; The Mid-
night Marauder; After the Ball; Three Sisters; The Poor Sick Men;
A Decree of Destiny; Fate's Turning; What Shall We Do With Our
Old; Priscilla's Engagement Kiss

1911: (as actor); Fisher Folks; The Lonedale Operator; Teaching
Dad to Like Her; Cured; Priscilla's April Fool Joke; Priscilla and
the Umbrella; The Chief's Daughter; Madame Rex; A Knight of the
Road; Misplaced Jealousy; Taking His Medicine; Enoch Arden,
Part Two; The Manicure Lady; Dave's Love Affair; The Delayed
Proposal; Fighting Blood; Bobby, the Coward; A Country Cupid;
The Diving Girl; A Convenient Burglar; The Making of a Man; Too
Many Burglars; The Long Road; Why He Gave Up; Through His
Wife's Picture; The Miser's Heart; The Failure; Sunshine Through
the Dark; The Baby and the Stork; The Old Bookkeeper; For His
Son; With a Kodak; A Blot in the 'Scutcheon; A String of Pearls;
The Root of Evil

1912: (as actor) The Engagement Ring; A Voice from the Deep;
Hot Stuff; The Would-Be Shriner; Help! Help!; Those Hicksville
Boys; Their First Kidnapping Case; Won by a Fish; The Fickle
Spaniard; The Leading Man (also au); When the Fire-Bells Rang;
A Close Call; Helen's Marriage; Algy, the Watchman; The Spirit
Awakened; A Dash Through the Clouds; What the Doctor Ordered;
The Mystery of the Milk; The Massacre; One-Round O'Brien;
Willie Becomes an Artist; An Interrupted Elopement; The Tragedy
of a Dress Suit; Stern Papa; Mr. Grouch at the Seashore; Through
Dumb Luck; Getting Rid of Trouble; Blind Love; Love's Messenger;
A Limited Divorce; A Ten-Karat Hero; At the Basket Picnic; A
Real Estate Deal; His Auto's Maiden Trip; Their Idols; An Absent-
Minded Burglar; The Club-Man and the Crook; Hoist on His Own
Petard; After the Honeymoon; Jinx's Birthday Party; "She is a
Pippin"; The Divorcee (au only); The Informer; Bill Bogg's Wind-
fall; Oh, What a Boob!; The Bite of a Snake; Kissing Kate; There
Were Hoboes Three; An Up-to-Date Lochinvar; Look Not Upon the
Wine; Among Club Fellows; What is the Use of Repining?; A Queer
Elopement; The Delivery Package; Edwin's Badge of Honor; Love
in an Apartment Hotel

1913: (as actor) The Spring of Life; Tightwad's Predicament; The
Power of the Camera; The Old Gray Mare; All Hail to the King;
Edwin Masquerades; Their One Good Suit; A Lesson To Mashers;
An "Uncle Tom's Cabin" Troupe; A Horse on Bill; He Had a Guess
Coming; A Rainy Day; The Little Tease; Cinderella and the Boob;
The Trimmer's Trimmed; Just Kids; Red Hicks Defies the World;
Jenks Becomes a Desperate Character; Almost a Wild Man; The
Rise and Fall of McDoo; The Mothering Heart; Mister Jefferson
Green; A Compromising Complication; Faust and the Lily; An Old
Maid's Deception; A Sea Dog's Love; The Noisy Suitors; The Sweat-
Box; While the Count Goes Bathing; Mr. Spriggs Buys a Dog;

Cupid and the Cook (also au); Come Seben, Leben (au only); An
Indian's Loyalty; The Suffragette Minstrels; The Lady in Black;
His Hoodoo (d only); The End of the World (d only); A Saturday
Holiday (d only); Dyed But Not Dead (d only); Scenting a Terrible
Crime; With the Aid of Phrenology (d only); A Circumstantial
Hero (d only); Never Known to Smile (d only); McGann and His
Octette (d only); Aunts, Too Many (also d); The Winning Punch
(d only); A Fallen Hero (d only); In the Hands of the Black Hands
(d only); An Evening with Wilder Spender (d only); A Barber Cure;
Boarders and Bombs; "Mixed Nuts" (d and au); A Cure for Suf-
fragettes (d only); Mrs. Casey's Gorilla (d only); He's A Lawyer
(d only); The Somnambulists; Bink's Vacation; How the Day Was
Saved (d only)

DILLON, JOHN T.: Actor (1866-1937) (aka Jack Dillon)

1908: Lonesome Junction

1910: In the Border States; The Marked Time-Table; A Child's
Impulse; A Midnight Cupid; What the Daisy Said; A Flash of Light;
As the Bells Rang Out!; An Arcadian Maid; The House With Closed
Shutters; Her Father's Pride; The Affair of an Egg; A Mohawk's
Way; The Iconoclast; That Chink at Golden Gulch; The Broken Doll;
The Banker's Daughters; His Trust Fulfilled; The Italian Barber;
The Two Paths; His Wife's Sweethearts; After the Ball; The Poor
Sick Men; A Decree of Destiny; Fate's Turning; Help Wanted; What
Shall We Do With Our Old

1911: Fisher Folks; Was He a Coward?; Teaching Dad to Like
Her; Cured; The Spanish Gypsy; The Broken Cross; The Chief's
Daughter; Madame Rex; A Knight of the Road; In the Days of '49;
The Two Sides; The New Dress; The Crooked Road; The Primal
Call; The Jealous Husband; The Indian Brothers; The Last Drop
of Water; Bobby, the Coward; The Ruling Passion; Out from the
Shadow; Caught with the Goods; The Transformation of Mike; The
Sunbeam; A String of Pearls; The Root of Evil

1912: Blind Love; A Disappointed Mamma; The Musketeers of Pig
Alley; A Ten-Karat Hero; Like the Cat, They Came Back; His
Auto's Maiden Trip; Their Idols; An Absent-Minded Burglar; Gold
and Glitter; My Baby; The Informer; Brutality; The New York Hat;
My Hero; The Burglar's Dilemma; A Cry for Help; The God Within;
Three Friends; The Telephone Girl and the Lady; The Tender-
Hearted Boy; Oil and Water; A Chance Deception; Fate; A Mis-
appropriated Turkey; Love in an Apartment Hotel

1913: A Welcome Intruder; The Sheriff's Baby; The Hero of Little
Italy; A Horse on Bill; He Had A Guess Coming; A Ragtime Ro-
mance; The Wanderer; Olaf - An Atom; A Dangerous Foe; Red
Hicks Defies the World; Almost a Wild Man; The Mothering Heart;
Her Mother's Oath; The Switch-Tower; In Diplomatic Circles; The
Enemy's Baby; Mr. Spriggs Buys a Dog; A Gambler's Honor; The
Mirror; Brute Force; The Monument; The Vengeance of Galora;

Under the Shadow of the Law; I Was Meant For You; The Work Habit; A Woman in the Ultimate; For the Son of the House; A Modest Hero; A Fallen Hero

DION, HECTOR: Actor (b. 1881)

1912: Just Like a Woman; A Lodging for the Night; A Father's Lesson; Drink's Lure; The Wrong Bottle

1913: The Crook and the Girl; A Tender-Hearted Crook; The Stopped Clock; No Place for Father; His Inspiration

DIXON, MR.: Employee. Noted in Moving Picture World, 19 August 1911, p. 449.

DONALDSON, ROBERT A.: Author

1913: A Barber Cure

DONNELLY, ANTHONY: Author

1910: Winning Back His Love; After the Ball

DOUGHERTY, LEE E.: Director of advertising (aka Lew Dougherty)

DOWNS, CHARLES: Assistant cameraman with the O'Sullivan unit.

DROUET, ROBERT: Actor (1874-1914) (aka Robert Druet)

1913: The Wife

DUNCAN, ALBERT "BUD": Actor, Author (1883-1960) (aka Bud Duncan)

1912: Bill Bogg's Windfall; Among Club Fellows; A Queer Elopement; A Delivery Package (au only)

1913: The Spring of Life; A Rainy Day; Frappe Love; The Trimmers Trimmed (also au); Just Kids; Red Hicks Defies the World; Jenks Becomes a Desperate Character; Almost a Wild Man; Mister Jefferson Green; A Compromising Complication; The Widow's Kids

DUNCAN, GRACE: Author

1910: A Gold Necklace

EAGLE EYE: Actor

1913: An Indian's Loyalty; The Chieftain's Sons

EARL, MISS: Actress

1908: Rescued From an Eagle's Nest

EGAN, GLADYS: Actress

1908: Behind the Scenes; The Zulu's Heart; Romance of a Jewess; After Many Years

1909: What Drink Did; The Lonely Villa; The Way of Man; The Faded Lilies; The Message; Was Justice Served?; The Country Doctor; Jealousy and the Man; The Seventh Day; A Convict's Sacrifice; They Would Elope; The Heart of an Outlaw; The Children's Friend; A Fair Exchange; Wanted, a Child; The Little Teacher; His Lost Love; In the Watches of the Night; What's Your Hurry?; A Corner in Wheat; In a Hempen Bag; A Trap for Santa Claus; In Little Italy; The Rocky Road; The Call; On the Reef; One Night, and Then---; The Englishman and the Girl

1910: The Newlyweds; Gold is Not All; As It Is In Life; Thou Shalt Not; The Way of the World; The Unchanging Sea; Unexpected Help; A Child of the Ghetto; In the Border States; A Child's Impulse; A Child's Faith; As The Bells Rang Out!; The House With Closed Shutters; A Salutary Lesson; The Usurer; The Sorrows of the Unfaithful; Rose O'Salem-Town; Little Angels of Luck; A Summer Tragedy; Examination Day at School; The Iconoclast; The Broken Doll; Waiter No. 5; A Troublesome Baby; A Child's Stratagem; His Sister-in-Law; His Trust Fulfilled; Conscience

1911: Paradise Lost; The Two Sides; The Crooked Road; A Romany Tragedy; Fighting Blood; The Last Drop of Water; Bobby, the Coward; The Ruling Passion; The Village Hero; The Making of a Man; The Sunbeam

1912: A Child's Remorse; In the North Woods; The Painted Lady; Fate; McGann and His Octette; Red and Pete, Partners

1913: Men and Women

ELIOT, GEORGE: Author (1819-1880) (pseud. for Mary Ann or Marian Evans)

1909: A Fair Exchange

ELMER, BILLY: Actor (1872-1945) (b. William E. Johns)

1913: A Horse on Bill; The Left-Handed Man; The House of Darkness; The Mothering Heart; The Suffragette Minstrels; The Reformers, or The Lost Art of Minding One's Business

ELMER, RUTH M.: Author

1912: A Mixed Affair

EVANS, FRANK: Actor (aka "Big" Evans)

1909: With Her Card; Leather Stocking; A Fair Exchange; His

Lost Love; Lines of White On a Sullen Sea; The Gibson Goddess;
The Expiation; What's Your Hurry?; The Restoration; Nursing a
Viper; The Light That Came; A Midnight Adventure; The Moun-
taineer's Honor; In the Window Recess; The Trick That Failed;
The Death Disc; Through the Breakers; A Corner in Wheat; The
Redman's View; In Little Italy; To Save Her Soul; The Day After;
The Rocky Road; The Dancing Girl of Butte; The Call; On the
Reef; The Last Deal; The Cloister's Touch; The Woman From
Mellon's

1910:   The Newlyweds; The Impalement; A Child of the Ghetto;
In the Border States; The Marked Time-Table; A Child's Impulse;
A Midnight Cupid; A Child's Faith; What the Daisy Said; An Ar-
cadian Maid; The House with Closed Shutters; The Usurer; In
Life's Cycle; The Modern Prodigal; Rose O'Salem-Town; A Mo-
hawk's Way; The Oath and the Man; The Iconoclast; That Chink
at Golden Gulch; The Broken Doll; The Banker's Daughters; The
Masher; The Fugitive; A Child's Stratagem; Winning Back His
Love; The Two Paths; Conscience; His Wife's Sweethearts; The
Poor Sick Men; Fate's Turning; What Shall We Do With Our Old

1911:   A Country Cupid; The Ruling Passion; Swords and Hearts;
The Village Hero; The Making of a Man; Her Awakening; The Ad-
ventures of Billy; The Long Road; Dooley's Scheme; A Woman
Scorned; The Miser's Heart; The Failure; A Terrible Discovery;
The Baby and the Stork; The Transformation of Mike; Billy's
Stratagem

1912:   Under Burning Skies; Iola's Promise; The Goddess of Sage-
brush Gulch; Help! Help!; One is Business, the Other Crime;
The Lesser Evil; Those Hicksville Boys; Their First Kidnapping
Case; Won by a Fish; A Lodging for the Night; When Kings Were
the Law; The Leading Man; When the Fire-Bells Rang; A Close
Call; Helen's Marriage; Algy, the Watchman; Home Folks; A
Temporary Truce; Neighbors; Heaven Avenges; Black Sheep; The
Tourists; One-Round O'Brien; His Own Fault; The Narrow Road;
The Inner Circle; The Tragedy of a Dress Suit; Friends; A Feud
in the Kentucky Hills; Blind Love; The Musketeers of Pig Alley;
Brutality; The Unwelcome Guest; My Hero; The Burglar's Dilemma;
The God Within; Three Friends; Oil and Water; Fate; A Misappro-
priated Turkey; Love in an Apartment Hotel

1913:   The Hero of Little Italy; The Left-Handed Man; Olaf - An
Atom; A Timely Interception; The Yaqui Cur; Red Hicks Defies the
World; Her Mother's Oath; The Switch-Tower; Brute Force; The
Suffragette Minstrels; The Reformers, or The Lost Art of Minding
One's Business; Judith of Bethulia; The Law and His Son; The
Stopped Clock; "Old Coupons"; The Detective's Stratagem; By Man's
Law

FELTUS, PAUL L.:   Author

1913:   His Secret

FIFE, M. SHANNON: Author

    1911: A Message from the Moon

    1912: The New Baby

    1913: Diversion

FINCH, FLORA: Actress (1869-1940)

    1908: Mrs. Jones Entertains; The Helping Hand; A Wreath in Time; Mr. Jones Has a Card Party

    1909: Those Awful Hats; Jones and the Lady Book Agent; The Way of Man

FLEMING, CHARLES: Actor

    1913: The Wife

FOOTE, COURTENAY: Actor (d. 1925)

    1912: So Near, Yet So Far

FORDE, VICTORIA: Actress (1897-1964)

    1910: Love in Quarantine

    1912: The Bite of a Snake; The Best Man Wins

    1913: The Yaqui Cur

FOSTER, EDNA: Actress

    1911: Bobby, the Coward; A Country Cupid; The Ruling Passion; The Old Confectioner's Mistake; The Adventures of Billy; The Long Road; The Battle; A Terrible Discovery; The Baby and the Stork; For His Son; The Transformation of Mike; A Blot in the 'Scutcheon; Billy's Stratagem; The Sunbeam; A String of Pearls

    1912: With the Enemy's Help; A Misappropriated Turkey; Dyed But Not Dead, "Old Coupons"

    1913: Men and Women

FRAMBERS, CLARENCE A.: Author

    1913: The Van Nostrand Tiara

FREDERICKS, WALTER S.: Author (b. 1873)

    1913: Slippery Slim Repents

FULTON, V.: Author

1912: After the Honeymoon

GARCELON, DONALD D.: Author

1913: With the Aid of Phrenology

GATES, HARVEY H.: Author

1913: I Was Meant For You

GAUDIO, TONY: Cameraman (1885-1951) (b. Gaetono Antonio Gaudio)

1913: Classmates; Strongheart; Men and Women

GAUNTIER, GENE: Actress, Author (1880-1966) (b. Genevieve Gauntier Liggett)

1908: The Music Master; Hulda's Lovers; The Romance of an Egg; Thompson's Night Out; The Man in the Box; The Girl and the Outlaw; Betrayed by a Handprint; Taming of the Shrew

GEBHARDT, GEORGE: Actor (1879-1919) (aka Frank Gebhardt)

1908: The Man in the Box; Deceived Slumming Party; The Black Viper; The Kentuckian; The Stage Rustler; The Fight for Freedom; The Redman and the Child; The Tavern-Keeper's Daughter; A Calamitous Elopement; The Greaser's Gauntlet; The Man and the Woman; For Love of Gold; The Fatal Hour; For a Wife's Honor; Balked at the Altar; The Girl and the Outlaw; The Red Girl; Betrayed by a Handprint; Monday Morning in a Coney Island Police Court; Behind the Scenes; The Heart of O Yama; Where the Breakers Roar; The Stolen Jewels; A Smoked Husband; The Zulu's Heart; The Vaquero's Vow; Father Gets in the Game; The Barbarian, Ingomar; The Planter's Wife; The Devil; Romance of a Jewess; The Call of the Wild; After Many Years; Mr. Jones at the Ball; Concealing a Burglar; Taming of the Shrew; The Ingrate; A Woman's Way; The Pirate's Gold; The Guerrilla; The Curtain Pole; The Song of the Shirt; The Clubman and the Tramp; Money Mad; The Feud and the Turkey; The Test of Friendship; The Reckoning; The Valet's Wife; One Touch of Nature; An Awful Moment; The Helping Hand; The Maniac Cook; The Christmas Burglars; A Wreath in Time; The Honor of Thieves; The Criminal Hypnotist; The Sacrifice; The Welcome Burglar; A Rural Elopement; The Joneses Have Amateur Theatricals; The Hindoo Dagger; The Salvation Army Lass; Love Finds a Way; Tragic Love

1909: The Cord of Life; The Fascinating Mrs. Francis; Those Awful Hats; Jones and the Lady Book Agent; The Brahma Diamond; Politician's Love Story; The Golden Louis; At the Altar

GENEVA, FLORENCE: Actress

1912: Two Daughters of Eve; So Near, Yet So Far

GIBBS, MR.: Employee. Noted in Moving Picture World, 19 August 1911, p. 449.

GIBNEY, JOHN J. A.: Author

1913: The Detective's Stratagem

GIDLEY, WILL S.: Author

1913: In the Hands of the Black Hands

GISH, DOROTHY: Actress, Author (1898-1968)

1912: An Unseen Enemy; So Near, Yet So Far; The Painted Lady; The Musketeers of Pig Alley; Gold and Glitter; My Baby; The Informer; My Hero; Oil and Water

1913: Broken Ways; The Perfidy of Mary; The Lady and the Mouse; Just Gold; His Mother's Son; Red Hicks Defies the World; Almost a Wild Man; Her Mother's Oath; The Widow's Kids; Those Little Flowers; The Suffragette Minstrels (also au); Papa's Baby; The Lady in Black; The Reformers, or The Lost Art of Minding One's Business; Judith of Bethulia; The Adopted Brother; By Man's Law; The Wife

GISH, LILLIAN: Actress (b. 1896)

1912: An Unseen Enemy; So Near, Yet So Far; In the Aisles of the Wild; The Painted Lady; The Musketeers of Pig Alley; Gold and Glitter; The Informer; Brutality; The Unwelcome Guest; The New York Hat; My Hero; The Burglar's Dilemma; A Cry for Help; Oil and Water

1913: A Misunderstood Boy; The Left-Handed Man; The Lady and the Mouse; The House of Darkness; Just Gold; A Timely Interception; The Mothering Heart; The Battle at Elderbush Gulch; During the Round-Up; An Indian's Loyalty; Judith of Bethulia; A Woman in the Ultimate; A Modest Hero; So Runs the Way; The Madonna of the Storm

GLASER, GEORGE E.: Author

1911: With a Kodak

GLASSMIRE, ALBERT: Author (1882-1926)

1913: All for Science

GOLDEN, OLIVE FULLER: Actress, Author (b. 1896) (aka Olive Deering; Olive Carey; Mrs. Harry Carey)

1913: The Perfidy of Mary; Just Kids (au only); The Sorrowful Shore

GOODMAN, HALLIE B.: Author

1910: The Recreation of an Heiress

1911: When Wifey Holds the Purse-Strings

GORMAN, CHARLES: Actor (aka Texas Gorman)

1911: The Blind Princess and the Poet; A Terrible Discovery; The Old Bookkeeper

1912: Under Burning Skies; Iola's Promise; The Goddess of Sagebrush Gulch; The Girl and Her Trust; The Lesser Evil; His Lesson; When Kings Were the Law; Home Folks; Algy, the Watchman; A Temporary Truce; Tomboy Bessie; A Dash Through the Clouds; Black Sheep; The Massacre; With the Enemy's Help; The Chief's Blanket; The Narrow Road; The Inner Circle; An Interrupted Elopement; The Painted Lady; A Sailor's Heart; The God Within; Fate; When Love Forgives

1913: Broken Ways; Her Wedding Bell; The Left-Handed Man; A Timely Interception; The Yaqui Cur; Red Hicks Defies the World; Jenks Becomes a Desperate Character; Almost a Wild Man; Her Mother's Oath; The Battle at Elderbush Gulch; The Mistake; The Reformers, or The Lost Art of Minding One's Business; The Adopted Brother; The Chieftain's Sons; His Inspiration; By Man's Law; The Blue or the Gray

GRANDON, FRANCIS J.: Actor, Author (1879-1929) (aka Frank Grandon, Francis Grandin)

1909: Two Women and a Man; The Light That Came; The Dancing Girl of Butte; The Call; The Honor of His Family; The Cloister's Touch; The Woman From Mellon's; The Course of True Love; The Duke's Plan; One Night, and Then---; The Englishman and the Girl

1910: The Love of Lady Irma; His Last Burglary; Taming a Husband; The Newlyweds; The Thread of Destiny; In Old California; The Man; His Last Dollar; Faithful; Gold Is Not All; A Rich Revenge; Up a Tree; The Way of the World; An Affair of Hearts; The Gold-Seekers; Love Among the Roses; Unexpected Help; Ramona; A Knot in the Plot; The Impalement; A Child of the Ghetto; In the Border States; The Face at the Window; The Marked Time-Table; The Purgation; The Call to Arms; A Midnight Cupid; What the Daisy Said; Serious Sixteen; An Arcadian Maid; The House with Closed Shutters; Her Father's Pride; The Usurer; In Life's Cycle; Wilful Peggy; Muggsy Becomes a Hero; The Modern Prodigal; Rose

O'Salem -Town; Little Angels of Luck; A Mohawk's Way; The Oath and the Man; Examination Day at School; The Iconoclast; That Chink at Golden Gulch; The Broken Doll; The Message of the Violin; Simple Charity; The Fugitive; The Song of the Wildwood Flute; Sunshine Sue; The Golden Supper; Happy Jack, a Hero; His Trust; A Wreath of Orange Blossoms; White Roses; His Wife's Sweethearts; The Poor Sick Men; Fate's Turning; What Shall We Do With Our Old; The Lily of the Tenements; Heart Beats of Long Ago

1911: Comrades; The Lonedale Operator; Was He A Coward?; Teaching Dad to Like Her; The Spanish Gypsy; The Chief's Daughter; A Knight of the Road; Madame Rex; In the Days of '49; The Two Sides; The New Dress; Enoch Arden, Parts One and Two; The Primal Call; The Indian Brothers; The Delayed Proposal; Fighting Blood; The Last Drop of Water; Bobby, the Coward; Swords and Hearts

GRAYBILL, JOSEPH: Actor (1887-1913) (aka Joe Grable)

1910: A Victim of Jealousy; The Face at the Window; The Marked Time-Table; A Child's Impulse; Muggsy's First Sweetheart; The Purgation; The Call to Arms; A Midnight Cupid; What the Daisy Said; A Flash of Light; As the Bells Rang Out!; An Arcadian Maid; The House with Closed Shutters; An Old Story with a New Ending; When We Were in Our 'Teens; In Life's Cycle; The Broken Doll; Effecting a Cure; Turning the Tables; The Lesson; Winning Back His Love; His Trust; White Roses; The Italian Barber; Conscience; A Decree of Destiny; Help Wanted

1911: Fisher Folks; The Lonedale Operator; Was He a Coward?; Teaching Dad to Like Her; Priscilla's April Fool Joke; Priscilla and the Umbrella; Madame Rex; How She Triumphed; The New Dress; Enoch Arden, Parts One and Two; The White Rose of the Wilds; The Crooked Road; The Primal Call; The Last Drop of Water; Bobby, the Coward; A Country Cupid; The Diving Girl; The Baron; Italian Blood; The Making of a Man; The Adventures of Billy; The Long Road; The Battle; Saved From Himself; Love in the Hills; Through Darkened Vales; The Failure; The Voice of the Child; A Blot in the 'Scutcheon

1912: The Painted Lady; Gold and Glitter; The Informer; Brutality; The God Within

GREGORY, JOSEPHINE T.: Author

1912: Their Idols

GRIBBIN, FRANK B.: Author (aka Frank B. Gribbins, F. C. Gribbon, Frank C. Griffin)

1913: Mr. Spriggs Buys a Dog; The Influence of the Unknown; Aunts, Too Many

GRIFFIN, C. A.: Author

1912: Hoist on His Own Petard

GRIFFITH, DAVID WARK: Director, Actor, Author, Producer
(1875-1948) (aka Lawrence Griffith)

1907: (as actor) Professional Jealousy; Falsely Accused!

1908: (as actor) Rescued From an Eagle's Nest; Classmates; Cupid's Pranks; The Princess in the Vase; The Yellow Peril; Her
First Adventure; Caught by Wireless; Old Isaacs, the Pawnbroker;
A Famous Escape; King of the Cannibal Islands; Hulda's Lovers;
The Music Master (also au); The King's Messenger; The Sculptor's Nightmare; When Knights Were Bold (au only); Mixed Babies
(au only); 'Ostler Joe (also au); The Invisible Fluid; The Outlaw
(au only); The Man in the Box; Deceived Slumming Party (also
co-d); At the French Ball; At the Crossroads of Life (also au);
The Black Viper (also co-d); The Kentuckian; The Stage Rustler

(as director) The Adventures of Dollie; The Redman and the Child;
The Tavern-Keeper's Daughter; The Bandit's Waterloo; A Calami-
tous Elopement (also au); The Greaser's Gauntlet; The Man and
the Woman; For Love of Gold; The Fatal Hour (also a); For A
Wife's Honor; Balked at the Altar; The Girl and the Outlaw; The
Red Girl (also a); Betrayed by a Handprint; Monday Morning in a
Coney Island Police Court; Behind the Scenes; The Heart of O
Yama (also a); Where the Breakers Roar; The Stolen Jewels (also
a); A Smoked Husband; The Zulu's Heart; The Vaquero's Vow;
Father Gets in the Game; The Barbarian, Ingomar; The Planter's
Wife; The Devil; Romance of a Jewess; The Call of the Wild;
After Many Years; Mr. Jones at the Ball; Concealing a Burglar;
Taming of the Shrew; The Ingrate; A Woman's Way; The Pirate's
Gold; The Guerrilla; The Curtain Pole; The Song of the Shirt; The
Clubman and the Tramp; Money Mad; Mrs. Jones Entertains; The
Feud and the Turkey; The Test of Friendship; The Reckoning; The
Valet's Wife; One Touch of Nature; An Awful Moment; The Helping
Hand; The Maniac Cook; The Christmas Burglars; A Wreath in
Time; The Honor of Thieves; The Criminal Hypnotist; The Sacri-
fice; The Welcome Burglar; A Rural Elopement; Mr. Jones Has A
Card Party; The Joneses Have Amateur Theatricals; Edgar Allen
Poe; The Roue's Heart; The Hindoo Dagger; The Salvation Army
Lass; Love Finds A Way; Tragic Love; The Girls and Daddy (also
a)

1909: (as director) Those Boys; The Cord of Life; The Fascinating
Mrs. Francis; Those Awful Hats; Jones and the Lady Book Agent;
Trying to Get Arrested; The Brahma Diamond; The Drive for a
Life; Politician's Love Story; His Wife's Mother; The Golden Louis;
His Ward's Love; At the Altar; The Prussian Spy; The Medicine
Bottle; The Deception; The Lure of the Gown; Lady Helen's Es-
capade; A Fool's Revenge; The Wooden Leg; I Did It, Mamma; A
Burglar's Mistake; The Voice of the Violin; "And A Little Child

Shall Lead Them"; The French Duel; Jones and His New Neigh-
bors; A Drunkard's Reformation; The Winning Coat; A Rude Host-
ess; The Road to the Heart; The Eavesdropper; Schneider's Anti-
Noise Crusade; Twin Brothers; Confidence; The Note in the Shoe;
Lucky Jim; A Sound Sleeper; A Troublesome Satchel; 'Tis An Ill
Wind That Blows No Good; The Suicide Club; Resurrection; One
Busy Hour; A Baby's Shoe; Eloping with Aunty; The Cricket on
the Hearth; The Jilt; Eradicating Aunty; What Drink Did; Her First
Biscuits; The Violin Maker of Cremona; Two Memories; The Lone-
ly Villa; The Peachbasket Hat; The Son's Return; His Duty; A New
Trick; The Necklace; The Way of Man; The Faded Lilies; The
Message; The Friend of the Family; Was Justice Served?; Mrs.
Jones' Lover or, "I Want My Hat"; The Mexican Sweethearts; The
Country Doctor; Jealousy and the Man; The Renunciation; The
Cardinal's Conspiracy; The Seventh Day; Tender Hearts; A Con-
vict's Sacrifice; A Strange Meeting; Sweet and Twenty; The Slave;
They Would Elope; Jones' Burglar; The Mended Lute; The Indian
Runner's Romance; With Her Card; The Better Way; His Wife's
Visitor; The Heart of an Outlaw; The Mills of the Gods; Pranks;
"Oh, Uncle"; The Sealed Room; "1776" or, The Hessian Rene-
gades; The Little Darling; In Old Kentucky; The Children's Friend;
Comata, the Sioux; Leather Stocking; Getting Even; The Broken
Locket; A Fair Exchange; The Awakening; Pippa Passes or, The
Song of Conscience; Fools of Fate; Wanted, A Child; The Little
Teacher; A Change of Heart; His Lost Love; Lines of White on a
Sullen Sea; The Gibson Goddess; In the Watches of the Night; The
Expiation; What's Your Hurry?; The Restoration; Nursing A Viper;
Two Women and a Man; The Light That Came; A Midnight Adven-
ture; The Open Gate; Sweet Revenge; The Mountaineer's Honor; In
the Window Recess; The Trick That Failed; The Death Disc; Through
the Breakers; A Corner in Wheat; In a Hempen Bag; The Redman's
View; The Test; A Trap for Santa Claus; In Little Italy; To Save
Her Soul; The Day After; Choosing a Husband; The Rocky Road;
The Dancing Girl of Butte; Her Terrible Ordeal; The Call; The
Honor of His Family; On the Reef; The Last Deal; The Cloister's
Touch; The Woman From Mellon's; The Duke's Plan; One Night,
and Then---; The Englishman and the Girl

1910: The Final Settlement; His Last Burglary; Taming a Husband;
The Newlyweds; The Thread of Destiny; In Old California; The
Man; The Converts; Faithful; The Twisted Trail; Gold Is Not All;
As It Is In Life; A Rich Revenge; A Romance of the Western Hills;
Thou Shalt Not; The Way of the World; The Unchanging Sea; The
Gold-Seekers; Love Among the Roses; The Two Brothers; Unex-
pected Help; Ramona; Over Silent Paths; The Impalement; In the
Season of Buds; A Child of the Ghetto; In the Border States; A
Victim of Jealousy; The Face at the Window; The Marked Time-
Table; A Child's Impulse; Muggsy's First Sweetheart; The Purga-
tion; The Call to Arms; A Midnight Cupid; A Child's Faith; What
the Daisy Said; Serious Sixteen; A Flash of Light; As the Bells
Rang Out!; An Arcadian Maid; The House with Closed Shutters; Her
Father's Pride; A Salutary Lesson; The Usurer; The Sorrows of
the Unfaithful; An Old Story with a New Ending; In Life's Cycle;

Wilful Peggy; A Summer Idyl; The Modern Prodigal; Rose O'Salem-
Town; Little Angels of Luck; A Mohawk's Way; The Oath and the
Man; Examination Day at School; The Iconoclast; That Chink at
Golden Gulch; The Broken Doll; The Banker's Daughters; The Mes-
sage of the Violin; Two Little Waifs; Waiter No. 5; Simple Charity;
The Fugitive; The Song of the Wildwood Flute; A Child's Strata-
gem; Sunshine Sue; A Plain Song; His Sister-In-Law; The Golden
Supper; When a Man Loves; The Lesson; Winning Back His Love;
His Trust; His Trust Fulfilled; A Wreath of Orange Blossoms;
The Italian Barber; The Two Paths; Conscience; Three Sisters;
A Decree of Destiny; Fate's Turning; What Shall We Do With Our
Old; The Diamond Star; The Lily of the Tenements; Heart Beats
of Long Ago

1911: Fisher Folks; His Daughter; The Lonedale Operator; The
Heart of a Savage; Was He a Coward?; Teaching Dad to Like Her;
The Spanish Gypsy; The Broken Cross; The Chief's Daughter; A
Knight of the Road; Madame Rex; His Mother's Scarf; How She
Triumphed; In the Days of '49; The Two Sides; The New Dress;
Enoch Arden, Parts One and Two; The White Rose of the Wilds;
The Crooked Road; A Romany Tragedy; A Smile of a Child; The
Primal Call; The Jealous Husband; The Indian Brothers; The Thief
and the Girl; Her Sacrifice; The Blind Princess and the Poet;
Fighting Blood; The Last Drop of Water; Bobby, the Coward; A
Country Cupid; The Ruling Passion; The Rose of Kentucky; Out
From the Shadow; The Sorrowful Example; Swords and Hearts;
The Stuff Heroes Are Made Of; The Old Confectioner's Mistake;
The Unveiling; The Eternal Mother; Dan, the Dandy; The Revenue
Man and the Girl; The Squaw's Love; Italian Blood; The Making
of a Man; Her Awakening; The Adventures of Billy; The Long
Road; The Battle; Saved from Himself; Love in the Hills; The
Trail of Books; Through Darkened Vales; A Woman Scorned; The
Miser's Heart; The Failure; Sunshine Through the Dark; As In a
Looking Glass; A Terrible Discovery; A Tale of the Wilderness;
The Baby and the Stork; The Voice of the Child; The Old Book-
keeper; A Sister's Love; For His Son; The Transformation of Mike;
A Blot in the 'Scutcheon; Billy's Stratagem; The Sunbeam; A String
of Pearls; The Root of Evil

1912: Under Burning Skies; A Siren of Impulse; Iola's Promise;
The Goddess of Sagebrush Gulch; The Girl and Her Trust; The
Punishment; Fate's Interception; The Female of the Species; Just
Like a Woman; One is Business, the Other Crime; The Old Actor;
The Lesser Evil; A Lodging for the Night; His Lesson; When Kings
Were the Law; A Beast at Bay; Home Folks; A Temporary Truce;
Lena and the Geese; The Spirit Awakened; The School Teacher
and the Waif; An Indian Summer; Man's Lust for Gold; Man's
Genesis; Heaven Avenges; The Sands of Dee; A Pueblo Legend;
The Massacre (also au); The Narrow Road; A Child's Remorse;
The Inner Circle; A Change of Spirit (also au); An Unseen Enemy;
Two Daughters of Eve (also a); Friends (also au); So Near, Yet
So Far; A Feud in the Kentucky Hills (also au); In the Aisles of
the Wild; The One She Loved; The Painted Lady (also au); The

Musketeers of Pig Alley (also au); Heredity; Gold and Glitter; My Baby (also au); The Informer; Brutality; Pirate Gold; The Unwelcome Guest; The New York Hat; My Hero (also au); The Burglar's Dilemma; A Cry for Help; The God Within; Three Friends; The Telephone Girl and the Lady; An Adventure in the Autumn Woods; The Tender-Hearted Boy; Oil and Water; A Chance Deception; Fate; A Misappropriated Turkey; Brothers; Drink's Lure; Love in an Apartment Hotel

1913: Broken Ways; A Girl's Stratagem; Near to Earth; A Welcome Intruder; The Sheriff's Baby; The Hero of Little Italy; The Perfidy of Mary; A Misunderstood Boy; The Left-Handed Man; The Little Tease (also au); The Lady and the Mouse (also au); If We Only Knew; The Wanderer (also au); The House of Darkness; The Stolen Loaf; Just Gold (also au); His Mother's Son; A Timely Interception; Death's Marathon; The Yaqui Cur; The Ranchero's Revenge; The Mothering Heart; Her Mother's Oath (also au); The Sorrowful Shore; The Battle at Elderbush Gulch; The Mistake (also au); The Coming of Angelo (also au); Brute Force (also au); Two Men of the Desert (also au); The Reformers, or The Lost Art of Minding One's Business; Judith of Bethulia; The Adopted Brother (co-d)

HALDEMAN, EDITH: Actress

1909: Leather Stocking; A Fair Exchange; Wanted, A Child; The Little Teacher; The Open Gate; The Death Disc; A Corner in Wheat; The Redman's View; The Rocky Road; The Last Deal; The Cloister's Touch

1910: The Final Settlement; In Life's Cycle; Little Angels of Luck; A Mohawk's Way; Examination Day at School; The Iconoclast; Two Little Waifs; His Trust; The Two Paths

1911: The Miser's Heart; The Baby and the Stork; Billy's Stratagem

1912: A Child's Remorse

HALE, ALAN: Actor (1892-1950) (b. Rufus Alan McKahan)

1913: His Inspiration; By Man's Law; Strongheart; Men and Women

HALL, ELLA: Actress (1897-1981)

1912: Hot Stuff; The School Teacher and the Waif

HALL, EMMET CAMPBELL: Author

1910: The House with Closed Shutters; Rose O'Salem-Town; That Chink at Golden Gulch; His Trust; His Trust Fulfilled

1911: Was He a Coward?; Teaching Dad to Like Her; The Primal Call; Out from the Shadow; Swords and Hearts; For His Son

HALM, FRIEDERICH: Author

1908: The Barbarian, Ingomar

HAMILTON, MR.: Employee. Noted in Moving Picture World, 19 August 1911, p. 449. This may be Gilbert P. Hamilton, listed in Appendix C.

HAMMER, W. H.: General manager in 1913

HARRIS, CAROLINE: Actress (1867-1937)

1909: The Necklace

HARRIS, JAMES: Actor

1913: Aunts, Too Many

HARRON, ROBERT: Actor (1894-1920) (aka Bobby Harron)

1907: Dr. Skinum; Mr. Gay and Mrs.; Professional Jealousy

1908: Bobby's Kodak; The Snowman; The Boy Detective - or - The Abductors Foiled; Her First Adventure; Mixed Babies; Thompson's Night Out; At the French Ball; At the Crossroads of Life; A Calamitous Elopement; Balked at the Altar; Monday Morning in a Coney Island Police Court; Behind the Scenes; Where the Breakers Roar; A Smoked Husband; Concealing a Burglar; The Song of the Shirt; The Clubman and the Tramp; The Feud and the Turkey; The Test of Friendship; The Reckoning; The Valet's Wife; The Helping Hand; A Wreath in Time; The Welcome Burglar; Mr. Jones Has a Card Party; The Hindoo Dagger; The Salvation Army Lass; Tragic Love; The Girls and Daddy

1909: Those Awful Hats; Jones and the Lady Book Agent; Trying to Get Arrested; The Brahma Diamond; The Drive for a Life; His Wife's Mother; At the Altar; A Burglar's Mistake; A Drunkard's Reformation; The Note in the Shoe; A Sound Sleeper; A Troublesome Satchel; 'Tis An Ill Wind That Blows No Good; One Busy Hour; The Peachbasket Hat; His Duty; The Message; They Would Elope; Pranks; "1776" or, The Hessian Renegades; In Old Kentucky; The Broken Locket; Sweet Revenge; Through the Breakers; A Corner in Wheat; In a Hempen Bag; To Save Her Soul; Her Terrible Ordeal; The Call

1910: The Newlyweds; The Converts; The Way of the World; A Child's Impulse; A Summer Idyl; The Modern Prodigal; Sunshine Sue; A Plain Song; When a Man Loves; The Lesson; Winning Back His Love; A Wreath of Orange Blossoms; The Italian Barber

1911: Enoch Arden, Part Two; The White Rose of the Wilds; The Primal Call; Fighting Blood; The Last Drop of Water; Bobby, the Coward; A Country Cupid; The Diving Girl; The Unveiling; Her Awakening; The Long Road; The Battle; The Miser's Heart; The Failure; For His Son; The Transformation of Mike; Billy's Stratagem; A String of Pearls

1912: Under Burning Skies; Iola's Promise; The Girl and Her Trust; Fate's Interception; Just Like a Woman; One Is Business, the Other Crime; The Old Actor; The Lesser Evil; A Lodging for the Night; A Beast at Bay; Home Folks; A Temporary Truce; The School Teacher and the Waif; Man's Lust for Gold; Man's Genesis; The Sands of Dee; A Pueblo Legend; The Massacre; A Child's Remorse; The Inner Circle; A Change of Spirit; An Unseen Enemy; Two Daughters of Eve; Friends; So Near, Yet So Far; A Feud in the Kentucky Hills; The Painted Lady; The Musketeers of Pig Alley; Heredity; The Informer; A Sailor's Heart; The New York Hat; My Hero; The Burglar's Dilemma; A Cry for Help; The Tender-Hearted Boy; Fate; A Misappropriated Turkey; Brothers; Love in an Apartment Hotel

1913: Broken Ways; Near to Earth; The Sheriff's Baby; The Perfidy of Mary; A Misunderstood Boy; The Little Tease; The Lady and the Mouse; The House of Darkness; His Mother's Son; A Timely Interception; Death's Marathon; The Yaqui Cur; Her Mother's Oath; The Sorrowful Shore; The Battle at Elderbush Gulch; Brute Force; The Reformers, or The Lost Art of Minding One's Business; Judith of Bethulia; The Adopted Brother; An Unjust Suspicion; The Influence of the Unknown; The Girl Across the Way; By Man's Law; The Blue or the Gray; In the Elemental World

HART, RUTH: Actress (d. 1952)

1909: The Restoration; Nursing a Viper; Two Women and a Man; The Light That Came; A Midnight Adventure; The Open Gate; The Mountaineer's Honor; The Trick That Failed; The Death Disc; Through the Breakers; A Corner in Wheat; In a Hempen Bag; The Redman's View; The Test; In Little Italy; To Save Her Soul; The Call; The Honor of His Family; On the Reef; The Last Deal; The Cloister's Touch; The Woman From Mellon's; The Duke's Plan; One Night, and Then---; The Englishman and the Girl

1910: The Love of Lady Irma; Taming a Husband; The Newly-weds; A Child of the Ghetto; A Victim of Jealousy; A Flash of Light

HASTINGS, SEYMOUR: Actor? A member of the comedy unit that remained in Los Angeles with Fred Mace in 1912.

HATTON, RAYMOND: Actor (1887-1971)

1908: Tragic Love

1909: A Fool's Revenge; A Burglar's Mistake; Confidence; Was Justice Served?

HAVEY, M. B.: Author

1910: His Sister-In-Law; The Diamond Star

1911: The Failure

1912: Blind Love

1913: The Madonna of the Storm

HAY, WALTER B.: Author

1913: Papa's Baby

HAYN, FRED: Author

1913: Boarders and Bombs

HEARN, F.: Actor

1913: Men and Women

HEDLUND, GUY: Actor (1884-1964)

1908: The Salvation Army Lass

1909: The Fascinating Mrs. Francis; Leather Stocking; The Expiation; The Restoration; The Light That Came; The Trick That Failed; In Little Italy; The Last Deal; The Woman From Mellon's

1910: The Love of Lady Irma; Taming a Husband; The Newlyweds; The Impalement; A Child of the Ghetto; In the Border States; A Victim of Jealousy; The Face at the Window; A Child's Impulse; The Call to Arms; A Child's Faith; A Flash of Light; The Usurer; Wilful Peggy; A Summer Idyl; The Modern Prodigal; Rose O'Salem-Town; A Mohawk's Way; The Oath and the Man; The Iconoclast; That Chink at Golden Gulch; The Broken Doll; The Banker's Daughters; Waiter No. 5; The Fugitive; A Child's Stratagem; Sunshine Sue; A Plain Song; His Sister-In-Law; The Golden Supper; When a Man Loves; The Lesson; Winning Back His Love; His Trust; His Trust Fulfilled; A Wreath of Orange Blossoms; Conscience; Three Sisters; Fate's Turning; What Shall We Do With Our Old; Heart Beats of Long Ago

1911: The Lonedale Operator; Was He a Coward?; Teaching Dad to Like Her; The Spanish Gypsy; Priscilla and the Umbrella; A Knight of the Road; In the Days of '49; The Two Sides; The New Dress; Enoch Arden, Part Two; The Manicure Lady; The Crooked Road; The Indian Brothers; The Blind Princess and the Poet; The Last Drop of Water; Bobby, the Coward; The Ruling Passion;

Swords and Hearts; The Diving Girl; The Eternal Mother; A Convenient Burglar; The Making of a Man; The Long Road; The Battle

1913: By Man's Law

HELLAWELL, RALPH E.: Author

1912: Look Not Upon the Wine

1913: An Old Maid's Deception; The End of the World; Just Boys

HENDERSON, DELL: Actor, Director, Author (1883-1956) (aka G.
Delbert Henderson; Del Henderson; George Delbert Henderson; G.
Dell Henderson)

1909: (as actor) The Last Deal; The Cloister's Touch; The Woman
From Mellon's; The Course of True Love; The Duke's Plan; One
Night, And Then---; The Englishman and the Girl

1910: (as actor) The Love of Lady Irma; Taming a Husband; The
Newlyweds; The Converts; Faithful; The Twisted Trail; Gold Is
Not All; The Tenderfoot's Triumph; A Romance of the Western
Hills; Thou Shalt Not; The Way of the World; The Unchanging Sea;
The Gold-Seekers; The Two Brothers; Unexpected Help; Ramona;
Over Silent Paths; The Impalement; A Child of the Ghetto; In the
Border States; The Face at the Window; The Marked Time-Table;
A Child's Impulse; The Purgation; A Salutary Lesson; The Usurer;
Wilful Peggy; Muggsy Becomes a Hero; The Modern Prodigal (also
au); Little Angels of Luck; The Oath and the Man; That Chink at
Golden Gulch; A Gold Necklace; The Broken Doll; The Banker's
Daughters; The Message of the Violin; Waiter No. 5; Simple Chari-
ty; The Fugitive; The Song of the Wildwood Flute; A Child's Strata-
gem; A Plain Song; When a Man Loves; The Lesson (also au);
Happy Jack, a Hero (also au); His Trust; A Wreath of Orange
Blossoms; The Two Paths; Conscience; The Poor Sick Men; Help
Wanted

1911: (as actor) The Lonedale Operator; Was He a Coward?;
Teaching Dad to Like Her; The Spanish Gypsy; The Broken Cross;
The Chief's Daughter; A Knight of the Road (also au); In the Days
of '49; The Two Sides; Enoch Arden, Part Two; The Crooked
Road; The Primal Call; The Jealous Husband; Fighting Blood;
Bobby, the Coward (au only); The Ghost; The Diving Girl; The
Baron; The Making of a Man; The Adventures of Billy; The Long
Road; The Battle; Love in the Hills (au only); A Victim of Circum-
stances; Through Darkened Vales; The Failure; Did Mother Get Her
Wish? (au only); Who Got the Reward?; For His Son; Brave and
Bold (au only); The Sunbeam; A String of Pearls; The Fatal Choco-
late; A Message from the Moon

1912: (as actor) A Spanish Dilemma; The Engagement Ring; A
Voice from the Deep (also au); Hot Stuff (also au); Help! Help!;
The Brave Hunter; Those Hicksville Boys (also au); Their First

Kidnapping Case; Won by a Fish; The Fickle Spaniard (also au);
The Leading Man; When the Fire-Bells Rang; The Furs; A Close
Call; Helen's Marriage; Algy, the Watchman; Neighbors (au only);
Katchem Kate; A Dash Through the Clouds; Trying to Fool Uncle;
What the Doctor Ordered (also au); The Massacre; The Speed
Demon (also au); The Tragedy of a Dress Suit; Stern Papa; Mr.
Grouch at the Seashore (d only); Through Dumb Luck (au and d);
Getting Rid of Trouble (d only); Love's Messenger (d only); A
Disappointed Mamma (also d and au); A Mixed Affair (also d); A
Limited Divorce (au and d); The Line at Hogan's (d only); A Ten-
Karat Hero (d only); Like the Cat, They Came Back (d only); At
the Basket Picnic (d only); A Real Estate Deal (au and d); His
Auto's Maiden Trip (d only); Their Idols (d only); An Absent-
Minded Burglar (d only); The Club-Man and the Crook (d and au);
Hoist on His Own Petard (d only); After the Honeymoon (d only);
Jinx's Birthday Party (d only); "She is a Pippin" (d only); The
Divorcee (also d); Papering the Den (d only); Bill Bogg's Windfall
(d only); A Day's Outing (d only); Oh, What a Boob! (d only); The
Press Gang (d only); The Bite of a Snake (d only); The Best Man
Wins (d only); Kissing Kate (also d); The Masher Cop (also d); A
Father's Lesson (d only); There Were Hoboes Three (d only); An
Up-to-Date Lochinvar (d only); Look Not Upon the Wine (d only);
Among Club Fellows (d only); The High Cost of Reduction (d and
au); What is the Use of Repining? (d and au); A Queer Elopement
(d only); A Delivery Package (d only); Edwin's Badge of Honor (d
only); A Motorcycle Elopement (d only)

1913: (as director) The Spring of Life; Tightwad's Predicament
(also au); The Power of the Camera (also a); The Old Gray Mare
(also au); All Hail to the King; Edwin Masquerades; Their One
Good Suit; A Lesson to Mashers; How They Struck Oil; An "Uncle
Tom's Cabin" Troupe (also au); A Horse on Bill; He Had a Guess
Coming; A Ragtime Romance (also au); The Cure; Blame the Wife
(also a); The Daylight Burglar (also a); A Rainy Day; Frappe Love;
The Coveted Prize; The King and the Copper (also au); Cinderella
and the Boob; The Hicksville Epicure; The Trimmers Trimmed;
Highbrow Love; Slippery Slim Repents; Just Kids; Red Hicks Defies
the World; Jenks Becomes a Desperate Character (also a); Almost
a Wild Man; The Rise and Fall of McDoo; The Mothering Heart
(a only); Mister Jefferson Green; A Compromising Complication;
Faust and the Lily; An Old Maid's Deception; A Sea Dog's Love;
The Noisy Suitors; The Sweat-Box; A Chinese Puzzle; Pa Says;
While the Count Goes Bathing (also a); Mr. Spriggs Buys a Dog;
The Widow's Kids (also a); Cupid and the Cook; Those Little
Flowers; Come Seben, Leben; The Suffragette Minstrels (also a);
Father's Chicken Dinner; Papa's Baby (also a); Black and White;
Baby Indisposed; Objections Overruled; Dan Greegan's Ghost; The
Lady in Black; A Woman in the Ultimate; For the Son of the House;
A Modest Hero

HENDERSON, GRACE: Actress, Author (1860-1944)

1909: Through the Breakers; A Corner in Wheat; In a Hempen
Bag

1910:   A Victim of Jealousy; The Face at the Window; The Marked Time-Table; Muggsy's First Sweetheart; The Purgation; The Call to Arms; A Midnight Cupid; A Flash of Light; As the Bells Rang Out!; The House with Closed Shutters; Her Father's Pride; The Usurer; Wilful Peggy; Muggsy Becomes a Hero; Little Angels of Luck; A Summer Tragedy; The Iconoclast; How Hubby Got a Raise; The Masher; The Message of the Violin; Two Little Waifs; Waiter No. 5; Simple Charity; Love in Quarantine; Not So Bad As It Seemed; The Golden Supper; When a Man Loves; Happy Jack, a Hero; His Trust Fulfilled; A Wreath of Orange Blossoms; The Recreation of an Heiress; The Two Paths; His Wife's Sweethearts; Three Sisters; The Poor Sick Men; A Decree of Destiny; Fate's Turning

1911:   Comrades; Was He a Coward?; The Broken Cross; Priscilla and the Umbrella; The Chief's Daughter; Misplaced Jealousy; The Country Lovers; The New Dress (au only); Enoch Arden, Part Two; The Manicure Lady; The Crooked Road; The Primal Call; Her Sacrifice; The Blind Princess and the Poet; Bobby, the Coward; The Old Confectioner's Mistake; The Unveiling; The Baron; A Convenient Burglar; The Making of a Man; The Adventures of Billy; Through Darkened Vales; The Failure; Sunshine Through the Dark; The Baby and the Stork; For His Son; The Transformation of Mike; A String of Pearls

1912:   Hot Stuff; Just Like a Woman; The Old Actor; Those Hicks-ville Boys; Won by a Fish; His Lesson; The Leading Man; When the Fire-Bells Rang; A Close Call; Helen's Marriage; Algy, the Watchman; Lena and the Geese; The School Teacher and the Waif; Trying to Fool Uncle; Heaven Avenges; The Sands of Dee; The Tourists; A Child's Remorse; The Tragedy of a Dress Suit; An Unseen Enemy; Through Dumb Luck; A Disappointed Mamma; A Mixed Affair

HENDLER, BERT: Actor

1912:   A Temporary Truce; The School Teacher and the Waif; An Indian Summer

HENDRIE, ANITA: Actress (1868-1940) (aka Anita Hendry; Mrs. David Miles)

1908:   The Helping Hand; The Maniac Cook; A Wreath in Time; The Honor of Thieves; The Criminal Hypnotist; The Welcome Bur-glar; Mr. Jones Has a Card Party; The Joneses Have Amateur Theatricals; Edgar Allen Poe; The Roue's Heart; The Salvation Army Lass; Love Finds a Way; Tragic Love; The Girls and Daddy

1909:   Those Boys; The Cord of Life; The Fascinating Mrs. Fran-cis; Those Awful Hats; Trying to Get Arrested; The Brahma Dia-mond; The Drive for a Life; Politician's Love Story; His Wife's Mother; The Golden Louis; At the Altar; The Medicine Bottle; The Deception; The Lure of the Gown; Lady Helen's Escapade; A Fool's

Revenge; I Did It, Mamma; The Voice of the Violin; "And a Little Child Shall Lead Them"; The French Duel; Jones and His New Neighbors; A Drunkard's Reformation; The Winning Coat; A Rude Hostess; The Road to the Heart; Schneider's Anti-Noise Crusade; Twin Brothers; Confidence; The Note in the Shoe; Lucky Jim; A Sound Sleeper; A Troublesome Satchel; 'Tis An Ill Wind That Blows No Good; Resurrection; One Busy Hour; A Baby's Shoe; Eloping With Aunty; The Cricket on the Hearth; What Drink Did; Her First Biscuits; The Lonely Villa; The Peachbasket Hat; The Son's Return

HENNESSY, GEORGE: Author, Actor

1911: An Interrupted Game; A Convenient Burglar; Why He Gave Up; Their First Divorce Case; Through His Wife's Picture; Saved From Himself; The Inventor's Secret; Dooley's Scheme; Won Through a Medium; A Woman Scorned; The Miser's Heart; As In a Looking Glass; Caught with the Goods; The Baby and the Stork; The Voice of the Child; Billy's Stratagem; The Sunbeam; The Root of Evil; "Got a Match?"

1912: The Girl and Her Trust; The Punishment; Fate's Interception; Just Like a Woman; One is Business, the Other Crime; The Old Actor; The Lesser Evil; Won by a Fish; A Lodging for the Night; His Lesson; A Beast at Bay; An Outcast Among Outcasts; A Temporary Truce; An Indian Summer; Man's Lust for Gold; Heaven Avenges; Black Sheep; The Narrow Road; A Child's Remorse (also a); The Inner Circle; Two Daughters of Eve; So Near, Yet So Far; The One She Loved; Heredity; Gold and Glitter; The Informer; Brutality; Pirate Gold; The Unwelcome Guest; Drink's Lure

1913: A Girl's Stratagem; The Perfidy of Mary; If We Only Knew; The Switch-Tower; Objections Overruled; A Modest Hero; The Strong Man's Burden; Red and Pete, Partners

HICKOX, SIDNEY: Camera boy

HICKS, ELEANOR: Author (1886-1936) (aka Mrs. Frank Powell)

1910: The Two Brothers

1911: Cured; Curiosity

1913: Blame the Wife

HIGGINSON, PERCY: Cameraman

1909: They Would Elope; Pippa Passes or, The Song of Conscience

1911: Cupid's Joke; Cured; Priscilla's April Fool Joke: The Broken Cross; Priscilla and the Umbrella; Paradise Lost; Priscilla's Capture; Misplaced Jealousy; Her Pet; The Country Lovers; Taking

His Medicine; Curiosity; The Manicure Lady; A Dutch Gold Mine;
Dave's Love Affair; Their Fates "Sealed"; Bearded Youth; The
Wonderful Eye; The Delayed Proposal; Stubbs' New Servants;
Jinks Joins the Temperance Club; Mr. Pecks Goes Calling; The
Ghost; The Ruling Passion; That Dare Devil; The Beautiful Voice;
An Interrupted Game; $500 Reward; The Diving Girl; The Villain
Foiled; Mr. Bragg, A Fugitive; The Baron; The Lucky Horse-
shoe; The Squaw's Love; The Village Hero; A Convenient Burglar;
When Wifey Holds the Purse-Strings; Trailing the Counterfeiter;
Josh's Suicide; Too Many Burglars; Why He Gave Up; Their First
Divorce Case; Through His Wife's Picture; The Inventor's Secret;
Dooley's Scheme; A Victim of Circumstances; Won Through a
Medium; The Joke on the Joker; Her Mother Interferes; Resource-
ful Lovers; Abe Gets Even with Father; Did Mother Get Her Wish?;
A Mix-Up in Rain Coats; Who Got the Reward?; Brave and Bold;
Pants and Pansies; With a Kodak; Lily's Lovers; A Near-Tragedy;
The Fatal Chocolate; "Got a Match?"; A Message from the Moon

1912: A Spanish Dilemma; The Engagement Ring; A Voice From
the Deep; Hot Stuff; The Would-Be Shriner; Help! Help!; The
Brave Hunter; Those Hicksville Boys; Their First Kidnapping Case;
Won by a Fish; The Fickle Spaniard; The Leading Man; When the
Fire-Bells Rang; The Furs; A Close Call; Helen's Marriage; Algy,
the Watchman; Tomboy Bessie; Neighbors; Katchem Kate; A Dash
Through the Clouds; The New Baby; Trying to Fool Uncle; What
the Doctor Ordered; The Tourists; One-Round O'Brien; The Speed
Demon; His Own Fault; Willie Becomes an Artist; An Interrupted
Elopement; The Tragedy of a Dress Suit; He Must Have a Wife;
Stern Papa; Mr. Grouch at the Seashore; Through Dumb Luck;
Getting Rid of Trouble; Love's Messenger; A Disappointed Mamma;
A Mixed Affair; A Limited Divorce; At the Basket Picnic; A Real
Estate Deal

HILL, VIOLETTE: Actress

1908: Cupid's Pranks

HIRSCH, EDMUND S.: Author (b. 1888)

1909: Comata, the Sioux

HODGE, EARL: Author

1910: The Banker's Daughters

1912: Helen's Marriage

HONKERS, MRS. WILLIAM L.: Author

1912: Fate

HOOD, THOMAS: Poet

1908: The Song of the Shirt

HORNE, BILLY: Actor

  1912: The High Cost of Reduction

HOWLEY, IRENE: Actress

  1913: His Inspiration; The Blue or the Gray; In the Elemental
  World

HOYT, EDWARD N.: Actor (b. 1859)

  1913: By Man's Law

HOYT, HARRY O.: Author

  1913: An Unjust Suspicion

HUBBARD, HAZEL H.: Author

  1913: The Mothering Heart

HUGHES, H. F.: Author

  1912: Algy, the Watchman

HUGO, VICTOR: Novelist (1802-1885)

  1909: A Fool's Revenge

HYDE, HARRY: Actor

  1910: The Passing of a Grouch; A Child's Stratagem; A Plain
  Song; His Sister-In-Law; The Golden Supper; Winning Back His
  Love; His Trust Fulfilled; A Wreath of Orange Blossoms; The
  Midnight Marauder; The Two Paths; Three Sisters

  1911: The Making of a Man; Her Awakening; The Adventures of
  Billy; The Long Road; The Battle; Through Darkened Vales; The
  Failure; The Old Bookkeeper; For His Son; A Blot in the 'Scutch-
  eon; Billy's Stratagem; A String of Pearls; The Root of Evil

  1912: Iola's Promise; The Goddess of Sagebrush Gulch; The
  Engagement Ring; A Voice from the Deep; Hot Stuff; The Would-
  Be Shriner; The Punishment; Fate's Interception; Just Like a
  Woman; The Lesser Evil; Their First Kidnapping Case; The Fickle
  Spaniard; His Lesson; When Kings Were the Law; When the Fire-
  Bells Rang; A Close Call; A Temporary Truce; Lena and the
  Geese; An Indian Summer; A Dash Through the Clouds; The Tour-
  ists; A Pueblo Legend; The Massacre; The Speed Demon; His Own
  Fault; Willie Becomes an Artist; The Tragedy of a Dress Suit;
  Two Daughters of Eve; A Feud in the Kentucky Hills; Blind Love;
  A Limited Divorce

1913: All Hail to the King; Edwin Masquerades; Her Wedding
Bell; How They Struck Oil; The Perfidy of Mary; The Stolen
Bride; The Lady and the Mouse; Death's Marathon; The Yaqui Cur;
Slippery Slim Repents; Red Hicks Defies the World; Almost a Wild
Man; The Mothering Heart; In Diplomatic Circles; The Mistake;
Brute Force; The Reformers, or The Lost Art of Minding One's
Business; Judith of Bethulia

INCE, THOMAS H.: Actor (1880-1924)

1910: His New Lid

INSLEE, CHARLES: Actor, Author (aka Charles E. Inslee; Charles
Insley)

1908: At The Crossroads of Life; The Adventures of Dollie; The
Redman and the Child; The Bandit's Waterloo; A Calamitous Elope-
ment; The Greaser's Gauntlet; The Man and the Woman; For a
Wife's Honor; The Girl and the Outlaw; The Red Girl; Behind the
Scenes; Where the Breakers Roar; The Stolen Jewels; The Zulu's
Heart; The Vaquero's Vow; Father Gets in the Game; The Bar-
barian, Ingomar; The Call of the Wild; After Many Years; Mr.
Jones at the Ball; Taming of the Shrew; The Pirate's Gold; The
Guerrilla; Money Mad; The Feud and the Turkey; The Test of
Friendship; One Touch of Nature; The Helping Hand; The Christmas
Burglars; A Wreath in Time; The Criminal Hypnotist; The Welcome
Burglar; Mr. Jones Has a Card Party; The Roue's Heart; The Sal-
vation Army Lass; Love Finds a Way; Tragic Love; The Girls and
Daddy

1909: The Cord of Life; The Fascinating Mrs. Francis; Those
Awful Hats; Trying to Get Arrested; The Brahma Diamond; His
Wife's Mother; The Golden Louis; At the Altar; The Deception; The
Lure of the Gown; Lady Helen's Escapade; A Fool's Revenge; A
Burglar's Mistake; The French Duel; Jones and His New Neigh-
bors; The Eavesdropper; Twin Brothers; Confidence; The Note in
the Shoe; Lucky Jim; 'Tis An Ill Wind That Blows No Good; One
Busy Hour

1911: A Dutch Gold Mine (au only)

1913: The Ranchero's Revenge (au only)

JACKSON, HELEN HUNT: Novelist (1830-1885)

1910: Ramona

JEANNIE: Actress

1908: Rescued From An Eagle's Nest

JEFFERSON, THOMAS: Actor (1859-1932)

1913: Olaf - an Atom; Classmates

JOHN, D. B.: Author

1913: The Winning Punch

JOHNSON, ARTHUR: Actor (1876-1916)

1908: The Adventures of Dollie; The Greaser's Gauntlet; For A Wife's Honor; Balked at the Altar; The Girl and the Outlaw; Where the Breakers Roar; A Smoked Husband; The Zulu's Heart; The Vaquero's Vow; The Barbarian, Ingomar; The Planter's Wife; The Devil; Romance of a Jewess; The Call of the Wild; After Many Years; Mr. Jones at the Ball; Concealing A Burglar; Taming of the Shrew; The Ingrate; A Woman's Way; The Guerrilla; The Curtain Pole; The Song of the Shirt; The Clubman and the Tramp; Money Mad; The Feud and the Turkey; The Test of Friendship; The Reckoning; The Valet's Wife; One Touch of Nature; The Helping Hand; The Christmas Burglars; A Wreath in Time; The Honor of Thieves; The Criminal Hypnotist; The Sacrifice; The Welcome Burglar; Mr. Jones Has A Card Party; Edgar Allen Poe; The Roue's Heart; The Hindoo Dagger; The Salvation Army Lass; Tragic Love; The Girls and Daddy

1909: The Cord of Life; The Fascinating Mrs. Francis; Those Awful Hats; Trying To Get Arrested; The Brahma Diamond; The Drive for a Life; Politician's Love Story; His Wife's Mother; The Golden Louis; His Ward's Love; At the Altar; The Prussian Spy; The Deception; The Lure of the Gown; Lady Helen's Escapade; A Fool's Revenge; A Burglar's Mistake; The Voice of the Violin; "And a Little Child Shall Lead Them"; The French Duel; A Drunkard's Reformation; The Winning Coat; A Rude Hostess; The Road to the Heart; Schneider's Anti-Noise Crusade; Twin Brothers; Confidence; The Note in the Shoe; Lucky Jim; A Sound Sleeper; A Troublesome Satchel; 'Tis An Ill Wind That Blows No Good; Resurrection; A Baby's Shoe; Eloping With Aunty; The Cricket on the Hearth; The Jilt; Eradicating Aunty; What Drink Did; Her First Biscuits; The Violin Maker of Cremona; Two Memories; The Lonely Villa; The Peachbasket Hat; The Son's Return; His Duty; A New Trick; The Necklace; The Way of Man; Was Justice Served?; Jealousy and the Man; The Cardinal's Conspiracy; The Seventh Day; Tender Hearts; A Convict's Sacrifice; A Strange Meeting; The Slave; They Would Elope; Jones' Burglar; The Mended Lute; The Indian Runner's Romance; With Her Card; The Better Way; The Heart of an Outlaw; The Mills of the Gods; Pranks; The Sealed Room; "1776" or, the Hessian Renegades; The Little Darling; Comata, the Sioux; Leather Stocking; Getting Even; The Broken Locket; A Fair Exchange; The Awakening; Pippa Passes or, The Song of Conscience; The Little Teacher; A Change of Heart; The Gibson Goddess; The Expiation; Nursing a Viper; Two Women and a Man; The Light That Came; A Midnight Adventure; Sweet Revenge; The Mountaineer's Honor; In the Window Recess; The Trick That Failed; The Death Disc; Through the Breakers; A Corner in Wheat; The Redman's View; The Test; To Save Her Soul; The Day After; All On Account of the Milk; The Cloister's Touch

1910: The Final Settlement; Taming a Husband; The Newlyweds; In Old California; The Converts; Faithful; The Twisted Trail; The Tenderfoot's Triumph; A Romance of the Western Hills; The Unchanging Sea; Love Among The Roses; The Two Brothers; Unexpected Help; Over Silent Paths

JOHNSON, GEORGE E.: Author

1912: Their First Kidnapping Case

JOHNSON, H. L.: Author

1913: No Place for Father

JOHNSON, MIN: Actress

1909: The Medicine Bottle; The Deception

JOHNSON, MISS C.: Author

1913: A Chinese Puzzle

KENNEDY, JEREMIAH J.: President of The Biograph Company, Banker, Industrialist. Left Biograph and the film industry in late 1916.

KERSHAW, ELINOR: Actress (1884-1971) (aka Nell Ince; Mrs. Thomas H. Ince)

1909: The Course of True Love; One Night, and Then---

1910: The Love of Lady Irma; Taming a Husband

KERZOG, F.: Actor

1913: Men and Women

KING, ROSE: Actress

1909: The Necklace; The Country Doctor; The Cardinal's Conspiracy; The Seventh Day; Tender Hearts

KINGSLEY, CHARLES: Poet (1819-1875)

1910: The Unchanging Sea

KIRBY, MADGE: Actress

1912: A Disappointed Mamma; A Mixed Affair; The One She Loved; The Painted Lady; The Musketeers of Pig Alley; The Line at Hogan's; At the Basket Picnic; Their Idols; An Absent-Minded Burglar; Heredity; Jinx's Birthday Party; My Baby; Brutality; The New York Hat; The Burglar's Dilemma; The Telephone Girl and the Lady

KIRKWOOD, JAMES: Actor, Director (1883-1963)

1909: The Lonely Villa; The Necklace; The Way of Man; The Faded Lilies; The Message; Was Justice Served?; The Mexican Sweethearts; Jealousy and the Man; The Renunciation; The Cardinal's Conspiracy; The Seventh Day; Tender Hearts; A Convict's Sacrifice; A Strange Meeting; Sweet and Twenty; The Slave; They Would Elope; The Mended Lute; The Indian Runner's Romance; The Better Way; His Wife's Visitor; The Heart of an Outlaw; "Oh, Uncle"; "1776" or, The Hessian Renegades; The Little Darling; In Old Kentucky; Comata, the Sioux; Leather Stocking; Getting Even; The Broken Locket; A Fair Exchange; Pippa Passes or, The Song of Conscience; Fools of Fate; A Change of Heart; His Lost Love; Lines of White On A Sullen Sea; The Gibson Goddess; The Restoration; Nursing a Viper; Two Women and a Man; The Light That Came; The Mountaineer's Honor; In the Window Recess; The Death Disc; Through the Breakers; A Corner in Wheat; The Redman's View; In Little Italy; To Save Her Soul; The Day After; The Rocky Road; The Call; The Honor of His Family; The Last Deal; The Woman From Mellon's; The Duke's Plan; One Night, and Then---

1910: The Final Settlement; His Last Burglary; A Victim of Jealousy; The Face at the Window

1913: (as director) Classmates; Strongheart; Men and Women

KOSTER, SIDNEY: Prop boy

KRUSCHKE, EMIL: Author

1913: The Crook and the Girl

LA BADIE, FLORENCE: Actress (1893-1917)

1911: The Spanish Gypsy; The Broken Cross; Paradise Lost; A Knight of the Road; The New Dress; Enoch Arden, Part Two; Dave's Love Affair; The Primal Call; The Thief and the Girl; Her Sacrifice; Fighting Blood; Bobby, the Coward

LA VARNIE, MRS. LAURA: Actress

1913: The Wife

LAMOTHE, JULIAN: Author

1911: The Joke on the Joker

LANDERS, SAM: Prop boy, Assistant cameraman on JUDITH OF BETHULIA. Joined Biograph in 1908.

LANGDON, LILLIAN: Actress (1860?-1943) (aka Mrs. Lillian Bolles)

1913: The Girl Across the Way

LANOE, J. JIQUEL: Actor (aka G. Jiquel Lanoe, J. Jiquel Lauve)

1910: The Oath and the Man; The Iconoclast; That Chink at Gold-
en Gulch; The Broken Doll; Waiter No. 5; The Fugitive; The Song
of the Wildwood Flute; A Child's Stratagem; Sunshine Sue; A Plain
Song; His Sister-In-Law; The Golden Supper; Winning Back His
Love; A Decree of Destiny; Fate's Turning; What Shall We Do
With Our Old; Heart Beats of Long Ago

1911: Bobby, the Coward; Swords and Hearts; The Eternal Mother;
A Convenient Burglar; The Making of a Man; Trailing the Counter-
feiter; Her Awakening; The Long Road; The Battle; Through Dark-
ened Vales; The Failure; A Terrible Discovery; The Baby and the
Stork; The Old Bookkeeper; For His Son; The Transformation of
Mike; A Blot in the 'Scutcheon; Billy's Stratagem; A String of
Pearls; The Root of Evil

1912: A Spanish Dilemma; Iola's Promise; The Engagement Ring;
A Voice from the Deep; The Would-Be Shriner; The Punishment;
Just Like a Woman; The Brave Hunter; The Old Actor; The Les-
ser Evil; The Fickle Spaniard; When Kings Were the Law; A
Beast at Bay; When the Fire-Bells Rang; A Close Call; Helen's
Marriage; An Outcast Among Outcasts; A Temporary Truce; Lena
and the Geese; Neighbors; A Dash Through the Clouds; What the
Doctor Ordered; Black Sheep; A Pueblo Legend; The Massacre;
One-Round O'Brien; His Own Fault; Willie Becomes an Artist;
With the Enemy's Help; The Narrow Road; The Inner Circle; Mr.
Grouch at the Seashore; Through Dumb Luck; A Feud in the Ken-
tucky Hills; Love's Messenger; A Limited Divorce; Pirate Gold;
The Unwelcome Guest; A Sailor's Heart; My Hero; The Burglar's
Dilemma; The God Within; Three Friends; Oil and Water

1913: The Old Gray Mare; Edwin Masquerades; Her Wedding
Bell; How They Struck Oil; The Hero of Little Italy; The Perfidy
of Mary; An "Uncle Tom's Cabin" Troupe; A Horse on Bill; The
Lady and the Mouse; The House of Darkness; Death's Marathon;
The Yaqui Cur; Slippery Slim Repents; Red Hicks Defies the World;
Almost a Wild Man; The Mothering Heart; The Sorrowful Shore;
The Mistake; Brute Force; The Reformers, or The Lost Art of
Minding One's Business; Judith of Bethulia; The Madonna of the
Storm; No Place for Father; By Man's Law

LANNING, FRANK: Actor

1912: My Hero

LAWRENCE, FLORENCE: Actress (1886-1938) (married to Harry
Solter)

1908: The Girl and the Outlaw; The Red Girl; Betrayed by a
Handprint; Behind the Scenes; The Heart of O Yama; Where the
Breakers Roar; The Stolen Jewels; A Smoked Husband; The Zulu's
Heart; The Vaquero's Vow; Father Gets in the Game; The Bar-

barian, Ingomar; The Planter's Wife; The Devil; Romance of a Jewess; The Call of the Wild; After Many Years; Mr. Jones at the Ball; Concealing a Burglar; Taming of the Shrew; The Ingrate; The Curtain Pole; The Song of the Shirt; The Clubman and the Tramp; Money Mad; Mrs. Jones Entertains; The Feud and the Turkey; The Test of Friendship; The Reckoning; The Valet's Wife; One Touch of Nature; An Awful Moment; The Helping Hand; The Christmas Burglars; A Wreath in Time; The Honor of Thieves; The Criminal Hypnotist; The Sacrifice; Mr. Jones Has A Card Party; The Joneses Have Amateur Theatricals; The Roue's Heart; The Salvation Army Lass; Love Finds a Way; Tragic Love; The Girls and Daddy

1909: Those Boys; The Cord of Life; The Fascinating Mrs. Francis; Those Awful Hats; Jones and the Lady Book Agent; Trying to Get Arrested; The Brahma Diamond; The Drive for a Life; His Wife's Mother; His Ward's Love; At the Altar; The Prussian Spy; The Medicine Bottle; The Deception; The Lure of the Gown; Lady Helen's Escapade; The Wooden Leg; The French Duel; Jones and His New Neighbors; A Drunkard's Reformation; The Winning Coat; The Road to the Heart; Schneider's Anti-Noise Crusade; Confidence; The Note in the Shoe; Lucky Jim; A Sound Sleeper; A Troublesome Satchel; 'Tis An Ill Wind That Blows No Good; Resurrection; One Busy Hour; A Baby's Shoe; Eloping With Aunty; The Jilt; Eradicating Aunty; What Drink Did; Her First Biscuits; Two Memories; The Peachbasket Hat; The Way of Man; Mrs. Jones' Lover or, "I Want My Hat"; The Country Doctor; Jealousy and the Man; The Cardinal's Conspiracy; Tender Hearts; Sweet and Twenty; The Slave; Jones' Burglar; The Mended Lute

LEE, FLORENCE: Actress, Author (1888-1962) (aka Mrs. Dell Henderson)

1911: Teaching Dad to Like Her; Cured; The Chief's Daughter; Enoch Arden, Part One; The Manicure Lady; The Diving Girl

1912: A Voice From the Deep; Won by a Fish; A Close Call (also au); Willie Becomes an Artist; Mr. Grouch at the Seashore; A Disappointed Mamma; A Mixed Affair; A Limited Divorce; A Ten-Karat Hero; Like the Cat, They Came Back; His Auto's Maiden Trip; Their Idols; Bill Bogg's Windfall; Oh, What a Boob!; The Best Man Wins; Kissing Kate; The Masher Cop; There Were Hoboes Three; An Up-to-Date Lochinvar; Look Not Upon the Wine; The High Cost of Reduction

1913: The Spring of Life; The Power of the Camera; Edwin Masquerades; A Lesson to Mashers; A Rainy Day (au only); Cinderella and the Boob (au only); The Trimmers Trimmed; Just Kids; Jenks Becomes a Desperate Character; The Rise and Fall of McDoo; Mister Jefferson Green (au only); Faust and the Lily (au only); An Old Maid's Deception; While the Count Goes Bathing; Baby Indisposed; Objections Overruled; For the Son of the House

LEE, JENNIE: Actress (1850-1925)

1913:   His Mother's Son; Almost a Wild Man; The Mothering
Heart; Her Mother's Oath; The Sorrowful Shore; The Battle at
Elderbush Gulch; The Coming of Angelo; Brute Force; Two Men
of the Desert; The Reformers, or The Lost Art of Minding One's
Business; Judith of Bethulia

LEHRMAN, HENRY: Actor (1886-1946) (aka "Pathe" Lehrman)

1909:   Nursing a Viper; Through the Breakers; A Corner in Wheat;
The Redman's View; In Little Italy; To Save Her Soul; The Day
After; The Rocky Road; The Last Deal; The Cloister's Touch; The
Woman From Mellon's; The Course of True Love

1910:   The Love of Lady Irma; A Child of the Ghetto; In the Bor-
der States; A Victim of Jealousy; The Face at the Window; A
Child's Impulse; A Child's Faith; A Flash of Light; As the Bells
Rang Out!; An Arcadian Maid; In Life's Cycle; Wilful Peggy; Rose
O'Salem-Town; Little Angels of Luck; A Mohawk's Way; The Mes-
sage of the Violin; A Child's Stratagem; Sunshine Sue; His Sister-
In-Law; Happy Jack, A Hero; White Roses; The Italian Barber;
The Midnight Marauder; The Two Paths

1911:   Comrades; The Broken Cross; Priscilla and the Umbrella;
Madame Rex; A Knight of the Road; The New Dress; Enoch Arden,
Part Two

1912:   Iola's Promise; A Beast at Bay; His Own Fault

LEIST, BERNARDINE R.:   Author

1910:   The Iconoclast; Waiter No. 5

1911:   Dan, the Dandy; Italian Blood; The Long Road; A String
of Pearls

LEONARD, MARION: Actress, Author (1880-1956) (aka Mrs. Stanner
E. V. Taylor)

1908:   At the Crossroads of Life; The Tavern-Keeper's Daughter;
The Bandit's Waterloo; The Greaser's Gauntlet; The Feud and the
Turkey; The Test of Friendship; One Touch of Nature; An Awful
Moment; The Helping Hand; The Maniac Cook; The Christmas Bur-
glars; The Criminal Hypnotist; The Sacrifice; The Welcome Bur-
glar; A Rural Elopement; The Joneses Have Amateur Theatricals;
The Roue's Heart; The Hindoo Dagger; The Salvation Army Lass;
Love Finds a Way; Tragic Love; The Girls and Daddy

1909:   The Cord of Life; The Fascinating Mrs. Francis; Trying
to Get Arrested; The Brahma Diamond; The Drive for a Life; Politician's Love Story; The Golden Louis; At the Altar; The Prussian
Spy; The Medicine Bottle; The Lure of the Gown; A Fool's Re-

venge; A Burglar's Mistake; The Voice of the Violin; "And A Little
Child Shall Lead Them"; A Drunkard's Reformation; The Winning
Coat; A Rude Hostess; The Eavesdropper; The Note in the Shoe;
Lucky Jim; 'Tis An Ill Wind That Blows No Good; Resurrection;
The Jilt; Her First Biscuits; The Violin Maker of Cremona; Two
Memories; The Lonely Villa; The Peachbasket Hat; His Duty; A
New Trick; The Way of Man; With Her Card; The Heart of an
Outlaw; The Mills of the Gods; Pranks; The Sealed Room; The
Children's Friend; Comata, the Sioux; Leather Stocking; The Bro-
ken Locket; Pippa Passes, or The Song of Conscience; Fools of
Fate; His Lost Love; Lines of White on a Sullen Sea; The Gibson
Goddess; In the Watches of the Night; The Expiation; The Restora-
tion; Nursing a Viper; The Light That Came; Sweet Revenge; In
the Window Recess; The Death Disc; Through the Breakers; The
Test; A Trap for Santa Claus; In Little Italy; The Day After; On
the Reef; The Cloister's Touch; The Duke's Plan

1910: In Old California; His Last Dollar; Gold Is Not All; As It
Is In Life; Thou Shalt Not; Love Among the Roses; The Two
Brothers; Over Silent Paths; The Call to Arms

1913: Those Little Flowers (au only)

LESTINA, ADOLPH: Actor

1909: The Honor of His Family; On the Reef; The Last Deal;
Winning Back His Love; His Trust; His Trust Fulfilled; A Wreath
of Orange Blossoms; The Italian Barber; The Two Paths; Con-
science; A Decree of Destiny; Fate's Turning; What Shall We Do
With Our Old; The Lily of the Tenements; Heart Beats of Long
Ago

1911: Through Darkened Vales; A Woman Scorned; The Miser's
Heart; The Failure; A Terrible Discovery; The Old Bookkeeper;
The Sunbeam; A String of Pearls

1912: A Lodging for the Night; The Chief's Blanket; The Narrow
Road; The Inner Circle; An Unseen Enemy; Friends; So Near, Yet
So Far; A Feud in the Kentucky Hills; The Musketeers of Pig
Alley; My Baby; The Unwelcome Guest; The New York Hat; My
Hero; The Burglar's Dilemma; The God Within; An Adventure in
the Autumn Woods; Oil and Water; A Chance Deception; Fate;
Brothers; Love in an Apartment Hotel

1913: Broken Ways; A Welcome Intruder; Her Wedding Bell; The
Lady and the Mouse; The Wanderer; The House of Darkness; Just
Gold; His Mother's Son; A Timely Interception; Death's Marathon;
Red Hicks Defies the World; Almost a Wild Man; The Mothering
Heart; Her Mother's Oath; The Sorrowful Shore; The Coming of
Angelo; The Reformers, or The Lost Art of Minding One's Bus-
iness; Judith of Bethulia; The Adopted Brother

LEWIS, GRACE: Actress

1912: Jinx's Birthday Party; Gold and Glitter; A Day's Outing; Oh, What a Boob!; The Press Gang; The Best Man Wins; Kissing Kate; There Were Hoboes Three; Look Not Upon the Wine; Among Club Fellows; The High Cost of Reduction; What is the Use of Repining?; A Queer Elopement

1913: The Spring of Life; Edwin Masquerades; A Lesson to Mashers; Her Wedding Bell; An "Uncle Tom's Cabin" Troupe; He Had a Guess Coming; The Cure; Cinderella and the Boob; The Noisy Suitors; A Chinese Puzzle

LEWIS, WALTER P.: Actor (1871-1932)

1912: The Chief's Blanket; Blind Love; The Painted Lady; The Musketeers of Pig Alley; Heredity; Gold and Glitter; My Baby; Brutality; The New York Hat; My Hero; Three Friends; The Telephone Girl and the Lady; An Adventure in the Autumn Woods; The Tender-Hearted Boy; Fate; A Misappropriated Turkey; Brothers

1913: The End of the World; A Saturday Holiday; Dyed But Not Dead; The Winning Punch; No Place for Father

LINCOLN, ELMO: Actor (1899-1952) (b. Otto Elmo Linkenhelter)

1913: The Battle at Elderbush Gulch; Brute Force; The Suffragette Minstrels; The Reformers, or The Lost Art of Minding One's Business

LONDON, JACK: Writer (1876-1916)

1908: For Love of Gold; Money Mad

LONGFELLOW, STEPHANIE: Actress

1909: A Convict's Sacrifice; A Strange Meeting; The Better Way; In Little Italy; The Rocky Road

1910: The Love of Lady Irma; His Last Burglary; A Flash of Light; As the Bells Rang Out!; Her Father's Pride; A Salutary Lesson; In Life's Cycle; Wilful Peggy; A Summer Idyl; The Banker's Daughters; The Message of the Violin; Love In Quarantine; A Child's Stratagem; Effecting a Cure; Turning the Tables; The Lesson; Winning Back His Love; The Recreation of an Heiress; Conscience; Fate's Turning

1911: Cured; Priscilla's April Fool Joke; The Chief's Daughter; Madame Rex; The Crooked Road; Stubbs' New Servants

LOOMIS, C. B.: Author

1913: The Daylight Burglar

LOONEY, J. F.: Author

1913: The House of Darkness

LOOS, ANITA: Author (1893-1981)

1912: The New York Hat

1913: The Power of the Camera; A Horse on Bill; The Hicksville Epicure; Highbrow Love; Pa Says; The Widow's Kids; The Lady in Black; His Hoodoo; A Fallen Hero; A Cure for Suffragettes; Bink's Vacation; How the Day Was Saved

LOVELL, MARIA: Translator

1908: The Barbarian, Ingomar

LOVERIDGE, LESLIE: Actress

1913: The Battle at Elderbush Gulch

LUCAS, WILFRED: Actor, Director, Author (1871-1940)

1908: (as actor) The Greaser's Gauntlet

1910: (as actor) The Marked Time-Table; Sunshine Sue; Winning Back His Love; His Trust; His Trust Fulfilled; The Two Paths; Three Sisters; What Shall We Do With Our Old; The Diamond Star; Heart Beats of Long Ago

1911: (as actor) Fisher Folks; The Lonedale Operator; Was He a Coward?; The Spanish Gypsy; His Mother's Scarf; In the Days of '49; The New Dress; Enoch Arden, Parts One and Two; The White Rose of the Wilds; The Primal Call; The Indian Brothers; The Thief and the Girl; The Ruling Passion (also au); The Rose of Kentucky; The Sorrowful Example; Swords and Hearts; The Old Confectioner's Mistake; Dan, the Dandy; The Making of a Man; The Long Road; Love in the Hills; A Woman Scorned; The Miser's Heart; The Failure; As In A Looking Glass; A Terrible Discovery; A Sister's Love; The Transformation of Mike (also au); Billy's Stratagem

1912: (as actor) Under Burning Skies; The Girl and Her Trust; Fate's Interception; Just Like a Woman; When Kings Were the Law (also au); Home Folks; An Outcast Among Outcasts (d only); A Temporary Truce; Man's Genesis; Black Sheep (d only); A Pueblo Legend; The Massacre; With the Enemy's Help (d only); The Chief's Blanket (d and au); In the North Woods (also d); Blind Love (d only); A Sailor's Heart (also d and au); Three Friends

MACE, FRED: Actor, Author (1879-1916)

1911: The Diving Girl; The Village Hero; A Convenient Burglar;

Trailing the Counterfeiter; Her Awakening; Too Many Burglars;
The Long Road; Why He Gave Up; Their First Divorce Case;
Through His Wife's Picture; Dooley's Scheme; A Victim of Circum-
stances; Through Darkened Vales; Caught with the Goods; Abe Gets
Even with Father; Brave and Bold; With a Kodak; A Near Tragedy

1912: A Spanish Dilemma; The Engagement Ring; A Voice From
the Deep; Hot Stuff; The Would-Be Shriner; Help! Help!; Those
Hicksville Boys; Their First Kidnapping Case; The Fickle Spaniard;
The Leading Man; When the Fire-Bells Rang; A Close Call; Helen's
Marriage; Algy, the Watchman; Neighbors; A Dash Through the
Clouds; One-Round O'Brien; The Speed Demon; His Own Fault;
The Bite of a Snake (au only)

MACKIN, MRS. LAURIE: Author

1909: All on Account of the Milk

MACPHERSON, JEANNIE: Actress (1884-1946)

1908: Mr. Jones at the Ball; Concealing A Burglar; Taming of the
Shrew; The Curtain Pole; The Clubman and the Tramp; Money Mad;
Mrs. Jones Entertains; One Touch of Nature; The Christmas Bur-
glars; A Wreath in Time; The Criminal Hypnotist

1909: The Winning Coat; Her First Biscuits; The Peachbasket
Hat; The Open Gate; Sweet Revenge; In the Window Recess; The
Trick That Failed; The Death Disc; Through the Breakers; A
Corner in Wheat; In A Hempen Bag; In Little Italy; To Save Her
Soul; The Day After

1910: A Child's Faith; A Salutary Lesson; The Usurer; An Old
Story with a New Ending; A Summer Idyl; Little Angels of Luck;
A Mohawk's Way; The Oath and the Man; A Gold Necklace; The
Message of the Violin; Two Little Waifs; Waiter No. 5; The Fugi-
tive; A Child's Stratagem; Sunshine Sue; A Plain Song; His Sister-
In-Law; The Golden Supper; The Lesson; Winning Back His Love;
His Trust; His Trust Fulfilled; A Wreath of Orange Blossoms;
The Italian Barber; The Two Paths; Conscience; Heart Beats of
Long Ago

1911: Fisher Folks; Comrades; The Lonedale Operator; The
Spanish Gypsy; The Broken Cross; The Chief's Daughter; Madame
Rex; A Knight of the Road; The New Dress; Enoch Arden, Parts
One and Two; The Crooked Road; The Blind Princess and the Poet;
The Last Drop of Water; Bobby, the Coward; The Ruling Passion;
Out From the Shadow; The Eternal Mother; The Village Hero

MAHR, JOHN: Camera Assistant (aka Johnny Mahr)

1911: The Squaw's Love

MAILES, CHARLES HILL: Actor (1870-1937)

1909:   The Faded Lilies

1910:   In Life's Cycle; A Summer Idyl; Rose O'Salem-Town; Little
Angels of Luck; A Mohawk's Way; The Oath and the Man; A Child's
Stratagem

1911:   The Ghost; Out From the Shadow; Swords and Hearts; The
Eternal Mother; The Making of a Man; Her Awakening; The Adven-
tures of Billy; The Long Road; The Battle; Through Darkened
Vales; Saved From Himself; A Woman Scorned; The Miser's
Heart; The Failure; A Terrible Discovery; The Baby and the
Stork; A Tale of the Wilderness; For His Son; A Blot in the
'Scutcheon; Billy's Stratagem; The Sunbeam; A String of Pearls;
The Root of Evil

1912:   Under Burning Skies; Iola's Promise; The Goddess of Sage-
brush Gulch; The Girl and Her Trust; Fate's Interception; Just
Like a Woman; The Old Actor; The Lesser Evil; Those Hicksville
Boys; Won by a Fish; A Lodging for the Night; When Kings Were
the Law; A Beast at Bay; Home Folks; A Close Call; Algy, the
Watchman; A Temporary Truce; Lena and the Geese; The School
Teacher and the Waif; Man's Lust for Gold; Man's Genesis; The
Sands of Dee; A Pueblo Legend; The Massacre; The Speed Demon;
With the Enemy's Help; The Narrow Road; A Child's Remorse;
The Inner Circle; A Change of Spirit; Friends; So Near, Yet So
Far; A Feud in the Kentucky Hills; In the Aisles of the Wild; The
Painted Lady; Brutality; Pirate Gold; The Unwelcome Guest; A
Sailor's Heart; The New York Hat; My Hero; The God Within; An
Adventure in the Autumn Woods; A Chance Deception; Fate; A
Misappropriated Turkey; Brothers; The Wrong Bottle; When Love
Forgives

1913:   A Welcome Intruder; Her Wedding Bell; The Hero of Little
Italy; He Had a Guess Coming; A Misunderstood Boy; The Wanderer; The House of Darkness; The Stolen Loaf; Olaf - An Atom;
Just Gold; The Yaqui Cur; A Dangerous Foe; The Ranchero's Revenge; Red Hicks Defies the World; Almost a Wild Man; The Mothering Heart; Her Mother's Oath; Faust and the Lily; The Battle at
Elderbush Gulch; The Mistake; The Coming of Angelo; Brute Force;
The Reformers, or The Lost Art of Minding One's Business; Judith of Bethulia; The Work Habit; A Woman in the Ultimate; For
the Son of the House; A Modest Hero; The Madonna of the Storm;
By Man's Law

MANNING, MILDRED: Actress

1912:   A Chance Deception

1913:   The Girl Across the Way; By Man's Law

MARSH, MAE: Actress (1895-1968) (b. Mary Wayne Marsh)

1912: A Voice from the Deep; The Lesser Evil; Those Hicksville Boys; Just Like a Woman; A Lodging for the Night; His Lesson; When Kings Were the Law; A Beast at Bay; Home Folks; A Temporary Truce; Lena and the Geese; The Spirit Awakened; The School Teacher and the Waif; An Indian Summer; Man's Genesis; The Sands of Dee; His Own Fault; Brutality; The New York Hat; Three Friends; The Telephone Girl and the Lady; An Adventure in the Autumn Woods; The Tender-Hearted Boy; Fate; Love in an Apartment Hotel

1913: A Girl's Stratagem; Near to Earth; The Perfidy of Mary; The Little Tease; The Wanderer; His Mother's Son; Her Mother's Oath; The Sorrowful Shore; The Battle at Elderbush Gulch; Brute Force; The Reformers, or The Lost Art of Minding One's Business; Judith of Bethulia; For the Son of the House; The Influence of the Unknown; The Girl Across the Way; By Man's Law

MARSH, MARGUERITE: Actress (1892-1925) (aka Marguerite Loveridge; Margaret Loveridge)

1912: Under Burning Skies; A Voice from the Deep; Just Like a Woman; The Old Actor; Their First Kidnapping Case; The Leading Man; The New York Hat

MARSTON, WILLIAM M.: Author

1912: Love in an Apartment Hotel

MARVIN, ARTHUR W.: Cameraman (1861-1911)

1907: Mr. Gay and Mrs.; Professional Jealousy

1908: Classmates; The Man in the Box; Deceived Slumming Party; At the Crossroads of Life; The Black Viper; The Kentuckian; The Stage Rustler; The Adventures of Dollie; The Fight for Freedom; The Redman and the Child; The Tavern-Keeper's Daughter; The Bandit's Waterloo; A Calamitous Elopement; The Greaser's Gauntlet; The Man and the Woman; For Love Of Gold; The Fatal Hour; For a Wife's Honor; Balked at the Altar; The Girl and the Outlaw; The Red Girl; Betrayed by a Handprint; Behind the Scenes; The Heart of O Yama; Where the Breakers Roar; The Call of the Wild; After Many Years; Taming of the Shrew; The Ingrate; A Woman's Way; The Pirate's Gold; The Guerrilla; The Feud and the Turkey; The Valet's Wife; One Touch of Nature; An Awful Moment; The Helping Hand; The Salvation Army Lass; Love Finds a Way; Tragic Love; The Girls and Daddy

1909: Those Boys; The Cord of Life; Trying to Get Arrested; The Drive for a Life; Politician's Love Story; His Wife's Mother; At the Altar; The Lure of the Gown; A Fool's Revenge; The Wooden

Leg; A Burglar's Mistake; The Voice of the Violin; "And a Little
Child Shall Lead Them"; The French Duel; The Road to the Heart;
The Eavesdropper; Schneider's Anti-Noise Crusade; Twin Brothers;
Confidence; Lucky Jim; A Sound Sleeper; A Troublesome Satchel;
'Tis An Ill Wind That Blows No Good; The Suicide Club; Resur-
rection; One Busy Hour; A Baby's Shoe; Eloping With Aunty; The
Cricket on the Hearth; The Jilt; Eradicating Aunty; The Lonely
Villa; The Peachbasket Hat; The Son's Return; His Duty; The
Necklace; The Way of Man; The Faded Lilies; The Message; The
Friend of the Family; Was Justice Served?; The Renunciation;
Jones' Burglar; The Heart of an Outlaw; Pranks; "1776" or, The
Hessian Renegades; Leather Stocking; Pippa Passes or, The Song
of Conscience; The Little Teacher; A Midnight Adventure; The
Test; To Save Her Soul; The Rocky Road; All On Account Of The
Milk; The Honor of His Family; The Cloister's Touch; The Course
of True Love

1910: The Love of Lady Irma; The Final Settlement; The Newly-
weds; The Smoker; His Last Dollar; Faithful; The Kid; The Ten-
derfoot's Triumph; Up a Tree; Never Again; May and December;
An Affair of Hearts; The Gold-Seekers; Love Among the Roses;
The Two Brothers; A Knot in the Plot; The Impalement; In the
Season of Buds; A Child of the Ghetto; A Child's Impulse; Serious
Sixteen; An Old Story with a New Ending; When We Were In Our
'Teens; The Affair of an Egg; Muggsy Becomes a Hero; A Summer
Tragedy; A Gold Necklace; How Hubby Got a Raise; A Lucky
Toothache; The Masher; The Proposal; The Passing of a Grouch;
Simple Charity; Love in Quarantine; A Troublesome Baby; Not So
Bad As It Seemed; His New Lid; Effecting a Cure; Turning the
Tables; Happy Jack, A Hero; White Roses; The Recreation of an
Heiress; The Midnight Marauder; His Wife's Sweethearts; After the
Ball; The Poor Sick Men; Help Wanted; Priscilla's Engagement
Kiss

MARVIN, HENRY NORTON: Co-founder and officer of the Biograph
Company.

MAUPASSANT, GUY DE: Writer (1850-1893)

1909: The Necklace

MCCABE, MRS. KATE: Author

1913: The Stolen Bride

MCCLELLAND, HARRY: Set Dresser, Lighting and Painting Assistant

MCCOY, BESSIE: Actress (1886?-1931)

1909: What's Your Hurry?

MCCULLOUGH, L.: Assistant cameraman with the comedy unit that remained in Los Angeles with Fred Mace in 1912.

MCCUTCHEON, WALLACE, SR.: Director, Cameraman

1908: Classmates; Bobby's Kodak; The Snowman; The Princess in the Vase; The Yellow Peril; The Boy Detective - or - The Abductors Foiled; Her First Adventure; Caught by Wireless; Old Isaacs, the Pawnbroker; A Famous Escape; King of the Cannibal Islands; Hulda's Lovers; The King's Messenger; The Music Master; The Sculptor's Nightmare; When Knights Were Bold; His Day of Rest; Thompson's Night Out; The Romance of an Egg; Mixed Babies; 'Ostler Joe; The Invisible Fluid; The Man in the Box; The Outlaw; At the French Ball; The Kentuckian; The Stage Rustler; Deceived Slumming Party; The Black Viper

MCCUTCHEON, WALLACE, JR.: Director (1881-1928)

1908: At the Crossroads of Life; The Kentuckian; The Stage Rustler; Deceived Slumming Party; The Black Viper

MCDERMOTT, JOSEPH: Actor

1911: The Old Bookkeeper; The Transformation of Mike; The Sunbeam

1912: The Chief's Blanket; The Inner Circle; A Change of Spirit; Blind Love; Like the Cat, They Came Back; Pirate Gold; Three Friends; The Telephone Girl and the Lady; An Adventure in the Autumn Woods; Oil and Water; A Chance Deception; Fate; A Misappropriated Turkey; Love in an Apartment Hotel

1913: Broken Ways; Near to Earth; A Welcome Intruder; A Misunderstood Boy; The Left-Handed Man; The Lady and the Mouse; The Wanderer; The House of Darkness; Just Gold; His Mother's Son; A Timely Interception; The Yaqui Cur; Red Hicks Defies the World; The Mothering Heart; Her Mother's Oath; The Battle at Elderbush Gulch; Brute Force; The Reformers, or The Lost Art of Minding One's Business; A Woman in the Ultimate; So Runs the Way; The Girl Across the Way; The Stopped Clock; Diversion; "Old Coupons"; The Detective's Stratagem; All for Science

MCDONAGH, JOHN: Author

1910: The Fugitive

MCDOWELL, CLAIRE: Actress (1877-1966) (aka Clare McDowell)

1908: The Planter's Wife; The Devil; The Call of the Wild

1910: A Flash of Light; The Usurer; Wilful Peggy; Muggsy Becomes A Hero; A Summer Idyl; Rose O'Salem-Town; A Mohawk's Way; The Oath and the Man; The Iconoclast; How Hubby Got A

Raise; A Lucky Toothache; The Message of the Violin; Two Little Waifs; Waiter No. 5; Simple Charity; The Fugitive; His New Lid; A Child's Stratagem; His Sister-In-Law; The Golden Supper; Happy Jack, A Hero; His Trust; His Trust Fulfilled; The Recreation of an Heiress; The Italian Barber; Conscience; Three Sisters; A Decree of Destiny; Fate's Turning; What Shall We Do With Our Old

1911: Fisher Folks; Cured; The Spanish Gypsy; The Broken Cross; The Chief's Daughter; Misplaced Jealousy; In the Days of '49; The Manicure Lady; The Crooked Road; A Romany Tragedy; The Primal Call; A Country Cupid; The Ruling Passion; The Sorrowful Example; Swords and Hearts; The Squaw's Love; The Making of a Man; The Adventures of Billy; The Long Road; A Woman Scorned; As In A Looking Glass; The Baby and the Stork; A Blot in the 'Scutcheon; Billy's Stratagem; The Sunbeam; A String of Pearls

1912: Under Burning Skies; The Female of the Species; The Old Actor; The Fickle Spaniard; When Kings Were the Law; The Leading Man; When the Fire-Bells Rang; A Temporary Truce; Lena and the Geese; The School Teacher and the Waif; Trying to Fool Uncle; Man's Genesis; The Sands of Dee; The Massacre; A Child's Remorse; In the North Woods; Two Daughters of Eve; So Near, Yet So Far; In the Aisles of the Wild; The Unwelcome Guest; A Sailor's Heart; The New York Hat; A Cry for Help; The God Within; The Telephone Girl and the Lady; A Father's Lesson; A Misappropriated Turkey; Drink's Lure; The Wrong Bottle

1913: A Welcome Intruder; The Stolen Bride; The Wanderer; The Tenderfoot's Money; The House of Darkness; Olaf - an Atom; The Ranchero's Revenge; The Well; The Switch-Tower; A Gamble with Death; The Enemy's Baby; A Gambler's Honor; The Mirror; The Vengeance of Galora; Under the Shadow of the Law; I Was Meant for You; The Work Habit; The Crook and the Girl; The Strong Man's Burden; The Stolen Treaty; The Law and His Son; A Tender-Hearted Crook; The Van Nostrand Tiara; The Stopped Clock; Diversion; The Detective's Stratagem; All for Science

MCEVOY, TOM: Actor 1913: Strongheart

MCGOWAN, ROBERT F.: Author 1910: The Affair of an Egg

MCWADE, EDWARD: Author 1913: "Old Coupons"

MEREDYTH, BESS: Actress (1890-1969) 1912: A Sailor's Heart

MERSEREAU, VIOLET: Actress (b. 1894)

1909: The Suicide Club; One Busy Hour; Eloping with Aunty; The Cricket on the Hearth; Her First Biscuits; The Violin Maker of Cremona; The Lonely Villa; The Peachbasket Hat; His Duty; The Way of Man; His Lost Love; What's Your Hurry?

MEYER, MINNIE: Author

1913: The Well

MILES, DAVID: Actor, Director (d. 1915)

1908: The Helping Hand; A Wreath in Time; The Honor of Thieves;
The Criminal Hypnotist; The Welcome Burglar; A Rural Elopement;
The Joneses Have Amateur Theatricals; Edgar Allen Poe; The
Roue's Heart; The Salvation Army Lass; Love Finds A Way; Tragic
Love; The Girls and Daddy

1909: The Cord of Life; Trying to Get Arrested; The Brahma
Diamond; Politician's Love Story; His Wife's Mother; At the Altar;
The Prussian Spy; The Medicine Bottle; The Deception; The Lure
of the Gown; Lady Helen's Escapade; A Fool's Revenge; The Wood-
en Leg; A Burglar's Mistake; The Voice of the Violin; "And A
Little Child Shall Lead Them"; The French Duel; Jones and His
New Neighbors; A Drunkard's Reformation; The Winning Coat; The
Road to the Heart; The Eavesdropper; Twin Brothers; Confidence;
The Note in the Shoe; Lucky Jim; 'Tis An Ill Wind That Blows No
Good; The Suicide Club; Resurrection; One Busy Hour; A Baby's
Shoe; Eloping with Aunty; The Cricket on the Hearth; The Jilt;
Eradicating Aunty; What Drink Did; Her First Biscuits; The Violin
Maker of Cremona; Two Memories; The Lonely Villa; The Son's
Return; His Duty; The Necklace; The Way of Man; The Faded
Lilies; Was Justice Served?

1913: (as director) The Wife

MILLER, MR.: Employee. Noted in Moving Picture World, 19
August 1911, p. 449.

MILLER, W. CHRYSTIE: Actor (1843-1922)

1909: A Corner in Wheat; The Redman's View; A Trap for Santa
Claus; In Little Italy; To Save Her Soul; The Day After; The Rocky
Road; The Dancing Girl of Butte; Her Terrible Ordeal; The Call;
The Honor of His Family; On the Reef; The Last Deal; The Clois-
ter's Touch; The Duke's Plan; One Night, and Then---, The Eng-
lishman and the Girl

1910: The Newlyweds; The Thread of Destiny; In Old California;
The Converts; Faithful; The Twisted Trail; Gold Is Not All; As It
Is In Life; Thou Shalt Not; The Way of the World; The Gold-
Seekers; The Two Brothers; Unexpected Help; Ramona; Over Silent
Paths; In the Season of Buds; A Child of the Ghetto; In the Border
States; The Marked Time-Table; The Call to Arms; A Midnight
Cupid; A Child's Faith; An Arcadian Maid; Her Father's Pride; The
Sorrows of the Unfaithful; An Old Story with a New Ending; In
Life's Cycle; Wilful Peggy; A Summer Idyl; Rose O'Salem-Town;
The Oath and the Man; Examination Day at School; That Chink at
Golden Gulch; The Broken Doll; A Lucky Toothache; Simple Charity;

The Fugitive; Sunshine Sue; A Plain Song; Effecting a Cure; The Lesson; His Trust; White Roses; His Wife's Sweethearts; What Shall We Do With Our Old; The Lily of the Tenements

1911: Fisher Folks; The Lonedale Operator; Was He a Coward?; Teaching Dad to Like Her; His Mother's Scarf; In the Day of '49; The New Dress; The White Rose of the Wilds; The Crooked Road; The Primal Call; Bobby, the Coward; The Village Hero; The Making of a Man; The Adventures of Billy; The Battle; Dooley's Scheme; The Old Bookkeeper; The Sunbeam; A String of Pearls

1912: Under Burning Skies; The Goddess of Sagebrush Gulch; The Old Actor; An Outcast Among Outcasts; A Temporary Truce; Lena and the Geese; The Spirit Awakened; An Indian Summer; Man's Genesis; Heaven Avenges; The Sands of Dee; The Massacre; The Chief's Blanket; Getting Rid of Trouble; Blind Love; My Baby; Pirate Gold; The Unwelcome Guest; An Adventure in the Autumn Woods; The Tender-Hearted Boy; Oil and Water; A Misappropriated Turkey

1913: A Welcome Intruder; An "Uncle Tom's Cabin" Troupe; The Little Tease; His Mother's Son; A Timely Interception; Her Mother's Oath; The Battle at Elderbush Gulch; The Monument; The Reformers, or The Lost Art of Minding One's Business; Judith of Bethulia; The Work Habit; The Adopted Brother; The Girl Across the Way; The Stopped Clock; The Blue or the Gray

MILLER, WALTER: Actor (1892-1940)

1912: A Change of Spirit; An Unseen Enemy; Two Daughters of Eve; Friends; So Near, Yet So Far; A Feud in the Kentucky Hills; The Painted Lady; The Musketeers of Pig Alley; My Baby; The Informer; Brutality; A Cry for Help; An Adventure in the Autumn Woods; Oil and Water; The Wrong Bottle; Love in an Apartment Hotel

1913: Broken Ways; Near to Earth; The Hero of Little Italy; The Perfidy of Mary; A Frightful Blunder; A Rainy Day; The Little Tease; The Wanderer; The House of Darkness; His Mother's Son; The Yaqui Cur; Death's Marathon; Red Hicks Defies the World; The Mothering Heart; In Diplomatic Circles; A Gamble with Death; The Coming of Angelo; Two Men of the Desert; Under the Shadow of the Law; The Reformers, or The Lost Art of Minding One's Business; A Modest Hero

MOLNAR, FERENC: Playwright (1878-1952)

1908: The Devil

MONTAGNE, E. J.: Author

1912: Oil and Water

MOORE, OWEN: Actor (1886-1939)

1908: The Honor of Thieves; The Criminal Hypnotist; The Welcome Burglar; A Rural Elopement; The Joneses Have Amateur
Theatricals; The Roue's Heart; The Salvation Army Lass

1909: Jones and the Lady Book Agent; Trying to Get Arrested;
His Wife's Mother; The Golden Louis; His Ward's Love; The
Prussian Spy; The Medicine Bottle; The Deception; The Lure of
the Gown; Lady Helen's Escapade; A Fool's Revenge; A Burglar's
Mistake; The Voice of the Violin; The French Duel; Jones and His
New Neighbors; A Drunkard's Reformation; The Winning Coat; A
Rude Hostess; The Eavesdropper; Schneider's Anti-Noise Crusade;
Twin Brothers; Confidence; The Note in the Shoe; Lucky Jim; A
Sound Sleeper; A Troublesome Satchel; 'Tis An Ill Wind That
Blows No Good; The Suicide Club; Resurrection; One Busy Hour;
A Baby's Shoe; The Cricket on the Hearth; The Jilt; Eradicating
Aunty; What Drink Did; Her First Biscuits; The Violin Maker of
Cremona; The Lonely Villa; The Peachbasket Hat; The Son's Re-
turn; His Duty; The Necklace; The Way of Man; The Faded Lilies;
The Message; The Friend of the Family; Was Justice Served?;
Jealousy and the Man; The Cardinal's Conspiracy; The Seventh
Day; A Convict's Sacrifice; A Strange Meeting; The Slave; They
Would Elope; Jones' Burglar; The Mended Lute; The Indian Run-
ner's Romance; With Her Card; The Better Way; His Wife's Visi-
tor; The Heart of an Outlaw; The Mills of the Gods; The Sealed
Room; "1776" or, The Hessian Renegades; The Little Darling; In
Old Kentucky; The Children's Friend; Leather Stocking; The Broken
Locket; A Fair Exchange; The Awakening; Pippa Passes or, The
Song of Conscience; A Change of Heart; His Lost Love; Lines of
White on a Sullen Sea; The Expiation; The Restoration; Nursing a
Viper; Two Women and a Man; The Light That Came; The Open
Gate; The Mountaineer's Honor; The Trick That Failed; The Death
Disc; Through the Breakers; A Corner in Wheat; The Redman's
View; In Little Italy; To Save Her Soul; The Dancing Girl of Butte;
Her Terrible Ordeal; The Last Deal; The Cloister's Touch; The
Course of True Love; The Duke's Plan

MOORE, TOM: Actor (1885-1955)

1908: The Test of Friendship; An Awful Moment; The Helping
Hand; The Christmas Burglars; The Criminal Hypnotist

1909: The Voice of the Violin; A Drunkard's Reformation

MORENO, ANTONIO: Actor (1887-1967)

1912: Iola's Promise; His Own Fault; An Unseen Enemy; Two
Daughters of Eve; So Near, Yet So Far; The Musketeers of Pig
Alley; Oil and Water

1913: A Misunderstood Boy; No Place for Father; By Man's Law;
Strongheart; Men and Women

MORRIS, DAVE: Actor (b. 1884)

1913: Jenks Becomes a Desperate Character; The Rise and Fall of McDoo; Mister Jefferson Green; A Compromising Complication; An Old Maid's Deception; A Sea Dog's Love; The Noisy Suitors; The Sweat-Box; A Chinese Puzzle; The Widow's Kids; Come Seben, Leben; The Suffragette Minstrels; Father's Chicken Dinner; Papa's Baby; Black and White; Baby Indisposed; Objections Overruled; Dan Greegan's Ghost; The Lady in Black; The Reformers, or The Lost Art of Minding One's Business; His Hoodoo; The End of the World; A Saturday Holiday; Dyed but not Dead; Scenting a Terrible Crime; With the Aid of Phrenology

MORRIS, REGGIE: Actor (1886-1928)

1913: The Stolen Treaty; The Law and His Son; So Runs the Way; The Winning Punch; The Van Nostrand Tiara; The Stopped Clock; Diversion; "Old Coupons"; The Detective's Stratagem; All for Science

MORRISON, David: Author 1911: The Villain Foiled

MORRISSEY, EDWARD: Production assistant to James Kirkwood, later director of comedy unit in 1913 (after Edward Dillon).

MOULAN, E.: Author

1910: His Wife's Sweethearts; The Poor Sick Men

MULHALL, JACK: Actor (1887-1979) (b. John Joseph Francis Mulhall)

1910: A Child's Stratagem; Sunshine Sue

1913: Strongheart

MURRAY, CHARLES: Actor (1872-1941)

1912: Mr. Grouch at the Seashore; Through Dumb Luck; Getting Rid of Trouble; Love's Messenger; A Disappointed Mamma; A Mixed Affair; A Limited Divorce; The Line at Hogan's; A Ten-Karat Hero; Like the Cat, They Came Back; At the Basket Picnic; A Real Estate Deal; His Auto's Maiden Trip; Their Idols; An Absent-Minded Burglar; The Club-Man and the Crook; Hoist on His Own Petard; Look Not Upon the Wine; A Delivery Package; Edwin's Badge of Honor

1913: Tightwad's Predicament; The Power of the Camera; The Old Gray Mare; All Hail to the King; Edwin Masquerades; Their One Good Suit; How They Struck Oil; An "Uncle Tom's Cabin" Troupe; A Horse on Bill; He Had a Guess Coming; A Ragtime Romance; The Daylight Burglar; A Rainy Day; Frappe Love; The King and the Copper; Cinderella and the Boob; Highbrow Love;

Slippery Slim Repents; Just Kids; Red Hicks Defies the World;
Jenks Becomes a Desperate Character; Almost a Wild Man; The
Rise and Fall of McDoo; The Mothering Heart; Mister Jefferson
Green; Faust and the Lily; An Old Maid's Deception; A Sea Dog's
Love; The Noisy Suitors; The Suffragette Minstrels; Father's Chick-
en Dinner; Baby Indisposed; Objections Overruled; The Lady in
Black; The Reformers, or The Lost Art of Minding One's Business;
His Hoodoo; The End of the World; For the Son of the House; Dyed
but not Dead; Scenting a Terrible Crime; With the Aid of Phreno-
logy; Never Known to Smile; McGann and His Octette; The Winning
Punch; A Fallen Hero; In the Hands of the Black Hands; An Eve-
ning with Wilder Spender; A Barber Cure; Boarders and Bombs;
"Mixed Nuts"; He's a Lawyer; The Somnambulists; Bink's Vacation;
How the Day Was Saved

MURRAY, MISS: Actress

1908: Cupid's Pranks

MYERS, TERRY: Author

1912: His Own Fault

NEILAN, MARSHALL: Actor (1891-1958) (aka Mickey Neilan)

1912: When the Fire-Bells Rang

1913: Classmates; Men and Women

NELSON, O. A.: Author

1913: The Work Habit

NEWTON, MARIE: Actress (b. 1899)

1911: The Ruling Passion

1912: The Musketeers of Pig Alley

1913: "Old Coupons"

NICHOLLS, GEORGE O.: Actor (1865-1927) (aka George Nichols)

1908: Behind the Scenes; The Heart of O Yama; The Jilt

1909: One Busy Hour; A Baby's Shoe; The Cricket on the Hearth;
What Drink Did; Her First Biscuits; The Sealed Room; "1776" or,
The Hessian Renegades; The Little Darling; In Old Kentucky;
Leather Stocking; Getting Even; The Broken Locket; A Fair Ex-
change; The Awakening; Pippa Passes or, The Song of Conscience;
Wanted, A Child; The Little Teacher; A Change of Heart; His Lost
Love; Lines of White on a Sullen Sea; The Gibson Goddess; In the
Watches of the Night; The Expiation; What's Your Hurry?; The
Restoration; Nursing a Viper; Two Women and a Man; The Light

That Came; A Midnight Adventure; The Open Gate; The Mountain-
eer's Honor; In the Window Recess; The Trick That Failed; The
Death Disc; Through the Breakers; A Corner in Wheat; The Red-
man's View; In Little Italy; To Save Her Soul; The Day After;
The Rocky Road; Her Terrible Ordeal; The Honor of His Family;
The Last Deal; The Cloister's Touch; The Woman From Mellon's;
One Night, and Then---; The Englishman and the Girl

1910: His Last Burglary; The Newlyweds; The Thread of Destiny;
The Converts; The Twisted Trail; Gold Is Not All; As It Is In
Life; A Rich Revenge; Thou Shalt Not; The Way of the World; Un-
expected Help; A Child of the Ghetto; The Face at the Window; The
Marked Time-Table; A Child's Impulse; Muggsy's First Sweetheart;
The Purgation; A Midnight Cupid; A Child's Faith; A Flash of
Light; As The Bells Rang Out!; An Arcadian Maid; Her Father's
Pride; The Usurer; In Life's Cycle; The Modern Prodigal; Rose
O'Salem-Town; Little Angels of Luck; A Mohawk's Way; The Icono-
clast; That Chink at Golden Gulch; The Broken Doll; The Banker's
Daughters; The Message of the Violin; Waiter No. 5; A Child's
Stratagem; Sunshine Sue; When A Man Loves; The Lesson; Winning
Back His Love; Conscience; A Decree of Destiny; What Shall We
Do With Our Old; The Lily of the Tenements; Heart Beats of Long
Ago

1911: The Lonedale Operator; Was He a Coward?; The Spanish
Gypsy; The Broken Cross; The Chief's Daughter; A Knight of the
Road; In the Days of '49; Enoch Arden, Part One; The Primal
Call; Fighting Blood; The Ruling Passion

NOLTE, H. M. L.: Author

1912: Brothers

NORCROSS, FRANK M.: Actor (1856-1926)

1913: For the Son of the House; The Detective's Stratagem; By
Man's Law; The Blue or the Gray; Men and Women

NORMAND, MABEL: Actress, Author (1894-1930)

1911: The Diving Girl; The Unveiling; The Eternal Mother; The
Baron; The Squaw's Love; The Making of a Man; Her Awakening;
Why He Gave Up; Through His Wife's Picture; Saved from Him-
self; The Fatal Chocolate

1912: A Spanish Dilemma; The Engagement Ring (also au); Hot
Stuff; Help! Help!; The Brave Hunter; The Fickle Spaniard; When
Kings Were the Law; The Furs; Helen's Marriage; Tomboy Bessie;
Neighbors; A Dash Through the Clouds; What the Doctor Ordered;
The Tourists; An Interrupted Elopement; The Tragedy of a Dress
Suit (also au); He Must Have a Wife

NORRIS, FRANK: Writer (1870-1902)

  1909: A Corner in Wheat

NORTON, JANE: Author

  1913: McGann and His Octette

NULTZ, E.: Employee in 1913

O. HENRY: Writer (1862-1910) (pseud. for William Sydney Porter)

  1908: The Sacrifice

  1909: Trying To Get Arrested; The Deception

  1910: A Summer Tragedy

OHNET, DOLLY: Author

  1913: The Rise and Fall of McDoo

OLSON, JEROME J.: Author

  1911: The Trail of Books

OPPERMAN, FRANK: Actor (b. 1861)

  1910: The Newlyweds; The Thread of Destiny; In Old California; The Smoker; The Converts; The Twisted Trail; Gold Is Not All; As It Is In Life; The Tenderfoot's Triumph; A Rich Revenge; Up a Tree; The Way of the World; The Unchanging Sea; The Gold-Seekers; Unexpected Help; Ramona; A Knot in the Plot

  1911: Paradise Lost; In the Days of '49; The Primal Call; The Indian Brothers; The Last Drop of Water

  1912: Iola's Promise; The Goddess of Sagebrush Gulch; The Would-Be Shriner; The Punishment; Fate's Interception; Just Like a Woman; One is Business, The Other Crime; The Old Actor; The Lesser Evil; A Lodging for the Night; When Kings Were the Law; Home Folks; When the Fire-Bells Rang; A Close Call; Helen's Marriage; An Outcast Among Outcasts; A Temporary Truce; Lena and the Geese; The School Teacher and the Waif; An Indian Summer; Tomboy Bessie; Neighbors; Trying to Fool Uncle; Man's Lust for Gold; The Sands of Dee; The Massacre; Willie Becomes an Artist; A Feud in the Kentucky Hills; Bill Bogg's Windfall; The Press Gang; An Adventure in the Autumn Woods; The Bite of a Snake; The Best Man Wins; Kissing Kate; The Masher Cop; Look Not Upon the Wine; Among Club Fellows; The High Cost of Reduction; A Queer Elopement; A Delivery Package

  1913: Broken Ways; The Spring of Life; The Power of the Camera;

Near to Earth; A Welcome Intruder; A Lesson to Mashers; The
Hero of Little Italy; An "Uncle Tom's Cabin" Troupe; A Misunder-
stood Boy; The Cure; The Little Tease; The Lady and the Mouse;
The Wanderer; The House of Darkness; Just Gold; His Mother's
Son; A Timely Interception; The Yaqui Cur; Red Hicks Defies the
World; Her Mother's Oath; The Sorrowful Shore; The Battle at
Elderbush Gulch; During the Round-Up; An Indian's Loyalty; Judith
of Bethulia

ORR, JAMES: Author

1913: Near to Earth

ORTH, LOUISE: Actress

1913: He's a Lawyer

OSBURN, S. R.: Author

1912: A Real Estate Deal

O'SULLIVAN, ANTHONY: Actor, Director, Author (d. 1920) (aka
Tony O'Sullivan)

1907: (as actor) Yale Laundry; Dr. Skinum; Mr. Gay and Mrs.

1908: (as actor) Lonesome Junction; The Yellow Peril; A Famous
Escape; King of the Cannibal Islands; Hulda's Lovers; The Sculptor's Nightmare; Thompson's Night Out; 'Ostler Joe; Over the Hills
to the Poorhouse; The Invisible Fluid; The Man in the Box; Deceived Slumming Party; At the Crossroads of Life; The Black Viper; The Kentuckian; The Stage Rustler; The Fight for Freedom;
The Greaser's Gauntlet; The Fatal Hour; Monday Morning in a
Coney Island Police Court

1909: (as actor) Twin Brothers; Confidence; The Note in the Shoe;
Lucky Jim; A Sound Sleeper; 'Tis An Ill Wind That Blows No
Good; The Suicide Club; Resurrection; One Busy Hour; A Baby's
Shoe; Eloping with Aunty; The Jilt; What Drink Did; Her First
Biscuits; The Violin Maker of Cremona; Two Memories; The Lone-
ly Villa; The Peachbasket Hat; The Son's Return; The Necklace;
The Way of Man; The Faded Lilies; The Message; Was Justice
Served?; Mrs. Jones' Lover or, "I Want My Hat"; Jealousy and
the Man; The Renunciation; The Cardinal's Conspiracy; The Seventh
Day; A Convict's Sacrifice; A Strange Meeting; They Would Elope;
Jones' Burglar; The Indian Runner's Romance; With Her Card; The
Better Way; The Heart of an Outlaw; The Mills of the Gods; Pranks;
The Sealed Room; "1776" or, The Hessian Renegades; The Little
Darling; In Old Kentucky; Leather Stocking; Getting Even; The
Broken Locket; A Fair Exchange; The Awakening; Pippa Passes
or, The Song of Conscience; Wanted, A Child; A Change of Heart;
His Lost Love; Lines of White on a Sullen Sea; The Gibson God-
dess; In the Watches of the Night; The Expiation; What's Your

Hurry?; Nursing a Viper; Two Women and a Man; The Light That
Came; A Midnight Adventure; The Open Gate; The Mountaineer's
Honor; In the Window Recess; The Trick That Failed; The Death
Disc; A Corner in Wheat; The Redman's View; The Test; A Trap
for Santa Claus; In Little Italy; The Day After; Choosing a Hus-
band; The Rocky Road; Her Terrible Ordeal; The Call; The Honor
of His Family; The Last Deal; The Woman from Mellon's; The
Englishman and the Girl

1910: The Final Settlement; Taming a Husband; The Newlyweds;
The Thread of Destiny; In Old California; The Converts; His Last
Dollar; Faithful; The Twisted Trail; Gold Is Not All; As It Is In
Life; A Rich Revenge; Up a Tree; Never Again; The Way of the
World; An Affair of Hearts; The Gold-Seekers; The Two Brothers;
Ramona; A Knot in the Plot; A Child of the Ghetto; A Victim of
Jealousy; A Child's Impulse; What the Daisy Said; A Flash of
Light; An Arcadian Maid; Her Father's Pride; The Usurer; In
Life's Cycle; Muggsy Becomes A Hero; The Modern Prodigal; Rose
O'Salem-Town; Little Angels of Luck; A Mohawk's Way; The Oath
and the Man; The Iconoclast; That Chink at Golden Gulch; How
Hubby Got a Raise; The Banker's Daughters; The Masher; The
Proposal

1911: (as actor) A Knight of the Road

1912: (as director) The Wrong Bottle; When Love Forgives

1913: (as director) Her Wedding Bell; The Stolen Bride; A Fright-
ful Blunder; The Left-Handed Man; The Tenderfoot's Money; The
Stolen Loaf; Olaf - An Atom; A Dangerous Foe; The Well; The
Switch-Tower (also a); In Diplomatic Circles; A Gamble with
Death; The Enemy's Baby; A Gambler's Honor; The Mirror; The
Monument (also au); The Vengeance of Galora; Under the Shadow
of the Law; I Was Meant for You; The Work Habit; The Crook
and the Girl; The Strong Man's Burden; The Stolen Treaty; The
Law and His Son; A Tender-Hearted Crook; Red and Pete, Partners; The Stopped Clock; Diversion; "Old Coupons"; The Detec-
tive's Stratagem; All for Science

PAGET, ALFRED: Actor, Director? (1880?-1925)

1909: The Slave; The Mended Lute; The Honor of His Family;
The Cloister's Touch; The Woman From Mellon's; The Duke's
Plan

1910: The Love of Lady Irma; The Newlyweds; The Thread of
Destiny; In Old California; The Converts; The Twisted Trail; Gold
Is Not All; A Romance of the Western Hills; The Way of the
World; The Unchanging Sea; The Gold-Seekers; Love Among the
Roses; The Two Brothers; Unexpected Help; Over Silent Paths;
The Impalement; A Child of the Ghetto; In the Border States; A
Victim of Jealousy; The Face at the Window; The Marked Time-
Table; A Child's Impulse; The Purgation; The Call to Arms; A

Midnight Cupid; A Child's Faith; What the Daisy Said; A Flash of Light; As the Bells Rang Out!; An Arcadian Maid; The House with Closed Shutters; Her Father's Pride; A Salutary Lesson; The Usurer; In Life's Cycle; Wilful Peggy; Muggsy Becomes a Hero; The Modern Prodigal; Rose O'Salem-Town; Little Angels of Luck; A Mohawk's Way; The Oath and the Man; Examination Day at School; The Iconoclast; That Chink at Golden Gulch; The Broken Doll; The Banker's Daughters; The Masher; The Message of the Violin; Two Little Waifs; Waiter No. 5; Simple Charity; The Fugitive; The Song of the Wildwood Flute; A Child's Stratagem; A Plain Song; The Golden Supper; The Lesson; Winning Back His Love; His Trust; A Wreath of Orange Blossoms; The Two Paths; Conscience; Three Sisters; The Poor Sick Men; A Decree of Destiny; Fate's Turning; What Shall We Do With Our Old; The Lily of the Tenements; Heart Beats of Long Ago

1911: Fisher Folks; Was He a Coward?; Teaching Dad to Like Her; Cured; The Spanish Gypsy; Priscilla and the Umbrella; The Chief's Daughter; Madame Rex; A Knight of the Road; His Mother's Scarf; In the Days of '49; The Two Sides; The New Dress; Enoch Arden, Part One; The Crooked Road; The Primal Call; The Indian Brothers; Fighting Blood; The Last Drop of Water; Bobby, the Coward; A Country Cupid; The Rose of Kentucky; Out From the Shadow; Swords and Hearts; The Squaw's Love; Trailing the Counterfeiter; The Adventures of Billy; The Long Road; The Battle; A Woman Scorned; The Miser's Heart; The Failure; A Terrible Discovery; The Baby and the Stork; The Old Bookkeeper; For His Son; Billy's Stratagem; A String of Pearls; The Root of Evil

1912: Under Burning Skies; Iola's Promise; The Goddess of Sagebrush Gulch; The Girl and Her Trust; The Would-Be Shriner; Help! Help!; The Old Actor; The Lesser Evil; A Lodging for the Night; When Kings Were the Law; A Beast at Bay; Home Folks; Algy, the Watchman; A Temporary Truce; Lena and the Geese; The Spirit Awakened; The School Teacher and the Waif; A Dash Through the Clouds; Black Sheep; The Tourists; A Pueblo Legend; The Massacre; One-Round O'Brien; The Chief's Blanket; The Narrow Road; A Child's Remorse; The Inner Circle; Two Daughters of Eve; In the Aisles of the Wild; Blind Love; The Musketeers of Pig Alley; Heredity; Gold and Glitter; My Baby; The Informer; Brutality; The New York Hat; My Hero; The Burglar's Dilemma; A Cry for Help; The Telephone Girl and the Lady; An Adventure in the Autumn Woods; The Tender-Hearted Boy; Oil and Water; Drink's Lure

1913: Broken Ways; Her Wedding Bell; The Sheriff's Baby; A Misunderstood Boy; The Left-Handed Man; A Rainy Day; The House of Darkness; Just Gold; A Timely Interception; Death's Marathon; The Yaqui Cur; Red Hicks Defies the World; Almost a Wild Man; The Mothering Heart; Her Mother's Oath; The Battle at Elderbush Gulch; Brute Force; Two Men of the Desert; The Reformers, or The Lost Art of Minding One's Business; Judith of Bethulia; A Woman in the Ultimate; A Modest Hero; An Unjust Suspicion; The

Chieftain's Sons; The Madonna of the Storm (d only); The Birthday Ring (d only); His Inspiration; By Man's Law

PARCINNICCI, [ ] Employee in developing room.

PARMALEE, PHILIP: Aviator

1912: A Dash Through the Clouds

PAYNE, GEORGE F.: Author

1912: The Press Gang

PEACOCKE, CAPTAIN LESLIE: Author

1911: The Wonderful Eye

PEARCE, PEGGY: Actress (b. 1896)

1913: The Mothering Heart

PERLEY, CHARLES G.: Actor (1886-1933)

1908: Edgar Allen Poe

1909: The Mexican Sweethearts; The Last Deal

1913: The Wife

PERRY, MRS. MONTAYNE: Author

1911: A Victim of Circumstances

PICKFORD, JACK: Actor (1896-1933) (b. Jack Smith)

1909: The Message; Pranks; Wanted, A Child; In A Hempen Bag; To Save Her Soul; The Call; All On Account of the Milk

1910: The Newlyweds; The Smoker; The Kid; The Tenderfoot's Triumph; An Affair of Hearts; Ramona; Muggsy Becomes a Hero; The Modern Prodigal; Rose O'Salem-Town; The Oath and the Man; Examination Day at School; The Iconoclast; The Broken Doll; Two Little Waifs; Waiter No. 5; A Child's Stratagem; A Plain Song; His Trust Fulfilled; White Roses; The Poor Sick Men; Fate's Turning

1911: The Would-Be Shriner; A Temporary Truce; The School Teacher and the Waif; An Indian Summer; A Dash Through the Clouds; What the Doctor Ordered; Man's Lust for Gold; Black Sheep; A Pueblo Legend; The Massacre; The Speed Demon; The Chief's Blanket; A Child's Remorse; The Inner Circle; Mr. Grouch at the Seashore; A Feud in the Kentucky Hills; The Painted Lady; The Musketeers of Pig Alley; A Ten-Karat Hero; Heredity; My

Baby; The Informer; Brutality; The Unwelcome Guest; The New
York Hat; My Hero; Fate; A Misappropriated Turkey; Love in an
Apartment Hotel

1913: For the Son of the House

PICKFORD, LOTTIE: Actress (1895-1936) (b.

Lottie Smith)

1909: The Cardinal's Conspiracy; Tender Hearts; A Strange
Meeting; The Slave; The Indian Runner's Romance; The Better Way;
Getting Even; His Lost Love; Through the Breakers; The Woman
From Mellon's

1910: A Gold Necklace; The Broken Doll; Simple Charity; A Plain
Song; His Sister-In-Law; The Golden Supper; Happy Jack, A Hero;
His Trust; White Roses; The Italian Barber; The Midnight Marau-
der; The Two Paths; Three Sisters; Help Wanted

PICKFORD, MARY: Actress, Author (1893-1979) (b.

Gladys Smith)

1909: Her First Biscuits; The Violin Maker of Cremona; Two
Memories; The Lonely Villa; The Peachbasket Hat; The Son's Re-
turn; His Duty; The Necklace; The Way of Man; The Faded Lilies;
The Country Doctor; The Renunciation; The Cardinal's Conspiracy;
The Seventh Day; Tender Hearts; Sweet and Twenty; The Slave;
They Would Elope; The Indian Runner's Romance; His Wife's Visi-
tor; The Heart of an Outlaw; "Oh, Uncle"; The Sealed Room; "1776"
or, The Hessian Renegades; The Little Darling; In Old Kentucky;
Getting Even (also au); The Broken Locket; The Awakening (also
au); The Little Teacher; His Lost Love; Lines of White on a Sullen
Sea; The Gibson Goddess; In the Watches of the Night; What's
Your Hurry?; The Restoration; The Light That Came; A Midnight
Adventure; The Mountaineer's Honor; The Trick That Failed; The
Test; To Save Her Soul; The Day After (au only); All On Account
of the Milk; The Woman From Mellon's; The Englishman and the
Girl

1910: The Newlyweds; The Thread of Destiny; The Smoker; The
Twisted Trail; As It Is In Life; A Rich Revenge; A Romance of
the Western Hills; Never Again; May and December (also au);
The Unchanging Sea; Love Among the Roses; The Two Brothers;
Ramona; In the Season of Buds; A Victim of Jealousy; A Child's
Impulse; Muggsy's First Sweetheart; The Call to Arms; What the
Daisy Said; An Arcadian Maid; The Sorrows of the Unfaithful; When
We Were In Our 'Teens; Wilful Peggy; Muggsy Becomes A Hero;
A Gold Necklace; A Lucky Toothache; Waiter No. 5; Simple Chari-
ty; The Song of the Wildwood Flute; A Plain Song; When A Man
Loves; White Roses; The Italian Barber; Three Sisters; A Decree
of Destiny

1911: Madame Rex (au only)

1912: Iola's Promise; Fate's Interception; The Female of the

Species; Just Like a Woman; The Old Actor; Won by a Fish; A Lodging for the Night; A Beast at Bay; Home Folks; Lena and the Geese (also au); The School Teacher and the Waif; An Indian Summer; A Pueblo Legend; With the Enemy's Help; The Narrow Road; The Inner Circle; Friends; So Near, Yet So Far; A Feud in the Kentucky Hills; The One She Loved; My Baby; The Informer; The Unwelcome Guest; The New York Hat

PIERCE, GRACE A.: Author

1913: Judith of Bethulia

PIERSON, MRS. E. C.: Author

1911: A Sister's Love

PIXLEY, GUS: Actor (1874-1923)

1909: The Last Deal

1911: Abe Gets Even with Father; For His Son; The Transformation of Mike

1912: He Must Have a Wife; Stern Papa; So Near, Yet So Far; Hoist on His Own Petard; After the Honeymoon; Jinx's Birthday Party; "She Is a Pippin"; Brutality; A Day's Outing; Bill Bogg's Windfall; Oh, What A Boob!; The Press Gang; My Hero; The Bite of a Snake; The Best Man Wins; Kissing Kate; There Were Hoboes Three; An Up-to-Date Lochinvar; Look Not Upon the Wine; Among Club Fellows; The High Cost of Reduction; A Delivery Package; Edwin's Badge of Honor

1913: The Spring of Life; Tightwad's Predicament; The Power of the Camera; The Old Gray Mare; All Hail to the King; Edwin Masquerades; Their One Good Suit; A Lesson to Mashers; How They Struck Oil; An "Uncle Tom's Cabin" Troupe; A Horse on Bill; He Had a Guess Coming; A Ragtime Romance; The Cure; The Daylight Burglar; Frappe Love; The Coveted Prize; Cinderella and the Boob; The Hicksville Epicure; The Trimmers Trimmed; Highbrow Love; Slippery Slim Repents; Jenks Becomes a Desperate Character; Almost a Wild Man; The Rise and Fall of McDoo; The Mothering Heart; Mister Jefferson Green; A Compromising Complication; An Old Maid's Deception; The Noisy Suitors; The Sweat-Box; A Chinese Puzzle; While the Count Goes Bathing; Those Little Flowers; Come Seben, Leben; The Suffragette Minstrels; Father's Chicken Dinner; Baby Indisposed; Dan Greegan's Ghost; The Reformers, or The Lost Art of Minding One's Business; His Hoodoo; The End of the World; A Saturday Holiday; Dyed but not Dead; Scenting a Terrible Crime; McGann and His Octette; Aunts, Too Many; A Fallen Hero; A Barber Cure; Boarders and Bombs

POLITO, SOL: Still Photographer/Laboratory and Camera Assistant/ Projectionist (1892-1960)

PORTER, EDWIN S.: Cameraman (1864-1941)

1908: Rescued From an Eagle's Nest; Cupid's Pranks

POSNER, GEORGE A.: Author

1912: A Queer Elopement

1913: The Law and His Son

POWELL, BADEN: Actor

1911: The Crooked Road; A Smile of a Child; The Thief and the Girl

POWELL, FRANK: Director, Actor

1909: (as actor) The Son's Return; His Duty; The Necklace; The Way of Man; The Faded Lilies; The Message; The Friend of the Family; Was Justice Served?; The Country Doctor; The Cardinal's Conspiracy; The Seventh Day; Tender Hearts; A Strange Meeting; The Slave; Jones' Burglar; The Mended Lute; The Indian Runner's Romance; With Her Card; His Wife's Visitor; The Heart of an Outlaw; The Mills of the Gods; "1776" or, The Hessian Renegades; In Old Kentucky; The Children's Friend; Leather Stocking; The Broken Locket; Fools of Fate; Lines of White on a Sullen Sea; In the Watches of the Night; Nursing a Viper; Two Women and a Man; The Light That Came; Sweet Revenge; The Death Disc; A Corner in Wheat; The Rocky Road; All On Account of the Milk (d only); The Last Deal; The Course of True Love (d only)

1910: (as director) The Love of Lady Irma; The Newlyweds (a only); In Old California (a only); The Man (a only); The Smoker; His Last Dollar; The Kid; The Tenderfoot's Triumph; Up A Tree; Never Again; May and December; An Affair of Hearts; A Knot in the Plot; The Impalement (a only); An Old Story with a New Ending; When We Were In Our 'Teens; The Affair of an Egg; Muggsy Becomes A Hero; A Summer Tragedy; A Gold Necklace; How Hubby Got A Raise; A Lucky Toothache; The Masher; The Proposal; The Passing of a Grouch; Love in Quarantine; A Troublesome Baby; Not So Bad As It Seemed; His New Lid; Effecting a Cure; Turning the Tables; Happy Jack, A Hero; White Roses; The Recreation of an Heiress; The Midnight Marauder; His Wife's Sweethearts; After the Ball; The Poor Sick Men; Help Wanted; Priscilla's Engagement Kiss

1911: (as director) Cupid's Joke; Cured; Paradise Lost; The Country Lovers

PREDMORE, LESTER: Actor

1910: The Modern Prodigal

PRESCOTT, VIVIAN: Actress

1910: The Face at the Window; A Child's Impulse; The Call to Arms; A Midnight Cupid; A Flash of Light; An Arcadian Maid; A Salutary Lesson; Winning Back His Love; His Trust; The Italian Barber; The Two Paths; Three Sisters; What Shall We Do With Our Old

1911: Fisher Folks; Comrades; Teaching Dad to Like Her; The Spanish Gypsy; The Broken Cross; Paradise Lost; Madame Rex; How She Triumphed; The New Dress; The Manicure Lady; The Primal Call; The Jealous Husband; The Delayed Proposal; Her Sacrifice; Mr. Peck Goes Calling; That Dare Devil; Italian Blood; The Making of a Man; Her Awakening; Dooley's Scheme; A Woman Scorned; Resourceful Lovers; Who Got the Reward?; The Old Bookkeeper; With a Kodak; A Message from the Moon

1912: The Old Actor; When the Fire-Bells Rang; Kissing Kate

PRIOR, HERBERT: Actor (1867-1954) (aka Herbert Pryor)

1908: The Joneses Have Amateur Theatricals; The Salvation Army Lass

1909: Trying to Get Arrested; Politician's Love Story; At the Altar; The Lure of the Gown; Lady Helen's Escapade; A Fool's Revenge; A Burglar's Mistake; The Voice of the Violin; Jones and his New Neighbors; A Drunkard's Reformation; Schneider's Anti-Noise Crusade; Twin Brothers; Confidence; Lucky Jim; A Sound Sleeper; A Troublesome Satchel; 'Tis An Ill Wind That Blows No Good; The Suicide Club; Resurrection; One Busy Hour; A Baby's Shoe; The Cricket on the Hearth; The Jilt; Eradicating Aunty; What Drink Did; Her First Biscuits; The Violin Maker of Cremona; Two Memories; The Lonely Villa; The Peachbasket Hat; The Son's Return; A New Trick; The Necklace; The Way of Man; The Faded Lilies; Was Justice Served?

PRUCHA, BEATRICE: Author

1913: Father's Chicken Dinner

PURDY, JULIA M.: Author

1913: The Stolen Treaty

QUIMBY, HARRIET: Author

1911: Fisher Folks; The Broken Cross; His Mother's Scarf; In the Days of '49; A Smile of a Child; The Blind Princess and the Poet; Sunshine Through the Dark

QUIRK, WILLIAM A.: Actor (1881-1926) (aka Billy Quirk)

1909: The Necklace; The Faded Lilies; Was Justice Served?; The

Mexican Sweethearts; The Renunciation; The Cardinal's Conspiracy; A Convict's Sacrifice; A Strange Meeting; Sweet and Twenty; They Would Elope; With Her Card; His Wife's Visitor; The Heart of an Outlaw; Pranks; "Oh, Uncle"; "1776" or, The Hessian Renegades; The Little Darling; Leather Stocking; Getting Even; The Broken Locket; A Fair Exchange; Pippa Passes or, The Song of Conscience; The Little Teacher; A Change of Heart; Lines of White on a Sullen Sea; The Gibson Goddess; What's Your Hurry?; Nursing a Viper; Two Women and a Man; The Light That Came; A Midnight Adventure; The Mountaineer's Honor; The Trick That Failed; Through the Breakers; A Corner in Wheat; The Redman's View; The Test; In Little Italy; Choosing a Husband; The Dancing Girl of Butte; The Call; The Last Deal; The Woman from Mellon's; One Night, and Then---

1910: The Newlyweds; The Smoker; His Last Dollar; Faithful; A Rich Revenge; Up a Tree; Never Again; May and December; An Affair of Hearts; The Two Brothers; A Knot in the Plot; The Face at the Window; Muggsy's First Sweetheart; A Midnight Cupid; Serious Sixteen; When We Were In Our 'Teens; Wilful Peggy; Muggsy Becomes A Hero

RACKHAM, WILLIAM J.: Author

1913: Mrs. Casey's Gorilla

RADNOR, LEONIA: Author

1912: An Up-to-Date Lochinvar

RANDOLPH, F. W.: Author

1913: A Gamble with Death

RAY, ALBERT: Prop boy circa 1908. This may be Al Ray (b. 1893), who appeared as a child actor for Biograph in 1900-01.

REARDON, M. S.: Author

1912: Three Friends

RED WING: Actress

1909: The Mended Lute

REID, PEGGIE: Actress

1912: "She Is a Pippin"

REYNOLDS, ISOBEL M.: Author

1911: The Jealous Husband; A Mix-Up in Raincoats; Who Got the Reward?; Lily's Lovers

1912: An Absent-Minded Burglar

1913: Edwin Masquerades; The Birthday Ring

RIDGELY, RICHARD: Author

1913: How They Struck Oil

RITCHIE, FRANKLIN B.: Actor (d. 1918)

1913: Red and Pete, Partners

ROBERTS, AUSTIN F.: Author

1912: Oh, What a Boob!

ROBINSON, GERTRUDE: Actress (1891-1962)

1908: The Feud and the Turkey; The Test of Friendship; One Touch of Nature; An Awful Moment; The Girls and Daddy

1909: The Cord of Life; The Fascinating Mrs. Francis; Those Awful Hats; Jones and the Lady Book Agent; The Drive for a Life; A Burglar's Mistake; Jones and His New Neighbors; Two Memories; The Way of Man; They Would Elope; The Heart of an Outlaw; The Sealed Room; "1776" or, The Hessian Renegades; The Little Darling; In Old Kentucky; Getting Even; The Broken Locket; A Fair Exchange; Pippa Passes, or The Song of Conscience; The Little Teacher; His Lost Love; Lines of White on a Sullen Sea; The Gibson Goddess; What's Your Hurry?; The Restoration; Nursing a Viper; Two Women and a Man; The Light That Came; The Open Gate; The Mountaineer's Honor; The Trick That Failed; The Death Disc; Through the Breakers; A Corner in Wheat; In Little Italy; To Save Her Soul; The Day After; The Woman From Mellon's; The Duke's Plan; One Night, and Then---; The Englishman and the Girl

1910: The Love of Lady Irma; The Newlyweds; The Purgation; A Midnight Cupid; A Child's Faith; What the Daisy Said; A Flash of Light; As the Bells Rang Out!; A Salutary Lesson; The Usurer; The Sorrows of the Unfaithful; An Old Story with a New Ending; In Life's Cycle; The Affair of an Egg; Wilful Peggy; A Summer Idyl; Rose O'Salem-Town; A Mohawk's Way; A Summer Tragedy; The Oath and the Man; Examination Day at School; That Chink at Golden Gulch; The Broken Doll; The Masher

1913: Classmates; Strongheart; Men and Women

ROBINSON, W. C.: Actor (1884-1942) (aka Walter Charles Robinson; "Spike" Robinson)

1910: A Flash of Light; As The Bells Rang Out!; A Salutary Lesson; The Usurer; The Sorrows of the Unfaithful; An Old Story with a New Ending; Wilful Peggy; A Summer Idyl; Rose O'Salem-Town;

Little Angels of Luck; A Mohawk's Way; The Iconoclast; That
Chink at Golden Gulch; The Message of the Violin; The Proposal;
Waiter No. 5; The Fugitive; His New Lid; A Child's Stratagem;
A Plain Song; The Golden Supper; Effecting A Cure; The Lesson;
Happy Jack, A Hero; Winning Back His Love; His Trust; A Wreath
of Orange Blossoms; White Roses; The Recreation of an Heiress;
The Italian Barber; The Two Paths; Conscience; His Wife's Sweet-
hearts; Three Sisters; The Poor Sick Men; Help Wanted; What
Shall We Do With Our Old; The Lily of the Tenements; Heart Beats
of Long Ago

1911: Fisher Folks; The Lonedale Operator; Teaching Dad to Like
Her; Cured; The Spanish Gypsy; Priscilla and the Umbrella; Ma-
dame Rex; A Knight of the Road; The New Dress; Enoch Arden,
Part Two; The Manicure Lady; The Crooked Road; The Primal
Call; The Indian Brothers; Fighting Blood; The Last Drop of Water;
Bobby, the Coward; The Ruling Passion; Swords and Hearts; The
Diving Girl; The Making of a Man; Trailing the Counterfeiter; Her
Awakening; The Long Road; Why He Gave Up; The Battle; The
Miser's Heart; The Failure; A Terrible Discovery; The Baby and
the Stork; The Old Bookkeeper; For His Son; The Transformation
of Mike; Billy's Stratagem

1912: Under Burning Skies; A Spanish Dilemma; The Goddess of
Sagebrush Gulch; The Girl and Her Trust; The Would-Be Shriner;
Help! Help!; One is Business, The Other Crime; The Old Actor;
The Lesser Evil; Those Hicksville Boys; Won by a Fish; A Lodg-
ing for the Night; His Lesson; A Beast at Bay; An Outcast Among
Outcasts; Home Folks; A Temporary Truce; Lena and the Geese;
Tomboy Bessie; Trying to Fool Uncle; Man's Genesis; Heaven
Avenges; Black Sheep; A Pueblo Legend; The Massacre; The Chief's
Blanket; The Narrow Road; The Inner Circle; A Change of Spirit;
Two Daughters of Eve; Friends; So Near, Yet So Far; A Feud in
the Kentucky Hills; Blind Love; Love's Messenger; The Musketeers
of Pig Alley; Heredity; Gold and Glitter; My Baby; The Informer;
Brutality; The Unwelcome Guest; The New York Hat; My Hero;
The Burglar's Dilemma; The God Within; Three Friends; The Ten-
der-Hearted Boy; Fate; The Wrong Bottle; Love in an Apartment
Hotel

1913: The Perfidy of Mary; A Misunderstood Boy; The Lady and
the Mouse; The House of Darkness; His Mother's Son; Death's
Marathon; Jenks Becomes a Desperate Character; Almost a Wild
Man; The Mothering Heart; Her Mother's Oath; Faust and the Lily;
The Battle at Elderbush Gulch; Brute Force; The Reformers, or
The Lost Art of Minding One's Business; Judith of Bethulia; The
Adopted Brother; A Saturday Holiday; The Chieftain's Sons; So
Runs the Way; The Madonna of the Storm; Strongheart

ROOSEVELT, THEODORE: 26th President of the United States (1858-
1919)

1908: Classmates

RYAN, MRS. JAMES H.: Author

1910: Two Little Waifs; The Song of the Wildwood Flute

SALTER, HARRY: See Solter, Harry

SARDOU, VICTORIEN: Playwright (1831-1908)

1908: The Heart of O Yama

SARNO, HECTOR V.: Actor (1880-1953)

1912: The Chief's Blanket; Blind Love; Heredity; Pirate Gold; My Hero

1913: The Stolen Bride; The Mistake; A Saturday Holiday; The Chieftain's Sons; The Law and His Son; The Detective's Stratagem

SAUNDERS, JACKIE: Actress (1892-1954)

1911: Through Darkened Vales; The Old Bookkeeper

SCARDON, PAUL: Actor (1878-1954)

1909: To Save Her Soul; The Day After

SCHAEFER, CHARLES: Assistant Property Man

SCHLIEBITZ, F. A.: Author

1913: Dyed but not Dead

SCHRODE, JOSEPH: Actor

1913: Aunts, Too Many

SCHULTZ, HENRY B.: Laboratory technician

SCOTT, EDWARD: Film cutter

SEABURY, INEZ: Actress (1909-1973) (aka Ynez Seabury)

1911: For His Son; The Sunbeam

SENNETT, MACK: Actor, Director, Author (1880-1960) (b. Michael [Mikall] Sinnott)

1908: (as actor) Old Isaacs, the Pawnbroker; The King's Messenger; The Sculptor's Nightmare; Thompson's Night Out; Over the Hills to the Poorhouse; The Invisible Fluid; The Man in the Box; Deceived Slumming Party; The Black Viper; The Kentuckian; The Stage Rustler; The Fatal Hour; The Girl and the Outlaw; The Red Girl; Betrayed by a Handprint; Monday Morning in a Coney Island

Police Court; Behind the Scenes; The Heart of O Yama; Where the
Breakers Roar; A Smoked Husband; The Vaquero's Vow; Father
Gets in the Game; The Barbarian, Ingomar; The Devil; Romance
of a Jewess; The Call of the Wild; After Many Years; Mr. Jones
at the Ball; Concealing a Burglar; Taming of the Shrew; The
Pirate's Gold; The Guerrilla; The Curtain Pole; The Song of the
Shirt; The Clubman and the Tramp; Money Mad; The Feud and the
Turkey; The Test of Friendship; The Reckoning; The Valet's Wife;
One Touch of Nature; An Awful Moment; The Helping Hand; The
Maniac Cook; The Christmas Burglars; A Wreath in Time; The
Honor of Thieves; The Criminal Hypnotist; The Sacrifice; The Wel-
come Burglar; A Rural Elopement; Mr. Jones Has A Card Party;
The Joneses Have Amateur Theatricals; The Roue's Heart; The
Salvation Army Lass; Love Finds A Way; Tragic Love; The Girls
and Daddy

1909:   The Cord of Life; The Fascinating Mrs. Francis; Those
Awful Hats; Jones and the Lady Book Agent; Trying to Get Arrest-
ed; The Brahma Diamond; Politician's Love Story; His Wife's
Mother; The Golden Louis; At the Altar; The Prussian Spy; The
Medicine Bottle; The Deception; The Lure of the Gown; Lady Helen's
Escapade; A Fool's Revenge; The Wooden Leg; A Burglar's Mis-
take; The Voice of the Violin; "And A Little Child Shall Lead
Them"; The French Duel; Jones and His New Neighbors; A Drunk-
ard's Reformation; The Winning Coat; A Rude Hostess; The Road
to the Heart; Confidence; The Note in the Shoe; Lucky Jim; A
Sound Sleeper; A Troublesome Satchel; 'Tis An Ill Wind That
Blows No Good; The Suicide Club; Resurrection; One Busy Hour;
A Baby's Shoe; Eloping with Aunty; The Cricket on the Hearth;
The Jilt; What Drink Did; Her First Biscuits; The Violin Maker
of Cremona; Two Memories; The Lonely Villa (also au); The
Peachbasket Hat; The Son's Return; A New Trick; The Necklace;
The Way of Man; The Faded Lilies; The Message; Was Justice
Served?; The Mexican Sweethearts; Jealousy and the Man; The
Cardinal's Conspiracy; The Seventh Day; A Convict's Sacrifice; A
Strange Meeting; The Slave; They Would Elope; Jones' Burglar;
The Mended Lute; The Indian Runner's Romance; With Her Card;
The Better Way; His Wife's Visitor; The Heart of an Outlaw; The
Mills of the Gods; The Sealed Room; "1776" or, The Hessian Rene-
gades; The Little Darling; In Old Kentucky; Leather Stocking; Get-
ting Even; The Broken Locket; A Fair Exchange; The Awakening;
Pippa Passes or, The Song of Conscience; A Change of Heart; His
Lost Love; Lines of White on a Sullen Sea; The Gibson Goddess;
In the Watches of the Night; The Expiation; What's Your Hurry?;
Nursing a Viper; Two Women and a Man; The Light That Came;
A Midnight Adventure; The Open Gate; The Mountaineer's Honor;
The Trick that Failed; Through the Breakers; A Corner in Wheat;
In a Hempen Bag; The Redman's View; A Trap for Santa Claus;
In Little Italy; To Save Her Soul; The Day After; Choosing a Hus-
band; The Dancing Girl of Butte; The Call; All On Account of the
Milk; The Last Deal; The Cloister's Touch; The Woman From
Mellon's; One Night, And Then---; The Englishman and the Girl

1910: The Love of Lady Irma; Taming a Husband; The Newlyweds; The Thread of Destiny; In Old California; The Converts; Faithful; The Twisted Trail; Gold Is Not All; As It Is In Life; A Rich Revenge; Up A Tree; Never Again; The Way of the World; An Affair of Hearts; The Gold-Seekers; The Two Brothers; Ramona; A Knot in the Plot; In the Season of Buds; In the Border States; A Victim of Jealousy; The Face at the Window; The Marked Time-Table; A Child's Impulse; The Purgation; The Call to Arms; A Midnight Cupid; A Child's Faith; Serious Sixteen; A Flash of Light; As the Bells Rang Out!; An Arcadian Maid; Her Father's Pride; When We Were In Our 'Teens; The Affair of an Egg; Wilful Peggy; A Summer Tragedy; Examination Day at School; A Gold Necklace; The Broken Doll; A Lucky Toothache; The Passing of a Grouch; Love in Quarantine; Not So Bad As It Seemed; Effecting A Cure; Happy Jack, A Hero; His Trust; The Italian Barber; His Wife's Sweethearts; Priscilla's Engagement Kiss

1911: (as director) Fisher Folks (a only); Comrades (also a and au); The Lonedale Operator (au only); Cured (a only); The Spanish Gypsy (a only); Priscilla and the Umbrella; Paradise Lost (also a); Priscilla's Capture; Misplaced Jealousy (also au and a); Her Pet; The Country Lovers; Taking His Medicine; Curiosity; The Manicure Lady (also a); A Dutch Gold Mine (also a); Dave's Love Affair; Their Fates "Sealed"; Bearded Youth; The Wonderful Eye; The Delayed Proposal; Stubbs' New Servants; Jinks Joins the Temperance Club; Mr. Peck Goes Calling (also a); The Ghost (also au and a); That Dare Devil (also a); The Beautiful Voice; An Interrupted Game; $500 Reward; The Diving Girl; The Villain Foiled; Mr. Bragg, A Fugitive; The Baron; The Lucky Horseshoe; The Village Hero (also a); A Convenient Burglar; When Wifey Holds the Purse-Strings; Trailing the Counterfeiter (also a); Josh's Suicide; Too Many Burglars (also a); Why He Gave Up; Their First Divorce Case (also a); Through His Wife's Picture; The Inventor's Secret; Dooley's Scheme; A Victim of Circumstances; Won Through a Medium; The Joke on the Joker; Her Mother Interferes; Resourceful Lovers; Caught with the Goods (also a); Abe Gets Even with Father; Did Mother Get Her Wish?; A Mix-Up in Rain Coats; Who Got the Reward?; Brave and Bold; Pants and Pansies; With a Kodak; Lily's Lovers; A String of Pearls (a only); A Near-Tragedy; The Fatal Chocolate (also a); "Got a Match?"; A Message from the Moon (also a)

1912: (as director) A Spanish Dilemma (also a); The Engagement Ring; A Voice from the Deep; Hot Stuff (also a); The Would-Be Shriner (also a); Help! Help!; The Brave Hunter (also a); Those Hicksville Boys (also a); Their First Kidnapping Case (also a); Won by a Fish; The Fickle Spaniard; The Leading Man; When the Fire-Bells Rang; The Furs (also a); A Close Call; Helen's Marriage (also a); Algy, the Watchman; Tomboy Bessie (also a); Neighbors; Katchem Kate; A Dash Through the Clouds; The New Baby; Trying to Fool Uncle; What the Doctor Ordered (also a); The Mystery of the Milk; The Tourists; One-Round O'Brien; The Speed Demon; His Own Fault; Willie Becomes an Artist; An Interrupted

Elopement; The Tragedy of a Dress Suit; He Must Have a Wife; Stern Papa

SHAKESPEARE, WILLIAM: Playwright (1564-1616)

1908: Taming of the Shrew

SHAY, DANIEL: Shipping Clerk (aka "Truck Horse" Shay)

SHELDON, EDWARD: Playwright

1908: The Salvation Army Lass

SHORT, FRANK: Employee. A member of the comedy unit that remained in Los Angeles with Fred Mace in 1912.

SHULTER, EDDIE: Set Painter, Set Dresser, Lighting Assistant (1908-1909)

SIEGMANN, GEORGE: Actor (1883-1928)

1909: Confidence; The Note in the Shoe; Resurrection; A Convict's Sacrifice; A Strange Meeting; The Slave; The Sealed Room; "1776" or, The Hessian Renegades; In Old Kentucky

1910: A Flash of Light; As the Bells Rang Out!

SIMONE, CHARLES: Author

1910: In Life's Cycle

SIMPSON, S. R.: Author

1911: Their Fates "Sealed"

SINDELEAR, PEARL: Actress (aka Pearl Sindelar)

1912: The Wrong Bottle

SKINNER, IRMA: Author

1913: An Evening with Wilder Spender

SMART, BILLY: Assistant to Henry McClelland

SMITH, JAMES EDWARD: Assistant to Shay, Film cutter

SNYDER, MATT B.: Actor (1839-1917)

1912: Oil and Water; Drink's Lure

SOLTER, HARRY: Actor (d. 1928) (aka Harry Salter, Hal Salter)
(married to Florence Lawrence)

1908: A Famous Escape; King of the Cannibal Islands; Hulda's
Lovers; The Sculptor's Nightmare; When Knights Were Bold;
Thompson's Night Out; 'Ostler Joe; Deceived Slumming Party; The
Kentuckian; The Stage Rustler; The Redman and the Child; The
Tavern-Keeper's Daughter; The Bandit's Waterloo; A Calamitous
Elopement; The Greaser's Gauntlet; The Man and the Woman; For
Love of Gold; The Fatal Hour; For A Wife's Honor; The Girl and
the Outlaw; The Red Girl; Betrayed by a Handprint; Monday Morn-
ing in a Coney Island Police Court; The Heart of O Yama; Where
the Breakers Roar; The Stolen Jewels; A Smoked Husband; The
Zulu's Heart; The Vaquero's Vow; Father Gets in the Game; The
Barbarian, Ingomar; The Planter's Wife; The Devil; Romance of
a Jewess; The Call of the Wild; After Many Years; Mr. Jones at
the Ball; Concealing a Burglar; Taming of the Shrew; A Woman's
Way; The Guerrilla; The Curtain Pole; The Song of the Shirt; The
Clubman and the Tramp; Money Mad; Mrs. Jones Entertains; The
Feud and the Turkey; The Test of Friendship; The Reckoning; The
Valet's Wife; One Touch of Nature; An Awful Moment; The Helping
Hand; The Maniac Cook; The Christmas Burglars; A Wreath in
Time; The Honor of Thieves; The Criminal Hypnotist; The Sacri-
fice; The Welcome Burglar; A Rural Elopement; Mr. Jones Has A
Card Party; The Roue's Heart; The Hindoo Dagger; The Salvation
Army Lass; Love Finds A Way; Tragic Love

1909: The Cord of Life; The Fascinating Mrs. Francis; Jones
and the Lady Book Agent; The Brahma Diamond; At the Altar; The
Prussian Spy; The Deception; The Lure of the Gown; A Fool's Revenge; A Burglar's Mistake; The French Duel; A Drunkard's Reformation; The Winning Coat; Lucky Jim; 'Tis An Ill Wind That
Blows No Good; One Busy Hour; A Baby's Shoe; The Cricket on
the Hearth; The Jilt; What Drink Did; The Violin Maker of Cremona; The Son's Return; Was Justice Served?; The Renunciation;
A Convict's Sacrifice; The Slave; They Would Elope

STACEY, MRS. J. W.: Author

1912: Papering the Den

STERLING, FORD: Actor (1883-1939)

1911: Taking His Medicine

1912: An Interrupted Elopement; The Tragedy of a Dress Suit;
He Must Have a Wife; Stern Papa

STEVEN, JAMES G.: Author

1913: A Tender-Hearted Crook

STEWART, ELDEAN: Actor (b. 1911)

1912: The One She Loved; My Baby

STEWART, LUCILLE LEE: Actress (b. 1894) (aka Mrs. Ralph Ince)

1910: Two Little Waifs; Love in Quarantine; His New Lid

STOCKTON, P. W.: Author

1913: The Coveted Prize

STOUGHTON, MABEL: Actress

1908: Balked at the Altar; Romance of a Jewess

STUART, WILLIAM G.: Employee

SUCKERT, LEON J.: Author

1912: The Wrong Bottle

SUMMERS, E. LYNN: Author

1913: Scenting a Terrible Crime

SUNSHINE, MARION: Actress (1897-1963)

1908: Mr. Jones at the Ball

1910: Sunshine Sue; His Trust Fulfilled; The Italian Barber; Three Sisters; The Poor Sick Men; A Decree of Destiny; Fate's Turning; Help Wanted

1911: Was He a Coward?; The Rose of Kentucky; Out from the Shadow; The Stuff Heroes are Made Of; Dan, the Dandy

SWEET, BLANCHE: Actress (b. 1896) (b. Sarah Blanche Sweet)

1909: A Corner in Wheat; In Little Italy; To Save Her Soul; The Day After; Choosing A Husband; The Rocky Road; All On Account of the Milk

1911: The Lonedale Operator; Was He a Coward?; Priscilla's April Fool Joke; Priscilla and the Umbrella; How She Triumphed; The Country Lovers; The New Dress; Enoch Arden, Part One; The White Rose of the Wilds; A Smile of a Child; The Indian Brothers; The Blind Princess and the Poet; The Last Drop of Water; A Country Cupid; Out from the Shadow; The Stuff Heroes are Made Of; The Eternal Mother; The Making of a Man; The Long Road; The Battle; Love in the Hills; Through Darkened Vales; The Voice of the Child; The Old Bookkeeper; For His Son; The Transformation of Mike; A String of Pearls

1912: Under Burning Skies; The Goddess of Sagebrush Gulch; The Punishment; One is Business, The Other Crime; The Lesser Evil; An Outcast Among Outcasts; A Temporary Truce; The Spirit Awakened; Man's Lust for Gold; The Tourists; The Massacre; With the Enemy's Help; The Chief's Blanket; A Change of Spirit; Blind Love; The Painted Lady; Pirate Gold; A Sailor's Heart; The God Within; Three Friends; Oil and Water; A Chance Deception; Love in an Apartment Hotel

1913: Broken Ways; Her Wedding Bell; The Hero of Little Italy; The Stolen Bride; If We Only Knew; Death's Marathon; The Mistake; The Coming of Angelo; Two Men of the Desert; Judith of Bethulia; Classmates; Strongheart; Men and Women

TANNURA, PHILIP: Cameraman/Laboratory technician (b. 1897)

TANSEY, JOHN: Actor (aka John Tanzy)

1908: The Redman and the Child; The Fatal Hour

1909: The Seventh Day

TAYLOR, BELLE: Author

1910: The Broken Doll; A Child's Stratagem; A Wreath of Orange Blossoms; Heart Beats of Long Ago

1911: His Daughter; The Old Bookkeeper

1912: Iola's Promise; Love's Messenger

1913: A Welcome Intruder

TAYLOR, STANNER E. V.: Author, Director (married to Marion Leonard) (d. December 1948)

1908: (as director) Over the Hills to the Poorhouse; (as author) The Ingrate

1910: (as author) His Last Burglary; The Man; The Tenderfoot's Triumph; A Rich Revenge; The Impalement; In the Season of Buds; A Child of the Ghetto; In the Border States; A Victim of Jealousy; The Face at the Window; A Child's Impulse; The Purgation; The Call to Arms; A Midnight Cupid; What the Daisy Said; Serious Sixteen; A Flash of Light; As the Bells Rang Out!; An Arcadian Maid; Her Father's Pride; The Sorrows of the Unfaithful; When We Were In Our 'Teens; A Mohawk's Way; The Oath and the Man; A Plain Song

1911: A Romany Tragedy; The Squaw's Love; Through Darkened Vales

1912: In the North Woods; In the Aisles of the Wild; The Line at Hogan's; A Day's Outing

1913: The Tenderfoot's Money; The Yaqui Cur; Dan Greegan's Ghost; In the Elemental World

TENNYSON, ALFRED LORD: Poet (1809-1892)

1908: After Many Years

1910: The Golden Supper

TERWILLIGER, GEORGE W.: Author (b. 1882)

1910: A Lucky Toothache; When A Man Loves

1911: The Beautiful Voice

1912: Jinx's Birthday Party; The Best Man Wins

THOMPSON, H. S.: Author

1913: A Circumstantial Hero

TIGOR, GROVER G.: Stuntman, Assistant Director?

TOLSTOY, LEV: Writer (1828-1910)

1909: Resurrection

TONCRAY, KATE: Actress

1909: The Cloister's Touch

1910: A Flash of Light; A Salutary Lesson; Rose O'Salem-Town; Little Angels of Luck; The Oath and the Man; The Golden Supper; His Trust; A Wreath of Orange Blossoms; Conscience; Three Sisters; A Decree of Destiny; Fate's Turning; Heart Beats of Long Ago

1911: Fisher Folks; Comrades; Was He a Coward?; Teaching Dad to Like Her; The Chief's Daughter; Paradise Lost; A Knight of the Road; The Two Sides; The New Dress; The Manicure Lady; The Crooked Road; The Primal Call; The Indian Brothers; Fighting Blood; The Last Drop of Water; Bobby, the Coward; The Ruling Passion; The Rose of Kentucky; The Making of a Man; Her Awakening; The Long Road; The Battle; Love in the Hills; Through Darkened Vales; The Miser's Heart; The Failure; Caught With the Goods; The Old Bookkeeper; For His Son; Brave and Bold; A String of Pearls

1912: Under Burning Skies; Iola's Promise; Hot Stuff; One is Business, The Other Crime; Those Hicksville Boys; Won by a Fish; The Fickle Spaniard; His Lesson; When Kings Were the Law; Home Folks; The Leading Man; When the Fire-Bells Rang; An Outcast Among Outcasts; An Indian Summer; Tomboy Bessie;

Neighbors; Trying to Fool Uncle; What the Doctor Ordered; Heaven Avenges; The Sands of Dee; The Tourists; The Massacre; The Speed Demon; His Own Fault; Willie Becomes an Artist; A Child's Remorse; The Inner Circle; A Change of Spirit; Blind Love; Love's Messenger; A Limited Divorce; Bill Bogg's Windfall; The Press Gang; The Bite of a Snake; The Best Man Wins; There Were Hoboes Three; An Up-to-Date Lochinvar; Look Not Upon the Wine; Among Club Fellows; The High Cost of Reduction; What is the Use of Repining?; Love in an Apartment Hotel

1913: Tightwad's Predicament; The Power of the Camera; A Welcome Intruder; The Old Gray Mare; A Lesson to Mashers; The Hero of Little Italy; He Had a Guess Coming; The Cure; Blame the Wife; The Lady and the Mouse; The Wanderer; Frappe Love; Cinderella and the Boob; The Hicksville Epicure; The Trimmers Trimmed; Highbrow Love; Slippery Slim Repents; Red Hicks Defies the World; Jenks Becomes a Desperate Character; Almost a Wild Man; An Old Maid's Deception; Mr. Spriggs Buys a Dog; The Widow's Kids; Cupid and the Cook; Those Little Flowers; Brute Force; The Suffragette Minstrels; Under the Shadow of the Law; Baby Indisposed; Objections Overruled; The Reformers, or The Lost Art of Minding One's Business; Judith of Bethulia; A Saturday Holiday; Dyed but not Dead; Scenting a Terrible Crime; So Runs the Way; The Winning Punch; Mrs. Casey's Gorilla

TOOHEY, JOHN P.: Author

1910: A Summer Tragedy; The Passing of a Grouch

TRUNELLE, MABEL: Actress (married to Herbert Prior)

1908: A Woman's Way

1909: Nursing a Viper; Two Woman and a Man; The Light That Came

TUCKER, VIRGINIA K.: Author 1910: A Decree of Destiny

TURNBULL, MARGARET: Playwright (d. 1942) 1913: Classmates

TWAIN, MARK: Writer (1835-1910) (pseud. for Samuel Langhorne Clemens)

1909: The Death Disc

URIE, JOHN: Cameraman

VAN BUREN, MABEL: Actress (1878-1947)

1910: Serious Sixteen; The House with Closed Shutters; The Usurer; An Old Story with a New Ending; Wilful Peggy; A Summer Tragedy

VAN LOAN, CHARLES: Writer

1912:   One-Round O'Brien

VERDI, GIUSEPPE: Composer (1813-1901)

1909:   A Fool's Revenge

VOLLMER, LULU S.: Author

1912:   When Love Forgives

WAINWRIGHT, BYRON C.: Author

1912:   A Motorcycle Elopement

WAKE, MR.: Made Mutoscopes in the evenings with G. W. Bitzer

WALDRON, JOHN A.: Cashier/Cost accountant (1910-1913); Studio Business Manager (1913-1916) (aka J. A. Waldern)

WALSH, JOHN A.: Author

1912:   He Must Have a Wife

WALSH, RAOUL: Actor (1889?-1980)

1912:   The Detective's Stratagem

WALTHALL, HENRY B.: Actor (1878-1936)

1909:   A Convict's Sacrifice; A Strange Meeting; The Slave; They Would Elope; The Mended Lute; With Her Card; The Better Way; The Heart of an Outlaw; The Mills of the Gods; Pranks; The Sealed Room; "1776" or, The Hessian Renegades; The Little Darling; In Old Kentucky; Getting Even; The Broken Locket; A Fair Exchange; A Corner in Wheat; In a Hempen Bag; The Test; A Trap for Santa Claus; In Little Italy; The Day After; Choosing a Husband; The Call; The Honor of His Family; On the Reef; The Cloister's Touch; One Night, And Then---

1910:   His Last Burglary; The Newlyweds; The Thread of Destiny; In Old California; The Converts; The Kid; Gold Is Not All; The Tenderfoot's Triumph; Thou Shalt Not; The Way of the World; The Gold-Seekers; Love Among the Roses; The Two Brothers; Ramona; The Impalement; A Child of the Ghetto; In the Border States; The Face at the Window; The Call to Arms; The House with Closed Shutters; The Usurer; The Sorrows of the Unfaithful; In Life's Cycle; Wilful Peggy; A Summer Idyl; Rose O'Salem-Town; The Oath and the Man; The Iconoclast; The Banker's Daughters

1912:   A Change of Spirit; Two Daughters of Eve; Friends; A Feud in the Kentucky Hills; In the Aisles of the Wild; The One She

Loved; The Painted Lady; My Baby; The Informer; Brutality; My Hero; The Burglar's Dilemma; The God Within; Three Friends; Oil and Water; Love in an Apartment Hotel

1913: Broken Ways; Her Wedding Bell; The Sheriff's Baby; The Perfidy of Mary; A Horse on Bill; The Little Tease; The Lady and the Mouse; If We Only Knew; The Wanderer; The Tenderfoot's Money; Death's Marathon; Red Hicks Defies the World; The Mothering Heart; Her Mother's Oath; The Switch-Tower; The Battle at Elderbush Gulch; The Mistake; A Gambler's Honor; During the Round-Up; The Mirror; Two Men of the Desert; Judith of Bethulia; A Woman in the Ultimate; The Influence of the Unknown; Diversion; Classmates; Strongheart

WALTHAM, J.: Actor

1909: The Gibson Goddess; What's Your Hurry?; Nursing a Viper; The Light That Came; Through the Breakers; In Little Italy; The Rocky Road

1910: A Child of the Ghetto

1911: The Diving Girl; The Making of a Man; Why He Gave Up; The Miser's Heart; The Failure

1912: Through Dumb Luck; Getting Rid of Trouble; So Near, Yet So Far; The Musketeers of Pig Alley; Jinx's Birthday Party; "She Is a Pippin"; Brutality; Three Friends; The Tender-Hearted Boy; Fate

1913: The Coveted Prize; His Hoodoo

WARD, AUGUST J. V.: Film cutter (?)

WATER, JOHN S.: Assistant director, Production assistant (b. 1893)

WEBBER, GEORGE F.: Cameraman

WEED, A. E.: Cameraman

1908: Classmates

WELLS, L. M.: Actor (1862-1923)

1912: So Near, Yet So Far

WEST, CHARLES H.: Actor (1885-1943) (aka Charles West)

1909: Two Women and a Man; The Redman's View; The Last Deal

1910: The Newlyweds; The Thread of Destiny; In Old California; The Converts; The Twisted Trail; Gold is Not All; As It Is In

Life; A Rich Revenge; A Romance of the Western Hills; Thou Shalt
Not; The Unchanging Sea; The Gold-Seekers; Love Among the
Roses; The Two Brothers; Ramona; The Impalement; In the Season
of Buds; A Child of the Ghetto; In the Border States; A Victim of
Jealousy; The Face at the Window; The Marked Time-Table; A
Child's Impulse; A Midnight Cupid; What the Daisy Said; A Flash
of Light; As the Bells Rang Out!; The House with Closed Shutters;
Her Father's Pride; A Salutary Lesson; In Life's Cycle; The Oath
and the Man; That Chink at Golden Gulch; A Lucky Toothache; The
Message of the Violin; Waiter No. 5; The Fugitive; Sunshine Sue;
The Golden Supper; When a Man Loves; The Lesson; His Trust;
The Recreation of an Heiress; Three Sisters; Fate's Turning

1911: The Lonedale Operator; Was He a Coward?; Teaching Dad
to Like Her; The Spanish Gypsy; The Broken Cross; Paradise
Lost; His Mother's Scarf; In the Days of '49; The Country Lovers;
The New Dress; Enoch Arden, Part Two; The Manicure Lady; The
Crooked Road; The Indian Brothers; Her Sacrifice; The Blind
Princess and the Poet; The Last Drop of Water; The Ghost; The
Rose of Kentucky; Out From the Shadow; Swords and Hearts; Dan,
the Dandy; Italian Blood; The Long Road; The Battle; Love in the
Hills; Through Darkened Vales; Resourceful Lovers; A Terrible
Discovery; The Baby and the Stork; The Old Bookkeeper; For His
Son; A Blot in the 'Scutcheon; A String of Pearls; The Fatal
Chocolate

1912: Under Burning Skies; A Siren of Impulse; Iola's Promise;
The Goddess of Sagebrush Gulch; The Girl and Her Trust; The
Engagement Ring; The Would-Be Shriner; Fate's Interception; The
Female of the Species; One Is Business, the Other Crime; The
Lesser Evil; A Lodging for the Night; His Lesson; A Beast at
Bay; A Close Call; Helen's Marriage; An Outcast Among Outcasts;
Home Folks; Lena and the Geese; Heaven Avenges; Black Sheep;
The Tourists; The Massacre; The Speed Demon; With the Enemy's
Help; The Chief's Blanket; In the North Woods; A Disappointed
Mamma; A Sailor's Heart; My Hero; The Burglar's Dilemma; The
God Within; Oil and Water; A Misappropriated Turkey; The Wrong
Bottle; When Love Forgives

1913: A Girl's Stratagem; A Welcome Intruder; Her Wedding Bell;
The Hero of Little Italy; The Stolen Bride; A Horse on Bill; A
Frightful Blunder; The Left-Handed Man; The Wanderer; Just Gold;
Slippery Slim Repents; Just Kids; Red Hicks Defies the World; The
Mothering Heart; Her Mother's Oath; The Switch-Tower; In Diplo-
matic Circles; A Gamble with Death; A Gambler's Honor; The
Mirror; The Vengeance of Galora; Father's Chicken Dinner; Under
the Shadow of the Law; I Was Meant for You; The Reformers, or
The Lost Art of Minding One's Business; For the Son of the House;
A Modest Hero; A Tender-Hearted Crook; Red and Pete, Partners;
The Stopped Clock; "Old Coupons"; The Detective's Stratagem; All
for Science; The Wife

WEST, DOROTHY: Actress

1908: One Touch of Nature; The Joneses Have Amateur Theatricals; The Roue's Heart; The Salvation Army Lass; Love Finds a Way; The Girls and Daddy

1909: Those Boys; The Cord of Life; Those Awful Hats; The Brahma Diamond; The Drive for a Life; Politician's Love Story; His Wife's Mother; The Golden Louis; At the Altar; The Medicine Bottle; The Deception; The Lure of the Gown; Lady Helen's Escapade; A Fool's Revenge; I Did It, Mamma; A Burglar's Mistake; The Voice of the Violin; The Cricket on the Hearth; His Lost Love; Lines of White on a Sullen Sea; The Gibson Goddess; In the Watches of the Night; What's Your Hurry?; Two Women and a Man; The Light That Came; A Midnight Adventure; The Open Gate; The Mountaineer's Honor; The Trick That Failed; The Death Disc; A Corner in Wheat; In a Hempen Bag; The Redman's View; In Little Italy; To Save Her Soul; The Day After; Choosing a Husband; The Rocky Road; The Honor of His Family; The Cloister's Touch; The Woman From Mellon's; The Duke's Plan; One Night, And Then---; The Englishman and the Girl

1910: The Love of Lady Irma; His Last Burglary; The Newlyweds; The Thread of Destiny; The Converts; Faithful; The Twisted Trail; A Romance of the Western Hills; Thou Shalt Not; The Way of the World; The Unchanging Sea; Love Among the Roses; The Two Brothers; Ramona; The Impalement; A Child of the Ghetto; In the Border States; A Victim of Jealousy; A Child's Impulse; The Call to Arms; A Midnight Cupid; A Child's Faith; A Flash of Light; As the Bells Rang Out!; The House with Closed Shutters; The Usurer; A Summer Idyl; Rose O'Salem-Town; The Oath and the Man; Examination Day at School; The Broken Doll; The Banker's Daughters; Waiter No. 5; The Fugitive; Sunshine Sue; A Plain Song; His Sister-In-Law; The Golden Supper (also au); Winning Back His Love; His Trust Fulfilled; A Wreath of Orange Blossoms; The Lily of the Tenements; Heart Beats of Long Ago

1911: The Spanish Gypsy; The Broken Cross; The Chief's Daughter; A Knight of the Road; His Mother's Scarf; In the Days of '49; The New Dress; Swords and Hearts; The Revenue Man and the Girl

WEST, MADELINE: Actress (aka Madeline Gebhardt; Mrs. George Gebhardt)

1908: The Adventures of Dollie

WEST, PAUL: Author

1912: Bill Bogg's Windfall; Edwin's Badge of Honor

1913: A Lesson to Mashers

WHEATON, CHARLES S.: Author

1913: Baby Indisposed

WHITAKER, CHARLES E.: Assistant Director, Production Assistant

WILLIAMS, KATHLYN: Actress (1888-1962)

1910: Gold Is Not All; A Romance of the Western Hills; Thou Shalt Not

WILLIS, L.: Actor

1912: Oil and Water

WING, WILLIAM E.: Author

1912: Tomboy Bessie; Trying to Fool Uncle; The Mystery of the Milk; Willie Becomes an Artist; Among Club Fellows

1913: All Hail to the King; He Had a Guess Coming; Frappe Love; Olaf - An Atom; Death's Marathon; Red Hicks Defies the World; Jenks Becomes a Desperate Character; A Compromising Complication; A Woman in the Ultimate; By Man's Law

WOODS, FRANK E.: Author, Head of Scenario Department in 1913 (1860-1939)

1908: His Day of Rest; A Smoked Husband; Mr. Jones at the Ball; Mrs. Jones Entertains; Mr. Jones Has a Card Party; The Joneses Have Amateur Theatricals

1909: His Wife's Mother; Jones and His New Neighbors; Jones and the Lady Book Agent; Her First Biscuits; The Peachbasket Hat; Mrs. Jones' Lover or, "I Want My Hat"; Jones' Burglar

1910: The Marked Time-Table; Muggsy's First Sweetheart; Muggsy Becomes a Hero; Simple Charity; Priscilla's Engagement Kiss

1911: Priscilla's April Fool Joke; Priscilla and the Umbrella; The Country Lovers; Dave's Love Affair; Stubbs' New Servants; Jinks Joins the Temperance Club; Mr. Peck Goes Calling

1912: Mr. Grouch at the Seashore; At the Basket Picnic

1913: The Left-Handed Man; In Diplomatic Circles; The Mirror; The Reformers, or The Lost Art of Minding One's Business; The Stopped Clock

WRAY, BEN: Employee

YOUNG DEER, JAMES: Actor

1909: The Mended Lute

YOST, HERBERT: Actor (1880-1945) (aka Barry O'Moore)

1908: The Criminal Hypnotist; Edgar Allen Poe; The Roue's Heart

1909: The Fascinating Mrs. Francis; The Brahma Diamond; Politician's Love Story; The Golden Louis; At the Altar; The Medicine Bottle; The Deception; The Road to the Heart; The Eavesdropper; Confidence; Lucky Jim; A Troublesome Satchel; 'Tis An Ill Wind That Blows No Good; The Suicide Club; The Cardinal's Conspiracy

APPENDICES

Appendix A: THE HEART OF AN OUTLAW

Appendix B: MUTOSCOPES

Appendix C: PERSONNEL

Appendix A: THE HEART OF AN OUTLAW

D. W. Griffith (d); G. W. Bitzer, Arthur Marvin (c); 14/16/20/28 July 1909 (f); Shadyside, New Jersey/Little Falls, New Jersey/Studio not noted (l); one reel; No release; No copyright

James Kirkwood (Husband/Outlaw); Marion Leonard (His wife); Gladys Egan (Their daughter, as a child); Mary Pickford (Their daughter, grown); Henry B. Walthall (Mexican lover); Arthur Johnson (J. Woodford, marshall/guardian); William A. Quirk, Mack Sennett, Frank Powell (Outlaw gang); Owen Moore, Anthony O'Sullivan (In posse); Anthony O'Sullivan, Mack Sennett, Gertrude Robinson, Linda Arvidson (Wedding guests); ? (Outlaw sentry); ? (Marshall's companion)

NOTE: This is the only known instance of a Griffith film left unreleased by Biograph due to censorship concerns. In its report on the film, the Board of Censorship recognized that THE HEART OF AN OUTLAW was

> a very well acted and a well staged play, and while the Board would prefer to save the film by judicious cutting, the plot is involved in such a way with a suggested seduction and the rather blood thirsty adventures of an outlaw that there seemed to be no way by which the film could be redeemed. An outlaw type of this kind is sure to arouse adverse criticism and when coupled with what is morally worse, this picture would undoubtedly work more or less harm to the Moving Picture interests. ("Report of the Board of Censorship on Film Shown August 6th, 1909, " Edison National Historic Site.)

Briefly told, the story involves a man who murders his wife and her lover, and confusedly believes he has also murdered his only daughter. However, the girl survives and is taken in by the local sheriff. The man becomes an outlaw, gathering about him a gang. Many years later, the same sheriff forms a posse to hunt down the outlaw, and in a shootout one of the gang members is killed. In vengeance, the outlaw has the sheriff's ward kidnapped and brought to the gang's shack. He instructs his companions to kill her after he is done with her (a rape is implied) and has her sent out of the shack. In the process of attacking the girl the outlaw comes to recognize her as his own daughter and relents, the horror of the situation dawning on him. He sends her safely away, and places her cloak over himself. Thus disguised, he leaves the cabin and is murdered by his own men, thereby atoning for his past.

THE HEART OF AN OUTLAW has recently been restored from the original negative in the Museum of Modern Art's vaults. Why this film was preserved by Biograph, unreleased and, apparently, unreleasable, is unclear. What is clear, however, is that the cuts suggested by the Board of Censorship would have dramatically altered the sense of the film, eliminating the motivation behind the husband's violent reaction to his wife's affair, and, at the finale, drastically reducing the horror of the scene by underplaying the potential for incest. The Board wanted Biograph to

> Cut out all that portion of the picture introducing the Mexican, save where he enters the automobile with the wife. Also all of the scene entitled "A Jealous Husband's Vengeance for a Fancied Wrong" where the husband shoots the wife, child and Mexican. In the scene entitled "Shoot when you see this cloak emerge from the shack," cut out the part where the girl is forced to look on the dead outlaw's face and also cut the choking scene so as to make it appear that the girl has fainted. To be consistent with this arrangement the titles, "The Temptation" and "The Husband Becomes a Social Outcast, thinking he has killed his child, whom the sheriff adopts," should be changed. (Letter from John Collier, Board Secretary, to Motion Picture Patents Company, 13 August 1909, Edison National Historic Site.)

The fact that the film went unreleased is ample proof that Biograph balked at these proposed cuts. In a second letter to the company from the Board, it was stated that

> the grounds upon which they [the Board] gave their decision upon this picture was, that in the form originally presented to the Board, it was an exhibition of gross immorality, presented in such a form that it would tend to corrupt the morals of the young. No new question was raised in giving this decision. (Letter from Collier to Motion Picture Patents Company, 16 August 1909, Edison National Historic Site.)

The entire film industry was sensitive to criticism at this time, especially criticism which implied immorality or impropriety of any kind. A few short months before, on Christmas day 1908, the mayor of New York City had closed down all movie houses in the city because of their supposed detrimental effect on the morals of the population. The Patents Company members had agreed to submit their films to the newly-formed National Board of Censorship (precursor of the present National Board of Review) for approval. This self-policing by the various film producers served to allay the fears of the several reform groups actively seeking the censorship of the industry, but the arrangement created tensions from the start. Whether or not the controversy surrounding THE HEART OF AN OUTLAW was a contributing factor in their decision is unknown, but in November of 1909, for a short time at least, Biograph released its films without first submitting them to the Board for approval. One would like to believe that Griffith himself was an instigator of this fight against censorship, especially in light of his later stand concerning THE BIRTH OF A NATION and the question of free speech, but there is no evidence that he was involved in the exchange over THE HEART OF AN OUTLAW. He never mentioned an unreleased film in later years, nor could Bitzer remember ever photographing a film that was not released. Their inability to recall a one-reel film representing only four days work out of a five-year collaboration is understandable, yet the fact that THE HEART OF AN OUTLAW was the only Griffith Biograph left sitting in the vaults due to censorship problems makes it too important to ignore.

Appendix B: MUTOSCOPES

In addition to films produced for theatrical projection, Biograph marketed a series of titles produced specifically for peep-show
machines. These were the mutoscopes. Running just a few seconds
and frequently containing, by turn-of-the-century standards, "blue"
material, the mutoscopes were an after-hours activity that brought
the studio, and its employees, extra revenue.

We do not know who actually directed these mutoscopes, although there is reliable testimony from Biograph employees that Wallace McCutcheon, Sr. probably staged most of them. It is also
probable that some were shot so quickly that the cameraman, in effect, became the director. Of the following thirty-three titles, three
were filmed after THE ADVENTURES OF DOLLIE, thus making possible Griffith's direction of at least that many. We know, by the
testimony of G. W. Bitzer and Linda Arvidson, that Griffith himself
acted in mutoscopes, and so the following list almost certainly includes titles containing Griffith performances. However, the fact
that mutoscopes were neither copyrighted nor systematically preserved
makes it impossible to determine their identity.

The following list of mutoscopes begins with the first title
filmed after D. W. Griffith's arrival at Biograph. The last title is
the final mutoscope entered in the Cameraman's Register at the Museum of Modern Art. The titles are recorded exactly as they appear
in the company's records, misspellings and abbreviations intact. The
codes used--"c, " "f, " "l"--are the same as those used in the rest
of the text; only "ol" has been added, to indicate the mutoscope's
original length at the time of production.

OH MAMA

G. W. Bitzer (c); 3 January 1908 (f); Studio (l); 174 feet (ol)

OH THAT CURTAIN

G. W. Bitzer (c); 3 January 1908 (f); Studio (l); 166 feet (ol)

CROWDED STREET - CONJESTED ST. SOCIETY

Arthur Marvin (c); 30 March 1908 (f); Brooklyn (l); 174 feet (ol)

MASKED POLICEMAN

G. W. Bitzer (c); 7 April 1908 (f); Studio (l); 146 feet (ol)

MRS. TROUBLE

G. W. Bitzer (c); 7 April 1908 (f); Studio (l); 147 feet (ol)

SELLING A MODEL

G. W. Bitzer (c); 7 April 1908 (f); Studio (l); 167 feet (ol)

GOLD-BUYS

G. W. Bitzer (c); 9 April 1908 (f); Studio (l); 148 feet (ol)

THAT AWFUL STORK

Arthur Marvin (c); 9 April 1908 (f); Studio (l); 152 feet (ol)

THE MERRY WIDOW AT A SUPPER PARTY

Arthur Marvin (c); 9 April 1908 (f); Studio (l); 145.75 feet (ol)

THE FISHERMANS MODEL

Arthur Marvin (c); 12 April 1908 (f); Studio (l); 150 feet (ol)

COLORED MAID GETTING RID OF A SUITOR

Arthur Marvin (c); 13 April 1908 (f); Studio (l); 145 feet (ol)

THEN TRAMP HE WOKE UP

Arthur Marvin (c); 13 April 1908 (f); Studio (l); 144 feet (ol)

THE HALLROOM BOYS REC'D. QUEER FRIGHT

Arthur Marvin (c); 14 April 1908 (f); Studio (l); 163 feet (ol)

SCENE IN A DRESSING ROOM

Arthur Marvin (c); 14 April 1908 (f); Studio (l); 153 feet (ol)

WHAT THE DUDE LOST IN THE DRESSING ROOM

Arthur Marvin (c); 15 April 1908 (f); Studio (l); 145 feet (ol)

NELLIE'S CAMERA

Arthur Marvin (c); 28 April 1908 (f); Studio (l); 160 feet (ol)

A FALSE ALARM

Arthur Marvin (c); 28 April 1908 (f); Studio (l); 122.5 feet (ol)

MAN UNDER THE BED

Arthur Marvin (c); 28 April 1908 (f); Studio (l); 150 feet (ol)

FARMER GREENE'S SUMMER BOARDERS

Arthur Marvin (c); 4 May 1908 (f); Little Falls, New Jersey (l); 164 feet (ol)

FUN IN THE HAY

Arthur Marvin (c); 4 May 1908 (f); Little Falls, New Jersey (l); 183 feet (ol)

JEALOUSY BEHIND THE SCENES

G. W. Bitzer (c); 7 May 1908 (f); Studio (l); 162 feet (ol)

THE GIRLS DORMITORY

G. W. Bitzer (c); 7 May 1908 (f); Studio (l); 187 feet (ol)

FLY PAPER

G. W. Bitzer (c); 7 May 1908 (f); Studio (l); 135 feet (ol)

THE GIRL AND THE GOSSIP

G. W. Bitzer (c); 8 May 1908 (f); Studio (l); 159 feet (ol)

SPECIAL MUTO REEL - MELLINS FOOD CO.

G. W. Bitzer (c); 20 May 1908 (f); Studio (l); 181 feet and 172 feet (ol)

THE GIRLS BOXING MATCH

Arthur Marvin (c); 21 May 1908 (f); Studio (l); 172 feet (ol)

TOO MANY IN BED

Arthur Marvin (c); 21 May 1908 (f); Studio (l); 163 feet (ol)

FLUFFYS NEW CORSETS

Arthur Marvin (c); 21 May 1908 (f); Studio (l); 155 feet (ol)

THE SOUL KISS

Arthur Marvin (c); 1 June 1908 (f); Studio (l); 166.5 feet (ol)

THREE WEEKS

Arthur Marvin, G. W. Bitzer (c); 1 June 1908 (f); Studio (l); 451 feet (ol)

THE CHORUS MAN'S REVENGE

G. W. Bitzer (c); 18 August 1908 (f); Studio (l); 163.5 feet (ol)

THE FORGOT THE MESSENGER

G. W. Bitzer (c); 12 October 1908 (f); Studio (l); 62/7 feet (ol)

WHAT THE COPPER SAW

G. W. Bitzer (c); 12 October 1908 (f); Studio (l); 56/4 feet (ol)

Appendix C: PERSONNEL

This list contains the names of those persons who claimed to have worked at Biograph, or who were remembered by former employees as having been at the studio during the years documented by this volume. We have been unable to verify such claims, and so have compiled this appendix, separate from the "Filmographies" section, as a guide for future research.

Abbott, Jack L., Actor (b. 1886)
Adamini, Arthur Marion, Actor (b. 1867) (aka Arthur A. Marion?)
Alexander, Baby Lois, Actress (b. 1910)
Anker, William, Actor (b. 1860)
Arnold, Lois, Actress (1877-1947)

Baker, Edwin, Actor (b. 1894)
Barrett, C. C., Actor (1871-1929)
Bassett, Russell, Actor (1846-1918)
Bentley, Alice, Actress (1898-1956)
Bergh, Albert Ellery, Author
Berry, Lilian, Actress
Betts, Peggy, Actress
Blanfox, David, Actor
Bonnell, Adrienne, Actress (b. 1897)
Bonner, Marguerite H., Actress (b. 1894) (aka Marjorie Bonner)
Boss, Yale, Actor (b. 1910)
Botter, Harry, Actor?/Director?
Bradley, Willard, Scenarist
Brooks, Alice E., Actress
Browning, Tod, Actor (1882-1962)
Burnett, Jessie, Actress (b. 1895)
Burns, Vinnie, Actress (aka June Daye)
Bylek, Rudolph, Actor/Director/Author (b. 1885)
Byrne, Jack, Scenarist (b. 1875)

Camp, Claude, Actor/Publicity man/Laboratory technician/Business-
man (b. 1888)
Carnaham, Junior, Actor (b. 1904)
Charles, John, Actor (b. 1885)
Cogan, James P., Scenarist/Author
Cooper, Miriam, Actress (1893-1976)
Cortes, Armand F., Actor (1880-1948)
Cosgrove, Larry Sheldon, Actor (b. 1882)
Crane, Ogden, Actor (1873-1940)
Cronjager, Henry, Cameraman

Crowell, Josephine Bonaparte, Actress (d. 1932)
Cummings, Robert, Actor (1867-1949)
Cunard, Grace, Actress (1894-1967)
Curley, Pauline, Actress
Cutting, Margaret, Actress (b. 1897)

Dailey, Joseph, Actor (1862-1940)
Davenport, Blanche, Actress
Davis, William S., Actor/Author/Director
Dawn, Norman O., Cameraman/Effects Artist (1886-1975)
Dean, Priscilla, Actress (b. 1896)
Deverich, Nat. G., Assistant Director (d. 1963)
Dillon, John Webb, Actor (1877-1949)
Dixon, Renee, Actress (b. 1894)
Dodsworth, Betty, Actress (b. 1895)
Dolberg, Camille, Actress (b. 1881) (aka Camilla Dalberg; Camilla
    D'Alberg)
Dubois, Philip R., Cameraman
Durning, Bernard J., Director (1893-1923)

Edwardy, Marie, Actress (b. 1895)

Fallon, Thomas F., Actor (b. 1885)
Farley, Dorothea, Actress (b. 1890) (aka Dot Farley)
Fay, Billy, Actor (1872-1947) (aka William George Fay)
Fayee, Aileen, Actress (b. 1895)
Fera, Gertrude M., Actress (b. 1892)
Foster, Fern, Actress
Franklin, Vera, Actress
French, Charles K., Actor (1860-1952)

George, Burton, Director
George, George, Actor (1889-1961)
Gereghty, Frank L., Assistant Director (1888-1934)
Gillies, Simon P., Actor (b. 1885)
Gish, Mrs. Mary, Actress (aka May Bernard)
Gittens, H. W., Scenario Editor
Gobbett, David William, Cameraman
Going, Frederica, Actress (1895-1959)
Goodwin, Eileen, Actress (b. 1887) (aka Aileen Goodwin)
Gorman, E. M., Actress (aka Em Gorman)
Gosden, A. G., Cameraman (d. 1941?)
Gowdy, James Edward, Actor (b. 1898)
Grandin, Ethel, Actress (b. 1896)
Grannison, Catheryne, Actress
Grant, Corinne, Actress (b. 1888?/1893?)
Grant, Nellie, Actress/Casting Director. Identified as a "former"
    Biograph actress in Moving Picture World, 29 October 1910, p.
    983.
Grey, John, Scenario staff (d. 1933?)
Grey, Margaret, Actress (b. 1875)

Appendix C / 319

Hamilton, Gilbert P., Cameraman/Laboratory Technician
Harding, Guy, Actor (b. 1888)
Harkness, Carter B., Actor (b. 1888)
Harrison, Estelle, Actress (b. 1898)
Harroun, Hazel, Actress (b. 1893)
Harvey, Harry, Actor (1873-1929?) (aka Herman Heacker?)
Hayes, Walter A., Actor (b. 1880)
Henderson, Jack (1878-1957) (aka Ogden M. Hoagland)
Henry, George, Actor
Hill, George, Cameraman?/Camera Assistant? Joined Biograph on
  THE BARRIER for Lionel Barrymore (aka "Tripod")
Hollingsworth, Alfred, Actor (1874-1926)
Holmes, Stuart; Actor (1887-1971)
Holton, Betty, Actress
Hulette, Gladys, Actress
Hunting, Harry L., Actor
Hutchins, Miriam, Actress (b. 1877)

Jefferson, William Winter, Actor (1876-1946)
Jenks, G. E., Scenarist
Jewett, Ethel, Actress
Johnson, Renee, Actress (b. 1897)
Johnson, Roswell, J., Cameraman
Jones, Marc Edmund, Author

Kearney, Joseph P., Actor (b. 1878)
Kellogg, Edwin J., Film cutter
Kennedy, Peter Benjamin, Actor
Kofstein, Jacques, Author/Scenarist (b. 1896)

Lehr, Anna, Actress
Lewis, Eugene B., Scenario staff
Lewis, Ralph, Actor (1872-1937)
Ligon, C. Grover, Actor (1885-1965)
Liston, M. N., Actor/Assistant Director (b. 1878) Worked on THE
  INFORMER (1912)?
Littell, Eddie, Actor/Cameraman (b. 1887)
Lloyd, Billy, Actor
Lyman, Laura, Actress
Lyons, Eddie, Actor (1886-1926)

Mack, Hayward, Actor (d. 1921)
Mackay, Rina, Actress (b. 1896)
Mackie, Laurie, Actress (b. 1878)
MacQuarrie, Murdock, Actor (1878-1942)
Madden, Golda, Actress (b. 1894)
Marion, Arthur A., Actor (aka Arthur Marion Adamini?)
McAlister, Mary, Actress (b. 1910)
McClellan, Robert F. E., Actor (1888-1976)
McCoy, Gertrude, Actress (1896-1967)
McCulley, William Thomas, Writer/Director (b. 1886)
McKey, Harry C., Actor (b. 1877)
Meader, J. E., Scenarist

Meuselbach, William C., Laboratory Technician
Midgley, Fannie, Actress (1877-1932)
Milasch, Robert E., Actor (1885-1954)
Miller, Ashley, Actor (1867-1949)
Mitchell, Yvette, Actress (b. 1898)
Modjeska, Felix B., Actor (b. 1887)
Mower, Jack, Actor (1890-1965)
Murphy, "Harlem Tom", Actor in THE MUSKETEERS OF PIG AL-
LEY? (1912)
Myers, Harry, Actor (1882-1938)

Newman, Walter H., Scenarist (b. 1876)
Nicholls, Fred, Actor
Noble, John W., Actor (b. 1880)
Norman, Gertrude, Actress (1848-1943)

O'Brien, Thomas E., Production Assistant (1889-1951)
O'Connor, Harry M., Actor (1873-1971)
O'Neil, Barry, Director (d. 1918) (b. Thomas J. McCarthy)
Orenback, Michael, Technical Director (b. 1891)
Orth, George, Director (b. 1894)
Osborne, Jefferson, Actor (1871-1932) (aka J. W. Schroeder)

Parmer, Devore, Actor
Pates, Vivian, Actress (aka Mrs. J. Kirkbrick)
Pearce, George C., Actor (1878?-1940)
Peters, George, Cameraman (b. 1890)
Peterson, Gus, Cameraman/Technician (aka G. C. Petersen)
Physioc, Wray, Director (b. 1890)
Pietz, Lucille, Actress (b. 1896)
Pixley, Mamie, Actress in comedy unit.
Powell, A. Van Buren, Scenarist (b. 1886)
Power, William H., Actor
Price, Anna Berger, Actress (aka A. Berger; Annie Theresa Ber-
ger)
Printzlau, Olga, Author/Scriptwriter (1893-1962)

Quinn, Edward, Actor (b. 1904)

Rader, William E., Actor (b. 1890)
Radford, Mazie, Actress
Rae, Zoe, Actress (b. 1910)
Reynolds, Vera, Actress (1899?-1962)
Riley, Claxton J., Actor (b. 1889)
Robinson, Daisy, Actress
Rogerson, Jack, Cameraman/Actor (b. 1888)
Rosee, Florence, Actress (b. 1896)
Ross, Budd, Actor
Rottman, Victor Jr., Actor (b. 1892)
Russell, James Gordon, Actor (1883-1935) (aka Z. William Russels?)
Russell, William, (1884-1929)

Saum, Clifford P., Production Assistant/Director (1883-1943)
Scarborough, Harry, Actor
Scott, Lester F., Jr., Production Assistant/Director (d. 1954)
Semels, Harry, Actor (1887-1946)
Sloan, William Hope, Actor (1864-1933)
Snyder, Flora B., Scenarist
Stewart, Loel, Actor (b. 1910)
Stewart, Maurice, Actor (b. 1908) (aka Maury Stewart)
Stone, George, Actor (b. 1910?)
Strong, Porter, Actor (1879-1923)
Sullivan, Daniel, Actor (d. 1914)
Sullivan, Joe, Actor (1910-1971)
Sullivan, John Maurice, Actor/Scenarist (1876-1949)

Talmadge, Constance, Actress (1900-1973)
Talmadge, Norma, Actress (1897-1957)
Templeton, Margaret, Actress
Thompson, Nicholas J., Actor
Tomek, Jack, Actor (b. 1889)
Trimmer, Mabel E., Actress (b. 1896)
Tuey, Bert, Actor (b. 1888)
Turner, Fred A., Actor (1866?-1923) (aka F. A. Turner)

Vale, Louise, Actress (d. 1918) (married to Travers Vale)
Vale, Travers, Director (1873?-1927)
Vale, Vola, Actress (aka Vola Smith)
Van, Polly, Actress (1882-1952) (aka Mrs. Bill Bailey)
Van Deusen, Cortland J., Director (b. 1890) (aka Cortland J. Van
   Deuren)
Vignola, Robert G., Actor (1882-1953)
Von Raven, Dorothy, Actress

Wade, John P., Actor (b. 1874)
Wadsworth, William, Actor (1873-1950) (confused by G. W. Bitzer
   with William Bechtel)
Waller, Jane, Actress
Weathersby, Jennie, Actress (1855-1931)
Wells, May, Actress (1862-1941)
Whitlock, Lloyd T., Actor (1891-1966)
Whitney, Claire, Actress (1890-1969)
Williams, Grace, Actress (b. 1891)
Wilson, Edna Mae, Actress (b. 1906)
Wing, Marie A., Scenarist (aka Mrs. W. E. Wing)
Woodruff, Henry F., Actor (1870-1916)
Woodward, Henry, Actor (b. 1891)

SOURCES

Arvidson, Linda (Mrs. D. W. Griffith). When the Movies Were Young. New York: E. P. Dutton, 1925; New York: Dover Publications, 1969.

Barry, Iris and Eileen Bowser. D. W. Griffith: American Film Master. New York: The Museum of Modern Art, 1940, 1965.

Bitzer, G. W. Billy Bitzer: His Story. New York: Farrar, Straus and Giroux, 1973.

Blum, Daniel. Collection. State Historical Society of Wisconsin, Madison, Wisconsin.

Bowser, Eileen, ed. Biograph Bulletins: 1908-1912. New York: Octagon Books, 1973.

Brownlow, Kevin. Hollywood: The Pioneers. New York: Alfred A. Knopf, 1979.

Copyright Collection. The Library of Congress, Washington, D.C.

Grau, Robert. The Theatre of Science. New York: Benjamin Blom, 1914; New York: Benjamin Blom, 1969.

Griffith, D. W. Papers. Museum of Modern Art, New York.

Henderson, Robert. D. W. Griffith: The Years at Biograph. New York: Farrar, Straus and Giroux, 1970.

Lauritzen, Einar and Gunnar Lundquist. American Film-Index 1908-1915. Stockholm: Film-Index, 1976.

Library of Congress Copyright Office. Catalog of Copyright Entries, Cumulative Series: Motion Pictures, 1912-1939. Washington, D.C.: Library of Congress, 1951.

Munden, Kenneth, ed. The American Film Institute Catalog: Feature Films, 1921-1930. 2 volumes. New York: R. R. Bowker, 1971.

Niver, Kemp R. D. W. Griffith: His Biograph Films in Perspective. Edited by Bebe Bergsten. Los Angeles: Locare Research Group, 1974.

. The First Twenty Years: A Segment of Film History. Edited by Bebe Bergsten. Los Angeles: Locare Research Group, 1968.

. Klaw & Erlanger Present Famous Plays in Pictures. Edited by Bebe Bergsten. Los Angeles: Locare Research Group, 1976.

and Bebe Bergsten, eds. and comps. Biograph Bulletins: 1896-1908. Los Angeles: Locare Research Group, 1971.

O'Leary, Liam. Cinema Ireland: 1895-1976. Dublin: Dublin Arts Festival, 1976.

Perry, Jeb H. Variety Obits: An Index to Obituaries in Variety, 1905-1978. Metuchen, N.J.: The Scarecrow Press, Inc., 1980.

Pickford, Mary. Sunshine and Shadow. Garden City, N.Y.: Doubleday and Company, Inc., 1955.

Quigley, Martin. Collection. Georgetown University Library, Washington, D.C.

Ramsaye, Terry. A Million and One Nights. New York: Simon and Schuster, 1926; New York: Simon and Schuster, 1964.

Slide, Anthony. The Griffith Actresses. New York: A. S. Barnes and Company, Inc., 1973.

Stars of the Photoplay. Chicago: Photoplay Publishing Company, 1916.

Truitt, Evelyn Mack. Who Was Who on Screen. Second edition. New York and London: R. R. Bowker, 1977.

. Who Was Who on Screen. Third edition. New York: R. R. Bowker, 1983.

Walls, Howard Lamarr. Motion Pictures, 1894-1912: Identified From the Records of the United States Copyright Office. Washington, D.C.: The Library of Congress, 1953.

Who's Who in Moving Pictures. New York: Robert E. Sherwood, 1915.

Who's Who in the Film World. Los Angeles: Film World Publishing Company, 1914.

Windeler, Robert. Sweetheart: The Story of Mary Pickford. New York: Praeger Publishers, 1974.

In addition to the above sources, we thoroughly examined the following periodicals:

The Biograph

The Bioscope

The Implet

Motion Picture News (including its several "Studio Directory" sections)

Motography

The Moving Picture World

The New York Dramatic Mirror

Photoplay

Picture-Play Magazine

Reel Life

Variety

TITLE INDEX

(Page Numbers Refer To Main Entries Only)

Professional Jealousy 13
Proposal, The 94
Prussian Spy, The 39
Pueblo Legend, A 153
Punishment, The 139
Purgation, The 84

Queer Elopement, A 171

Ragtime Romance, A 178
Rainy Day, A 181
Ramona 80
Ranchero's Revenge, The 183
Real Estate Deal, A 159
Reckoning, The 31
Recreation of an Heiress, The 100
Red and Pete, Partners 202
Red Girl, The 25
Red Hicks Defies the World 185
Redman and the Child, The 21
Redman's View, The 67
Reformers, The 193
Renunciation, The 54
Rescued from an Eagle's Nest 13
Resourceful Lovers 127
Restoration, The 64
Resurrection 48
Revenue Man and the Girl, The 122
Rich Revenge, A 77
Rise and Fall of McDoo, The 186
Road to the Heart, The 43
Rocky Road, The 70
Romance of a Jewess 27
Romance of an Egg, The 18
Romance of the Western Hills, A 77
Romany Tragedy, A 112
Root of Evil, The 137
Rose O' Salem Town 91
Rose of Kentucky, The 120
Roue's Heart, The 40
Rude Hostess, A 43
Ruling Passion, The 118
Rural Elopement, A 33

Sacrifice, The 34
Sailor's Heart, A 162
Salutary Lesson, A 87

Salvation Army Lass, The 40
Sands of Dee, The 149
Saturday Holiday, A 199
Saved from Himself 129
Scenting a Terrible Crime 201
Schneider's Anti-Noise Crusade 43
School Teacher and the Waif, The 147
Sculptor's Nightmare, The 17
Sea Dog's Love, A 189
Sealed Room, The 58
Serious Sixteen 85
"1776" or, The Hessian Renegades 59
Seventh Day, The 57
"She Is a Pippin" 163
Sheriff's Baby, The 175
Simple Charity 95
Siren of Impulse, A 136
Sister's Love, A 134
Slave, The 55
Slippery Slim Repents 183
Smile of a Child, A 113
Smoked Husband, A 25
Smoker, The 76
Snowman, The 14
So Near, Yet So Far 156
So Runs the Way 201
Somnambulists, The 207
Song of the Shirt, The 29
Song of the Wildwood Flute, The 96
Son's Return, The 51
Sorrowful Example, The 119
Sorrowful Shore, The 188
Sorrows of the Unfaithful, The 88
Sound Sleeper, A 44
Spanish Dilemma, A 137
Spanish Gypsy, The 108
Speed Demon, The 148
Spirit Awakened, The 146
Spring of Life, The 172
Squaw's Love, The 121
Stage Rustler, The 20
Stern Papa 154
Stolen Bride, The 176
Stolen Jewels, The 26
Stolen Loaf, The 181
Stolen Treaty, The 198
Stopped Clock, The 204
Strange Meeting, A 55